BREAKING THE POVERTY CYCLE

Breaking the Poverty Cycle: The Human Basis for Sustainable Development

SUSAN PICK
JENNA SIRKIN

OXFORD
UNIVERSITY PRESS
2010

OXFORD

UNIVERSITY PRESS

Oxford University Press, Inc., publishes works that further
Oxford University's objective of excellence
in research, scholarship, and education.

Oxford New York
Auckland   Cape Town   Dar es Salaam   Hong Kong   Karachi
Kuala Lumpur   Madrid   Melbourne   Mexico City   Nairobi
New Delhi   Shanghai   Taipei   Toronto

With offices in
Argentina   Austria   Brazil   Chile   Czech Republic   France   Greece
Guatemala   Hungary   Italy   Japan   Poland   Portugal   Singapore
South Korea   Switzerland   Thailand   Turkey   Ukraine   Vietnam

Published by Oxford University Press, Inc.
198 Madison Avenue, New York, New York 10016

www.oup.com

Oxford is a registered trademark of Oxford University Press, Inc.

Library of Congress Cataloging-in-Publication Data

Pick, Susan.
 Breaking the poverty cycle: the human basis for sustainable development /
 by Susan Pick, Jenna Sirkin; developmental editing by Shoshana Grossman-Crist
    p. cm.
 ISBN 978-0-19-538316-4
 1. Sustainable development. 2. Poverty. I. Sirkin, Jenna. II. Title.
 HC79.E5.P515 2010
 338.9`27—dc22   2009038264

Cover design by Katie Clark/Collaboration from Giovanna Escobar
Cover photograph by Arturo Weiss Pick

9 8 7 6 5 4 3
Printed in the United States of America
on acid-free paper

In loving memory of Martin Fishbein and Henry David for their mentorship, support and friendship

To me, poor people are like bonsai trees. When you plant the best seed of the tallest tree in a six-inch-deep flower pot, you get a perfect replica of the tallest tree, but it is only inches tall. There is nothing wrong with the seed you planted; only the soil-base you provided was inadequate. Poor people are bonsai people. There is nothing wrong with their seeds. Only society never gave them the base to grow on. All that is required to get poor people out of poverty is for us to create an enabling environment for them. Once the poor are allowed to unleash their energy and creativity, poverty will dissapear very quickly.

—Muhammad Yunus (2009, p. 54)

PREFACE

My Personal Story (Susan Pick)

Everything in life begins with sex, so does this book.

"Yes, we are tired of so many children. But that is what God wants for us."

"The priest says it is a sin to control the number of children we have, but he is not the one who has to pay for them and raise them."

"If I even talk about those things [sex, contraception, pleasure], [my husband] will beat me up."

These are the words of adult women in Ciudad Netzahualcoyotl, one of the largest and poorest shanty-towns on the outskirts of Mexico City. As a prospective Ph.D. student at the University of London, I became interested in determinants of women's contraceptive behavior and how to facilitate family planning practices among women living in marginalized areas of the city. This was a key aspect of development in Mexico, because the government had recently legalized the use of contraceptives.[1]

My interest developed into a dissertation (Pick, 1975), where I collected qualitative data in the form of personal interviews with adult women in Ciudad Netzahualcoyotl. A recurring theme was the lack of control that these women felt over their own lives. *"Si Dios quiere," "No puedo trabajar porque mi esposo me agarraría a golpes, mejor me aguanto," "Me da pena preguntar, mejor me quedo callada."* Meaning: "God willing," "I cannot work because my husband would hit me, better that I bear it," "I feel ashamed asking, I better keep quiet." Goals, intentions, or plans did not resonate with these women because they did not have control over day-to-day events, much less their future actions. They expressed their desires in the form of dreams or wishes, and often attributed events to fate: "… it was in the hands of God." When I asked the women, "Do you plan to use contraception? How do you decide how many children you want to have? Do you plan to send your kids to school?" Their answers contained expressions such as: "It depends …" "I would like to, but I do not know …" "Who knows?" or "If God wills it …" rather than expressions you might hear from women who perceive control over their life decisions.

Although most of the women had positive attitudes about contraception, there was a large discrepancy in the data between their attitudes and what they did in practice. They admired the idea of being able to choose how many children to have rather than leaving it up to chance but did not have the necessary information to take action. I argued that part of the gap between attitudes and practice could be explained by the women's reluctance to contradict what they *perceived* as the social norm. Instead, they followed what they assumed everyone else was doing, without knowing or asking what precisely it was that others were doing—especially if it had to do with sexuality.

There also existed considerable discrepancy between a woman's perception of what was acceptable to talk about concerning sexuality and what she wanted to talk about. When my colleagues and I began to discuss sexuality as naturally as talking about tacos and beans, the women tended to relax. Once they felt comfortable, they did not want to stop talking. They had an enormous need to express their views and doubts about issues surrounding sexuality; this was the first time in their lives that the discussion of these taboo topics was encouraged, and someone finally cared enough to listen.

The results of my dissertation highlighted some key factors responsible for women's failure to use contraceptives in Mexico City in 1975. These included: *(1)* lack of knowledge about how to use contraceptives correctly; *(2)* inadequate psychosocial support surrounding contraceptive use—for example, fear and shame regarding what others would think, specifically men and pharmacists; *(3)* lack of decision-making and communication skills; *(4)* an expressed feeling of powerlessness over their decisions; and *(5)* little awareness that they were entitled to make such choices (Pick de Weiss, 1978).

Beyond sexual behaviors, these themes seemed to be inherent to the Mexican way of life. For years I had listened to my father argue that the Mexican formal and informal education system failed to incorporate the concept of what he called "inner responsibility," meaning responding to one's obligations, interests, and needs because one realizes the importance of doing so rather than merely as a response to external pressures. Although he was born and raised in Germany, he had worked in Mexico for decades, and often struggled with the implications of passive Spanish idioms such as *"se cayó,"* meaning "it fell down," and *"fíjese que así pasó,"* meaning something like "so it came to pass." These phrases imply that any control over consequences is outside a person's responsibility. These expressions made my father uncomfortable. He would ask: *Who* was in control? *Who* was taking responsibility for decisions and for their consequences? Of course, these questions raised the larger issue of whether this worldview was the result of a legitimate inability to predict the environment or whether it had become part of the cultural mindset.

The lack of "inner responsibility" occurs not only at the individual level but also at the institutional level. The education system in Mexico, as in many other developing countries, is based on a paternalistic, hierarchical structure that emphasizes rote memorization and the expectation that students unquestioningly comply with norms. Such a system does not encourage the students to ask questions, to be analytical, and to address their needs, leaving little room for personal initiative, analytical thinking, or creativity. I would often get into trouble for asking too many questions or for asking the "wrong thing at the wrong time." At the level of educational policy, emphasis has often been placed on the politics of the system and personnel administration rather than focusing on improving quality, updating teaching methods and strengthening educational content. Similarly, in national politics, priorities tend to emphasize the passing of laws rather than their just execution, implementation, and enforcement; and inaugural ceremonies for libraries and bridges rather than their cost-effective and sustainable operation.

I was able to establish the link between these cultural realities and theoretical concepts thanks to the lectures on axiology by Robert S. Hartman at the Faculty of Philosophy at the National University of Mexico (UNAM). Axiology is the theory of value, and the focus of Hartman's course was to define and measure different values. He had developed a scale to understand which values, or combination thereof, were the most important in individuals' lives and had categorized them into three types: *(1)* extrinsic values, which emphasize material goods such as money; *(2)* systemic values, which are based on rules, norms, and laws; and *(3)* intrinsic values, which refer to one's innermost values (Hartman, 1967). In class, Hartman would often refer to Mexico, arguing that the most important values in Mexican culture were the systemic values, defined by strong pressure and expectations to follow socio-cultural norms.

A few years later, the principles of behavior change theory enriched my theoretical knowledge of psycho-social development. Fishbein and Ajzen's Theory of Reasoned Action categorizes determinants of behavior change into separate components—namely, attitudes, beliefs, and perceived social norms regarding the behavior. Each of these determinants affects the intention to perform the behavior, and such segmentation allows behavior change to be assessed and addressed in a step-by-step manner (Fishbein & Ajzen, 1975); several components were added as the theory evolved (Ajzen, Albarracín, & Hornik, 2007).

As part of my studies at the University of London, I attended an economic theory course with Professor Amartya Sen, the 1998 Nobel Laureate in Economics. I understood his classes and later writings as examples of how economics and psycho-social approaches may be paired to conceptualize the way in which quality of life could be improved for people in developing countries.

The work of Hartman, Fishbein, and Sen enhanced my understanding of the inadequacies of many programs and policies in Mexico, and reflected the reality for many Latin American people, such as the women in the Mexico City shantytowns. Hartman's work emphasized the relationship between social compliance and external control as well as the associated lack of intrinsic motivation. He linked these ideas to his criticism of the Latin American education system, which he argued was the underpinning of many development problems in the region. The repercussions of this system affected school performance, future work productivity, and the quality of interpersonal and institutional relationships. Sen's work—such as "Well-being, agency and freedom" (1985)—articulated the reality that I had experienced in my interviews with these women and many other groups in Mexico.

IMIFAP Programs and Development

My personal experiences combined with these theories have provided the foundation for the Mexican civil society organization (CSO)[2] known as the Mexican Institute of Family and Population Research (IMIFAP). The organization's slogan, *I want to, I can* [*Yo quiero, yo puedo*], encapsulates IMIFAP's mission to promote intrinsic values—rather than, or complementing, systemic and extrinsic values—to enable people and communities to expand their choices. The expansion of individual choice helps to promote community understanding about the importance of enhancing individual freedoms, responsibilities, rights, and capabilities. In academic terms, behavior change theory elucidates how individual freedoms can be enhanced and communities can be empowered. All of these factors are key components for sustainable development.

This book draws from IMIFAP's experiences with marginalized communities in Latin America, highlighting the obstacles to accessing choice and opportunity, and seeking to present a framework as to how freedom and development can be achieved and maintained. Sustainable human development is key to sustainable societal and economic development. In short, this book addresses how individual and contextual capabilities can be expanded and how a mindset of freedoms as an entitlement can be sustained. We must invest in the *people* that build families, institutions, communities, and policies in order to break the poverty cycle in a sustainable way.

We include a brief, anecdotal history of IMIFAP's development, intended to provide a context for the presentation of the Framework for Enabling Empowerment (FrEE), later in the book. The framework we present is rooted in Sen's (1983, 1999) Capability Approach. The central principle of the Capability Approach is to enhance the alternatives or choices people have to promote human capabilities and freedoms. In actual programs, we have operationalized these concepts through Programming for Choice, which encompasses the context in which we grow up, targets behaviors through the development of life skills in response to specific situations, and aims to promote the development of individual processes such as personal agency.[3] Personal agency is a key concept that will be used throughout the book, and is a foundational component of the framework that is presented. Although the concept of an "agent" is used to convey other meanings in fields such as economics, we promote Sen's conceptualization of agency as both the process and the state in which a person carries out informed and motivated decisions in an autonomous fashion. An agent will be more likely to promote choice as an entitlement—and support personal and institutional growth and development—than an individual who is subject to external decisions and is neither in control of nor held responsible for them.

In this book, Jenna Sirkin and I hope to show how enabling individuals to enhance their capabilities, and thus their potential, can have an effective and sustainable impact. Ours is an agent-oriented view of development. Most of the empirical data presented is based on IMIFAP's experiences in Latin America, with Mexico as the primary example. But there are common themes found in development programs worldwide. We hope that our theory and framework will be adapted and applied cross-culturally, so that our research and programs—through constructive policies, market, education and health reforms, and collaborative program implementation—can enhance not only sustainable economic development, but also human and social well-being.

The Early Years of IMIFAP: Health Education in Mexico

After my dissertation research with the women of Ciudad Netzahualcoyotl, it became clear that to make a difference in sex education, we would need to start working with youth. After presenting this idea at the 1980 XXIII International Congress of Psychology, Henry David, Director of the Transnational Family Research Institute, invited me to give a talk in Norway. I had proposed targeting prevention efforts early in adolescence[4] and from a psychosocial point of departure, rather than a demographic or medical perspective.

A few weeks later, at a Pan American Health Organization (PAHO) meeting on adolescent pregnancy prevention, Joao Yunes, coordinator of the Maternal Child Health Program at PAHO, approached me. "I want to fund that work. If you are interested, please form an NGO before the end of September," he said. After quickly learning the process of forming an NGO, the end result was the conceptualization of the Mexican Institute of Family and Population Research (IMIFAP) in 1984.

Before developing our first program in the mid 1980s, IMIFAP researchers conducted a number of diagnostic studies of adolescents in Mexico City to understand the specific needs of adolescents regarding reproductive health, sexuality, and life skills. Our research primarily aimed to identify protective sexual behaviors among adolescents. The results identified socio-cultural norms as a significant explanatory factor of adolescent behaviors and sexual health in Mexican youth. Sexually active adolescent girls who were less accepting of broad socio-cultural norms in Mexico were: *(1)* more likely to use contraceptives and *(2)* less likely to become pregnant.[5] The research also identified other variables that influenced the sexual health and behaviors of adolescents in Mexico, including: knowledge and attitudes about sexuality, family and friends' perceptions of sexuality, and the adolescents' communication skills (Pick de Weiss, et al., 1991; Pick, Díaz-Loving, & Atkin, 1988).[6]

Our findings were not surprising considering that the existing sex education programs in Mexico were very basic, focusing exclusively on menstruation, using technical language, and excluding the personal, psychological, and emotional aspects of sexuality. Educators were authoritarian and unconcerned with student participation. Feminine product companies and medical providers developed and provided most of the programming, using technical diagrams along with medical terminology. Concurrently, IMIFAP found that programs in other Latin American countries also lacked the psychosocial aspects of sexuality education. This style stemmed from the contemporary application of "sex" education as a means of population control. Thus, most of the research and programs that existed were developed from a demographic perspective (Isaacs, Cairns, & Heckel, 1985; Wolfson, 1978).

The issue was that this style of educating did not resonate with the participants' needs and therefore did not translate into useful knowledge or protective behaviors. I recall several arguments with key national and international authorities regarding the importance of psychosocial factors (e.g., decision making, communication, and sexuality) being part of sexuality education. One high level official, a demographer, responded to my argument for more comprehensive programming, *"Por favor no metas lo cursi … las cosas de niñas al asunto. Enfócate en control de la población"* [Keep the matters of the heart … the girly things out of it. Focus on population control]. His reaction paralleled a common message of economists, that improving the overall economic situation would reduce poverty and promote development, and a common message of policymakers, that better laws and policies would provide the solution. A multidisciplinary, needs-based perspective was lacking.

At IMIFAP we realized the need for life skills and sexuality education that was participatory and based on the observations and needs of the adolescents. We determined that the goals of the new program would be for participants to develop communication and decision-making skills, acquire factual information about sexuality in accessible language, increase classroom participation, learn strategies to overcome fears and insecurities regarding their sexuality, understand their rights, obtain a sense of autonomy and control over their own lives, and increase cross-gender awareness. After many pilot trials, "Planning Your Life"[7] would become the first program and didactic material that we developed (Pick de Weiss, Montero, & Aguilar, 1988). We believed that it would foster in our participants new skills and intentions with important behavioral impacts.

After implementing the program in the late 1980s and early 1990s, the World Health Organization (WHO) invited IMIFAP to discuss the antecedents of adolescent risk-taking behaviors at the 1995 Program on Mental Health in Geneva.[8] Before these meetings, a group of CSOs had come to an informal consensus that knowledge-based programming was not enough to change behaviors. The proposed remedy to this program and policy gap was the concept of "life skills,"[9] which would be incorporated into future health promotion programming on a larger scale (WHO, 1999). The Program on Mental Health marked a historical change in the public health field, because it was the first time that life skills programs were officially named, recognized, and promoted at an international level. IMIFAP research around this time found that providing life skills-based sexuality education programs before adolescents had sex increased the likelihood that they would adopt safe sex practices (Pick de Weiss et al., 1994). As a result, we began to develop programs for youth of younger ages, initially targeting 7th through 9th grade and later designing programs with a focus on still younger children, from pre-school onward. Future programs applied the same concepts in programs for parents, as the manifestation of parental frustration revealed that children participating in the program knew more about sexuality than their parents.

Prior experience had demonstrated to IMIFAP that facilitating programs for men in particular was an integral component of community development, yet it was not until this point that there was the support to do so. Unfortunately it became clear in subsequent years that providing programs for men would always be a challenge, because of the limited availability of funds for programs with men. Indeed this initiated a gender bias in programs, which is unfortunate because it is bringing with it negative consequences for both male and female well-being.

Overcoming the Opposition and Scaling Up the Programs

In parallel with the work to develop programs for younger children and parents, and after determining how to effectively implement our programs at the local level, we were ready to expand. We soon realized that scaling-up was harder than we thought. We wanted to offer our life skills and sexuality education program for adolescents to the Ministry of Education for broader testing, with the hope that it could be institutionalized over the long term. After a long wait and much perseverance, including establishing my office on a bench outside the Minister of Education's office where I sat, waiting and working for 3 weeks, I was given an appointment with the then Minister of Education, Manuel Bartlett. He referred me to his Undersecretary, Jesus Liceaga, who had apparently conducted some research on IMIFAP while I was waiting to meet him. And a few days later Minister Bartlett approved the training of a nationally representative sample of secondary[10] and high school level public school teachers and supervisors, under the auspices of the Ministry of Education. The decision was an impressive step for Mexico's Ministry of Education.

The Ministry invited teachers representing all states to Queretaro, Mexico for a training workshop on "Planning Your Life", and IMIFAP was hired to conduct the training. The first days were tense because members of groups opposing sexuality education had unified in protest; they interrupted the training and encouraged teachers to boycott the sessions. Initially, teachers themselves were uncomfortable with the subject matter and with the degree of participation and analysis required. It was also difficult for them to accept that young facilitators were providing the program. However, as they began the training, they became more comfortable with the style and the materials. Not only did the program teach them strategies for working with their students, but it helped them address personal issues within their own lives and with other staff members. They also realized they could use the life skills-building lessons in courses beyond sexuality education. By the end of the training, the teachers were so excited about the programs that they invited a mariachi band to perform for the IMIFAP facilitators to show their gratitude.

The excitement was interrupted a few weeks later when a member of a pro-life group threatened one of IMIFAP's workers at gunpoint. After consulting lawyers, IMIFAP decided against following up on the incident. We thought that by ignoring the episode, and not politicizing it, we could continue our work without further pressure from opposing groups. A few days later, however, *EL Heraldo de Mexico*, a conservative Mexican newspaper, carried various one-page advertisements[11] quoting select lines of "Planning Your Life" (Pick de Weiss et al., 1991) and its corresponding question and answer book "I am an adolescent"[12] (Pick de Weiss & Vargas Trujillo, 1990). We realized that trying to avoid politics while attempting to institute sexuality education would be impossible. We feared that conservative forces would create obstacles, even before sexuality education was institutionalized. Yet, some colleagues and friends noted that the press could be positive—in fact, the advertisements became a form of free publicity for IMIFAP. The course books sold out the same day the advertisements were published and reached record-breaking sales that week (more than 10,000 copies). Even Manuel Bartlett, Secretary of Public Education at the time, spoke out for us, making front-page news a few days later.

> The possibility of including sexuality education classes in the country's secondary schools has been extensively discussed in the Technical Council on Education, so regarding the content of the program Adolescence and Sexuality, there is nothing further to discuss, declared Secretary of Public Education, Manuel Bartlett Díaz. (Miranda, 1991)[13]

A few months later, Bartlett became governor of the state of Puebla, and Dr. Ernesto Zedillo became the Secretary of Public Education. Zedillo immediately expressed support for our work and the integration of the program into official school textbooks: "I have read your books and think they are very useful, but we need to negotiate with the groups opposed to it. Bring me data regarding national public opinion. It may be useful for dissemination purposes." This was an indication of another breaking point: A key policymaker was asking for data to back up a negotiation and hopefully to make a decision.

Ian Reider, then president of Gallup, Mexico, agreed to insert some questions about sexuality education into one of the Gallup Poll surveys. The results showed that 95% of Mexicans nationwide thought sexuality education should begin in first grade. We disseminated the sexuality education results nationally through education authorities, and the results received wide press coverage (IMIFAP, 1993).

Zedillo, who would become president of Mexico a few months later, was amazed by the results. He suggested I meet with members of the opposition groups and with prominent conservative women in Mexico. Although these women publicly opposed the essence of our work, it was critical to gain their support because their husbands held prominent positions and controlled both economic and political power in Mexico City. The predominant view within this circle is a conservative one, which aims at preserving the status quo. Their voice in greater economic and political matters is often decisive.

Our first strategy was to convene a meeting with a group of Mexican women, including the prominent conservative individuals we intended to target. It turned out to be a disaster. The more we explained, the more opposition we received. The women believed our programs were promoting "sexual debauchery" and "excessive freedom of thought and action," which would lead to the destruction of Mexican youth. They asked how we could "even entertain the possibility of talking about such threatening matters as gender equality, autonomous decision making, and contraceptives in school." In their view, sexuality education—if it was to be provided at all—should be done within the domain of the home. The topics should include only menstruation and pregnancy and should only be for youth well into their adolescence. Working with these women was often more challenging than working with government officials; neither research nor poll statistics could sway the centuries-old social norms and moral beliefs. They stood united against our proposal. We definitely needed a new strategy.

Soon after, at a wedding in a conservative area of central Mexico City, a middle-aged woman sitting next to me explained to me how she helped women:

> I convince maids that God put them in this world to serve, that they must be thankful for that opportunity and must make the best out of it. Imagine, what would happen if they started going out to study all sorts of things and to make their own decisions, then women like you and me would have nobody to serve us.

The phrase "people like you and me" felt unreal, but I realized that I could leverage these perceived similarities to my advantage. I replied, "We have quite a bit in common. I also work with women ..."

After a few tequilas, my new friend was telling me her life story and sobbing, "My husband does not allow me to work outside of the home except for my volunteer work ... I am confined to the house. He decides every move I make, every move my children make, and they are all over 21." As the conversation progressed, she became increasingly personal, "I had a hysterectomy because that was the only way I could stop having children ... and 'those' nasty thoughts which were so shameful." However, now that she had decreased her sexual drive, "as all good women must do once they are finished having children," her husband had found another woman. "And my sons are turning out exactly like him," she continued. One of them raped the neighbor's daughter and paid for her to have an abortion in Texas. They were opposed to sexuality education and abortion on a national level, but in her son's case, they "simply had to decide." In the case of *her* son and neighbor, they had made the right choice.

This conversation made me realize that if I spoke to women on a personal level, free of the barriers created by the institutions each of us represented, I could develop a better rapport. I also realized that regardless of this woman's socio-economic status, her story was similar to those of the poor women with whom IMIFAP had been working. The most difficult barriers for women of all classes were the psychological and social pressures to conform, such as the fear, guilt, and shame. For development to be successful, these obstacles had to be overcome. My new strategy was to meet individually with key women in the conservative opposition groups, where I could relate to them on a personal level. Dressed in an elegant and sober fashion (as they did), I would meet them for breakfast before work. I began by telling them about myself.

This strategy was so successful that these key women eventually hired Martha Givaudan and me to facilitate workshops for them behind their husbands' backs. Martha and I learned a lot about Mexican norms regarding sexual role expectations while teaching these courses. After about 30 breakfasts and a few months of sexuality education groups with the women, the avenue for sexuality education in the Mexican school system had opened.

With Zedillo's support, IMIFAP then developed a short *telenovela* (or soap opera) that ran daily on national television for a year. It was called, *Talk to Me About "That"*[14] and was paired with a series of short films on various themes of sexuality education, adapted from the Canadian video *Joy of Life* (Girerd, 1991). In these films a friendly grandmother talks to her grandchildren about sexuality related issues such as menstruation, changes in puberty, homosexuality, and falling in love in a warm and sensitive manner. Within that year, the Ministry of Education received over 2,000 phone calls regarding the show; only 1 opposed the program. It was then that Zedillo decided the Ministry of Education was ready to introduce sexuality education into the official school curriculum, specifically into the national fifth- and sixth-grade textbooks.

With the aid of Patricia Mercado,[15] an opportunity was created for IMIFAP to address a congressional committee meeting about the need for sexuality education. Legal measures could significantly advance the introduction of sexuality education nationwide. The wording was proposed in a subsequent discussion with members of the Mexican legislature, and the following clause was adopted in Article 7 of the General Law of Education:

> Education ... shall, besides the aims established in the second paragraph of Article 3 of the Mexican Constitution, do the following: . . . Develop attitudes of solidarity in individuals, to raise awareness about the maintenance of health, family planning and responsible parenting, without undermining the freedom and absolute respect of human dignity, and promoting the rejection of vices. [16] (Diario Oficial de la Federación, 1993)

The new law had a problem: the ambiguous wording left space for interpretation. Nevertheless, even an ambiguous law was an important move. It would take extensive training sessions and increased public awareness to successfully implement the law, but it was a beginning.

From Sexuality Education to Comprehensive Health Education

Parallel to the scaling up and institutionalization of sexuality education in the 1990s, IMIFAP continued developing new programs and expanding its theoretical knowledge. Based on the results of a Population Council study, John Townsend (then a program officer at the Population Council in Mexico) suggested that we conduct an additional evaluation to identify whether the determinants of unprotected sex were correlated with determinants of substance abuse. The study showed that the acquisition of life skills was inversely associated with both behaviors (Pick de Weiss, Andrade Palos, & Townsend, 1990). Consequently, IMIFAP developed multithematic health programs that focused not only on sexuality education but also on other health and prevention topics, such as substance abuse prevention, general health, and nutrition (Pick et al., 1988). It was the first step toward IMIFAP's comprehensive prevention programs.

After various program evaluations, we noticed that more comprehensive programs generated a stronger sense of personal agency in the participants. Furthermore, we found that through repeated success of behavior change in situations targeted by Programming for Choice, individuals developed control in other spheres of their lives as well. How this came to light requires another story.

One morning a number of women came to IMIFAP. They explained that as a result of their participation in the "Planning Your Life" program,[17], they were taking care of their health, using contraceptives, getting Pap smears, cooking and eating more nutritiously, and vaccinating their children; they felt stronger, had more power, and were ready to undertake what they saw as a next stage in their development. The women told me they now needed a source of income. We persuaded the Finnish Ambassador to Mexico to provide a grant, and a few months later the Finnish government sent over an oven, trays, cake and pastry molds, and an enormous mixer. Meanwhile, the women had successfully convinced the well-known local French bakery, La Baguette, to provide baking classes. After about 6 months, the women's bakery opened with a large community gathering, mariachis, and media attention. The ambassador was delighted; the women even more so. The families of the women gazed at the bakery in disbelief. Thereafter, many of the family members commented on the changes they had observed in these women and, consequently, in their community.

When we asked the women why they had inquired for help starting a business, they attributed their courage to the skills and confidence they had gained from their new behaviors and the outlook on life that came as a result of the health course. The success of actions such as communicating with their partner, negotiating for their needs within the family, or questioning a doctor about their health gave them confidence in their capacity to transcend the norms. Although the need for income had always been an issue, it was only after demonstrating that they were capable of taking risks and initiative, caring for themselves—and doing all of this successfully—that these women dared to take a larger step. So began the micro-enterprise programs at IMIFAP.

From "Planning Your Life," the women became aware of opportunities that they might not have recognized without first developing the self-knowledge and critical consciousness to understand how they could improve their lives. In psychological terms, these women felt more self-efficacious and autonomous and were moving toward a more internal locus of control; they had developed a sense of personal agency. They were increasingly taking initiative, talking about difficult matters, and taking control of their lives. The bakery constituted not only a confirmation of the value of multithematic programs but a step toward more comprehensive programming; it was the first effort on the part of IMIFAP to integrate economic well-being into its health promotion programs. At the same time, IMIFAP launched its first international program, demonstrating the effectiveness of life skills-based programs elsewhere in Latin America and, a few years later, in Europe and other regions of the world as well.

Institutionalizing Comprehensive Health Education

This more comprehensive approach to programs proved useful when the Ministry of Education launched a life skills course for secondary schools with a focus on civics and citizenship. The course would address new thematic content and be delivered for 3 consecutive years from first through third grade of secondary school (grades seven through nine). Additionally, for the first time in the history of the Ministry of Education, publishing companies were invited to write, design, and illustrate books that the Ministry would distribute in accordance with teachers' preferences. IMIFAP was invited by a publishing company to participate and pulled together a diverse group of experts, including educational psychologist Martha Givaudan, philosophers Antonio Tenorio and Alfredo Troncoso, civil rights lawyer Francisco Fernández, and myself. Having such an interdisciplinary perspective was useful to look at the enhancement of freedoms, and responsibility through these freedoms, from different viewpoints using a participatory and reflection-based methodology; the course was meant to be fun for students.

Teachers nationwide selected books from 10 finalists. The book the majority of the teachers selected from those final 10 was IMIFAP's "Civics and Ethics Formation."[18] Three million copies were printed initially and more than three times that number were printed within a few years, representing about one-third of the total circulated and reaching close to 12 million students.

By 2000, a substantive portion of secondary school youth in Mexico had access to a book that contained a life skills education program.[19] Additionally, almost all of the books the teachers chose incorporated a participatory teaching methodology, life skills training, and competency development. This advancement reached far beyond the establishment of sexuality education; it became a revolution in teaching methodology and philosophy in an interactive style that promoted self-reflection, learning, creativity, and participation. An added accomplishment of the initiative was the effective CSO and public sector partnership, which had historically been challenging. Much of the success of "Civics and Ethics Formation" can be attributed to the substantive work of many CSOs for better sexuality education and sexuality education training programs, as well as the advocacy and dissemination undertaken by a number of government officials.[20]

The subsequent step was to train teachers, as they would be conducting the programs in the secondary schools nationwide. One of the primary obstacles here was that many government officials felt that providing teachers with the program books was enough, and therefore they were not interested in investing teacher time or federal funding in training. Consequently, CSOs pursued an additional round of negotiations with various groups of influence[21] to ensure the teachers would be properly trained to provide the program to their students. The government agreed that CSOs would provide the training, and they would ensure 4 hours of time set aside for this training each year. Although this seemed insufficient, it helped to sensitize the teachers to the material and make them aware of the need for a life skills orientation. Additionally, groups such as the Office of the Undersecretary of Education for Mexico City facilitated longer training sessions and made available an optional diploma for 120 hours of training.

Similarly to the previous trainings, the change in teacher reception of the programs over time demonstrated how motivation can shift from extrinsic or systemic to instrinsic. Vivian, one of the teacher participants, illustrates this transformation in her testimony:

> I only came because if not, they would discount [payment for] the days. After a few hours, things started to make sense, and after a few days much more so. I started connecting what I was hearing with my life, with questions I had asked myself many times. It was as if pieces of a puzzle were coming together. I understood my needs, that I had rights and how to make them valid. I then started attending because I wanted to, not only because I was supposed to.

The teachers affirmed that the programs motivated students to participate, to be responsible, and to do their homework. As a result, the teachers' jobs became more interesting and rewarding. "It helps me solve personal problems, and helps me feel sure of myself," said José Juan, a secondary school student in Chihuahua, Mexico. And teachers' relationships with their students improved. "I now realize I have a say ... not only in the class, but also at home. That makes it easier for me to allow my children, both in school and at home, to have a say too," commented Amparo, a teacher in Guanajuato, Mexico. Finally, the teachers expressed increased empowerment and motivation in the classroom:

> I was no longer afraid of speaking my mind, of trying new things, and even more importantly of saying the truth, of not hiding it. It became clear to me that I have

rights and that I can say what I need and think without shame. It made me grow, and helped me help the kids to be better citizens, to be more sure of themselves.

—Crisóforo, a young male teacher, Campeche, Mexico

Based on professor Robert Hartman's theory of axiology, a good part of the success of "Civics and Ethics Formation" can be attributed to the intrinsic motivation of the teachers, which can lead to feelings of program ownership and motivation to extend new skills to other classroom subjects and to improved personal lives. His theories support the argument that teachers implementing programs based on extrinsic and systemic factors (e.g., money, trying to please the administration, orders from the Ministry of Education) would lead to less sustainable program outcomes. Years later, follow-up interviews with teachers in Coahuila and Mexico City, where the program had been most widely implemented, showed that those teachers who felt the program benefited their personal development were more motivated and thus continued replicating the program far beyond the intended time period (Pick & Givaudan, 2007).[22]

This framework provided the initial foundation for identifying the needs and defining the problems with sex education[23] in Mexico. It has since driven the successive health promotion and poverty reduction programs that IMIFAP has developed for marginalized communities in Mexico and Latin America. It has made the difference between a knowledge base for programs and a practical behavior base, between short-lived efforts that are externally imposed and needs based sustainable development that expands individual and community freedoms and can break the poverty cycle.

—Susan Pick, Mexico City, March 2, 2010

Notes

1. Mexico legalized the use of contraceptives in 1973 with the General Law of Population.

2. We have elected to use "civil society organization" as the operative word to describe IMIFAP and the host of other existing organizations engaging in similar work. We have chosen this term over the more widely utilized "not for profit" and "nongovernmental organization" as it includes and acknowledges the for profit entities that too are undertaking human and community development work in the region.

3. *See* Chapter 4.

4. Later we would reform this view, advocating for prevention programs to be implemented in pre-adolescents (before the onset of sexual activity) (Pick & Givaudan, 2007; Pick et al., 2007).

5. Comments from adolescents reflected the strong influence of norms: "What will people think of me if I talk about those things?" "Whether or not to have sex is the man's decision. He uses us ... that is the woman's role." "Don't you know that saying 'no' is bad manners, especially to a male?" "But if I come prepared to have sex, he will think that I want to have sex." "Yes, we have had sex education. We have been told that menstruation is dangerous because it is when you can get pregnant, that contraceptive use is sinful, that men only want 'that,' and that we have to protect our virginity." "Yes, we have had sex education but I did not understand anything. The doctor just mentioned

lots of difficult names for all these parts. I guess it is done like that so that we do not ask too many questions."

6. The discrepancy in the dates is because it often took us many years to write and publish our research findings and evaluation results.

7. The original Spanish title was *Planeando Tu Vida*.

8. Ten CSOs from seven different countries came together to talk about their work on prevention of risk behaviors (Weisen & Orley, 1996).

9. Life skills-based programs integrate knowledge with its application, promoting opportunities to utilize the newly learned skills. Life skills-based programs, for example, have individuals making decisions, not just talking about them; practicing assertive communication and reflecting on the individual's strengths and weaknesses in confronting a difficult negotiation. Also, they often employ a small group structure because the group provides feedback, critical for skills building, and the social permission to learn and use the skills, key in populations that rely centrally on others' approval. After incorporating life skills into prevention programming, program developers recognized the instrumental value of this approach in areas such as children's education (Cronin, 1996; Van Biema & Dowell, 1996), business (IMIFAP, 2008), health, nutrition, and environmental protection (Atchoarena & Gasperini, 2003). Businesses have also turned to life-skills based capacity-building in recruitment and training (Callieri, 2001; Gibb, 1995). Such diverse application of life skills programming reinforces its applicability and capacity to improve performance in many settings.

10. Secondary school in Mexico refers to seventh through ninth grade.

11. The ads decried: "[L]ow-level officials of the S.E.P. [Ministry of Education], are determined to trample the dignity of the individual through pushing youth into sexual debauchery...In the final week of August last year, in the city of Querétaro, a "training" course was given to teachers of the second year of secondary school [eighth grade] who as part of the pilot program are already teaching an adolescence and sexuality class, renamed adolescence and development. The Mexican Institute of Family and Population Research was in charge of the course, and although various texts were proposed, they finally decided on the books "I Am an Adolescent" and "Planning Your Life," co-edited by IMIFAP itself." (Unión Nacional de Padres de Familia, 1991)

12. The Spanish title was "Me, an Adolescent" [Yo adolescente] (Pick de Weiss & Vargas Trujillo, 1990), which in its most recent edition was renamed "I Am an Adolescent: My Challenges, My Risks and My Expectations" [Soy adolescente: mis retos, mis riesgos y mis expectativas] (Pick & Givaudan, 2004).

13. "La posibilidad de incluir clases de educación sexual en las escuelas secundarias del país ya ha sido ampliamente discutida en el seno del Consejo Técnico de la Educación, por lo que sobre el contenido del Programa Adolescencia y Juventud, no hay nada que argumentar, manifestó el secretario de Educación Pública, Manuel Bartlett Díaz."

14. The Spanish title was *Platícame de "eso"*.

15. A colleague who in 2006 would run in the presidential election.

16. "La educación ... tendrá, además de los fines establecidos en el segundo párrafo del artículo 3o. de la Constitución Política de los Estados Unidos Mexicanos, los siguientes: ... Desarrollar actitudes solidarias en los individuos, para crear conciencia sobre la preservación de la salud, la planeación familiar y la paternidad responsable, sin menoscabo de la libertad y del respeto absoluto a la dignidad humana, así como propiciar el rechazo a los vicios..."

17. This account is written about a time when IMIFAP was piloting a new version of the life skills and sexuality education program "Planning Your Life" with a group of

about 70 women in the Center for Community Development of *Desarrollo Integral para la Familia*, which is comparable to a Ministry for Family Affairs. The piloted program expanded the thematic focus to include cancer, among other health topics.

18. The Spanish title was *"Formación cívica y ética: yo quiero, yo puedo."* This program was initially entitled *"Adolescencia y sexualidad"* [*Adolescence and sexuality*].

19. They even included controversial topics such as emergency contraception.

20. Negotiations occurred both between and within states, between CSOs and the Ministry of Education, and with the National Labor Union of Education Workers [*Sindicato Nacional de Trabajadores de la Educación*].

21. With the development of teachers' sense of ownership over the program, "Civics and Ethics Formation" became more sustainable at a national level, nowadays implemented from elementary through secondary school.

22. In this book, the term "sex education" refers to those programs which aim to teach only about biological occurrences, such as menstruation, and do not include emotional elements. The term "sexuality education" refers to those programs which aim to teach not only about sex and the body, but also about psychosocial barriers, personal values, life skills, gender, emotions, rights and self-reflection, among other topics.

References

Ajzen, I., Albarracín, D., & Hornik, R. (Eds.). (2007). *Prediction and change of health behavior: Applying the reasoned action approach.* Mahwah, NJ: Lawrence Erlbaum Associates, Inc.

Atchoarena, D., & Gasperini, L. (2003). Education for rural development: Towards new policy responses. Retrieved February 6, 2009, from United Nations Educational, Scientific and Cultural Organization/International Institute for Educational Planning and Food and Agriculture Organization: http://unesdoc.unesco.org/images/0013/001329/132994e.pdf.

Callieri, C. (2001). The knowledge economy: A business perspective. In D. S. Rychen & L. H. Salganik (Eds.), *Defining and selecting key competencies* (pp. 228–231). Seattle: Hogrefe & Huber Publishers.

Cronin, M. E. (1996). Life skills curricula for students with learning disabilities. *Journal of Learning Disabilities, 29*(1), 53–68.

Diario Oficial de la Federación (1993). *Ley general de la educación [General law of education].* Retrieved July 27, 2007, from www.ordenjuridico.gob.mx/Federal/PE/PR/Leyes/13071993(1).pdf.

Fishbein, M., & Ajzen, I. (1975). *Belief, attitude, intention, and behavior: An introduction to theory and research.* Reading, MA: Addison-Wesley.

Gibb, A. A. (1995). *Learning skills for all: The key to success in small business development.* Paper presented at the International Council for Small Business 40th World Conference. Sydney, Australia. Retrieved September 14, 2008.

Girerd, J.-R. (Writer) (1991). The joy of life. Canada: The Multimedia Group of Canada [MGC].

Hartman, R. S. (1967). *The structure of value: Foundations of scientific axiology.* Carbondale, Illinois: Southern Illinois University Press.

Instituto Mexicano de Investigación de Familia y Población [IMIFAP] (2008). *Colaboración de organizaciones México-Guatemala-Honduras para el fortalecimiento de capabilidades humanas: Fase I [Colaboration of Mexican, Guatemalan and Honduran organizations for the fortification of human capabilities: Phase I].* Mexico City: IMIFAP.

Instituto Mexicano de Investigación de Familia y Población [IMIFAP] (1993). *Final report on the project: Development of support for national sex education in Mexico. Report presented to The Moriah Fund, The Prospect Hill Foundation and The John Merck Fund.* Mexico City: IMIFAP.

Isaacs, S., Cairns, G., & Heckel, N. (1985). *Population policy: A manual for policymakers and planners.* New York: Columbia University.

Miranda, G. O. (1991, November 11). La SEP no hará modificaciones al programa: El Conalte tomó la decisión por consenso [The Ministry of Public Education will not make modifications to the program: The National Technical Council on Education made the decision by consensus]. *El Heraldo de Mexico,* p. 1A.

Pick de Weiss, S. (1978). *A social psychological study of family planning in Mexico City.* Unpublished Thesis, University of London, London.

Pick de Weiss, S., Aguilar Gil, J. A., Rodriguez, G., Trujillo, E. V., & Pardo, J. R. (1991). *Planeando tu vida [Planning your life]* (5th ed.). Mexico City: Editorial Limusa.

Pick de Weiss, S., & Andrade Palos, P. (1989). Development and longitudinal evaluation of comparative sexuality education courses, *Report presented to the United States Agency for International Development.* Mexico City: IMIFAP.

Pick de Weiss, S., Andrade Palos, P., & Townsend, J. (1990). *Planeando tu vida: Development and testing of a family life education program for young adults.* Mexico City: IMIFAP.

Pick de Weiss, S., Andrade Palos, P., Townsend, J., & Givaudan, M. (1994). Evaluación de un programa de educación sexual sobre conocimientos, conducta sexual y anti-concepción en adolescentes [Evaluation of a sexuality education program on knowledge, behavior and contraception in adolescents]. *Salud Mental,* 17(17), 25–31.

Pick de Weiss, S., Atkin, L. C., Gribble, J. M., & Andrade Palos, P. (1991). Sex, contraception, and pregnancy among adolescents in Mexico City. *Studies in Family Planning,* 22(2), 74–82.

Pick de Weiss, S., Montero, M., & Aguilar, J. (1988). *Planeando tu vida [Planning your life]* (1st ed.). Mexico City: Editorial Pax México.

Pick de Weiss, S., & Vargas Trujillo, E. (1990). *Yo adolescente: Respuestas claras a mis grandes dudas [I, adolescent: Clear answers to my greatest doubts].* Mexico City: Editorial Planeta.

Pick, S. (1975). *Relationship between risk taking and cognitive processes.* Unpublished B.Sc., London School of Economics and Political Science, University of London, London.

Pick, S., Aguilar, J., Rodríguez, G., Reyes, J., Collado, M. E., Pier, D., Acevedo, M. P., & Vargas, E. (1988). *Planeando tu vida: Programa de educación sexual y para la vida dirigido a los adolescentes. [Planning your life: Sexual education program and life skills program for adolescents].* Mexico City: Editorial Planeta Mexicana.

Pick, S., Díaz-Loving, R., & Atkin, L. (1988). Adolescentes en la Ciudad de México: Estudio psicosocial de prácticas anticonceptivas y embarazo no deseado [Adolescents in Mexico City: Psychosocial study of contraceptive practices and unwanted pregnancy], *Report presented to the Pan American Health Organization and the United Nations Fund for Population Activities.* Mexico City: IMIFAP.

Pick, S., & Givaudan, M. (2004). *Soy adolescente: mis retos, mis riesgos y mis expectativas [I am an adolescent: My challenges, my risks and my expectations].* Mexico City: Editorial IDEAME.

Pick, S., & Givaudan, M. (2007). Yo quiero, yo puedo: estrategia para el desarrollo de habilidades y competencias en el sistema escolar [I want to, I can: Strategy for the development of skills and competencies within the school system]. *Psicologia da Educação: Revista do Programa de Estudos Pós-Graduados em Psicologia da Educação/ Pontifícia Universidade Católica de São Paulo, 23*, 203–221.

Pick, S., Givaudan, M., Sirkin, J., & Ortega, I. (2007). Communication as a protective factor: Evaluation of a life skills HIV/AIDS prevention program for Mexican elementary-school students. *AIDS Education and Prevention,* 19(5), 408–421.

Sen, A. (1983). Poor, relatively speaking. *Oxford Economic Papers,* 35(2), 153–169.

Sen, A. (1985). Well-being, agency and freedom: The Dewey Lectures 1984. *The Journal of Philosophy,* 82(4), 169–221.

Sen, A. (1999). *Development as freedom.* New York: Anchor.

Unión Nacional de Padres de Familia, A. C. (1991, November 5). ¿Porque se insiste en empujar a la juventud al libertinaje sexual? [Why must they insist on pushing the youth toward sexual debauchery?]. *El Heraldo de Mexico,* p. 10A.

Van Biema, D., & Dowell, W. (1996, November 11). Just say life skills. *Time,* 148(22), 70.

Weisen, R. B., & Orley, J. (1996). *Life skills education planning for research as an integral part of life skills education development, implementation and maintenance.* Paper presented at the Program on Mental Health. Geneva.

Wolfson, M. (1978). *Changing approaches to population problems.* Paris: OECD.

World Health Organization [WHO] (1999). Partners in life skills education: Conclusions from a United Nations inter-agency meeting, Geneva.

Yunus, M. (2009). *Creating a world without poverty: Social business and the future of capitalism.* New York: Public Affairs.

CONTENTS

FIGURES

BREAKING THE POVERTY CYCLE

CHAPTER 1

Introduction

Recent development efforts failed because they were aimed at symptoms rather than at underlying causes.

—David Dollar (2003, p. 50)

The roots of sustainable development lie, to a great degree, in the capacity of people to overcome their psychological, social, and contextual barriers, to view the world through a new lens, as *agents* (rather than passive recipients) of change. From this perspective, both personal and social change begins at the psychological level. People must learn to exercise control over their own lives and make choices. The difficulty is that the population at large experiences a lack of control because the needs, interests, and plans of a few prevail, and this dominant logic becomes the lens through which we view the world (Prahalad, 2006). Sofia, a young woman in Panajachel, Guatemala, expresses such constraints and lack of control over her life:

> The clinic is very close, but I don't like going there. It is for people that know how to ask things. I am ashamed of going there. Anyway, if I get sick that is fate, there is nothing I can do. It is much better to let fate decide than to feel ashamed of going there.

Antonio Manuel, a middle-aged man in Arequipa, Peru expresses a similar sentiment:

> Things do not depend on me, others decide my life. For example, it makes no sense to vote. We are supposed to be a democracy but the reality is I don't feel my vote leads to anything that will benefit me or my family. It is for the benefit of a powerful group. They come and talk and talk and offer and offer and they don't listen to us. They don't care. I don't feel anyone represents my needs and my problems. Politics is about the interests of the parties and the powerful people

not about the needs of the people they are supposed to govern or to serve. So my vote does not really help us, it only helps them.

In the presence of these seemingly insurmountable obstacles, which are especially prominent in developing countries and marginalized communities, breaking the poverty cycle may seem far-fetched. Yet programs and policies have the capacity to affect people on this most basic psychosocial level. Development and improvements in well-being occur only through the expansion of choice—that is, the enhancement of alternatives, of being able to make decisions in an informed, autonomous and responsible manner, and taking responsibility for the outcomes. Programs can be designed to promote this transformative process, where individuals gain the confidence and skills to take control of their own lives and go from being *objects* of change to *agents* of change. This is the basis of sustainable, expandable, and scalable development.

Most programs and public policy, however, tend to focus solely on contextual issues—mainly economic and legal aspects—seeing them as prerequisites for personal development and policy changes. Yet human development programs can mobilize individuals so effectively that this sequence that many take for granted is reversed. After all, it is individuals who make the decisions that shape the health, education, political, legal, economic, and cultural contexts. Despite recent recognition of this, and movement in the development field away from exclusively contextual focuses to include psychological and social components as well, the concepts have not been fully developed, and political will is still lacking. We continue to focus much more on political goals than on people's needs. This is why we see hype placed on short-term photo opportunities rather than on real, long-term development. Such changes are more easily visible and therefore more interesting to politics and the media; it is easier to show off a new road than an employee with initiative and responsibility, a luxurious clinic than an adolescent who is able to prevent unnecessary health risks, a shiny new school than teachers who know how to use participatory teaching strategies.

The aim of this book is to present a framework and a strategy of how to expand individual choice and contextually based opportunities to improve well-being beyond that which is provided by traditional socio-economic development theory. This expanded conceptualization of development requires an interdisciplinary approach, incorporating psychology, political philosophy, community psychology, and economics. Drawing from theories and methods across these disciplines, we provide the conceptual and methodological background for programs in resource-limited settings, with an emphasis on Mexico.

In most of the world, a powerful minority has control—both explicitly and implicitly—over the rest of the population; the majority is subject to the needs, interests, and plans of the few. For powerful groups—governments, private enterprises, and individuals in positions of power—a paternalistic and autocratic approach to governing and leadership proves comfortable. The lack of control that "the rest" experience may be objective or subjective, the former means that they do not have access to choice, and the latter results from their perceptions (psychological view) of the world. Both scenarios are problematic. A power imbalance restricts the opportunities available to those who are not members of influential groups. This context of inequality contributes to psychological barriers that constrain choice, which, in turn, limit access to those opportunities that do exist. Barriers often become self-perpetuating inhibitors of development. As C. K. Prahalad describes, "We are prisoners of our own socialization and a resultant dominant logic" (2006, p. 50).

Citizens of the Majority World[1] often view the world through a lens of subjugation and obedience, the consequence of a system that suppresses reflection, participation, the development of individual competencies, and the practical application of knowledge. Individuals struggle to reach their full potential because choice and autonomy are limited from their childhood years onward, and therefore when the opportunity is later presented, it can be anxiety producing (Iyengar & DeVoe, 2003). In addition, the negative effects of poverty and lack of opportunity permeate a range of domains at the individual and community level (e.g., education, psychological and physical health, and finances) and accumulate across generations (Morán, Sen, & Brundtland, 2004). This lack of psychological access to opportunities represents a "poverty trap." From this perspective, the poor exhibit behaviors that make them and keep them poor (Banerjee & Newman, 1994, p. 71). Even if opportunities and resources exist (e.g., a health clinic located nearby), the psychological access may be remote because of a lack of essential perceived or actual control.

Of course, there are genetic, personal, and contingent factors that might affect how poverty, or conversely an enabling context, will affect a person. After all, "the poor" are not monolithic, and response to situational changes will vary. At the same time, a context of exaggerated inequality has devastating effects on the process of personal and collective growth. It results in a permeating sense of futility in the poorest sector, stunting both psychological and "real" access to choice and opportunities. Systemic inequalities diminish both perceived and existing opportunities and can easily lead to a self-perpetuating condition of social injustice, in turn contributing to further inequality.

The Gini coefficient[2] indicates that there are high levels of inequality across Latin America (Lopez & Perry, 2008). The origins of this pronounced disparity in resources and opportunities can be traced to "a colonization strategy that led to highly exclusionary institutions in much of Latin America and the Caribbean, where a large fraction of the [indigenous population] remained for a long time excluded from access to land, education and political power" (Lopez & Perry, 2008, p. 13). Although the factors contributing to prevalence of contemporary inequality have become increasingly complex, efforts to address historical inequities and remedy present-day inequalities are complicated by low educational attainment, lack of political and socio-economic access, and, by extension, human rights across ethnic groups. The legacies of colonization have morphed into the current situation, where inequalities still permeate society and present both psychological and contextual barriers across domains and sectors.

This inequality has many repercussions at the contextual and individual (psychological) levels. Indicators at the contextual level demonstrate this lack of opportunity: high rates of unemployment (and underemployment), absence of schools and health clinics, unpredictable quality of public services, and laws that are differentially enforced and applied. High levels of inequality tend to be associated with low income mobility and reduced incentives to work, effectively taking a toll on the economy and reducing the positive effects of education. Although the cost to families of keeping their children in schools is higher in poorer populations, the benefits these children receive are lower[3] (Lopez & Perry, 2008). Psychological implications go hand-in-hand with contextual implications. Informal education in the home and through the media and formal education in the schools establishes a normative environment that fosters fear, shame, and guilt. Each of these factors strongly deters the development of personal initiative and the ability to reflect on one's rights and opportunities. Resource-based, educational, and psychological inequalities accumulate and compound the already damaging effects of economic disparities.

The influence of economic inequality and poor psychological access is especially evident when development services fail to reach their target populations. Objectively having opportunities is not sufficient; the individual must perceive having access. In other words, a person must emotionally and cognitively see the opportunities and understand that he has the right to access them, that he need not feel ashamed, fearful, or guilty for making use of them. When the psychological effects of poverty and inequality remain unaddressed, development programs often report underutilization, low participation, and even low awareness of the available services. It may not be sufficient to have information about existing services, just like it may not be sufficient to provide clinics and schools. The individual must be enabled to understand his rights to actively participate, to access these services, and, even further, to push for changes so that they better address his needs. If one is accustomed to always asking for permission and being denied with little or no explanation, or to simply following orders, then it will be very difficult for her to make use of opportunities. She needs to understand and have the emotional and cognitive elements to view contextual opportunities as an entitlement rather than a privilege.

Many services are underutilized because of direct barriers to care, including lack of available services, not knowing where or how to access them, financial and transportation barriers, and time constraints (Saldivia et al., 2004). At the same time, indirect, social barriers can also deter people from seeking the care and services that are technically available to them (Saldivia et al., 2004). This is particularly the case of socially and politically sensitive development initiatives, including mental health, contraception, and abortion. In India, for example, many women living in rural areas are unaware that abortion is legal. Some women who seek abortions encounter resistance from medical professionals, who at times even "insist that a woman undergoing a legal abortion also have an IUD inserted or be sterilized" (Alan Guttmacher Institute, 1999, p. 32). Because India's abortion legislation failed to address the social and psychological barriers still in place, it actually encouraged women to seek riskier extralegal abortions (Alan Guttmacher Institute, 1999, p. 32). In Mexico, one of the factors contributing to underutilization of health services are the prevalent myths surrounding health service use; women resisted cervical cancer treatment for fear that it would leave them sexually disabled (Bingham et al., 2003). The mere availability of care was not enough to ensure its delivery. Other obstacles to seeking care include low levels of confidence in government services (Barnes-Josiah, Myntti, & Augustin, 1998; Gilson, 2003), a lack of translators in indigenous areas, fear of breaches in confidentiality, and discomfort around male providers (Bingham et al., 2003).

Psychological and contextual factors are interrelated, both as barriers and as solutions to poverty. Addressed together, in an integrated manner, they can serve to enhance the options individuals and communities have for growth and development. Although a theoretical discussion exists on the relationship between the macro- and microfactors as well as successful programs to address them, the link between the theoretical and practical application is infrequently emphasized. This book aims to fill this gap in the literature.

Here we should mention that we have chosen to use the pronouns "he" and "she" interchangeably throughout this book. The exclusive use of "he" brings up questions of gender inequality and can be seen as excluding the women who are the focus of many of IMIFAP's programs. The exclusive use of "she" equally excludes men and can sound self-conscious. By using the terms interchangeably, we address both these issues and avoid the cumbersome "he or she." Hereafter, we refer to the generic individual using the pronouns interchangeably.

The Capability Approach and Its Implications for Development

Traditionally, development theory has grown from the field of economics, taking precedence over the contributions of other disciplines. The macroeconomics (promotion of national growth) and micro-economics (incentives for individuals and firms) of developing countries represent central arenas of the development field. While we recognize the importance of attaining economic security, we must adjust our theories of progress to include the many other facets of well-being that human beings strive to attain. A Human Development Report produced by the United Nations Development Program (UNDP) points out the shortcomings of a purely economic interpretation:

> As Aristotle argued, "Wealth is evidently not the good we are seeking; for it is merely useful and for the sake of something else." That "something else" is the opportunity of people to realize their potential as human beings. Real opportunity is about having real choices—the choices that come with a sufficient income, an education, good health and living in a country that is not governed by tyranny. (UNDP, 2006, p. 263)

By largely neglecting research surrounding the psychological, structural, and social barriers impeding sustainable development, theoretical discussion has failed to explain why people have difficulty accessing and expanding the opportunities available to them. Research on the effectiveness of international aid has found that financial assistance is often not linked to human development and national growth (Boone, 1996; Ovaska, 2003). Just as democracy does not provide an automatic remedy against political apathy and new clinics cannot promise solutions to poor community health, large budgets will not serve as the silver bullet for poverty reduction. Sen writes that the opportunities opened up by improvements in contextual spheres must "be positively grabbed in order to achieve the desired effect" (Sen, 1999, p. 155).

Sen views poverty as capabilities deprivation. Capabilities are "what real opportunities you have regarding the life you may lead" (Sen, 1987, p. 36)—they are opportunities to realize one's potential. They are freedoms that are comprised of accessible[4] opportunities dependent on psychological and social circumstances. In Sen's view, poverty should be explained in terms of a lack of substantial freedoms and capabilities instead of mere income deprivation. He argues for a comprehensive view of development that goes beyond the usual assessment of changes in resources, income, or utility (Robeyns, 2005; Sen, 1999). In the midst of the range of poverties that a person may experience—economic, psychological, social, political, and physical—an individual with expanded capabilities will be able to expand her freedoms in accordance with her interests and needs.

In his Capability Approach, Sen (1999) argues that freedoms are the essence of development, pointing to "functionings" and "capabilities" as the means to achieve these freedoms. Within the category of functionings, he refers to "doing functionings," which are actual behaviors, and "being functionings," which are the more stable characteristics within a person that are preceded by behaviors. An individual's capability is defined by the "various combinations of functionings that a person can achieve" (Sen, 1992, p. 40). Capability, then, is what one is able to do, regardless of whether she chooses to do it. Sen argues that development should be measured through capability rather than income, utility, or primary goods. The latter indicators may not necessarily translate into desired ends or even well-being. Capabilities, however, measure particular ends that are of value to the individual.

Based on Sen's work, we can conceptualize the Capability Approach as a broad framework for sustainable development that sees enhancement of capabilities as the goal of development, valuing both individual and contextual factors as essential components of policies, programs, and evaluation for social change. We use the Capability Approach to build a framework for a psychosocial, people-centered approach to development programs, making operative the work of Amartya Sen.

Psychology as Related to Development

In contrast to economists, psychologists mainly focus on change at the individual level. The discipline addresses topics such as asserting control, building self-efficacy, and increasing autonomy. Recently, psychologists have begun to focus more consistently on the effects of poverty on well-being (Evans, 2004) and on the role that psychology may play in economic and social development issues (Kagitcibasi, 2005). Evans (2004), for example, found significant negative correlations between extreme poverty and well-being. Low-income parents tend to have less time and resources to invest in their children, poorer quality daycare centers, and noisier and more crowded homes; live in poor neighborhoods (with few municipal services); and have children who attend inferior schools and who have limited access to or receive poor quality health care. All of these factors detract from the well-being of families across generations. A study of children under age 6 years in developing countries who were living in absolute poverty, showed that they performed poorly in school and were likely to transfer their impoverished condition to future generations (Grantham-McGregor et al., 2007). All of these psychological, social, and structural barriers accumulate and feed off one another and create a cycle of poverty. McClelland (1961), laid the theoretical groundwork for breaking this cycle, suggesting that people with a high need for achievement were more successful in entrepreneurship and less influenced by others than those with low achievement needs. He argued that intrinsic motivation could be learned and that fostering this motivation was important to economic development. Providing insight for initiatives looking to do just that, he found that intrinsic motivation will be strongest when feelings of challenge, competence, and self-determination are fostered (Nakanishi, 2002).

Although the specific environment affects individual behavior, much of McClelland's psychological theory can be implemented cross-culturally. The universality of psychological processes allows for diverse applications. Psychology provides an immense resource for policy developers. Recently some economists, realizing that poverty may negatively affect "rational" decision making, have encouraged changes in development economics; they are giving new attention to the benefits of human and social capital and to distributional issues (Mkandawire, 2001; Sachs, 2005; Woolcock & Narayan, 2000). There has been more recognition, for example, that mistrust in governments may reduce participation rates in government programs and that poor women might have multiple sexual partners to pay their expenses even though it increases their risk of HIV/AIDS. The ability to translate aspects of behavior into economic terms such as human capital and social capital has facilitated the shift in focus.

The explicit link between psychology and policy is only rarely acknowledged in economic and social development literature. Moreover, recommendations from the psychology discipline are often not translated into development practices. The application of psychosocial understandings is often met with skepticism (Antonides, 1996; Nakanishi, 2002; Sternberg & Lyon, 2002). This is especially apparent in developing countries where psychology often does not figure as a social science. Over the last two decades, however, some authors have emphasized that psychology could play an important role in development if the field focused on macrolevel analyses (e.g., Ogbu, 1987 in [Kagitcibasi,

2002]; [Fernández-Ballesteros, 2002]). The UNDP's and OECD's recent incorporation of psychosocial metrics in their indicators is evidence of the expanding perspective in the development arena (OECD, 2006; UNDP, 2007).

Although a broader perspective is emerging, these new ideas still need to be put into practice. IMIFAP's experience and gradual program development exemplify this process. When we began work in this field, we were trying to find the means through which to enhance the well-being of poverty-stricken individuals and communities, who faced an overwhelming number of constraints on growth and development. We used the Theory of Reasoned Action and the work of Prochaska and Diclemente as a guide and sought to identify the obstacles these individuals and communities faced, as well as the needs they expressed. From there, we worked to find the best means of tackling the challenges they experienced.

There is a need to strike a balance in development initiatives between the context and the individual. Individual-focused strategies must be complemented by "strategies that affect the larger political, media, family and community environment" (Mangrulkar, Whitman, & Posner, 2001, p. 6). Social networks are particularly important, as they play a key role in making an individual feel sufficiently supported by his environment to transfer new skills to everyday situations. There is a reciprocal relationship between enhancing individual choice and contextually based opportunities; each feeds on the other. Furthermore, an intention to expand freedoms, capabilities, and choices must rest at the core of all efforts. This central intention is often left out of the discussion and planning of development policy, as "most governments favor policies that offer easily perceived short-term benefits, such as subsidies, protection, and arranged mergers—the very policies that retard innovation" (Porter, 1998, p. 185).

We offer a framework and strategy for achieving freedom and development in a sustainable way that views the role of the individual within a dynamic context. Doing so includes support for continued social connectedness—it is in no means in opposition to it. We will address the needs of groups with few opportunities and little realization that they have rights or that they can gain the skills to access and further them. Without an agent-oriented view of development through expanding choice and freedoms, development is limited; the possibilities for participating as responsible individuals and citizens are diminished. Moreover, without the personal tools and characteristics to make individual rights a reality, personal and community freedoms are severely hampered. Investing in the capacity of the individual can have an effective and sustainable impact at the community level.

The Foundation of the Framework: Personal Agency and Intrinsic Empowerment

Freedoms provide people with a range of alternatives for action, and when these individuals are supplied with a toolbox of competencies and are enabled to see opportunities as their own, they are further able to make decisions and prioritize these in an autonomous fashion. If people are not enabled to choose and to act on the choices they make, then they will not be able to take advantage of the opportunities within their reach. We propose the term *personal agency* to describe the process through which a person carries out informed and intrinsically motivated decisions in an autonomous fashion. It is a multifaceted concept, emerging from the literature, qualitative results, and field experience. The term is adapted from Sen's conception, defined as "what a person is free to do and achieve in pursuit of whatever goals or values he or she regards as important" (Sen, 1985, p. 203). Personal agency focuses on the role of internal development, integrating several concepts from social psychology and personality literature that describe personal qualities: control (Rotter, 1966), autonomy (Kagitcibasi, 2005), and self-efficacy (Bandura, 1997). Central to these concepts are the intentions, meanings, and motivations that an individual brings to his behaviors (Kabeer, 1999). Intrinsically derived intentions, meanings, and motivations are central in the formation and state of personal agency. A sense of personal agency forms as the actual or perceived results of intrinsically driven behaviors affect a variety of domains.

As a result of this internal change, the individual is in a position to influence his context in a sustainable fashion. We have termed this *intrinsic empowerment*—that is, the sense and the ability to change the context, and therein promote development at the contextual level. The process of developing intrinsic empowerment is based on the reciprocal relationship between the individual's competencies (personal agency) to address situational demands and the existing contextual barriers or facilitators. Most empowerment strategists define empowerment by contrasting it with disempowerment and "unfreedoms." They focus on the impact that "unfreedoms" have on social and welfare inequalities and how powerlessness can be a risk factor that adversely affects quality of life and health (Moser, 1989; Rowlands, 1995; Sen, 1999). Empowerment has also been defined as a means of enhancing an individual's or group's capacity to make choices and transform those choices into desired actions and outcomes (Alsop & Heinsohn, 2005). A distinction should be made between internally driven action and action brought about through external factors. The difference is crucial because externally driven change, through rewards or external pressure, is likely to remain dependent on the continued availability of its external motivator. In other words, externally driven change is not self-sustaining.

The Framework for Enabling Empowerment (FrEE)

Out of this perspective comes our Framework for Enabling Empowerment (FrEE) (*see* Fig. 4–1a and Fig. 4–1b), which emphasizes the role of personal agency and intrinsic empowerment, focusing on the "real freedoms that people enjoy" (Sen, 1999, p. 3). FrEE provides the conceptual and strategic foundation for this book and a means for analyzing, designing, and implementing sustainable development programs. It provides a roadmap for increasing people's capabilities in an integrated and sustainable manner through a dialectical relationship between the individual and the varying components of the context. These components are economic, political, educational, and sociocultural. We present FrEE as a practical means of bringing Sen's Capability Approach into practice, incorporating the psychosocial perspective as a means to promote sustainable development.

We briefly discuss the framework here to introduce the reader to the central ideas of the book. The core concepts of personal agency and intrinsic empowerment within this framework emphasize the individual's centrality in development programs. The individual's fundamental and continuous role in the development process is a pillar of our strategy. It is the people themselves who develop the programs and policies that can make a difference in their lives and in their communities. The individual's ability to affect change—both on a personal level and within the greater community—has important implications for policy design. By recognizing this potential, FrEE goes beyond the traditional framework of aid programs, paternalistic government policies, and services that have viewed people as passive players in the development process. It is based on the notion that there is a complementary relationship between externally derived and intrinsically motivated empowerment; FrEE recognizes that the latter is more likely to be sustainable, and the former has been traditionally addressed more in development programs.

FrEE uses the needs people express in concrete situations to design programs that aim to foster development through targeting specific behavioral changes within a life skills-based methodology. This is the only sustainable way to encourage individuals to establish their own objectives and to pursue them in a way that is socially supported within their communities. The framework incorporates related psychological processes to promote specific changes among communities that share common skills and face similar psychological barriers. Such barriers occur for many, and such skills are needed by many— from the politician and the bureaucrat who are afraid of delegating and thus losing control, to the parent who is not sure how to let go of his adolescent children, to the authoritarian teacher who controls her students' behaviors and decision-making processes, and the demanding boss who knows no other way but to humiliate her employees as a means of controlling them.

Implementation of this framework is done through the strategy we have termed "Programming for Choice." It begins with teaching individuals relevant skills, providing encouragement, and opening opportunities to practice behaviors in situations of increasing complexity within an umbrella of foresight, prevention, and the promotion of human development. This process leads to the acquisition of competencies, which, in turn, serve as protective factors that facilitate the development and use of one's potential. Given that not all capabilities and outcomes are equally valuable, the focus of development programs must be on the underlying concerns and values of the targeted community. In other words, the foundation of development programs that aim to expand people's freedoms must rest on the needs and problems expressed by the people themselves. The programs are conducted in a highly participatory manner, where it is the task of the individual to make decisions and solve problems, with a focus on reflection. In this way, the development of personal agency is not only enhanced through the program content (the acquisition of specific skills) but also through the methodology itself (safe opportunities to make one's own decisions).

A middle-aged woman who was a participant in the micro-enterprise program in Mexico City explained the benefits of these teaching methods:

> In the course they made us think, they made us solve problems instead of telling us what the solutions were. That made me feel good. It made me realize I could solve problems and not just listen to other people's solutions. It also made me realize that when I was the one looking for a solution to a problem, like in my daughter's foot disease, I could not blame my husband if it went wrong.
>
> The trainer was very good because she would say the group has to solve it … that was new to us. We were accustomed to hearing "do this or do that." Now WE are the ones deciding.
>
> —Ana Laura, middle-aged female participant in "I Want to,
> I Can … Start My Own Business," Mexico City, Mexico

The development of analytic thinking, problem solving, decision making, and assertiveness skills lays the groundwork from which people begin to take initiative and responsibility for choosing and carrying out their own behaviors. People generally possess these skills; they are very much part of the human psychological make-up. Yet many individuals in Latin America have been socialized to emphasize modes of behavior that are socially constrained. With successful program results, individuals are able to make and communicate personal decisions and develop a sense of their own personal agency. And the status quo of resignation and passivity gradually begins to change. Juana, a middle-aged woman in Honduras, explains how her opportunities have expanded:

> I have more life options … there are always things that require me to think and work outside of the box, now I can confront many of those because I believe in myself and I can think by myself. When you count as a person you feel you count for everything else and you want to do more. When you do not count as a person like before when we only counted for the government because they wanted to use us for their politics or our husbands to use us to serve them or our children to care for them, I did not feel I counted. Now I do. Counting means you are important, you can believe in what you believe without having to ask others if it is okay … you count simply because you count, not because you do something … and that makes you feel important, free, and intelligent.
>
> —Juana, participant in "I Want to, I Can… Care for My Health and
> Exercise My Rights," Lempira, Honduras

As a result of this personal change, individuals begin to share their knowledge and attitudes with family and community members, exercising their new behaviors, and thus impacting the attitudes and norms of their immediate community. They become contributors of their own growth process, as well as of the social, economic, and political development of their communities.

Considerations for Development of Programs

This book attempts to bridge the gaps between research, programming, policy, and disciplines. Programming must focus primarily on increasing people's access to choices and, thus, expanding their freedoms. The effective elements we are proposing to achieve this are skills, knowledge, and opportunities for reduced psychological barriers. We assess choice in terms of achieved behavioral changes, which are exercised in a way that, when repeatedly reached, can also lead to changes at a more stable personal level. We identify program content and methods necessary to expand opportunities in accordance with people's needs. The outcomes of this self-change process (at the individual level) are decisions and behaviors that are pro-active and reflective. The outcome at the community level is a change in communities and institutions so that they promote contextual freedoms, opportunities, and increase psychological choice.

Our program strategy differs from those that try to address personal characteristics by simply telling program participants that they are worthy or capable of accessing choices and of developing new behaviors. It also diverges from programs that target solely economic, political, and/or social variables without placing the individual at the center of the strategy for change. The lack of people-oriented approaches may be detrimental to development programs and policies: before individuals can experience improved well-being—a more pro-active identity, higher self-esteem, or an improved self-concept—they need to experience proof of what they can accomplish. The approach we offer for human development recognizes the individual needs and potential of marginalized people and promotes the further development of their internally derived capabilities to build personal agency and, eventually, intrinsic empowerment. It is our aim that this book will assist governments and CSOs to recognize the key role of psychological factors in shaping social functioning so that these bodies may join the effort to enable choice, personal agency, and intrinsic empowerment, to break the poverty cycle and ensure sustainable human development.

The results presented have been seen in our programs in several countries across the world (Anaya et al., 2008; Leenen et al., submitted; Leenen et al., 2008; Martínez, Givaudan, & Pick, 1995; Osorio-Belmon, submitted; Osorio & Givaudan, 2006; Osorio, Givaudan, Oka, & Pick, 2008; Pick et al., in press; Pick & Reyes, 1994; Ramón et al., 2000; Ramón, Givaudan, & Pick, 1997; Ramón et al., 2002; Tacher et al., 2008; Tacher et al., 2009; Vera et al., 2002). IMIFAP programs have been implemented in 14 countries and have reached over 19 million individuals. Informal conversations with individuals from additional countries across Latin America, Africa, Europe, Asia, and the United States have confirmed the relevance of program themes in these countries as well, despite variations in cultural and institutional factors.

The main empirical evidence for the approach outlined here is threefold. The first source of evidence is formed by the numerous testimonies that are scattered throughout the book. We can only report a small percentage of the large number of similar accounts that we hear time and again. More recently, we have begun to conduct more rigorous experimental studies with control groups and pre- and post-program measurements where this has been demonstrated. These include the measurement of behaviors as well as of the variables that lead up to them, such as knowledge and skills (Anaya et al., 2008; Beltrán, Elizalde, & Givaudan, 2009; Givaudan, Barriga, & Pick, 2008; Givaudan, García, & Pick, 2007; Givaudan, Leenen, & Pick, submitted; Givaudan & Osorio, 2009; Givaudan, Vitcla, & Osorio, 2008; Leenen et al., 2008; Osorio & Givaudan, 2008; Pick, Givaudan, & Poortinga, 2003; Pick et al., submitted; Pick, Poortinga, & Givaudan, 2003; Pick et al., 2008; Universidad Autónoma de Aguascalientes, 2008a, 2008b, 2008c, 2009; Venguer, Pick, & Fishbein, 2007). In the last few years, we have started to pursue a third kind of evidence, in the form of psychometric scales that contain items reflecting personal agency and intrinsic (previously called agentic) empowerment (Pick, Leenen, & García, submitted; Pick et al., 2007).[5] Testimonies provide essential evidence that is difficult to obtain through standard program evaluation. Conducted largely as part of program needs assessments, evaluation, and other qualitative studies, they capture the scope of change attributed to the type of development programs advocated in this book. To make these testimonies as clear and readable as possible for the reader, we have edited them for sentence structure (and translated most of them to English), while ensuring that we preserve the speakers' words.

Summary of the Chapters

We begin the book with a section on setting the scene. Chapter 2, Socio-Cultural Norms as Impediments to Individual and Social Change: The Case of Mexico, illustrates how socio-cultural norms can be both barriers to and facilitators of personal and community development. Psychological barriers, such as shame, guilt, and fear, often originate in contexts of tight social norms that impede personal choices and behaviors. Both social norms and psychological barriers must be addressed for programs that focus on changing behaviors to be implemented sustainably. Chapter 3, Testimonies, serves as an introduction to some IMIFAP programs where the outcomes went beyond the directly targeted changes in knowledge, skills, and behaviors. It was these nontargeted results and our analysis of the underlying factors that lead to the development of our framework (FrEE). Three sets of testimonies of IMIFAP program participants provide the "human face" of development and emphasize the role of the individual in community development. The final chapter of the section, Chapter 4, The Framework for Enabling Empowerment (FrEE), provides a theoretical framework that we hope will contribute to programs and policies that make development more successful and more sustainable. The chapter outlines the Framework for Enabling Empowerment, illustrating how it works in practice, and establishes its foundation in psychology and development literature.

The second section of this book is on sustainable human development. Chapter 5, Development as Enhancing Capabilities, introduces Sen's Capability

Approach as an alternative model to traditional development economics. It also discusses the role of behavioral economics and psychology at the policy level, and shows how FrEE makes Sen's Capability Approach operational. Chapter 6, The Elements of FrEE: Enhancing Opportunities and Reducing Barriers to Development by Addressing Situational Demands, outlines the basic tools that individuals need to respond to situational demands: knowledge, skills, reduction of psychological barriers, and competencies. These tools are developed through participatory and reflective methodology and repetitive practice. Chapter 7, Behavior as Choice, focuses on behaviors and their subsequent impact on personal norms and attitudes as a means to developing personal agency. The importance of perceived and repeated behavioral success, the reflection process, and how behaviors can generalize across domains are also highlighted. We conclude the section on sustainable human development with Chapter 8, Context. This chapter discusses the interaction between the individual and the various levels of context. We analyze specific barriers and opportunities for personal agency in different domains, including education, economics, government, and health.

The final section of this book addresses development strategies. Chapter 9, Strategy for Program Development and Implementation, is the practical section of the book, which highlights the essential link among research, policy, and understanding community needs. The chapter aims to demonstrate how FrEE can be employed in program development and implementation through a series of programmatic stages. Programs following this approach further enable new choices, supporting the expansion of personal agency and intrinsic empowerment. IMIFAP programs provide examples that illustrate the practical application of our methodology. How sustainability can be achieved both at the individual and the replication levels of programs is also explained in this chapter. The concluding chapter summarizes the most salient points making up the framework and strategy for human development program design and implementation presented in this book. The chapter also points a way forward for policy. The ultimate goal is to bring into the government a human development program shown to work both at the small and scaled-up levels, institutionalizing and implementing it on a macroscale. Governments and CSOs must join in this effort to enable choice, personal agency, and intrinsic empowerment. Finally, an appendix located at the end of the book provides descriptions of the IMIFAP school and community programs for life skills, health promotion, and poverty reduction.

Notes

1. The Majority World is the world in which most people are living—that is, in conditions of poverty and limited access to education.

2. The Gini coefficient, the most common measure of inequality, compares income distribution. It is expressed on a scale from 0 to 1, with zero being complete equality and 1 being complete inequality. The average for the Latin American region is 0.52.

3. Lopez and Perry (2008) explain that the inequality of educational returns may be due to a variety of factors. Among them, "lower quality of schools, lower availability of assets that are complementary to education in income generation (land, public infrastructure, credit), discrimination in labor markets, and unobservable factors (linked to differential access to pre schooling facilities, in nutrition levels, etc.)" ("The Americas: "The teacher" holds back the pupils," p. 16).

4. Accessible opportunities are those that are logistically available (affordable health clinics and schools exist) *and* psychologically available (barriers such as shame or embarrassment to see a clinician are reduced).

5. In Pick et al. (2007), we have reported the first results obtained with such a questionnaire on personal agency and agentic empowerment (now called intrinsic empowerment) applied to over 1,000 high school and university students from both urban and rural areas in Mexico. The key result relevant for the present chapter is that the distinction between personal agency and intrinsic empowerment was reproduced. Factor analysis showed that the items could be characterized into these two groups, demonstrating that the theoretical concepts of personal agency and agentic empowerment were indeed two distinct factors. The first factor was exemplified by items like (with negative loading) "It is hard for me to publicly express my opinion" [*Me es difícil expresar mi opinión públicamente*], "I feel unsure of my decisions" [*Me siento inseguro de mis decisiones*), and (with positive loading) "I have the initiative to do things" [*Tengo iniciativa para hacer las cosas*] clearly reflected personal agency. The second factor with items like "In my community I help solve the conflicts that arise" [*En mi colonia/comunidad ayudo a resolver los conflictos que se presentan*], and "In my community I participate in the local assemblies or neighbor meetings" [*En mi colonia/comunidad participo en las asambleas o juntas vecinales*] fitted the notion of agentic (intrinsic) empowerment. In the concluding chapter of this book we refer to further data that was collected while the writing of this book was in progress and that has not yet been published.

References

Alan Guttmacher Institute (1999). Sharing responsibility: Women, society, & abortion worldwide. Retrieved January 8, 2008 from www.guttmacher.org/pubs/sharing.pdf.

Alsop, R., & Heinsohn, N. (2005). *Measuring empowerment in practice: Structuring analysis and framing indicators* (Policy Research Working Paper No. 3510). Washington DC: World Bank Poverty Reduction and Economic Management Network [PREM Network], Poverty Reduction Group.

The Americas: "The teacher" holds back the pupils (2007, July 19). *The Economist, 384*(8538), 48.

Anaya, M., Leenen, I., Givaudan, M., & Pick, S. (2008). México-Centroamerica: Educación en sexualidad, salud y habilidades para la vida. Fase III: Reporte Final [Mexico-Central America: Education on sexuality, health and life skills. Phase III: Final Report], *Report presented to the World Bank*. Mexico City: IMIFAP.

Antonides, G. (1996). *Psychology in economics and business: An introduction to economic psychology*. Dordrecht, Netherlands: Kluwer Academic Publishers.

Bandura, A. (1997). *Self-efficacy: The exercise of control*. New York: W.H. Freeman & Co.

Banerjee, A. V., & Newman, A. F. (1994). Poverty, incentives, and development. *American Economic Review, 84*(2), 211–215.

Barnes-Josiah, D., Myntti, C., & Augustin, A. (1998). The "three delays" as a framework for examining maternal mortality in Haiti. *Social Science & Medicine,* 46(8), 981–993.

Beltrán, M., Elizalde, L., & Givaudan, M. (2009). Formación en habilidades para la vida y metodología participativa para personal de salud [Life skills training and participatory methodology for health workers], *Report presented to Public Health Services of Mexico City.* Mexico City: IMIFAP.

Bingham, A., Bishop, A., Coffey, P., Winkler, J., Bradley, J., Dzuba, I., & Agurto, I. (2003). Factors affecting utilization of cervical cancer prevention services in low-resource settings. *Salud Pública de México,* 45(Supplement 3), S408–S416.

Boone, P. (1996). Politics and the effectiveness of foreign aid. *European Economic Review,* 40, 289–329.

Dollar, D. (2003). Eyes wide open. *Harvard International Review,* 25(1), 48–52.

Evans, G. W. (2004). The environment of childhood poverty. *American Psychologist,* 59(2), 77–92.

Fernández-Ballesteros, R. (2002). Determinants and structural relation of personal efficacy to collective efficacy. *Applied Psychology: An International Review,* 51(1), 107–125.

Gilson, L. (2003). Trust and the development of health care as a social institution. *Social Science & Medicine,* 56(7), 1453–1468.

Givaudan, M., Barriga, M. A., & Pick, S. (2008). The children left behind: Researching the impact of migration on the development of children and developing, piloting and evaluating a program that answers their special needs, *Report presented to the Bernard van Leer Foundation.* Mexico City: IMIFAP.

Givaudan, M., García, A., & Pick, S. (2007). Programa de prevención de cáncer cérvico uterino en áreas de extrema pobreza rural de Michoacán [Cervical cancer prevention program in areas of extreme rural poverty in Michoacan state], *Report presented to the Inter-American Development Bank.* Mexico City: IMIFAP.

Givaudan, M., Leenen, I., & Pick, S. (submitted). Health education and life skills: Building life skills and knowledge in rural children in Mexico.

Givaudan, M., & Osorio, P. (2009). Yo quiero, yo puedo... prevenir y controlar obesidad, diabetes y enfermedades cardiovasculares [I want to, I can... prevent and control obesity, diabetes and cardiovascular diseases], *Report presented to the Pfizer Foundation.* Mexico City: IMIFAP.

Givaudan, M., Vitela, A., & Osorio, P. (2008). Estrategia fronteriza de promoción y prevención para una mejor salud [Border strategy of promotion and prevention for improving health], *Report presented to the Pfizer Foundation.* Mexico City: IMIFAP.

Grantham-McGregor, S., Cheung, Y. B., Cueto, S., Glewwe, P., Richter, L., Strupp, B., & International Child Development Steering Group (2007). Developmental potential in the first 5 years for children in developing countries. *Lancet,* 369(9555), 60–70.

Iyengar, S., & DeVoe, S. E. (2003). Rethinking the value of choice considering cultural mediators of intrinsic motivation. In V. Murphy-Berman & J. J. Berman (Eds.), *Nebraska symposium on motivation* (Vol. 49, pp. 129–174). Lincoln, NE: University of Nebraska Press.

Kabeer, N. (1999). Resources, agency, achievements: Reflections on the measurement of women's empowerment. *Development and Change,* 30, 435–464.

Kagitcibasi, C. (2002). Psychology and human competence development. *Applied Psychology: An International Review,* 51(1), 5–22.

Kagitcibasi, C. (2005). Autonomy and relatedness in cultural context: Implications for self and family. *Journal of Cross-Cultural Psychology,* 36(4), 403–422.

Leenen, I., Pick, S., Tacher, A., Givaudan, M., & Prado, A. (submitted). Facilitating sexual and reproductive health among migrants in Central America.

Leenen, I., Venguer, T., Vera, J., Givaudan, M., Pick, S., & Poortinga, Y. H. (2008). Effectiveness of a comprehensive health education program in a poverty-stricken rural area of Guatemala. *Journal of Cross-Cultural Psychology,* 39(2), 198–214.

Lopez, J. H., & Perry, G. (2008). *Inequality in Latin America: Determinants and consequences* (Policy Research Working Paper No. 4504). Washington, DC: World Bank.

Mangrulkar, L., Whitman, C., & Posner, M. (2001). *Life skills approach to child and adolescent human development.* Washington, DC: Pan American Health Organization.

Martínez, A., Givaudan, M., & Pick, S. (1995). Training and supervision in family life and sexuality education programs and provision of teaching materials in Latin America, *Report presented to the David and Lucile Packard Foundation.* Mexico City: IMIFAP.

McClelland, D. (1961). *The achieving society.* Princeton, NJ: Van Nostrand.

Mkandawire, T. (2001). *Social Policy in a Development Context.* Geneva: UN Research Institute for Social Development.

Morán, R., Sen, A., & Brundtland, G. H. (2004). *Escaping the poverty trap.* Washington, D.C: Inter-American Development Bank.

Moser, C. (1989). Gender planning in the Third World: Meeting practical and strategic gender needs. *World Development,* 17(11), 1799–1825.

Nakanishi, T. (2002). Critical literature review on motivation. *Journal of Language and Linguistics,* 1(3).

Organisation for Economic Co-operation and Development [OECD] (2006). Society at a glance: OECD social indicators - 2006 edition Retrieved December 27, 2008, from www.oecd.org/els/social/indicators/SAG.

Osorio-Belmon, P. (submitted). Exporting strategies: A cross-cultural adaptation of a pregnancy prevention curriculum for teenagers.

Osorio, P., & Givaudan, M. (2006). Mexico-Central America: Education in sexuality, health and life skills, Phase II, *Report presented to the World Bank.* Mexico City: IMIFAP.

Osorio, P., & Givaudan, M. (2008). Formación en microcréditos para mujeres indígenas y rurales en Oaxaca [Training in microfinance for rural indigenous women in Oaxaca State, Mexico], *Report presented to the Finnish Embassy in Mexico, Fund for Local Cooperation.* Mexico City: IMIFAP.

Osorio, P., Givaudan, M., Oka, S., & Pick, S. (2008). My voice, my life: A pregnancy prevention curriculum for teenagers in Alameda, California, *Report presented to the Public Health Institute.* Mexico City: IMIFAP.

Ovaska, T. (2003). The failure of development aid. *Cato Journal,* 23(2), 175–198.

Pick, S., Givaudan, M., & Poortinga, Y. H. (2003). Sexuality and life skills education: A multistrategy intervention in Mexico. *American Psychologist,* 58(3), 230–234.

Pick, S., Leenen, I., & García, G. (submitted). Programa piloto para la promoción de la salud en comunidades marginadas, a través del desarrollo de agencia y empoderamiento [Pilot program for health promotion in marginalized communities, through the development of agency and empowerment].

Pick, S., Leenen, I., Givaudan, M., & Prado, A. (in press). I want to, I can... prevent violence: Raising awareness of dating violence through a brief intervention. *Salud Mental.*

Pick, S., Poortinga, Y. H., & Givaudan, M. (2003). Integrating intervention theory and strategy in culture-sensitive health promotion programs. *Professional Psychology: Research & Practice, 34*(4), 422–429.

Pick, S., & Reyes, J. (1994). Training project for Latin American health and population institutions, *Report presented to the John D. and Catherine T. MacArthur Foundation*. Mexico City: IMIFAP.

Pick, S., Romero, A., Arana, D., & Givaudan, M. (2008). Programa formativo para prevenir la violencia a nivel primaria y secundaria [Training program for the prevention of violence at the primary and secondary school levels], *Report presented to the Chamber of Deputies of the Congress of the Union, 60th Legislature*. Mexico City: IMIFAP.

Pick, S., Sirkin, J., Ortega, I., Osorio, P., Martínez, R., Xocolotzin, U., & Givaudan, M. (2007). Escala para medir las capacidades de agencia personal y empoderamiento (ESAGE) [Scale for the measurement of personal agency and empowerment]. *Revista Interamericana de Psicología, 41*(3), 295–304.

Porter, M. (1998). *On competition*. Boston: Harvard Business School Press.

Prahalad, C. K. (2006, Nov. 16). *Democratizing commerce: The challenge for the 21st century*, Lecture at Tilburg University.

Ramón, J., Bendezu, A., Pick, S., & Givaudan, M. (2000). Replicación y evaluación del programa de la vida familiar y educación sexual Yo quiero, Yo puedo, con maestros de 5° y 6° grado en áreas marginalizadas de Perú [Replication and evaluation of family life and sexual education program I want to, I can, with teachers from 5th and 6th grade in marginalized areas of Peru], *Report presented to the World Bank*. Mexico City: IMIFAP.

Ramón, J., Givaudan, M., & Pick, S. (1997). Replication of sexual health and family life education programs for parents in Mexico and Latin America, *Report presented to Public Welfare Foundation*. Mexico City: IMIFAP.

Ramón, J., Zárate, M., Pick, S., & Givaudan, M. (2002). Fortalecimiento y expansión de un programa integral de educación sexual y habilidades para la vida, en Bolivia y Panamá a través de la capacitación, supervisión y evaluación de multiplicadores [Strengthening and expansion of a comprehensive sexuality education and life skills program in Bolivia and Panama through training, supervision and evaluation of replicators]. Phase II, *Report presented to the World Bank*. Mexico City: IMIFAP.

Robeyns, I. (2005). The Capability Approach: A theoretical survey. *Journal of Human Development, 6*(1), 93–114.

Rotter, J. B. (1966). Generalized expectancies for internal versus external control of reinforcement. *Psychological Monographs, 80*(1), 1–28.

Rowlands, J. (1995). Empowerment examined. *Development in Practice, 5*(2), 101–107.

Sachs, J. D. (2005). *The end of poverty: Economic possibilities for our time*. New York: Penguin Press.

Saldivia, S., Vicente, B., Kohn, R., Rioseco, P., & Torres, S. (2004). Use of mental health services in Chile. *Psychiatric Services, 55*(1), 71–76.

Sen, A. (1985). Well-being, agency and freedom: The Dewey Lectures 1984. *The Journal of Philosophy, 82*(4), 169–221.

Sen, A. (1987). *The standard of living*. Cambridge: Cambridge University Press.

Sen, A. (1992). *Inequality reexamined*. Oxford: Oxford University Press.

Sen, A. (1999). *Development as freedom*. New York: Anchor.

Sternberg, R. J., & Lyon, G. R. (2002). Making a difference to education: Will psychology pass up the chance? *Monitor On Psychology, 33*(7), 76–78.

Tacher, A., Beltrán, M., Givaudan, M., & Pick, S. (2008). Colaboración de organizaciones México-Guatemala-Honduras para el fortalecimiento de capabilidades humanas: Fase I [Collaboration of Mexican, Guatemalan and Honduran organizations for the strengthening of human capabilities: Phase I], *Report presented to W. K. Kellogg Foundation*. Mexico City: IMIFAP.

Tacher, A., Leenen, I., Pick, S., Givaudan, M., & Prado, A. (2009). Facilitating sexual and reproductive health among migrants in Central America, *Report presented to the World Bank*. Mexico City: IMIFAP.

United Nations Development Program [UNDP] (2006). *Human development report 2006: Beyond scarcity*. New York: United Nations Development Program.

United Nations Development Program [UNDP] (2007). Indicators - 2007/2008 report Retrieved December 27, 2008, from http://hdrstats.undp.org/indicators/.

Universidad Autónoma de Aguascalientes (2008a). Implementación del Modelo de transmisión de conocimientos para el desarrollo de capacidades entre el personal de Diconsa, los Consejos Comunitarios y los Comités Rurales de Abasto. Primer reporte parcial: Sensibilización [Implementation of a knowledge transmission model for capacity development of Diconsa, Community Council and Rural Supply Committee personnel. First partial report: Developing awareness], *Report presented to Diconsa*. Mexico City: IMIFAP.

Universidad Autónoma de Aguascalientes (2008b). Implementación del Modelo de transmisión de conocimientos para el desarrollo de capacidades entre el personal de Diconsa, los Consejos Comunitarios y los Comités Rurales de Abasto. Segundo reporte parcial: Formación [Implementation of a knowledge transmission model for capacity development of Diconsa, Community Council and Rural Supply Committee personnel. Second partial report: Training], *Report presented to Diconsa*. Mexico City: IMIFAP.

Universidad Autónoma de Aguascalientes (2008c). Implementación del Modelo de transmisión de conocimientos para el desarrollo de capacidades entre el personal de Diconsa, los Consejos Comunitarios y los Comités Rurales de Abasto. Tercer reporte parcial: Réplica y Acompañamiento [Implementation of a knowledge transmission model for capacity development of Diconsa, Community Council and Rural Supply Committee personnel. Third partial report: Replication and follow-up], *Report presented to Diconsa*. Mexico City: IMIFAP.

Universidad Autónoma de Aguascalientes (2009). Implementación del Modelo de transmisión de conocimientos para el desarrollo de capacidades entre el personal de Diconsa, los Consejos Comunitarios y los Comités Rurales de Abasto. Informe ejecutivo final. [Implementation of a knowledge transmission model for capacity development of Diconsa, Community Council and Rural Supply Committee personnel. Final executive report], *Report presented to Diconsa*. Mexico City: IMIFAP.

Venguer, T., Pick, S., & Fishbein, M. (2007). Health education and agency: A comprehensive program for young women in the Mixteca region of Mexico. *Psychology, Health & Medicine*, 12(4), 389–406.

Vera, J., Venguer, T., Givaudan, M., & Pick, S. (2002). Encuentro: México-Guatemala: Educación de la sexualidad y habilidades para la vida [Encounter: Mexico-Guatemala: Sexuality and life skills education], *Report presented to the World Bank*. Mexico City: IMIFAP.

Woolcock, M., & Narayan, D. (2000). Social capital: Implications for development theory, research, and policy. *The World Bank Research Observer*, 15(2), 225–228.

SECTION I

Setting the Scene

CHAPTER 2

Socio-Cultural Norms as Impediments to Individual and Social Change

The Case of Mexico

> *The crucial role of social opportunities is to expand the realm of human agency and freedom, both as an end in itself and as a means of further expansion of freedom. The word 'social' in the expression 'social opportunity' … is a useful reminder not to view individuals and their opportunities in isolated terms. The options that a person has depend greatly on relations with others.*
>
> —Jean Dréze & Amartya Sen (1995, p. 6)

Socio-cultural norms are societal standards of conduct that determine appropriate behavior and serve to regulate manners to uphold social order (Segall et al., 1999). In an ideal society, socio-cultural norms encourage the expansion of choice and the empowerment of individuals. Moreover, the community as a whole thrives when it supports individual growth. However, most societies have not traditionally functioned in this way; norms generally block decision making and action rather than encourage choice. According to Sen, norms can present one of the main barriers to realizing entitlements because they are socially defined and often entail the pressure to conform (1998). When norms are so restrictive that they take precedence over an individual's own decision-making processes, the potential of the individual suffers. Additionally, their families, communities, and the institutions to which they belong are also negatively affected. Therefore, in such societies, people need to develop their skills and knowledge to reduce these barriers to action.

Being socially and politically expected to "behave well" and simply wait for things to happen limits the possibility of taking risks, making decisions, and changing social norms. Recognizing one's right to these possibilities would move a man toward realizing his potential and making it a reality. However, in a tight society (Pelto, 1968), there is strong pressure to conform to social roles and expectations. In this case, norms are largely detrimental to individual growth, and social and psychological barriers develop that constrain clear and uninhibited, autonomous, responsible, and informed decision making. The alternative of fighting, lying, and cheating becomes a necessary means of meeting his basic needs in life while maintaining social appearances.

Norms are reproduced through formal and informal agreements between participants of a group and are often utilized as a means of social control (Coser, 1967; Giddens, 1993). They influence cultural facets as trivial as table manners and as critical as political decisions, institutional values, and the accessibility of community programs. Norms are encompassed within a culture's larger system of shared symbols that are learned and passed on through generations, consistently influencing how people perceive the world and how they interact with each other (Lipson, Dibble, & Minarek, 1996). Socially accepted cultural meanings become part of individual decision-making processes. Norms are natural phenomena; they are part of individual and social development and whether the impact they have leads to the expansion of capabilities, to the maintenance of the *status quo,* or to the detriment of freedoms and well-being depends both on their actual content and on the strictness with which each is expected to be followed.

Societal norms transform into personal norms (Valsiner & Lawrence, 1997), especially when the system is tight and does not easily allow for alternative courses of action. "Either you comply or you're out," is a message that makes diverging difficult. The pervasiveness of social norms depends not only on the tightness of the society but also on the public perception of their legitimacy. The latter is often based on the perceived legitimacy of the "promoters," by nature those with some form of social, political, or economic influence in society: the upper class, the popular girls in school, teachers, government officials, professionals, or any revered member of a community. These powerful members of society are likely to set normative standards in their own interest; this is especially true of those in governments and institutions with limited transparency, nepotism, and corruption. It is important to recognize that the media, in the hands of powerful economic and political elite across Latin America, often serves as a tool for the promotion of those norms that serve the promoters' interests.

Those individuals who are more autonomous about their personal goals allow themselves more space within the set of socio-cultural norms to reach their own decisions and determine their own actions. Being part of the process for change and achieving these goals are elements of personal agency (Sapp, Harrod, & Zhao, 1994). Individuals possessing a strong sense of personal agency are more likely to make value judgments about which norms they deem important for their own development and for the development of their families, communities, institutions, and their society as a whole and which norms might be ignored. This chapter reflects on the traditional societal structure and the prevailing socio-cultural norms[1] that limit human and, therefore, social development in Mexico.

The Pressure to Conform in Mexico

Based on the degree to which norms influence a society, that society may be classified as "loose" or "tight" (Gelfand, Nishii, & Raver, 2006; Pelto, 1968). In tighter societies, there is strong pressure on the individual to adhere to societal roles, which in such cases tend to be very restrictive, with a focus on maintaining external control over decisions. The individual is "embedded in a web of relationships and roles" (Fiske et al., 1998, p. 923), and interdependence is the defining feature of the self and self-regulation; behavior is oriented toward the harmonious functioning of relationships (Fiske et al., 1998). In contrast, there is less pressure to adhere to social roles in looser societies. The size and diversity of urban societies often makes the content of socio-cultural norms as well as the pressure to conform to them less of a behavioral constraint than in traditional rural communities, where there are fewer structural (e.g., economic) and social (e.g., peer support) opportunities for choice (Bond & Smith, 1996). As opportunities arise (e.g., improved quality of education, greater access to media and to clinics, better judicial system), socio-cultural norms change and possibilities for acting outside of the normative tightness expand; the society becomes "less tight." Additionally, expansion of opportunities is likely to lead to changes in the norms themselves. For example, until a few years ago, it would have been unheard of to think that one day the necessary social and political openness would exist to allow the largest poverty alleviation program in Mexico (*Oportunidades*) to be focused on providing funds to women (Levy, 2006).

Although the strength and value placed on specific socio-cultural norms depends on the particular community, social scientists and cultural commentators point to a variety of traditional characteristics as being prominent elements in Mexican communities: high conformance to socio-cultural norms, emphasis on the family, participation in in-group activities, and subordination of personal goals to group goals, all making norms more powerful (Gregory & Munch, 1997; Hubbell, 1993; Malloy et al., 2004; Peterson & Hennon, 2006). Here, behavior is "principally oriented toward the harmonious functioning of ... social entities" (Fiske et al., 1998, p. 922). Although globalization, education, and other impetuses for change are altering both norms and the cultural elements that make norms more powerful, this is a slow process, and historical trends and long-held mindsets continue to hold fast, particularly in those communities with lower educational levels and those that are more rural.

"Bien Educado" [Well-Brought-Up]

Being *bien educado*, a well-educated, well brought-up person, refers throughout Latin America to both social and formal education (Peterson & Hennon, 2006).

A person *bien educado* has strong principles and good manners; is respectful, obedient, caring, capable in social settings; and, above all, follows what is socially expected of her. She maintains these characteristics even if doing so requires her to override her own personal interests and desires. A person without these principles or values is seen as *mal educado*; she is perceived as crude, disobedient, disrespectful, disheveled, and not worthy of receiving any attention or love (Gongora Coronado, Cortes Ayala, & Flores Galaz, 2002). The marked difference between *bien educado* and *mal educado* is whether or not the individual adheres to prescribed social norms.

Being *bien educado* entails avoiding direct confrontation in interpersonal relationships, including work interactions (Zubieta et al., 2006); it is part of being congenial (Triandis et al., 1984). An important feature of norms is that in conversation, people tend not to be direct or explicit, but rather say what the other person expects to hear. To make a point, the individual must wait until the other can infer the meaning and "read between the lines"[2] of what is being said (Zubieta et al., 2006, p. 6). There are highly complicated rituals of courtesy, extreme formality in political institutions, and a strong inclination toward respecting and upholding socio-cultural norms (Paz, 1950). In fact, it is a norm to uphold norms.

A study conducted in Toluca, Mexico, found that youth interpreted *rebelliousness* as "behaving badly" and disliked peers considered to be acting as such (Medina, Mondragón, & Morelato, 2005). Expressing disagreement, anger, or discontent signified dissidence toward hierarchical relationships and, therefore, was considered a threat to the perceived social harmony. The high valuation of adhering to what is viewed as socially acceptable—to make sure the person has the "right social image"—can make certain situations particularly demanding, even within academic environments:

> All along my supervisor had been telling me how well I was doing in my studies. Then the day of the public exam she asked many questions. I was surprised. How was I supposed to "show off" and uphold my professor's and my good name with *those* kinds of questions being asked? I thought she would just ask me to talk about what I had learned, not to have to explain in detail the statistics I had used in my analyses. I cannot believe she did this to me. I don't want to talk to her again.
> —Ph.D. student in Mexico City after her dissertation defense
> (which she successfully passed).

The student perceived the public interrogation of her knowledge and skills in front of her friends and family as threatening, whereas the professor understood the academic exercise as one where she should highlight both strengths and weaknesses in the student's knowledge. Thus, the defense was viewed as a threat to the interpersonal and social harmony among her, the teacher, and those who attended her exam.

A common way of reinforcing adherence to socio-cultural norms is punishing those people who overstep them. A municipal president[3] in Oaxaca, Mexico, explained his view:

> The governor's wife wanted the municipal presidents to support her project of starting tortilla factories so the women would not have to grind corn by hand.

She did not care that in doing so she was destroying the way things are done around here . . . Imagine how [by not having to grind the corn] the women would have all that time free to do who knows what! The community would be ruined, they would not care for their husbands and children anymore, and they would go mad doing their own thing, who knows what ideas they would get into their heads! . . . She may be the wife of the governor, but I am the municipal president. I make the rules around here. So I had to put a stop to her. I did so through political pressure on her husband. No more support from this town for him. Even the wife of the governor has to learn to conform to what is socially accepted.

The pressure to please—to be *bien educado*—and to adhere to social norms can be so strong that it discourages recognizing mistakes (e.g., Jáuregui, 2010) — taking the normal risks that should be part of everyday life. Risks inherently imply willingness to fail, to err. And this willingness is necessary for someone to take initiative, make autonomous decisions, and be an agent rather than an object of change. As development specialist Lincoln Chen stated, "If you are taking risks, you are having successes and failures" (Chen, 2007). If the focus is on doing everything "perfectly" to be *bien educado,* incentive for risk-taking is strongly reduced, and so too the possibility of becoming an agent of change.

These dynamics also create a high value for social and self-deception. If an individual desires to achieve his goals, but doing so by acting autonomously (Rotter, 1990) is unacceptable, he must find ways that don't make him appear to be contravening that which is socially expected or accepted. Covert approaches such as lying and cheating become rational.

When valued more than individual growth, conformity represents a strong and rigid barrier to autonomy and, therefore, to choice and freedoms. In contrast, if individual needs and interests are respected and supported in conjunction with rule and order, then personal development can be enhanced. As Alicia, a secondary school teacher in Santiago, Chile, argued:

When there is so much pressure to conform, it becomes like a pressure cooker ... the moment there is a way to get the pressure off, kids explode [and manifest themselves in all sorts of ways that may even be dangerous]. If instead of all this vigilance they had information, had choice, felt parental and teacher trust to make their own decisions, they would decide in a responsible way, there would be no need to lie and hide.

Socio-cultural norms and role expectations can promote or limit freedoms.

Fatalism

Another cultural obstacle to autonomous decision making in Mexico and Latin America at large is the broad acceptance of things as they stand—in other words, fatalism. As exemplified in some testimonies in the prologue, this is the belief that a higher power determines a person's destiny. It leads to high levels of external control,[4] a mindset of passivity, and inability to change the environment, because life "is regulated by a higher force"[5] usually associated with "a distant and powerful God... whose infinite wisdom... cannot be questioned by a little creature"[6] (Martin-Baró, 1987, p. 137). For this reason, individuals accepting beliefs of fatalism resign themselves, even when they have a negative experience. Tiburcio, a young apple picker in Chihuahua, Mexico, demonstrates this passivity in his statement about his future prospects: "To me they should give, to me it should come... I have my whole life to wait... the One up there should know when it is my turn." A Mexican saying goes "*La divina providencia decidirá cuando me toca*" [Divine providence will know when it is my turn].

Fatalism can be counterpositioned with internal control. In the case of the latter, the individual is an active agent of her course, whereas in the former, the individual is a passive receptor of others' determinations. Fatalism results in a highly counterproductive vision of life and is a self-fulfilling prophecy, reducing the individual's vision of the future and thus blocking all initiative for both social and personal progress. When people believe that they have no control over outcomes, they are less inclined to face difficult situations despite potentially beneficial outcomes. A teacher exemplifies how in the midst of fatalism, shame and fear easily serve as barriers to action:

> I am ashamed to ask, who knows what people will think. They will see that I don't know much about sicknesses or medicine or they might think that I am asking for too many things that I don't deserve and that I am trying to take advantage of them. Anyway I am already 42 years old; if I die it is because God wanted me to.
>
> —Maria Teresa, a female teacher, Huancayo, Perú

Through their passive and constraining outward-directed view, these beliefs in turn strengthen the perception of people across all domains of life that external control is the way to maintain order.

The pressure in Mexico to conform—encapsulated in the concept of *bien educado*, together with a broad acceptance of fatalism—limits autonomous decision making. In doing so, it strengthens socio-cultural norms to the point that individual development is inhibited. The specific norms that are "empowered" to this extreme and have negative societal consequences are detailed in the following section.

Examples of Prevailing Mexican Socio-Cultural Norms

Gender Roles and Sexuality

In Mexican literature it has been commonly depicted that all women are considered to be whores, except for one's mother and one's sister (Cypess, 2008). In Mexico, there has historically been an intricate pattern of socio-cultural norms regarding sexuality and gender roles that impact individuals' beliefs and subsequently their decision making and behavior. Social control over sexuality and gender roles is exercised through these norms and is strengthened by the social pressures to conform that institutions, sanctions, and group behavior propagate (Szasz, 1998). Sen writes that even women internalize traditional conceptions of their roles as "natural" (Sen, 1995).

The role of the mother continues to be one of responsibility, care, commitment, respect, calmness, and seriousness. A woman is supposed to be docile, domestic, faithful, and fully dependent on men (Guendelman et al., 2001). "Women are defined by others, including their spouses and the internalized expectations of what women's roles… should be" (Guendelman et al., 2001, p. 1808). In daily household interactions, women are expected to abide by their husbands' decisions. In many rural areas, as well as marginalized urban ones, women are even expected to eat only after their husbands have finished eating.

> The women in the village cook, and serve their families. They carefully watch that they have everything they need (of course within their economic means). It is only once the family finishes eating and leaves the table that [the mother] serves herself some of the leftover food, and generally eats it standing up.
> —Luisa, rural health promoter, highlands of Puebla, Mexico

Although childbearing and motherhood are highly valued, a women's sexual autonomy is not (Amuchástegui & Aggleton, 2007; Szasz, 1998). Women are not regarded as "equal subjects of desire and pleasure" (Amuchástegui & Aggleton, 2007, p. 73): a mother is not supposed to have sexual desires, nor to openly express sexual feelings. Social disapproval, which generates fear, shame, and guilt, is used to maintain this gender inequality. Hypocritically, although sexual initiative or pleasure on the part of the woman is seen as a sign of loose morals, her modesty and restraint in sexual matters is an alleged reason for her husband to seek pleasure elsewhere. The counter-figure to the mother– wife is this woman who is used only for sex (Paz, 1950). She is regarded as promiscuous, untrustworthy, and inappropriately initiatory. The sexual rela- tions with these women are kept hidden and secret from family members, yet this frequent extramarital situation is often justified by the lack of emotions involved (Szasz, 1998). Because it is impossible for women to fulfill both the maternal and sexual roles expected of them, women are trapped by pervasive and conflicting messages regarding sexuality. Ximena, a middle-aged woman from Jalisco, Mexico, explained to us that, "If you show pleasure you will be seen as a prostitute, if you don't, he will leave you for someone else."

These norms extend to the gender roles taught to young girls. Those not yet married are taught to value being a virgin at marriage, and they learn that engaging in premarital sex risks harm to their reputation (Carrillo, 2002). An article in the Mexican newspaper Reforma discusses prevalent attitudes toward female virginity in Mexico. It quoted an elderly woman of the village Jucatán, in Chiapas, as saying, "Women who do not bleed the first time they have sex are worthless"[7] (Izquierdo, 2007, p. 18). A teacher interviewed for the article agreed, stating that it is important for a woman to show the sheet used during her first engagement in sexual intercourse to demonstrate that her husband is the first man in her life. The teacher explained that it is the way to build his trust and acceptance. According to this conceptualization, it is the woman who has to go the extra mile to maintain the marriage and whose status is threatened if she does not have a partner. Beatriz, an elementary school teacher from Jucatán, Chiapas, Mexico, explained to us, "My cousin still keeps the handker- chief [where she bled] as a good remembrance [of her value]. This custom is by no means an aggression towards women; on the contrary, it is a way of showing a woman her place." Yet concurrently, premarital sex is implicitly encouraged as a means for a woman to coerce a man to marry her (Pick, Givaudan, & Aldaz, 1996). A range of sources reinforce these mixed messages, emphasizing the contradictory danger and necessity of sexual relationships:

> The most widely used word in sexual education is "*careful!*"[8] ... Mothers tell their daughters, "Careful with menstruation because you can get pregnant ... *careful* with men because all they want from you is sex." Men tell their friends, "*Careful* with women because they manipulate you to get things out of you." Parents tell their daughters, "*Careful* if you have sexual pleasure because he will think you are an easy woman, *careful* if you do not show sexual pleasure because he will go look for it elsewhere." How are people supposed to be clear about what to do or how to behave? This lack of clarity leads to lies, trying to hide, insecurities, and fears.
>
> —Tatiana, secondary school teacher, participant in
> "I Want to, I Can... Prevent Pregnancies," Guanajuato, Mexico

These socio-cultural norms are a dominating force among individuals from various socio-economic levels.

Often, an individual finds incompatibilities between different norms or between norms and the reality of everyday life. As shown above, there are many contradictions for girls to address. For boys in Mexico, there are two basic traditional messages: sleep with as many women as you can and make a lot of money (Marston, 2004). These norms emphasize an external appearance of sexual prowess and masculinity (Amuchástegui & Aggleton, 2007; Szasz, 1998). A deviating interest can result in social disapproval:

> I am exhausted. It is so hard to try to do everything my family expects from me, and they don't really care so much what I do as long as the neighbors get the impression that I do the right thing. I am not really interested in having many women or getting drunk and I can't get the job that I am "expected" to have, to make a lot of money, so that my family can show it off. But "real men" are supposed to do those things. It is somehow supposed to bring pride to the family and to the community.
>
> —Sergio, a man in his 40s, Michoacan, Mexico

A study in Mexico City found that there exists strong admiration for men who have many children (including those conceived out of wedlock) and many sexual partners, and that this negatively affects condom and contraceptive use (Brito, 1996). As occurs in many countries, there is little support provided for the social and emotional development of males. Although it is common to see a mother hug her crying daughter, it is equally common for her to tell her son that he should be strong because "real men don't cry." Girls are also more likely to be expected to care for their younger siblings or elderly family members. Parental influence, coupled with the media, peer interactions, and the classroom all affect the development of male identity (Barnes, 2008).

The prevailing socio-cultural norms that support the imbalance in sexual rights between genders and the pressure to conform to them strongly limit communication as well as autonomous decision-making. When the topic of sex is referred to, it is often spoken about indirectly and alluded to in a way that is in accordance with the established norms. For example, girls will be encouraged to stay away from the "forbidden fruit." Maintaining norms also serves to construct a body of quasi-factual knowledge, especially in matters related to sexuality, where a large number of myths have developed to propagate those norms. The myths and centrality of moral pressures create barriers to accessing and accepting existing factual information, thus leading to sexual (mis)education.

Limited communication also means that partners are simply not accustomed to speaking openly about their concerns and sexuality. Instead, people must lie, hide their feelings and desires, and relegate talking about sexual issues to conversations with others. Such social pressures reinforce norms, compelling people to abide by the norms and function with limited autonomy. Resulting feelings of fear, guilt, and shame can be so strong as to make a person feel invisible at the personal level and actually be invisible at the social level. It is not the person that is of importance, but rather, it is compliance with social expectations; her voice is secondary. Such pressure imposes formidable limitations on the possibility of exploring and expanding what could otherwise be a wide horizon of options—that is, her capability set. A clear example in this direction is provided by Sen, who opposes faith-based schools because he sees them as places where children are boxed into identities without the possibility of knowing different alternatives from which they later may be able to choose (Sen, 2006).

As with culture, the prevalent gender norms are beginning to change. This is largely because of social policy and opportunities brought about by the feminist movement (Guzmán, 2002), the influence of global institutions such as the World Bank and the United Nations, and the increasing role of CSOs (Guendelman et al., 2001; World Bank, 2003). Normative changes are also occurring in the mass media, where women exhibit increasingly autonomous roles, and in the greater society, as women make up an increasing proportion of the labor force. The rise of women in the market sector has certainly challenged the idea that the position of the woman is solely that of "mother" and "wife" (Peterson & Hennon, 2006). In the household, women are also experiencing noneconomic benefits of their growing role in the workforce, including greater decision-making power within the family. Nevertheless, men and women still adhere to gender roles, which are largely established within the household (Gates, 2001). Older social norms indicate that the wife should be at home waiting for the husband; these contradictory norms often position a woman's respectability and dignity in conflict with her working outside of the home (Gates, 2001).

Over 30 years ago, well-known Mexican psychiatrist Santiago Ramírez described the situation of the home, in which the father is rarely present. When he is present, he is there only to be admired, served, and answered. This typical image of the household often involves emotional and physical violence (Ramírez, 1978). Recent work has shown that this has not changed much (PAHO, 2005; Pick et al., 1998; Pick & Givaudan, 2006). The new opportunities and alternative roles for women have yet to be accompanied with corresponding new roles for men. Males are still raised with the pressure to be the dominant figure in the family and professional spheres, and they are not given the basis of emotional and social development with which to address these changes. Consequently, conflict is occurring as women are demanding more rights and control, whereas men are trying to maintain those traditional gender roles. One of the unfortunate consequences of the transformation of female roles but the static nature of the traditional male role (*machismo*) is the prevalence of violence. This may stem from men seeing violence as their only means to address the perceived threat to their traditional social roles. The pervasiveness of domestic violence and the limited social support for men highlights the need for a significantly larger investment in programs focused on males and the family—particularly, building their emotional and social skills, which is largely absent in the social education of boys.

Family Values

The changes in the workplace and the home in Mexico are undoubtedly forcing family dynamics to shift, although certain concepts of the family continue to be propagated through TV and radio programs (such as the widely viewed soap operas), movies, the church, and other social institutions (Salles & Tuirán, 1996). The differential gender roles are part of the bread and butter of the most popular TV and radio programs. On the other hand, the "until death do us part" assumption is no longer a reality because of changes in both norms and laws. Yet in the midst of these changing family concepts, the family unit continues to maintain its central role in Mexican life and therefore serves as a common promoter and supervisor of social norms (Peterson & Hennon, 2006).

The Mexican family unit is traditional: parental authority, blind respect, obedience, interdependence, and discipline are emphasized (Gregory & Munch, 1997). The ensuing behaviors of respect—not questioning or contradicting, simply obeying and following instructions (or at least putting on an appearance of doing so)—can be a key impediment to the autonomous development of youth. This is especially the case for girls, who are granted less autonomy than boys. Every member of the family is subject to certain expectations about individual behavior. These expectations are held beyond just the familial sphere and apply to individuals' behavior within the community setting as well. Thus, children's obedience toward their parents extends to other authority figures. As such, authoritarianism and submission pervade relationships in Mexican society: woman to man, citizen to public authority, student to teacher. The role of pleasing one's superior, also largely attributable to the value of *bien educado* which we discussed earlier, is a central component of the *modus vivendi*, which puts strong limitations on the possibility of expanding freedoms.

The hierarchical structure of families and the related cultural values of external control and appearance also result in violent parenting (Frías Armenta & McCloskey, 1998). Slapping, spanking, and other physically punitive measures are common (Frías Armenta et al., 2004; Peterson & Hennon, 2006),[9] and this maltreatment is considered to be "corrective" (Corral Verdugo et al., 1995; Frías Armenta & McCloskey, 1998; Frías Armenta et al., 2004), and viewed as a means of providing necessary control. The emphasis in raising children continues to be on providing, meeting basic needs, and disciplining to ensure that family cohesion be maintained and that social norms be closely followed. Objectives that are not central to this conception are not a focus of parenting; these include management and expression of emotions, autonomous and informed decision making, and open, direct communication. The outcomes of a system based on external control rather than internal growth as a means of addressing conflicts begin with the family and are reproduced at other levels of society.

Parent–child communication on socially taboo topics can be difficult because of the hierarchical relationship. Research has shown a gap between the adolescent–parent communication that is socially expected and that which psychologists perceive as ideal, especially in the case of boys (Prieto, 2002). In an IMIFAP report about intergenerational communication within the family, male adolescents reported talking very little with their mothers and even less with their fathers. Female adolescents similarly reported a low level and poor quality of communication with parents. Communication was perceived by the adolescents as being directive rather than informative (meaning that parents placed pressure on choosing certain behaviors rather than providing information with which the adolescent could choose the course of action best for him or investigate further). The lack of informative communication—and subsequent open exchange of ideas—is something that also occurs at the community level. In our view, this is one of the primary factors preventing community members from being able to exercise autonomous decision making, which is the basis of participatory citizenship and democratic rights.

The lack of knowledge about how to be autonomous manifests itself throughout society. If parents, authorities, teachers, and bosses do not understand the importance of informed choice and are unable to make or communicate informed decisions, this results in a social failure to exercise and encourage self-determination, autonomy, growth, and opportunities. Consequently, restrictiveness begins to permeate decisions at each level of society. Conversely, citizens who know their rights and obligations and exercise them in a free way can take responsibility for social problems. Peón (2007) asserts that nations whose citizens take such responsibility recognize problems as part of "their" community, and therefore claim ownership of and take responsibility for "their" problems. Citizens who take control of their own destinies and choices do not see the solutions coming from authorities as necessarily valid or as the only possible option (Estrada, 1991).

Political Culture

A nation's political culture is important not only because it affects a country's economic and infrastructure development but also because it can enhance or reduce individual and contextual opportunities for personal well-being. The political culture in Mexico is replete with socio-cultural norms, many of which are restrictive and pervade society so deeply that they are central to political processes and part of the individual mindset.

The long history of a passive and conforming Mexican citizenry is strongly linked to government domination, manipulation, and the corrupt focus on personal gain. In the newspaper *Milenio*, journalist Arturo Pérez-Reverte discussed these norms:

> The time has passed in which the kings impoverished us, the priests ruled over our families and social lives, and the generals kept us in line. We now live in democracy. But we continue to follow our traditions with a monstrous faith[10] (Pérez-Reverte, 2007, p. 44).

Pérez-Reverte stated that Mexicans continue to create new social castes that maintain the old customs of exploiting each other and their communities. It is a system associated with excessive bureaucracy, electoral fraud, corruption, and feelings of deception and vulnerability. Di Costanzo writes in the newspaper *La Jornada* that "the State creates its own monsters and in many cases the citizens feed them with our complacency"[11] (2009, p. 20).

In the closed system of nepotism and distribution of power among cronies, a feeling of ownership over political decisions is generated among high-end politicians. The focus is on power for personal gain, and thus value is placed on protecting those in the inner circle and on trying to keep all others out; family relationships are commonly privileged (Estrada, 1991). These dynamics trap politicians in a situation in which maintaining and advancing one's position is based not on merit but on obliging relationships. Mexican columnist Luis Rubio (2006) argues that such a lack of independence in Mexican institutions and individuals greatly hinders the institutional development of Mexican society. Politicians are not expected to render results, recognize liabilities and mistakes, or increase the transparency of their dealings. For example, it would be very difficult for a judge to make an objective judicial decision in a case involving a member of his "clan"; a disciplinary ruling would be considered a lack of loyalty. According to Rubio, "In Mexico, even someone caught in a delinquent act expects his buddy to get him out of jail; it is his friend's responsibility"[12] (Rubio, 2007, p. 17).

Furthermore, because this system is based on nepotism and a lack of transparency, many bureaucrats are not held accountable for their actions. Such practices have become socially accepted; it could even be said that they are normative. Rubio has criticized Mexican bureaucrats for propagating corruption, among other political norms, without the interests of the people in mind.

> Resources are directed at maintaining the status quo and the favorite projects of the people in power, which rarely are the most profitable, the most desired by the population, or the ones that could constitute the foundation of the economy and future society[13] (Rubio, 2006, p. 19).

Many people in power seem oblivious to their role as public servants or their duty to administer taxed wealth and elected power for the improvement of the community. The personal wealth seen in the wages of politicians displays an evident lack of social consciousness. Editorialist Miguel Angel Granados Chapa wrote,

> In a country in which tens of millions of people can hardly cover their basic needs, the legislative diets and their raises constitute an offense which no parliamentary faction has been willing to denounce and consequently step down[14] (2007, p. 15).

Politicians have noted, however, that the fear of making mistakes brings about the "save your own skin, forget the people you are supposed to be serving" attitude (Alberto Jonguitud, personal communication). Regardless, the lack of social responsibility among the upper tiers of society severely limits the social and contextual scope for change and development.

Lack of popular interest in politics stems from this traditional failure of politicians and political parties to address substantively the interests and needs of the populations whose interests they claim to represent (Peschard, 1991). If an individual's needs have historically encountered little valuation by those in politics, why bother voting or expressing those desires? Yet because livelihoods are often tied up in politics—sometimes simply through a relationship with the local politician—dissent is frowned upon, and many Mexicans feel that they have no option but to obey whichever person has more power in society, regardless of personal opinion. Their political capabilities, understood in terms of the power or options to undertake action, are therefore limited.

Obedience and the resulting lack of autonomy lead to citizens' own feelings of incompetence and powerlessness in politics, which, in turn, feed greater feelings of passivity and lack of initiative and competence (Peschard, 1991). Voting justifications often result from hopelessness, fear, and resignation (Valdespino, 1999, p. 10): "He always wins," or "The opposition is worse than the government," are explanations commonly heard. For several decades, the *Partido Revolucionario Institucional* (PRI) was in control of the country. Even when opinions about the PRI and the corruption associated with it were generally negative, it took a long time for people to stop voting for the PRI because the status quo was being preserved (Irízar, 2007; Reyes-Heroles, 1993). Individuals adopt this normative passive-dependency from an early age, which develops into both social and psychological constraints to civic participation. Parents have traditionally taught their children that political choice is limited and that active participation makes little sense (Segovia, 1991), rather than explaining to their children how to implement change in the political system.

To develop a political agenda focused on benefiting citizens, the well-being of the population must be the central objective of all political premises. Unfortunately, the concept of politicians as "public servants" is not common in many developing countries, including Mexico. For citizens and authorities to transform their respective political roles, it will require knowledge, sensitivity, openness to change, planning capacities, and willingness (by all) to take political risks that may benefit the community at large. This will necessitate a shift in policies and norms from paternalism to responsibility, from obedience to participation, and from submission to decision making. Change will also entail a realization that citizens have not only the right but also the obligation to be active citizens and hold congressmen and other key authorities accountable for their actions.

Paternalism

Paternalism has been defined as "the interference of a state or an individual with another person, against their will, and justified by a claim that the person interfered with will be better off or protected from harm" (Dworkin, 2005). In Mexico, paternalism results from lack of personal responsibility, feelings of fatalism, and concentration of power, both inside and outside of the political sphere. At the same time, paternalism further perpetuates this complex environment. Under a paternalistic system, the normal pathway for resolving problems does not involve proactively exercising individual rights. Rather, the pathway is one of personal favors and other actions determined by someone or some system other than oneself; it is "they" who are responsible for us, "they" who have the choice and the opportunities. We wait for "their" decisions and hope that they will benefit us. This, of course, contributes to a situation in which there is little predictability regarding where a person stands and how he can make a difference. The course of action that is taken very often depends minimally on oneself, once again leading to an externally focused decision-making process.

Individuals in positions of power often act paternalistically toward their constituents as a means of maintaining control over them. This is linked to a belief (rarely expressed openly) that it is a select few who are capable of making the decisions, including decisions on behalf of others. It is seen with politicians and citizens, teachers and students, parents and children, and employers and employees. A well-known entrepreneur recently stated:

> The best thing we [the entrepreneurial class], the people who have had the good fortune of having so many opportunities, can do is protect *al pueblo*, which does not have the capacity to make its own decisions, and teach [the people] the importance of being merciful, honest and obedient. (Servitje Sendra, 2007)

Such cases of paternalism are not unusual in nations such as Mexico, where since the Spanish conquest, the white population's superiority and right of control over the indigenous peoples has been held as a conviction by both groups. Because ancestry is closely linked with social class and occupation, paternalism easily manifests itself as an interface between classes.

The limitations that such views and systems bear on the development of individual and community freedoms are apparent. A paternalistic attitude implies that the figurehead is wiser than and in some way superior to the person or group he "protects." Yet the interfering actor often makes his decisions without the necessary information or skills to guarantee that these decisions will benefit the constituents. And in reality, as seen through the testimonies cited, paternalistic actions often serve the actors' interests at the expense of others. Instead of promoting change, paternalism manipulates people into accepting dependence on the prevailing political system, which requires pleasing the paternalistic figure.

Norms as Psychological Barriers to Change

Socio-cultural norms can be internalized by individuals and adopted as their personal norms. Transgression of internalized norms will likely be accompanied by feelings of shame, fear, or guilt, as well as an impact on identity and motivation as described earlier. Individuals can impose norms on others. Exerting control in interpersonal relationships is common in all human groups (Fiske & Depret, 1996) and can be achieved through cultivating negative feelings in the other person, either consciously or unconsciously. A person can say to someone, "If you don't do X, I will feel ashamed. What will people think if you don't do it?" or "Obedience is the most important thing; if you do not obey, God will punish you." Such comments enhance feelings such as *pena* and *vergüenza* in traditional Mexican communities.

Such emotions serve as psychological barriers to action—that is, limitations on an individual's potential to make decisions and choices and to act on them. When living up to the standard of the community is required, as we have shown to be predominant in Mexico, these emotions are powerful regulators that cultivate the fear of being scorned if one transgresses social norms. In traditional communities, regulators such as the need to keep up appearances and to conform can present an individual's main source of motivation. When this ideal has not been met, it is tempting to lie or act behind another's back; this is preferable to entering situations in which one might make a mistake or contravene what is perceived as socially expected or accepted. Those regulators also serve to maintain discrimination against groups such as children, indigenous peoples, and females, who traditionally have been accustomed to feel fear, shame, and guilt for making demands and who are both perceived and treated as inferior. Such patterns stand in stark contrast to the actions of a woman who stands up for her actions and accepts the consequences. Negative emotions can present a barrier to action, making a person passive. That individual aims at keeping a low profile rather than acting and exerting choice.

Psychological barriers, as identified through the testimonies and experiences of development work in Latin America, in principle apply at all socio-economic levels (Pick & Pérez, 2006). This section focuses specifically on groups of low socio-economic status and education levels. Within such groups, psychological barriers fit the history of cultural, social, and economic imperialism. For centuries in Latin American countries, external actors have employed negative emotions to cultivate among indigenous peoples the belief that they are inferior and incapable of making the "right choices" ("Piden a México," 2007) and that other, more capable individuals should make the decisions. As a domestic worker explained:

> I am ashamed of saying what I believe in because I am not rich. It is the white and rich people that have the right to say what they think and what they need.

They know more. And maybe we would get into trouble if we say what we want. Who knows, but better not to risk it ... I did not even dare ask for medicine when I was sick.
—Marta, a middle-aged woman working in a private home in Jalisco, Mexico

In summary, feelings of inferiority mix with other psychological barriers, which derive from tight social norms; together, they hinder individual initiative as well as agentic identity. As such, psychological barriers can be a major constraint to individual and community development, hampering interpersonal relations (Barriga, 2001), utilization of health services (Bingham et al., 2003), use of financial services (Pick & Pérez, 2006), and political participation (Segovia, 1991).[15] When looking to improve individuals' quality of life, major obstacles that must be confronted are psychological barriers, often built through generations.

Pena and Vergüenza

In the Mexican context, the example *par excellence* of an emotion serving as an impediment to action is *"pena."* This is translated into English as "shame." Closely related is *vergüenza*, a similar feeling, although *vergüenza* is somewhat closer in meaning to embarrassment. The two are expressed as shyness, insecurity, or timidity, manifested in daily behaviors by using defensive body language, avoiding eye contact, not answering a question, responding "I don't know" even if the individual has the correct answer, and dressing conservatively. In Mexico, such behavior is seen as modest, and its expression is considered socially appropriate and even expected. It is expected because *pena* and *vergüenza* imply the personal dignity, conscience, responsible behavior, and trustworthiness (Barriga, 2001) that are part of being *bien educado*.

The expression *"me da pena"* is equivalent to saying "sorry" in English. The difference is that it is not only the notion of "being sorry" that is expressed but "being sorry *and* ashamed"—that is, she is at fault, while others judge her. Making mistakes is seen as an opportunity for social reprimand, for showing others the error. It is not exceptional that *pena* and *vergüenza* create such extreme feelings of doubt, panic, and insecurity that individuals reach the point of being paralyzed by the fear that they may engage in an unacceptable behavior. Such a fear can grow from one or a few situations to become a constant feeling: a "mindset" that limits thoughts and actions. The value of *pena* in particular is so ingrained and associated with socially expected submission that people are expected to demonstrate and say they feel *pena* even if there is no real reason for it. Also, this outward emphasis stifles expression of actual feelings and needs by placing priority of culturally accepted expressions over conveying true feelings and thoughts.

These psychological barriers tend to affect women more strongly than men because they have a gendered component (Amuchástegui, 2001). Men are supposed to be attracted to women with *pena*, who are obedient, virginal, sweet, and feminine. Whereas it is socially accepted for males to have *pena* and *vergüenza,* it is *expected* for females. As expressed by a program participant from Campeche, Mexico: "As women we keep our opinions to ourselves." "Good women"—that is, those who are deemed apt for marriage—are expected to show *pena* in sexual relations; this is a way to comply with norms regarding sexual behaviors and gender roles. Those who do not are perceived as too sexually liberal and not worthy of marriage. Elderly women significantly help maintain this socio-cultural norm, pressuring the younger generations to express *pena* and *vergüenza* in their interpersonal interactions.

Guilt

Guilt is remorse over not having done what appears to have been most appropriate—that is, acted according to norms—and can be inflicted by an individual's own conscience or by others in society. Eliciting guilt by criticizing is an effective mechanism for dominating others and limiting their ability to assert themselves and their own life choices. Guilt is used at different levels and by various actors: mother-in-law to daughter-in-law, parents to children, and institutions—namely, religious ones.

In many communities in the region, invoking guilt is a socially accepted means of raising children both in the home and in school, as it is a means of exerting control over the younger and less educated child. Practice of this can be seen in the following testimony of a young woman who wanted to continue her studies in a city about 2 hours away from her home village. The young woman quoted her mother, trying to discourage her from leaving, as saying: "I have raised you all by myself. Your father was a drunkard who left when you were born and now you want to go off to study when you could stay here and keep me company!" Eric, a high school student from Panajachel in Guatemala and a participant in an IMIFAP program, was able to reflect on dynamics in his house and understand the guilt that was inappropriately inflicted on him by his family:

> It was hard for me to understand that I should not have been held accountable for everything that happened in my house. They always made me feel that things were my fault ... they made me feel bad for anything that happened. I was the oldest one, so if my brother got sick or my sister did not get to school on time or the food was not right, they made me feel guilty.

Inducement of guilt is also a strong means of restricting choice, making the individual feel as if he is undeserving of happiness and justifying punishment or social rejection. In Latin America, the influence of the Catholic Church has notoriously employed guilt as a means of controlling individual's sexuality. The concept of sin, *pecado*, is repeated in mass, homes, and schools in Latin America and is central to the widespread use of guilt that has permeated educational methodology, educational contents, and interpersonal relationships. In fact, it is so common and so widely accepted that it can be called a "cultural guilt." Guilt is induced as part of cultural practices, serving to restrict pleasure or the "wrong type" of pleasure.

Passivity is a common result of guilt. As a young child put it after leaving Sunday mass, "So why make an effort? I am bad, even without doing anything wrong." It simply does not make sense under these circumstances for someone to make any effort. Such views are beyond constraining—they paralyze choice and action. Mónica, a young adolescent from Mexico City, described, "I was always told that having too much fun could be bad for me, that only bad girls have too much fun. But I never understood what 'too much' meant so I just stayed home." The immobilizing effect of guilt, whether valid or not, impedes autonomous decision making. You are not capable of making your own decisions, so your choices belong to your superiors rather than to you. Furthermore, people become stuck in situations in which their problems are viewed by themselves and others as rightful punishment.

Socially imposed guilt can also lead to feelings of envy or contempt for those who do act in an autonomous fashion and are able to advance (Staller & Petta, 2001). A young woman in Oruro, Bolivia, once remarked to us, "She has this really good business. Let's see how long it will last. She was always the preferred one in my house. She did everything right, I was always asked why I was not be as obedient as my sister, why I did not behave as well as she did". Feelings of envy and jealousy are themselves psychological barriers when repeatedly present in an individual, a family, a community, or an institution, just like other negative emotions. In many ways they serve as psychological poison leading to psychological paralysis, which prevents the individual from seeing options and therefore severely constrains access to or creation of choice. Similarly to *pena* and *vergüenza*, when guilt is used as a central means of raising children, it generates insecurity that can grow from one situation to become a constant feeling and a limiting mindset.

Fear

As seen in the case of sexual and gender roles, instilling fear is a means of exerting social control. It is generally cultivated with threats or strong directives, which define "proper behavior" and serve to prevent "rebellious behavior." Similarly to the other psychological barriers, fear also represents a constraint on clear and uninhibited, autonomous decision making, decisions that may move a person toward realizing her potential. In a community in which compliance and appearance are of utmost importance, individuals may refrain from accessing opportunities for fear of making a mistake (e.g., it may lead to punishment) or even for fear of being successful (e.g., it may lead to being seen as different or as trying to go over others' heads) and consequently being socially ostracized. A municipal president played on this at a community meeting in Tabasco, Mexico: "It is important that the whole community join in building the new school. If you do not, the children will not have education, and who knows what will become of them and the community."

Being fearful of trying new things, of taking even measured and well-planned risks, also has implications for productivity and competitiveness (Ducci, von Uchtrup, & Oetken, 2001). The Mexican national fencing trainer told her team at the opening ceremony of the 1994 World Championships in

Mexico City, "Look, I know you won't make it to the finals, so just aim for not tripping or falling down in the inaugural march. I don't want to be embarrassed. Just walk well and don't try to do anything else." Fear of mistakes and diminishing efforts, has severe implications for performance. Additionally, fear of making a mistake may lead to escaping responsibilities. After all, if a person does not take any initiative or accept any responsibility, she does not need to worry about the concurrent commitment to respond to the consequences. When asked why he did not participate more in the classroom, a student in Arequipa, Peru, said, "If I don't participate, I can't do anything wrong, if I don't ask questions, they can't accuse me so easily of not knowing things. Better to just watch others do, and not do myself ... it makes life easier." Fear is an immensely restrictive emotion that goes beyond limiting decisions; like so many other negative emotions, it limits the possibilities of discovery, experimentation, and learning.

Health Consequences of Psychological Barriers

These psychological barriers are one of the factors contributing to the underuse of necessary and preventative health-care services. For example, many women avoid wellness and preventative visits, such as Pap smears, because they include exposure of their intimate body parts, which violates the prevalent norms of sexual modesty and shame (Givaudan et al., 2005; Pick, Givaudan, & Aldaz, 1996). A study in resource-poor settings analyzed the factors affecting underutilization of cervical cancer prevention services (Bingham et al., 2003).[16] Socio-cultural norms affected the women's personal beliefs, misunderstandings, and psychological barriers. Women were repeatedly afraid to be tested for sexually transmitted infections (STIs), which could develop into cervical cancer, because it required exposure of their genitals. The women were also afraid to receive the test results because positive results would be viewed as evidence of unfaithfulness. Thus, shame and fear of explaining exam results to their husbands reduced the women's willingness to get tested for cervical cancer:

> For many years we read on the [village] fences that we should prevent cancer ...
> my husband threatened to leave me if someone else touched or saw "those" parts
> of me. I went behind his back to the doctor because I did not want to die and
> leave all my kids. The doctor said the [Pap smear] was very easy to do and that I
> did not need the permission of my husband. But what if he could see it in my
> eyes,[17] that another man touched me? I was afraid.
> —Luz del Carmen, middle-aged female, participant in "I Want to, I Can...
> Prevent Cancer," Michoacán, Mexico

For many women, the pressure to conform to norms and fear of nonconformance are great enough that they will fail to be proactive about their health. This woman, however, obtained the information to make a choice, but making a personal choice without contextual and social support is much more difficult. We see that interpersonal relations, including partner relations, are hindered by a lack of open communication stemming from the strong presence of psychological barriers.

Studies have shown that mental health services are underutilized because of economic and logistical barriers of service scarcity, limited knowledge of existing services, and lack of funds, insurance, time, and transportation (Saldivia et al., 2004). But psychological barriers, such as misconceptions and fear of stigmatization, are persistent barriers as well. In a study about mental healthcare in Chile, more than two-thirds of the respondents misunderstood psychiatric illnesses to be disorders that could be cured without any medical attention (Saldivia et al., 2004). In the same study, one-third of the participants expressed fear of the stigmatization that would accompany a diagnosis of mental illness, and almost one-fourth were worried about others learning of their diagnosis. Another study of Latinos in the United States, showed that women feared bringing shame to their family members by relying on behavioral healthcare outside of the family, which would signify incompetence and irresponsibility within the family (Gloria & Peregoy, 1996). *Pena, vergüenza*, fear, and guilt also largely contribute to the high rates of underreported rapes. Many victims do not report their rape for fear of being branded, stigmatized, or blamed; fear of the family's reaction, tarnishing the family name, anger, or shame; and fear of attacker retaliation (Rivera-Rivera et al., 2004). Blame is often attached to the victim, pointing to personal attributes such as insufficient timidity, physical characteristics, and moral values rather than to the attacker.

In the case of reproductive healthcare, fear is one of the most prevalent methods of control. The countless myths (that parents, teachers, and health providers employ) generate fear of the body and of expressing doubts (Pick, Givaudan, & Aldaz, 1996). Social pressure and (mis)information serve to enhance the psychological barriers outlined in this section. The boundaries between shame and fear are nebulous: they are strongly intertwined and each feeds into the other. Embodiment of these emotions also has a negative impact on the individual's physical health (Fredrickson, 2004). For these reasons, understanding the impact of *pena, vergüenza*, guilt, and fear on psychological and physical health is imperative to promoting healthier behaviors.

Conclusions: Overcoming Psychological Barriers

Enhancing both the contextual and psychological access to choice empowers individuals and communities and can diminish the negative effects of a constraining culture. This will change both the power of restrictive norms and the norms themselves, opening opportunities for individuals and communities. As individuals start taking initiative to realize their own goals and life plans according to their self-identified needs, detrimental norms are modified and more productive norms adopted. For example, one of IMIFAP's early studies found that young girls who challenged social norms regarding contraceptive use were the least likely to become pregnant during adolescence (Pick de Weiss et al., 1991). Once individuals begin to exercise choice and autonomy, parting with them is difficult. In such cases, fatalism starts to be replaced with tolerance, acceptance, and even the promotion of choice and freedom. Fear, shame, and guilt to act begin to be substituted for what we call an "agency culture."

The development framework presented throughout the book is centered on this agent-oriented view. The Framework for Enabling Empowerment (FrEE) and its concomitant Programming for Choice emphasize the role of the individual in challenging constraining norms and promoting those that value agency and autonomous choice. Revisiting the earlier account of the struggle for local corn mills, we can see the value of such a focus. Guadalupe Murat, the late wife of the ex-governor of Oaxaca, Mexico, José Murat, had talked to all the municipal presidents of the state asking them to allow corn mills to be introduced in their villages so that women would have more time to themselves than they currently had while individually grinding the corn by hand. It was not an easy task, as she carefully explained:

> At the end I convinced many of them using economic arguments. One never gave in. He explained that it would mean too much choice for the women, and a loss of the control for him and the other men in the village; the women would not follow the social norms anymore, and would start making decisions on their own.

He was aware of exactly what keeping control in his own hands and those of other men meant in terms of power. Development is realized as individuals choose to transform not only their own personal norms but also the norms of social institutions. For those in control, allowing others to have similar opportunities may not come with ease, as parting with power is often difficult. Therefore, it is important to understand the benefits that enhancing opportunities for citizens at large may bring to the citizens as well as to the actors who have traditionally been in control. Indeed, this multi-level transformation is integral for changes at the societal level to occur.

As new choices are made, the probability of engaging in new behaviors and thus expanding one's capabilities is significantly expanded. Yet when choice is not accompanied by the necessary personal tools and contextual support (legal, educational, and structural), it can create problems instead of enhancing well-being; the introduction of choice without proper support brings about conflict, as decisions are made without viable solutions. This was the particular case of the woman afraid of getting a Pap smear despite the health promotion programs around town. Yet if this possibility for action is presented in the midst of a supportive social and structural context, along with knowledge, skills, and clarification of myths, expanding capabilities and entitlements can become normative behavior. Moreover, a social context supportive of informed, autonomous decision making should facilitate "giving oneself the necessary permission" to overcome psychological barriers. After all, these barriers to action both come about and can be let go of as part of learning experiences.

Notes

1. Although these norms may not be strong within all communities, they have been identified as pervasive norms within Mexico, and focusing on them allows for a discussion on how norms can impact individual development.
2. "sepa leer entre líneas"

3. The position of municipal president is comparable to that of mayor in the United States.

4. For a fuller discussion on external and internal sources of control, *see* Chapter 4: The Framework for Enabling Empowerment (FrEE) in this book.

5. "esta regida por fuerzas superiores"

6. "un Dios lejano y todopoderoso … cuya infinita sabiduría … no podría ser cuestionada por un simple creatura"

7. "Las mujeres que no sangran no valen nada."

8. The Mexican slang *"Aguas"* is the actual word used in this case.

9. The law allows such punishment, with slight injuries that go away within 15 days not being punishable crimes.

10. "Pasó el tiempo en que los reyes nos esquilmaban, los curas regían la vida familiar y social, y los generales nos hacían marcar el paso. Ahora vivimos en democracia. Pero sigue siendo el nuestro un esperpento fiel a las tradiciones."

11. "el Estado crea sus propios monstruos y en muchos casos los ciudadanos los alimentamos con nuestra complacencia."

12. "En México, hasta un acusado sorprendido en flagrancia espera que su cuate lo saque del tambo: es su responsabilidad de amigo."

13. "los recursos se dirigen hacia la preservación del status quo y los proyectos favoritos de los gobernadores, que rara vez son los más rentables, los deseados por la población o los que podrían construir los cimientos de la economía y sociedad del futuro."

14. "En un país donde decenas de millones de personas apenas pueden remediar sus necesidades básicas, las dietas legislativas y sus incrementos en términos reales constituyen una ofensa que ninguna fracción parlamentaria ha mostrado estar dispuesta a denunciar y, en consecuencia, a renunciar."

15. Details on contextual factors such as health, education and politics are discussed in more detail in Chapter 8.

16. The study was conducted in Bolivia, Peru, Kenya, South Africa, and Mexico.

17. There is the belief that if a man touches a woman's genitals, she will get pleasure from it and it will be apparent in her eyes.

References

Amuchástegui, A. (2001). The hybrid construction of sexuality in Mexico and its impact on sex education. *Sex Education,* 1(3), 259–277.

Amuchástegui, A., & Aggleton, P. (2007). 'I had a guilty conscience because I wasn't going to marry her': Ethical dilemmas for Mexican men in their sexual relationships with women. *Sexualities,* 10(1), 61–81.

Barnes, L. (2008). Influences and challenges of male gender construct. *Journal of Education and Human Development,* 2(1), 1–8.

Barriga, M. D. (2001). Vergüenza and changing Chicano and Chicana narratives. *Men and Masculinities,* 3(3), 278–298.

Bingham, A., Bishop, A., Coffey, P., Winkler, J., Bradley, J., Dzuba, I., & Agurto, I. (2003). Factors affecting utilization of cervical cancer prevention services in low-resource settings. *Salud Pública de México,* 45(Supplement 3), S408–S416.

Bond, R., & Smith, P. B. (1996). Culture and conformity: A meta-analysis of studies using Asch's (1952b, 1956) Line Judgment Task. *Psychological Bulletin,* 119(1), 111–137.

Brito, A. (1996, November 7). Identidad masculina y el uso del condón [Masculine identity and the use of the condom]. *La Jornada*, Retrieved August 3, 2007, from www.jornada.unam.mx/1996/11/07/ls-identidad.html

Carrillo, H. (2002). *The night is young: Sexuality in Mexico in the time of AIDS.* Chicago: University of Chicago Press.

Chen, L. (2007). Talk on occasion of the inauguration of the Instituto Carso de la Salud, *(September 18)*. Mexico City.

Corral Verdugo, V., Frías Armenta, M., Romero, M., & Muñoz, A. (1995). Validity of a scale measuring beliefs regarding the "positive" effects of punishing children: A study of Mexican mothers. *Child Abuse & Neglect*, 19(6), 669–679.

Coser, L. A. (1967). *Continuities in the study of social conflict* (1st Free Press paperback ed.). New York: Free Press.

Cypess, S. M. (2008). *La Malinche in Mexican literature: From history to myth.* Austin, Texas: University of Texas Press.

Di Costanzo Armenta, M. (2009, April 19). Después no nos preguntemos por qué [Let's not ask ourselves why after the fact]. *La Jornada*, p. 20.

Dréze, J., & Sen, A. (1995). *India: Economic development and social opportunity.* Oxford: Clarendon Press.

Ducci, M., von Uchtrup, H., & Oetken, M. (2001). Spontane Oszillationserscheinungen am Kupfer [Spontaneous oscillations: Findings on copper]. *Monatshefte für Chemie*, 132(3), 367–372.

Dworkin, G. (2005). Paternalism. In E. N. Zalta (Eds.), *The Stanford Encyclopedia of Philosophy* Available from http://plato.stanford.edu/archives/win2005/entries/paternalism/.

Estrada, G. (1991). La cultura popular de la transición democrática [Popular culture of the democratic transition]. In R. C. Campos (Ed.), *La nueva reforma política: Las perspectivas de la reforma política a partir de las elecciones de 1991 [The new political reform: Perspectives of political reform after the elections of 1991]* (pp. 189–197). Mexico City: El Nacional.

Fiske, A. P., Kitayama, S., Markus, H. R., & Nisbett, R. E. (1998). The cultural matrix of social psychology. In D. T. Gilbert, S. T. Fiske, & G. Lindzey (Ed.), *The handbook of social psychology* (4th ed., Vol. 2, pp. 915–981). New York: McGraw-Hill.

Fiske, S. T., & Depret, E. (1996). Control, interdependence and power: Understanding social cognition in its social context. In W. Stroebe & M. Hewstone (Eds.), *European Review of Social Psychology* (Vol. 7, pp. 31 61). New York: Wiley.

Fredrickson, B. L. (2004). The broaden-and-build theory of positive emotions. *Philosophical Transactions of the Royal Society B: Biological Sciences*, 359(1449), 1367–1377.

Frías Armenta, M., & McCloskey, L. A. (1998). Determinants of harsh parenting in Mexico. *Journal of Abnormal Child Psychology*, 26(2), 129–139.

Frías Armenta, M., Sotomayor Petterson, M., Corral Verdugo, V., & Castell Ruiz, I. (2004). Parental styles and harsh parenting in a sample of Mexican women: A structural model. *Revista Interamericana de Psicología*, 38(1), 61–72.

Gates, L. (2001). The strategic uses of gender in household negotiations: Women workers on Mexico's northern border. *Bulletin of Latin American Research*, 21(4), 507–526.

Gelfand, M., Nishii, L., & Raver, J. L. (2006). On the nature and importance of cultural tightness-looseness. *Journal of Applied Psychology*, 91(6), 1225 1244.

Giddens, A. (1993). *New rules of sociological method: A positive critique of interpretative sociologies* (2nd ed.). Cambridge: Polity Press.

Givaudan, M., Pick, S., Poortinga, Y. H., Fuertes, C., & Gold, L. (2005). A cervical cancer prevention program in rural Mexico: Addressing women and their context. *Journal of Community & Applied Social Psychology,* 15(5), 338–352.

Gloria, A. M., & Peregoy, J. J. (1996). Counseling Latino alcohol and other substance users/abusers. *Journal of Substance Abuse Treatment,* 13(2), 119–126.

Gongora Coronado, E., Cortes Ayala, M. d. L., & Flores Galaz, M. M. (2002). Creencias y acciones de los padres en la crianza de los hijos: un estudio exploratorio [Beliefs and actions of fathers in raising their children: An exploratory study]. *La Psicología Social en México,* 9, 849–855.

Granados-Chapa, M. A. (2007, June 17). Plaza Pública/De qué están hechos los legis-ladores [Public Forum / What legislators are made of]. *Reforma,* Retrieved June 18, 2007, from www.reforma.com.mx

Gregory, G. D., & Munch, J. M. (1997). Cultural values in international advertising: An examination of familial norms and roles in Mexico. *Psychology & Marketing,* 14(2), 99–119.

Guendelman, S., Malin, C., Herr-Harthorn, B., & Vargas, P. N. (2001). Orientations to motherhood and male partner support among women in Mexico and Mexican-origin women in the United States. *Social Science & Medicine,* 52(12), 1805–1813.

Guzmán, V. (2002). *Gobernabilidad democrática y género: una articulación posible [Democratic governability and gender: A possible articulation].* Paper presented at the Proyecto CEPAL/DAW "Fortalecimiento de las capacidades de las oficinas nacionales de la mujer en América Latina y el Caribe para la Gobernabilidad". Trigésima cuarta reunión de la Mesa Directiva de la Conferencia Regional sobre la Mujer de América Latina y el Caribe [CEPAL/DAW Project "Strengthening of the capacities for governability of the national offices of women in Latin America and the Caribbean." Thirty-fourth meeting of the Director's Board of the Regional Conference on Women in Latin America and the Caribbean]. Santiago de Chile.

Hubbell, L. J. (1993). Values under siege in Mexico: Strategies for sheltering tradi-tional values from change. *Journal of Anthropological Research,* 49(1), 1–16.

Irízar, G. (2007, September 29). Niegan 51% de PRI en 1988 [51% refuse the PRI in 1988]. *Reforma,* Retrieved September 31, 2007, from www.reforma.com.mx

Izquierdo, M. (2007, January 14). Persiste en etnias ritual de virginidad [The ritual of virginity persists in ethnic groups]. *Reforma,* p. 18.

Jáuregui, M. J. (2010, February 26). La disculpa [The apology]. *Reforma,* p. 18.

Levy, S. (2006). *Progress against poverty: Sustaining Mexico's Progresa-Oportunidades program.* Washington, DC: Brookings Institution Press.

Lipson, J. G., Dibble, S. L., & Minarek, P. A. (1996). *Culture and nursing care: A pocket guide.* San Francisco: UCSF Nursing Press.

Malloy, T. E., Albright, L., Diaz-Loving, R., Dong, Q., & Lee, Y. T. (2004). Agreement in personality judgments within and between nonoverlapping social groups in col-lectivist cultures. *Personality and Social Psychology Bulletin,* 30(1), 106–117.

Marston, C. (2004). Gendered communication among young people in Mexico: Implications for sexual health interventions. *Social Science & Medicine,* 59(3), 445–456.

Martin-Baró, I. (1987). El Latino indolente: Carácter ideológico del fatalismo latino-americano [The lazy Latino: Ideological character of Latin-American fatalism]. In M. Montero (Ed.), *Psicología política latinoamericana [Latin-American political psychology]* (pp. 135–162). Caracas, Venezuela: Editorial Panapo.

Medina, J. L. V. M., Mondragón, J. A., & Morelato, G. S. (2005). El autoconcepto en niños mexicanos y argentinos [Self-conception in Mexican and Argentine children]. *Revista Interamericana de Psicología,* 39(2), 253–258.

Pan American Health Organization [PAHO] (2005). Chapter one. Gender-based violence: A public health and human rights problem *Violence against women: Health sector responds:* Pan American Health Organization.

Paz, O. (1950). *El laberinto de la soledad [The labyrinth of solitude]* (3rd ed.). Mexico City: Fondo de la Cultura Economica.

Pelto, J. P. (1968). The difference between "tight" and "loose" societies. *Transaction,* 5, 37–40.

Pérez-Reverte, A. (2007, June 17). Nuestros nuevos amos [Our new owners]. *Milenio,* p. 44.

Peschard, J. M. (1991). El debate actual de la cultura política en México [The current debate about political culture in Mexico]. In R. C. Campos (Ed.), *La nueva reforma política: Las perspectivas de la reforma política a partir de las elecciones de 1991 [The new political reform: Perspectives of political reform after the elections of 1991]* (pp. 175–181). Mexico City: El Nacional.

Peterson, G. W., & Hennon, C. (2006). Influencias parentales en la competencia social de los adolescentes en dos culturas: Una comparación conceptual entre los Estados Unidos y México [Parental influences in the social competency of adolescents in two cultures: A conceptual comparison between the United States and Mexico]. In R. Esteinou (Ed.), *Fortalezas y desafíos de las familias en dos contextos: Estados Unidos de América y México [Strengths and challenges of families in two contexts: The United States and Mexico].* Mexico City: Publicaciones de La Casa Chata - DIF.

Pick de Weiss, S., Atkin, L. C., Gribble, J. M., & Andrade Palos, P. (1991). Sex, contraception, and pregnancy among adolescents in Mexico City. *Studies in Family Planning,* 22(2), 74–82.

Pick, S., Fawcett, G., Venguer, T., & Gamboa, M. (1998). *Domestic violence and reproductive health: Training for assessment and intervention in health care settings.* New York: INOPAL/Population Council.

Pick, S., & Givaudan, M. (2006). *Violencia: Cómo identificar y evitar la violencia en cualquiera de sus formas [Violence: How to identify and avoid violence in any of its forms].* Mexico City: Editorial IDEAME.

Pick, S., Givaudan, M., & Aldaz, E. (1996). Adolescent sexuality: A qualitative study in Mexico City, *Report presented to the Rockefeller Foundation.* Mexico City: IMIFAP.

Pick, S., & Pérez, G. (2006). Las barreras psicológicas para la democracia y el desarrollo [Psychological barriers to democracy and development]. *NEXOS,* 28(347), 17–19.

Piden a México reconozca derecho de indígenas en toma de decisiones. [Mexico asked to recognize right of indigenous people in decision making] (2007, November 11). *La Crónica de Hoy,* Retrieved November 11, 2007, from www.cronica.com.mx/nota.php?id_nota=332562

Prieto, M. I. (2002). *Sexualidad Infantil [Child sexuality].* Mexico City: Instituto Mexicano de Sexología.

Ramírez, S. (1978). *El mexicano, psicología de sus motivaciones [The Mexican, psychology of his motivations].* Mexico City: Grijalbo.

Reyes-Heroles, F. (1993, November 30). Colosio no es incitatus. *Reforma,* Retrieved August 3, 2007, from www.reforma.com.mx

Rivera-Rivera, L., Lazcano-Ponce, E., Salmerón-Castro, J., Salazar-Martínez, E., Castro, R., & Hernández-Avila, M. (2004). Prevalence and determinants of male partner violence against Mexican women: A population-based study. *Salud Pública de México,* 46(2), 113–122.

Rotter, J. B. (1990). Internal versus external control of reinforcement. A case history of a variable. *American Psychologist,* 45(4), 489–493.

Rubio, L. (2006, December 3). Oportunidad [Opportunity]. *Reforma*, p. 19.

Rubio, L. (2007, June 17). Independencia [Independence]. *Reforma*, p. 17.

Saldivia, S., Vicente, B., Kohn, R., Rioseco, P., & Torres, S. (2004). Use of mental health services in Chile. *Psychiatric Services*, 55(1), 71–76.

Salles, V., & Tuirán, R. (1996). Mitos y creencias sobre la vida familiar [Myths and beliefs about family life]. *Revista Mexicana de Sociología*, 58(2), 117–144.

Sapp, S. G., Harrod, W. J., & Zhao, L. (1994). Socially constructed subjective norms and subjective norm-behavior consistency. *Social Behavior and Personality: An International Journal*, 22(1), 31–40.

Segall, M. H., Dasen, P. R., Berry, J. W., & Poortinga, Y. H. (1999). *Human behavior in global perspective: An introduction to cross-cultural psychology*. Boston: Allyn and Bacon.

Segovia, R. (1991). Conducta y educación política en México [Behavior and political education in Mexico]. In R. C. Campos (Ed.), *La nueva reforma política: Las perspectivas de la reforma política a partir de la elecciones de 1991 [The new political reform: Perspectives of political reform after the elections of 1991]* (pp. 199–207). Mexico City: El Nacional.

Sen, A. (1995). Gender inequality and theories of justice. *Women, Culture, and Development*, 16, 259–274.

Sen, A. (1998, November 17). *Reason before identity*, Romanes Lecture at Oxford University.

Sen, A. (2006). *Identity and violence: The illusion of destiny*. New York: W.W. Norton and Company.

Servitje Sendra, L. (2007, May 28). Paper presented at the the the presentation of the book: *Urge un líder con sentido humano [A leader needs human consciousness]*, Mexico City.

Staller, A., & Petta, P. (2001). Introducing emotions into the computational study of social norms: A first evaluation. *Journal of Artificial Societies and Social Simulation*, 4(1). Retrieved August 2, 2006, from http://jasss.soc.surrey.ac.uk/4/1/2.html.

Szasz, I. (1998). Masculine identity and the meanings of sexuality: A review of research in Mexico. *Reproductive Health Matters*, 6(12), 97–104.

Tello Peón, J. E. (2007). Reflexiones sobre el impacto de la inseguridad en las empresas [Reflections on the impact of insecurity on businesses]. *Foreign Affairs en Español*, 7(2), 36–47.

Triandis, H. C., Marin, G., Lisansky, J., & Betancourt, H. (1984). Simpatia as a cultural script of Hispanics. *Journal of Personality and Social Psychology*, 47(6), 1363–1375.

Valdespino, M. (1999, July 23). Miedo de cambiar [Fear of change]. *Reforma*, p. 10.

Valsiner, J., & Lawrence, J. (1997). Human development in culture across the life span. In J. W. Berry, P. R. Dasen & T. S. Saraswathi (Eds.), *Handbook of cross-cultural psychology: Vol. 2. Basic processes and human development* (2nd ed., pp. 69–106). Boston: Allyn and Bacon.

World Bank (2003, March 5). Desafíos y oportunidades para la equidad de género en América Latina y el Caribe [Challenges and opportunities for the gender gender equity in Latin America and the Caribbean] Retrieved October 12, 2007, from www.ilo.org/public/english/region/ampro/cinterfor/temas/gender/doc/not/wban.htm.

Zubieta, E., Fernández, I., Vergara, A. I., Martínez, M. D., & Candia, L. (2006). *Cultura y emoción en América [Culture and emotion in America]*. San Sebastian, Spain: Vicerrectorado de Investigación de la Universidad del País Vasco.

CHAPTER 3

Testimonies

This chapter illustrates some of the results of the Mexican Institute of Family and Population Research (IMIFAP) programs for which outcomes exceeded the directly targeted changes in knowledge, skills, and behaviors. The programs from which the testimonies expounded in this chapter derived, began with the objective of targeting specific situational demands — enhancing specific needs for knowledge acquisition and skill building that would lead to particular behavioral changes. Although programs focused on a single topic, they always included transversal content on rights and gender equality. The behavioral changes were quantified, for example, in terms of: adolescents more frequently using contraceptives, women getting Pap smears, trash being adequately disposed of, and participants more regularly eating vegetables and brushing their teeth. In schools students were rejecting alcohol and drugs, and in businesses women were saving and employing others.

These results in themselves provided a good basis for individual and community development, but we also qualitatively observed a more complex phenomenon. In some participants, the impact of programs went beyond targeted, specific behavior changes and manifested a more general transformation in their approach to engaging with their social environment. Participants noted changes in: specific behaviors that enhanced their well-being; their initiative; their views on what rights they had and how to transform them into entitlements; and in how they could impact their contexts (Givaudan et al., 1997a; Givaudan et al., 1997b; Pick & Givaudan, 1995). We hypothesized that the agent-oriented view of development extended beyond targeted behaviors, enhancing individual and community choices, entitlements, and freedoms. These additional findings are the focus of this chapter and of much of the remainder of the book. They form the basis for the conceptual approach that we discuss in Chapter 4, where we present the Framework for Enabling

51

Empowerment (FrEE). We see this as a psychosocial approach to making Sen's Capability Approach operative.

We have chosen for this chapter three sets of testimonies, which cover the six IMIFAP programs that have reached the largest number of people (*see* Appendix A).

Silvia and Lorena

Silvia and Lorena both participated in the "I Want to, I Can … Prevent Pregnancies" program, which focuses on preventing unwanted pregnancies in adolescence. It was also the antecedent of all "I Want to, I Can" programs. The women attended the program 15 years before their testimonies (which are gathered in the interviews and reported here) were taken. They began work soon after their training as community facilitators and advocates. In this role they replicated the "I Want to, I Can… Prevent Pregnancies" program both informally and formally. They later received formal training for providing the "I Want to, I Can… Prevent Violence" program, which focuses on domestic violence prevention. This testimony is the joint discussion of Silvia and Lorena, which offers significant insight so many years after their participation in the programs.

> Our names are Silvia and Lorena. I am Lorena. I am 46 years old and have been a school teacher for 12 years. Silvia is 64 years old and has been a school teacher for 18 years.
>
> Once I started taking these [workshops], I began to realize many things and started thinking about many mistakes and situations in the past that I had thought were normal. For example, if my father got angry and yelled, "Why isn't dinner ready if your obligation is [to make it]?" I would see it as very normal because I thought, "This is the way life is." [In the workshops] though, I learned that this was not normal, no, this is a type of violence, even if it is my father, my brother, or whoever. So, I realized, "Oh, I don't like that." Then I started to tell him, "Dad, you're being aggressive."
>
> I think that I learned a lot from the program. First, for [building my] personal fulfillment, I learned how to look at mistakes and how to move on from them, and second, it served as a stimulus for me, to know that I could do other things that I didn't know about. In fact, I [eventually] taught the program "I Want to, I Can … Prevent Violence" to a number of groups in my community, where many of the women also changed their way of thinking, of acting, and of speaking. They became able to say, "I don't want this, I want that."
>
> I am now working in the Ministry of Public Education as a volunteer. [I teach] groups for parents. We teach them an initial education program about child development, where we cover 39 or 40 different themes, from getting children off diapers, to emotions, learning and sexuality. … [A]lways within those themes there's something that I [originally] learned in the IMIFAP workshops that I remember, and can use. For example, the importance of participating, not just sitting there like a sack of potatoes, and of inviting everyone to be part of the group, not just your favorites, and of helping people think and solve things by themselves and not just telling them "do this" or "do that." There are occasions when parents are uncomfortable [with this] because they're stirred … Sometimes they say, "You don't know that my life is like that, teacher, [but] everything you say I think is happening to me. What can I do?" Then there are suggestions,

comments, and other women's experiences … [Just as long as] they're suggestions, and they're not impositions, [it's fine.]

Before we took "I Want to, I Can … Prevent Pregnancies", we walked straight in only [one] direction, we didn't look anywhere else. We did not realize there were many other possibilities. Then "I Want to, I Can … Prevent Pregnancies" arrived and we started opening our eyes. We started to realize that there were many barriers: of being afraid to speak out, of being ashamed to say what we think, of not counting, of people not even seeing me, and this helped mothers to open their eyes. Why do I say this? Because we learned that there was more than one way of doing things and that it was okay to choose between different ways.

Everything that we learned has been bearing fruit because many women are now realizing that what they have lived is not normal (for example, in the case of violence) and that they should say, "That's it, no more." [They realize] that it's not only physical violence, not like [when they used to say], "No, he didn't hit me. He doesn't hit me. He only insults me or he forces me to have sexual relations, or he threatens me, or maybe he takes my money, but he doesn't hit me." And now they realize that violence is not only the actual strike, but [that] there are also the emotional, psychological, sexual, and economical aspects of violence, and there are threats to the children. There exist many situations where the woman realizes and says, "I don't want that. I can't stand it," and they do manage to set their limits. Most women who have been part of the workshops don't stay quiet anymore. Now at least they protest, and many also take action.

"I Want to, I Can … Prevent Pregnancies" didn't just help us. Back then it opened our eyes, little by little, like a newborn. We could see things differently where we were living. We worked with 1,060 women. Of those 1,060 women, most of them weren't beaten, but they were victims of abuse—different kinds of abuse.

First and foremost the program helped me in terms of valuing myself—bettering myself—in terms of learning certain norms that one needs, as well as learning to read, to study, to be emphatic. I also learned that you need to be honest—in what you do, in what you say to yourself and to others.

Passivity or the desire not to grow [may be a factor] limiting some people's development, but for me, it's different. In my house, my husband was the kind of person who wanted to know that I was always over there [in the corner], waiting in case he needed anything. But I started to change. I started to bring the workshop into the house. And because I took it into the house, I have a daughter who is now an educational psychologist. And ever since the program, my husband clears the table, he helps me, cooperates, and sweeps the floor. He's a different person—not that "Mr. Eduardo Lazy" who got handed everything. He picks up for himself. And he passes it on, to his brothers. They have changed a lot too, and their families are much better off now. It is like we now have teams instead of some individual people simply demanding things and others doing all these things to please them.

This workshop didn't just stay in me; it has also led to transformations in my friends and in the community. I have always told them what I have learned and they come to me for ideas, and they tell it to their kids and friends. It is like a ball of cotton candy that keeps growing.

The mothers [we work with] accept us program leaders and see us as people who can give them a hand—at least by listening to them—which is the main thing, right? And, also, by pointing them in the right direction. But despite the recommendations that we give them, the final decision about what they do … is their own. Other people cannot solve [their problems], but maybe their opinions, their experiences, can help [them with their] decision making.

And there are many challenges. My challenge has always been for the program to be understood; that's why I'm teaching the mothers what can really be put into practice. It's no good if they only come and hear it and have it go in one ear and out the other. My challenge with the parents in the basic education groups is to get to them in terms of the message: that even if they change a little ... it's a gain, it's something positive. Sometimes we program leaders don't see the gain, possibly because there's little follow-up; [however], they have told us, "I have changed. I don't yell at my child anymore. I try not to hit him; sometimes I slap his hand, but I don't hit him like I used to." And "No, I don't let my husband hit me anymore," which is ... a testimony that [we're doing] something good.

There were abused women who went [to the anti-violence program] with their small children, and now they're great women because they've gotten over all of those barriers. They surpassed them and they're doing very well. They work, go to the doctor when they are sick, [and] even do check-ups for prevention. Their children adore them.

Patricia and Silvia also worked with young male drug addicts in their community. Of the groups they initiated with these men, one consisted of 70 employees from a gas company. One participant in particular was very quiet; he had physically abused his wife and went to the program for help. Patricia recounted what he said:

"Well, I dedicated this week to my wife and my two children, and we were very happy all this week. And, guess what, teacher? I was really craving *mole negro*, but I made it myself." This was a great testimony. That man from the gas company... I used to see him with a mean expression, very ugly. I had never seen him smile. Now, he's totally different, very kind and smiling.

Once when [a young man came to the training] with his mother, we gave them a reading for reflection about "the worst mother in the world." When he read it, he started crying and crying, and his mother was surprised, and also his sister—she was even distraught—and asked, "What's happening to my brother?" And all the mothers were saying, "What's happening that a man is crying? And he is a boxer!" Once he was calm, we asked, "Well, what do you think of the reading? What happened? How did it feel to read it?" He said, "I felt very moved because I have never told my Mom that I love her. I have never given her hugs. But she hasn't hugged me either, and so now I want to hug her." So he asked: "Mom, will you let me hug you?" And then the mother hugged him tightly, and they cried and cried, and the sister and everyone, they were all crying there, from seeing that.

I have a picture of [that young man to remind me that there are] things that [make] you say, "How far can we go?" Reading that reflection sheet got to him so deeply. He was moved that from that session on, there was a lot of communication. In fact, they never skipped a session, and I was surprised that a young man like him, who could be anywhere, was there at the training, giving his opinions, and sharing his feelings.

I think that [people] have many skills and much knowledge. What's lacking is that faith that is needed within themselves to recognize those skills and knowledge, to defend them, and put them into practice. ... It's culture, right? The culture we have from generations of our ancestors. Always that patriarchy has existed, where man has ruled, he has had the last decision. Be careful if you turn around and say "No," because here only my [man's] voice counts. This culture is learnt from our own grandmothers and mothers who said, "You, shut up. Don't say anything. Let's avoid problems." Or, "No, no, don`t say anything, you look prettier when you're quiet." It's that culture which is still rooted in [us.] And then again, it's not so much what we're told, but it's what we see. [Certainly] there are also those who decide to break an established pattern, right? And then there are those who decide to follow it and say, "Well I'm better off like this." "Why look for something else?" Or, "The bad I know is better than the good that I don't know."

If there's no desire [to change], the workshop is not enough; and if I have the desire and the workshop is not there with someone to help me, to teach me, it's not enough either.

There have been many barriers in the community with abused women that we [have] worked with. There were many barriers, starting with the husband who was a real Mexican *macho*. That was the first barrier in the community. Are we changing that? We're getting there. We work a lot with women who have been beaten, to get them out of [their houses], to get out of that environment of psychological and economic violence. Sometimes we manage to, but not always, because [the husband will say], "If you leave, let's see who supports you, and your children. I won't." I remember clearly the case of a beaten woman with a lot of fear. She didn't separate from her husband, but she was in treatment. She didn't end her marriage ... but she became independent. She works, she's helped her children to move forward ... and she's still with her husband. So, in that, she took down all the barriers that she had.

In giving support to the participants, teachers do what they can to remove participants' feelings of blame. However, the workshops do not always work for women in the beginning. Patricia continued:

Sometimes that is very heavy; the guilt. [We tell workshop participants], "You're very valuable, you can do it. You're able [and] intelligent." I always give them an example of the exercise of the staircase of self-esteem. "Let's see, imagine that you want to climb the highest mountain in the world or the smallest one, or a pyramid, or even to the last flight of a building. What would you do?" Some will say, "I would prepare myself physically to be strong, right?" Another, "Well I would pack my food and make sure I had enough water." And another [would say], "Well I would take with me all the tools to climb, and appropriate clothing, and many other things." So I say, "Well, everything's there, now what are you going to do? How are you going to do it?" And they respond, "Well ... [by] climbing." Yes, but, how? And they would all say, like, "Hmmm ..." By taking the first step, step by step, that's why there's a staircase; I will not [be able to] climb if I don't take the first step. ... I have to react and do something. If I really want to change, or if I want to do better, or if I don't want to hit my children anymore, I have to do something. I have to.

Felipe, Luisa, and Carmen

Felipe is the principal of a private school in Mexico City. Prior to that, from 1988 to 2002, he was the principal of a local public school. Both schools implemented the "I Want to, I Can... Integral Human Development" program for students and the parallel "I Want to, I Can... Learn to Be Dad and Mom" program for parents. The programs aim to contribute to healthy interpersonal relationships within families and childrens' social groups. Teachers were trained in both of these curricula. Felipe said:

When I first arrived at the school, I had the idea that our school could be one of the best ones in the neighborhood and even in Mexico City. So we directed our steps towards that; we walked slowly, taking firm steps in terms of programs that were implemented. We looked for the ideal ones to use at the school, and by chance, one of my colleagues who worked part-time told us about a very pleasant experience with one of the "I Want to, I Can" books that she had seen in photocopy form. She brought it to me and told me, "Look, they're taking this program to the school where I work in the afternoons." We skimmed through it, and she explained more or less what the dynamics were like, and I told her, "Listen, this is a wonderful manual. What can we do to get more books?"

[Shortly after], we got together 70 parents who took the whole program, including about 3 or 4 men. We organized one specifically for fathers only a while after, because they would tell me, "We don't have time, teacher." And I told them, "Well, let's find the time. Do you think we can do it on a weekend?" So, we organized one for Friday afternoon, I think at 3 P.M., and we finished at 10 P.M. And [another one] on Saturday from 8 A.M. to 2 P.M., and Sunday at the same. It was truly an extraordinary thing for them, and then we kept having follow-up workshops[1] over other weekends. Still today, when they see me, they ask me, "How's it going teacher? What about those courses?"

These courses move consciences, structures, that sometimes are square [or rigid], and makes them more flexible.

[One] of the ladies who took the course told me, "I thought that I had a democratic family, and that we made the decisions together, but the other day when I asked them—after taking the family dynamics part of the course—I realized that I'm an overbearing person and that my family shouldn't have to live with that."

We supported many people in terms of [helping them learn how to] make decisions, as in the case of Mr. A. who was an alcoholic [and a father of one of the students.] He said to me, "You know teacher, they're offering me a job in the well-known, national Amalia Hernández Ballet," and I asked him, "And what are you waiting for?" He replied: "I don't know if I can do it." "Sure you can, you have proved it—look [back at what you learned] at the training." He said, "Well, I did use it to find a job in the Fine Arts Hall in Chiapas, and I now learned that I can do things if I really want to ... and ... to decide based on my feelings, and, yes maybe I can go for it." Then he went to work at the ballet. When [the ballet management] saw him perform, they [chose him to go on tour] in Europe. I was really happy when he sent me a postcard from Europe, in which he thanked us for the support we gave him, which enabled him to make the decision.

According to Felipe, it is the adults, particularly teachers and parents, who impose barriers on children and reject new information provided by workshops. At the private school where he is principal, they are trying to revolutionize education by implementing the "I Want to, I Can... Integral Human Development" approach.

I've been there for 3 years now, and I'm the technical director of the primary school. First of all, there's a lot of rigidity in terms of the programs. We are going to have to start changing our strategies, so that the teachers start changing. They have to change because a private school is supposed to give parents a plus. The plus does not mean having more notebooks filled, and more exercises, and more of this and that; the plus needs to be something meaningful. How are we going to do that? We're going to train the teachers with the "I Want to, I Can" courses. That's because we need to be refreshing constantly. We just finished on Monday, and look, changing strategies. Changing mentalities means also giving more time; giving ourselves more time at the school for the "I Want to, I Can" courses for the personal development of the teachers. We offered them [during] vacations, and I thought we weren't going to have any response for the program. But everybody, every single one went. With the parents we also organized them [during] vacations. They had already heard about what the courses do to one's life.

The issue of changes in strategies [is challenging for the teachers], because maybe a traditionally [minded] person just tells you how to divide. But the change in strategies [makes you think], "Maybe I'll present it with beans." And they're using other materials because children are in the stage of concrete operations. It's a total change.

The change in methodology has also helped us as teachers because now we have more fun. If we're going to spend so much time at work throughout our lives, then we need to get along well with everyone and we have to have fun, which is what we want at our school. We want our school to be a true oasis. Maybe children come here after being hit to get them to wake up early. And so when they arrive at school, we want it to be paradise, a place for them to enjoy all the time that they're here. That's why we do things this way.

To me, the most important thing is that children have a truly significant learning experience, that they really learn and apply it later in their daily lives—like the "I Want to, I Can" program, which teaches them the skills to be applied in daily life. We no longer want children to only study so they can pass a test with a mark of 10 on their report card.

We don't [assume that it will be easy] to break that mentality of parents, which is in fact quite difficult. [They might say "My child is] just playing." … They want to see something more practical, and that's why we need to work with parents so they are convinced that our approach will really help the children and the parents too. [By teaching the children] that we need to become more responsible, for instance in using water … we're benefiting parents [as well].

Education is something so difficult, [yet so] beautiful and so enjoyable. Sometimes other people can't wrap their heads around the fact that school is precisely where change is generated: changes in [just about] anything; democratic changes.

Luisa is the mother of three girls, ages 15, 10, and 4 years. The little she earns as a cook in a restaurant goes toward her daughters' education. After taking the course "I Want to, I Can… Learn to Be Dad and Mom," she has seen a change in her relationships with her husband and with her daughters.

Since I took the course, I continue to be a loudmouth, but not like I used to be. I used to scream and occasionally hit the children. Now I've learned to understand my older daughter as an adolescent. It was very difficult, raising her but not knowing how to educate her, not knowing what to say to her. When she was 13 or 14, I said: "I just don't know how to understand her, how to help her as an adolescent, how, now that she's growing up."

I don't think she is rebellious; it's just that her friends influence her. I say to her, "Don't hang out with her, she's rude and smokes, and I don't want you to have such [bad] habits, and [what] if one gets pregnant." She always gets angry. Now I know that moms always say this to their children, and the daughters always get angry. After the training I began to talk to her, and I told her she should choose her friendships carefully; she shouldn't confide in just anyone. If she goes to a party, she shouldn't drink. So I learned how to talk to her more calmly, I think before I answer her rudely.

At home our family is doing better because I talk things over more with my husband. Of course we communicated before, but now we are talking more and because it is clear and direct we understand and accept each other better. Before, the idea that dads—say, my husband—would do something like sweeping would be thought to mean they were "apron-wearers" *(mandilón)*. So I would say, "You are not an apron-wearer." It's just that nowadays the wife does some things, the husband others—for example, doing the dishes. It's all about communication now. It's just a matter of practice that we always discuss everything. I now tell him everything I think.

And what's happening with our daughters is that now we discuss their friendships. I tell [my teenage daughter] examples of what I've seen. After the workshop I was able to give her these examples, instead of just saying "Do this because I say so!" The examples make her think and analyze. They also help in getting her to do things because she understands [that she needs to do] them not just because I say so, and that makes her do them with more joy and initiative. I used to have this wrong idea about how things should be, but now I know that as parents we also have to respect the decisions of our children, and that it is valid for them to point out mistakes.

And I speak with many women in the neighborhood about how I have learned to talk to my family. I do the exercises with them, and they are using this too in their own families. When family members who live in other states come to visit us, they cannot believe what they see. Some now call and ask to be taught too. I have sent them to the school to take "I Want to, I Can … Learn to Be Dad and Mom."

Luisa's 15-year-old daughter Carmen is in high school. She spoke of her experience with the course "I Want to, I Can… Integral Human Development."

After 4 years—which flew by; time is so short—I still have [the "I Want to, I Can" book], because it covers experiences from your life in which you're learning to be better. If you make a mistake, well, don't make it again; don't fall into the same trap. Know how to express yourself to people, [and] how to treat others. Learn something more about education. And don't just stay forever in the same place.

Before the ["I Want to, I Can"] program, if I had wanted to belong to a group, then I would have [said that I had] to be the same [as everyone else]. But in the workshop I learned that you have to respect yourself and your decisions, and not be afraid to say "yes" or "no." Because sometimes you're afraid that if you say "yes," it will create problems with your parents, and if you say "no," then [it's a problem] with your friends. So, then it's like you start forming part of your independence and being yourself. You know that if you do something wrong, it will bring serious consequences, but if you do something that you feel is right, then you'll be okay with yourself and with others. I used to care a lot about belonging to a group of friends, but when I saw that for that you have to smoke, cut school, skip classes, I thought "obviously not." And not because of my parents, since in any case, my parents already had their lives, right? Today it's about me and the benefit is for me, so I would say, "If I know that this is going to harm me, why do it?" If I'm [to be] someone in life, which I hope, and to have an excellent future, it will be for my parents and for me.

Also from the workshop I learned to relate better to the world. Because I realized not everybody thinks like me—everyone has [different] assumptions looking at life. I see it in a certain way, and other people see it in a different way. I used to think I was the only one who was right, but now I have learned to respect the points of view of each person. With the course I became more tolerant of the different ways of doing things that people have and now think things through before speaking. And if I don't have anything positive to say, I'd rather keep quiet.

And I also act without hurting people, because there are a lot of people who speak [their minds], and they don't know how much it can hurt people. If someone asks for a favor, I try to do it. But it's not merely to please people superficially, as if I have to do what people ask me to, [but] to somehow praise them. I do what I think is right and convenient for me as a person and also for other people. I respect myself and the people around me, because respect starts with yourself. If not, where else? I [no longer] do anything just to please others; I do much more to be happy with myself. And I understand that if I am okay, it will be easier to help others be okay too. I used to think the opposite—that I had to be the least important, that only others mattered, and that in that way people would like me.

[Parents] get scared of everything. But that's bad, because if a child goes and asks his father a question, but the father avoids the question with a silly answer, then the child will still want to find out. Maybe he will find out at school. Or he will look for an answer [on his own]. That's not the [best] way, when the father could have given it to him correctly. So that's when the consequences come. Sometimes it's like parents shut the doors. [They think] that if the children ask about something, then they're going to do it, and thinking like that is bad. The child is interested in knowing what's happening in his world and what could happen to him. Youth want to have information so they can make up their own mind, not just copy what others tell them, and for that they need to know that it is okay to make their own decisions, to not just obey. They need information to be able to choose between different things.

Since I began the program, I started thinking, "If this is going to help me, and if I do it myself, then in the same way that it helped me it can help more people." So I would go into the training sessions, and I would talk to many people. When I was in sixth grade, I talked to my classmates, and to my teachers; they were very timid. And then they learned from these things, and they all went in and signed up, and they supported each other.

Carmen said she went from house to house, telling her neighbors what she had learned and how she had promoted change at the school and community levels.

Many people told me, "Congratulations for what you have done." And a teacher called me and told me, "I want you to help me [with] my ['I Want to, I Can'] program." And [some] ladies saw me and asked me, "When can you come to my house to talk? So people approach me because they're interested in the program.

UNICEF invited a group from school to do a discussion openly on TV, urging TV viewers to avoid exploiting minors, to take care of the environment, and to support education. These were themes that I enjoyed a lot because in this country you never know, right? Especially with the prostitution and everything. This process [of taking the workshop, getting the courage and skills to speak in public, and then using it on TV] helped me a lot because I learned a new way of life, like how you can help people by speaking up, not just staying quiet. It was very nice.

After the UNICEF thing, and the dialogue, I went with many people to talk in schools, asking them to take care of their environment, not to let other people destroy what has taken so much work to create. And [in the case of] any sort of crime taking place, to report it. And it has worked. For example, in my house, I have also told my mother, and we have a kind of alarm that the county set up. My mother and some neighbors and my friends and I went to the authorities so they would do this.

I also stopped by [the neighbors] and told them about my experience with the alarms, and the neighbors talked about it. Representatives from the municipality came, and an agreement was made [to add more alarms]. [I told the neighbors] that they shouldn't just let themselves go along with what they see; if they see something wrong, rather than worry about what's going to happen to them they should fight against it and report it. [I want] for them to speak up and not to stay quiet.

Many people fail to act out of fear. If I see something bad, I speak up. I don't stay quiet, and so I'm inviting people to build a better municipality together. If we don't do it ourselves, then no one will do it.

Susana

Derived from the "I Want to, I Can… Integral Human Development" program, the rural and indigenous community-based version "I Want to, I Can… Care for My Health and Exercise My Rights" has expanded greatly over the years. This program aims to teach basic skills and knowledge for health promotion. Susana not only participated in "I Want to, I Can… Care for My Health and Exercise My Rights," but also in the "I Want to, I Can… Start My Own Business" program. The following is her testimony.

> I'm 45 years old and live in this village with my husband and three children. My oldest daughter, Marta, is 19 and studying to be a veterinarian. Her brothers are 17 and 8 years old.
>
> I'm originally from the State of Mexico, but I've lived in Oaxaca for some 20 years. All of my kids were born here. I have been back to Mexico City a few times but just to visit my family there.
>
> One comes with a heritage from one's family—how our parents were and how we were in the past. My parents were strict. We studied what they wanted us to study. And they made us do what they wanted: no boyfriends, no hanging around in the street, going to church every Sunday, and lowering our heads when they scolded us. But my oldest daughter decided to study to become a veterinarian because she loves the countryside. She heard about the career in school, and since my husband and I wanted our kids to do what they chose, we supported her in her decision. We both learned in the IMIFAP courses the importance of being able to choose and what one needs to be able to do that.
>
> Since I was 13 years old, when my mother taught me, I have been a seamstress—making repairs, dressmaking, anything having to do with clothing. And then there's the store. What happened is that my father-in-law owned a store. When he died the store was left, closed. That's how we ended up with the store. But we needed the money to restock it. We needed to get a loan, but aside from the bank, we didn't know where to go for this. We didn't go to the bank because they ask for things we don't have—pay stubs—but we are not salaried employees. And deeds; but here most of us don't have registered ownership of the land. We just have the piece of land we were given to build our houses on, and I couldn't go to my family for a loan, never. We are, after all, all in the same situation. And my relatives weren't here.
>
> I was used to putting money aside when I was single. But from the time I was 23 and I got married, I couldn't manage to save much money. Before that, I always had hopes of owning my own sewing shop. I even bought some sewing machines. For years after we were married, we never put our money into a savings account.

For Susana, it was the IMIFAP course "I Want to, I Can… Start My Own Business" that enabled her to develop the store, more efficiently manage the business, and reinvest in it to expand the operation.

Since my training, we've been able to save more for reinvesting. We do it by percentages. We always used to say: "I've made 10 cents, 20 cents, 30 cents." Since I'm in charge of the money, and because of what I've learned about percentages, I now say: "How much will I make on these products?" So the money comes in, and I see how much I make on each product. Then I divide the total according to the products and take out the percentage I had planned to earn, which is from 20% to 22% of the receipts. And from there I say: "This much goes to pay the invoices, this much is to reinvest, and this much is what I can put aside for the kids." In doing this, I think my business has grown 50% since we started. It's different now also, since we plan by the week. Every week we receive an order of goods, check them, stock the store, and we have a full inventory again. Then a week later we restock.

And aside from that, we now produce pickled cacti (*nopales*). ... Since there is no market here, we sell some of it directly, but most of it goes to a girl who then sells them at the market in Huajuapan. We also sell some when there are festivals here. And we sell honey. An engineer who owns an apiary brings the honey here in little buckets ... and we bottle it.

Now I look for ways to expand the store, any way I can; even more than before. When this helps the children, and when you figure out the way to sell things, you see more opportunities, and then that moves you on to others. And with the help of my husband, well, we are very eager to increase our sales.

In addition to allowing our kids to get an education, we've been able to get things for the house that we couldn't afford before. We now have a refrigerator and a microwave oven—which we also need for the business—but we use them for ourselves too. And the cell phones. We don't have telephone lines here, so there's no other way. We have to use them because the kids travel so far away to school. Just for that purpose. And it's running the business that gives us the opportunity to do this.

Having my own business has also led to other changes. Right after I got married, I wanted to work. But my husband said no, because the children were young, [and] because if I were to go out to work, people might say that he was not working. But he's changed his opinion and now he says, "Haven't you gone out yet to do your selling?" It's different now.

I don't ask his permission anymore to do things. Rather, I ask his opinion, or I say, "You know what? I'm going here or there, because I need this or that." Of course, I don't say, "I'm going, but I'm not asking your permission," but [instead] I simply say to him, "I'm going to Temazulapan now."

My relationship with him has gotten better. Because of the ["I Want to, I Can ... Care for My Health and Exercise My Rights"] training, there has been more communication between us. And I explain to him everything they teach us. He says that this is a good thing, and he hopes that all the other women will take the courses.

The whole family has benefited, because now after the health and empowerment program ["I Want to, I Can ... Care for My Health and Exercise My Rights"] and the starting a business program ["I Want to, I Can ... Start My Own Business"], there is more openness in expressing opinions. We even ask our children their opinions when there is a problem in the house, or with work, or at school. Whenever they come home, it's, "How did things go today? How are you doing at school? How are the exams going?" Also, my son needed to select a career, and we let him choose what he wanted. And he said, "It's just that I don't know, you choose for me." And I said, "If I were to choose everything, you'd be a priest." And he said, "No! I don't want to be a priest." So I said, "Then choose for yourself, because I'm not the one who will be doing the work or studying for what you want to do." So he chose; he is going to be a mechanic. We suggest options, and if he doesn't like them, he can choose for himself.

Things have changed for other families too, since the training. Although my husband was never a drinker, the majority of the men [here] drink. The most serious problem here is alcoholism. Just this year, three people died from alcohol. There have been many cases of abuse because of alcohol. But now, with all the training the women have been given, they talk to their husbands, saying to them that it's not necessary to drink so much nor to hit them nor to fight with them. And now, many really listen to them and get help or drink much less. Of course they talk to their husbands about this only when they are not drunk, because if the men are drunk and if the women get angry and they fight, they won't be able to accomplish anything.

Training about preventing health problems [in the "I Want to, I Can ... Care for My Health and Exercise My Rights" program] has also helped. For example, before, people used to get sick every month or every other month. And when they would send a nurse to vaccinate the kids, the people here would not allow it and would hide. They said it would make the kids sick. Now everyone agrees to it, and to the point where the women check to find out when the nurses will come to vaccinate the kids. Now there is more information. Before we didn't know what would happen to us if we didn't have a Pap smear or a breast examination ... or we didn't boil the water. Now we do all of these things and so we have more control over prevention and more opportunity to go to the doctor.

We've accomplished a lot that we couldn't have if we had not formed our women's community group. It is difficult to bring women together as a group. For example, a husband of one woman wouldn't let us meet in his house. Or when we formed a committee for the project to get sheep, one woman came to us and said, "I can't, my husband won't let me join." And we said, "Of course you can." We all know she had problems with him. "You need to explain it to him and tell him that all of us have to participate." She was a young woman, just married, a year at most, and she said, "Alright, I'll talk with him." Her sister said that she could do it, but we were worried that she would come back and tell us that her husband refused to allow it. So we all went to talk with her. So first we succeeded in attaining our autonomy, then the support of the group.

To be able to negotiate we need to be organized, or we cannot do anything. So we began from there, and began to make changes through requests and then demands of the authorities, submitting proposals for the health center, the school, the kids, and the women.

I think the men are taking us more seriously now. Before, they hardly ever listened to the women. The committees were all composed of men. I think I was one of the first women to join the kindergarten committee. At that point most people did not want to send their kids to kindergarten because they didn't have the money for supplies. So I said we would have dances and carnivals to raise money, and then the committee would buy supplies for the children. And we did it.

Since my training, I have become a leader in the community. One feels more capable. I think you could say I feel more prepared to speak to the people, to speak in public, to speak with women. Before, it was difficult to raise my hand and to express my opinion. What helped me a lot also was becoming a facilitator because I kept repeating and putting into practice what I had learned in the course, and every time I do, I see it from a different perspective.

Have I imagined myself as an elected official in my community? Yes. We women have discussed it. I say to them, "Why don't you want to be officials?" But they answer, "No, but we will help you." Sometimes we joke about these things, right? But I think one day it could be possible, because we women now would like to change many things that we do not like [in our community].

I didn't always think this way. It's recent. Because I know that we didn't understand things [before], and we thought we just had to follow what others said and we did not have a chance to decide, we just did as we were told, and so we didn't participate much. And now that we have this, we don't like the idea of giving it away. Before we didn't have the opportunities to express ourselves. We now exercise our right to present our opinions to the community: first to our family, our husbands, and then to the community.

The life skills training has helped me with teamwork and with business—so that I can administer it properly. I think that I've lost the fear of offering new products and the tendency of backing away, saying it's better not to invest in something, that I'm not going to accept the risk of selling something. It's taught us that we have to take some risks in order to accomplish things. Also, it has made me think more about what I want, not necessarily personally, but for my kids. What I want for them is that they succeed in their careers, that they not have what we have but, rather, more opportunities than we do. And, I want them to know to value their health and how to take care of it.

Now I don't think that what we accomplish necessarily has to do with luck but more with having [done the] work. If we are going to be waiting for God to give us everything, we aren't going to do anything by ourselves.

One goes on acquiring experience. I always had a problem of fear, of being in front of the public, of speaking publicly, of the microphone, and, above all, of hearing my own voice. Now I speak in public, and have discussions with the women. In the IMIFAP course, they told me to put a mirror in my room so that I could see myself and listen to my voice—that I had to learn to listen to my own voice.

Do I consider myself an honorary leader in the community? Yes. I have assumed more responsibility. But I always tell them "You have to do this your-selves." Above all, it's all about self-esteem, right? First, a person has to want something to be able to do it, and it is only if you really want it that it makes sense and that it really opens doors. And that is very different from just doing things because you are supposed to.

Conclusions

These testimonies have been included to bring attention to the participants' voices from which our framework emerged. These participants represent the *human* basis of sustainable development. These are select cases, and not all participants report a more agentic attitude toward their lives, nor do all favor making choices rather than waiting to be bestowed with miracles and favors. We do not have testimonies of those who did not participate in programs (i.e., a control group). They are not the ones who come forward with comments; they are far less likely to respond openly and directly express why they are not interested or perhaps more afraid of change. Responding in this way would mean that these individuals already are willing to contravene the socio-cultural norms of pleasing others and of not speaking openly about their wishes and needs. At the time of writing of this book, IMIFAP is in the process of putting together and analyzing the data of quantitative studies which systematically show such differences between experimental and control groups. Initial results are referred to in Chapter 4.

An example showing a range of reactions to a single situation occured when some villages in northern Oaxaca, Mexico, were invited to participate in a micro-enterprise training program. After the program, loans would be provided to participants. Some of the women did not show up to the training sessions.

Most did not say anything; they simply stayed away. When asked why, these women tended to shrug their shoulders or gave answers such as "I can't," "I don't know," "What would my husband say?" "Who knows if the funds will ever come?" or, "What will you give us in exchange?" There were also women who did not attend the training but who pressured us for the loan nonetheless. At the same time, there were many requests from neighboring villages asking for training even if loans were not available. Word had spread that the training was, as some women relayed, a way to help them "count," to "be someone," and "to make decisions."

These participant stories and testimonies demonstrate the psychological processes integral to sustainable development. Working at the individual level facilitates the expansion of knowledge, skills and a supportive normative structure among families, peer networks, communities and organizations. In turn, this results in an environment where *human* development can be fostered and sustained. We formalize these processes that have emerged from our participants in the framework presented in the following chapter.

Note

1. Such follow-up workshops are an integral component of IMIFAP programs. Often referred to as "actualizing and follow-up," the sessions are focused on connecting what students have practiced outside the classroom with the topics taught in class. Discussions often take place as students work through problems they have encountered and make linkages between skills sets and new thematic areas.

References

Givaudan, M., Ramón, J., Camacho, D. & Pick, S. (1997a). Multiplication of the family life and sex education program "Yo quiero, yo puedo" in marginalized areas of Mexico City, *Report presented to the Compton Foundation.* San Francisco, CA: IMIFAP.

Givaudan, M., Ramón, J., Camacho, D. & Pick, S. (1997b). Qualitative evaluation of the "Yo quiero, yo puedo" program for 5th and 6th grades, *Report presented to the World Bank.* Washington, DC: IMIFAP.

Pick, S. & Givaudan, M. (1995). Evaluación de diferentes tipos de intervenciones para la instrumentación de un programa de educación para la salud y vida familiar para los niveles de preescolar y primaria [Evaluation of different types of interventions for the instrumentation of a health and family life education program for preschool and elementary school], *Report presented to the Ministry of Education.* Mexico City: IMIFAP.

CHAPTER 4

The Framework for Enabling Empowerment

It is essential for the oppressed to realize that when they accept the struggle for humanization they also accept, from that moment, their total responsibility for the struggle. They must realize that they are fighting not merely for freedom from hunger, but for " ... freedom to create and to construct, to wonder and to venture. Such freedom requires that the individual be active and responsible, not a slave or a well-fed cog in the machine" ... The oppressed have been destroyed precisely because their situation has reduced them to things.

—Paulo Freire (1970, p. 55)

As we have argued in the previous chapters, in the developing world, the poor are not customarily afforded the freedom to make personal choices, nor the autonomy and rights to determine their own course of action. The deficiency of such fundamental freedoms undermines the prospects for human development in many countries. Individuals accustomed to decisions imposed externally, through pressure, threat, guilt, or even force, similarly place the responsibility for the outcomes of their choices and behaviors on outside forces. Instead of fostering individual capabilities and agency, a system of external control creates, in the terms of Freire (1970), a society of "slaves or well-fed cogs," whose lives are dictated by contextual realities and normative pressures.

The following discussion focuses on the individual components of development. We outline a way to make Amartya Sen's Capability Approach operational, through a psychosocial framework where investment in human capabilities and understanding individual needs is the point of departure. We begin with an exploration of our framework's conceptual foundations in psychology, and an extensive discussion of *personal agency*. We then introduce

65

extrinsic and intrinsic empowerment and, finally, present an outline of the *Framework for Enabling Empowerment* (FrEE), which illustrates how fostering individual capabilities and contextual factors can improve the sustainability of development initiatives. FrEE is based on the results of evaluations of development programs carried out with people in urban and rural communities in 10 countries in Latin America, as well as with Latinos in the United States, CSOs in Uzbekistan, and teachers in Greece. The strategy used to develop programs based on FrEE—namely, Programming for Choice—is presented in Chapter 9.

Foundations of the Framework: Access to Choice and Behavior Change

Amartya Sen has written extensively about agency and choice. In his conception, which contrasts that of traditional economics, "agent" refers to a person who is not performing according to external expectation and evaluation. Rather, he defines agent according to its "grander" meaning, as "someone who acts and brings about change, and whose achievements can be judged in terms of her own values and objectives, whether or not we assess them in terms of some external criteria as well" (Sen, 1999, p. 19). Subject to her own judgment, the agent also assumes more freedoms and responsibilities, increasing her sense of personal investment in development. As such, programs targeting human development have the potential to make a profound, sustainable impact on individuals and communities.

Behavior change is one of the most practical means through which human development can be assessed. Behaviors, after all, are the clearest means through which rights and choices can be made operative. Development programs can lead to a broad range of behavioral changes because successful change tends to gain momentum after the initial impetus, expanding the scope for more extensive transformation (Prochaska & DiClemente, 1982). Even programs that are narrowly focused, such as those directed at reducing drug use, for example, have the potential to affect a broad spectrum of behaviors. At the same time, appreciation of this human potential can be enhanced by a more dynamic interpretation of behavior change than traditional psychological theories offer. This interpretation is one that integrates psychology in order to address the broad range of behavioral domains and other determining factors such as common skills and cultural and psychological barriers to action.

We propose the term personal agency to describe such a dynamic interpretation; behavioral change as the means through which an individual realizes choice—seeing options and alternative courses of action. The term *agency* describes the process through which a person carries out informed, motivated, and autonomous decisions; the term *personal* serves to expand Sen's concept of agency to emphasize the individual level and how the changes are occurring at the stable level of the person's characteristics.

Personal agency is a consequence of experience-based success in the application of choice. It may develop as a result of a training program, a change in socio-cultural norms, or from institutional expectations, such as those set by the educational system. Personal agency also generalizes to other behaviors after individuals realize that their newly acquired sense of agency can be applied to different needs. For example, the realization that one is able to participate in class by asking a question can generalize to increased participation outside the classroom or to engaging in new actions within the school setting. Choosing to engage in new behaviors in various situations is likely to result in stronger feelings of self-efficacy, autonomy, competence, and self-esteem. This multifaceted concept has emerged from the existing literature, field experience, and results, and has been adapted from Sen's approach. It integrates concepts from the personality and social psychology fields that explain personal qualities: control (Rotter, 1966), autonomy (Kagitcibasi, 2005), and self-efficacy (Bandura, 1997). Key to understanding these psychological concepts—and the concept of personal agency that encompasses them—are the motivations for individual actions (Kabeer, 1999).

Agency implies autonomous—in other words, free and independent—and knowledge-based decision making, which allows individuals to foster a greater sense of control over their immediate environment. As choices and actions become more agentic, people develop greater personal responsibility; the individual responds, or is held responsible for, the consequences of her decisions (both positive and negative). They also develop heightened control over their lives, and freedoms are enhanced. Comin writes that agency "is behind individual initiative and social effectiveness" (2001, p. 4). A program participant who has formed a more holistic sense of herself—and is beginning to foster her personal agency—has greater potential to see herself as a member of a larger entity and to have a voice and to be heard. A transformation occurs from the initial reasoning of: "I was told to ..." or "I am supposed to ..." and develops into "I want to ..." or "I can ..." This new sense of ability allows the individual to sustain a greater effect on her family, community, and regional and national politics. We have termed this phenomenon of the sense and ability to extend personal agency into one's community and institutions "intrinsic empowerment". A supportive environment or development program can expedite this process, whereas a restrictive context will diminish the probability of change and of its maintenance once it has taken place.

Personal Agency

The person figures as one of the central concepts in the framework presented later in this chapter. We define the "person" as distinct from, yet interdependent with the context. Our definition contrasts somewhat with other terms, such as *personality*, which is used in the field of personality research to refer to lasting traits that are consistent over time and across a broad range of situations

(Allport, 1966; Mischel, 1968). The term *self* refers to how an individual perceives himself or herself (Shavelson & Bolus, 1982) and to the association of the self with various attributes (Greenwald et al., 2002). Within this perspective, the person is seen as formed through experience. For us, the term *person* does not refer to a relatively unchanging, static entity, but to a dynamic being that is capable of change in attitudes, thoughts, identity, and behavior—in essence, incorporating aspects of both "personality" and "self".

Defining Personal Agency

The term *agency* has been used in psychological (Martin, 2007), philosophical (McGeer, 2008), economic (Karni, 2008), and socio-economic development (Sen, 1985) literature as a means of explaining aspects of autonomous human functioning. Our use of the term "personal agency" is partly inspired by the currency of "agency" in developmental economics and in psychology, allowing it to serve as a bridge between these two fields. It connects the microlevel psychological approaches with the macrolevel economic approaches to development. We have added "personal" because agency is part of the more stable characteristics of the individual and part of a mindset that facilitates the expansion of freedoms. The decision to use "personal agency" is intended to emphasize the psychological aspects of freedoms; there is a bidirectional relationship between the development of agency and identifying as an active agent. This section serves to place the idea of personal agency within the context of existing research by defining components we see as integrated into the concept.

Sen (1999) defines agency as the ability to define one's goals in an autonomous fashion and act on them. The psychological extension of Sen's concept of agency includes "the meaning, motivation and purpose which individuals bring to their activity" (Kabeer, 1999, p. 438). The expression of agency is thus ultimately more than a mere behavior or decision because it incorporates the goals and obligations of a person (Sen, 1985). Agency implies control over the choices, decisions, and actions for which the person is responsible. In fact, the ability to take responsibility depends on the predictability and level of control a person has over events and situations within his life. Sen's writings have emphasized the centrality of agency in development:

> [T]he freedom of agency that we individually have is inescapably qualified and constrained by the social, political and economic opportunities that are available to us. There is a deep complementarity between individual agency and social arrangements. It is important to give simultaneous recognition to the centrality of individual freedom *and* [italics in original] to the force of social influences on the extent and reach of individual freedom ... (Sen, 1999, pp. xi–xii)

For Sen, agency is an integral aspect of freedom, while freedom and agency are necessary components for development (Dréze & Sen, 1995; Sen, 1999). A person's freedom may well be assessed in terms of his power to achieve chosen results in his life (Sen, 1999).

In psychology, agency has been defined as "the degree of autonomous functioning" (Kagitcibasi, 2005, p. 403), implying that agency is the volitional control that underlies autonomy. Other authors also include agency as self-governance and as a part of autonomy. For purposes of measurement, some authors make a distinction between "attitudinal autonomy", "emotional autonomy", and "functional autonomy" (Beyers et al., 2003; Noom, Dekovic, & Meeus, 2001), whereas others emphasize the behavioral components, referring to agency as competence and the possibility for self-directed behavior (Frank, Avery, & Laman, 1988). Albert Bandura's definition of agency is threefold: "direct personal agency, proxy agency that relies on others to act on one's behest to secure desired outcomes, and collective agency exercised through socially coordinative and interdependent effort" (Bandura, 2001, p. 1). He sees agency as occurring within a context where "people are producers as well as products of social systems" (Bandura, 2001, p. 15).

No matter what term is used to explain agency, the overall thrust is the crucial importance of informed, autonomous decision making and choice in dynamic interaction with one's environment. It is key to understand that capabilities expansion ideally occurs within a supportive context. Agency does not imply isolation or disconnection from one's surroundings; in fact, ideally there is a close coordination between the two in enabling the expansion of individual and contextual freedoms. A sense of personal agency resonates in the testimony of a fourth-grader in Chiapas, Mexico, who explains how he has changed as a result of Programming for Choice:

> I learned that it is okay to ask questions—of everyone—even the director and the teacher. It is okay not to know and to ask how to know better. I never used to ask anything or question anyone. Whatever they said, I would just say yes by nodding my head. Now I say yes, *or no*, with words as well as with my eyes.
> —Fourth-grade student, "I Want to, I Can … Prevent Drug Use,"
> Chiapas, Mexico

A middle-aged community health promoter in Santa Rosa de Copan, Honduras put it in the following terms:

> I now know things depend on me; I am part of the world. I can be seen and heard, and I can believe in myself because I can do things. And I can do them differently than I usually do and differently than the way others always do them. I can talk for myself and about myself. I woke up.

Renowned Mexican columnist and CNN reporter Carmen Aristegui astutely noted, "A society which searches for democracy cannot allow itself the luxury of abandoning itself to conformity"[1] (Aristegui, 2008). She highlights the aim for a better balance between individual choice and social support networks: It is about both working together in unison. Individual agency provides the foundation for democracy and democracy the basis for individual freedom.

As Alsop and Heinsohn explain, "Agency is built up by the *assets* that individuals or groups possess. People can have material assets, like financial and productive capital, and non-material assets like skills, knowledge, social networks and the psychological capacity to aspire and imagine change" (Holland, 2007, p. 43). Although material assets are important, they can only be an asset when people have the skills, knowledge, psychological strengths, and social support to utilize them. Because it is easier to implement new behaviors in young children who have not yet developed a sense of helplessness than to change existing behaviors, preventative development is ideally the focus (Nation et al., 2003; Schwab, 2003).

Specific capabilities, such as the ability to communicate or make autonomous decisions, build on each other and bring about both psychological and social changes during the process of developing personal agency. For example, Susana (whose story we recounted in Chapter 3) developed a view of herself as an agent through a number of specific life changes that she began to make—she decided to open a store, overcame her fears of speaking in group settings, and was able to analyze and modify her child-raising techniques. She attributed her achievements to hard work and to the changes that came from within. She stated:

> I knew that it was up to me to make a difference, that if I did not take my life in my own hands, there was nothing God could do to help me and that I could do it even if people frowned upon this new attitude.

This experience highlights the essential psychological changes—improvements in self-worth, in confidence, and in responsibility—that must occur for an individual to develop personal agency.

Once an individual has developed agency at the personal level, she is more capable of seeing herself as part of a social group and of broadening her perspective:

> When I realized that it was up to me to care for my well-being and that of my family and I learned how to do it, changes started to take place. First in me, then in my kids ... nowadays in my relationship with my husband and in my friends with whom I meet every week to talk about what we learn and how we can teach it to more and more people. Having and giving that social support makes a big difference.
> —Alejandra, program participant, "I Want to, I Can ... Start My Own Business," Hidalgo, Mexico

The individual is also better able to monitor and give self-feedback as well as anticipate new behaviors:

> I am not looking back anymore to get approval for everything I do. I now know I can decide if I am on the right track and how to get back on track. I started a new job, working in a factory that manufactures steel products. I feel that I can plan and say what I have to do next without others telling me. I feel confident that if I am able to continue administering my work and my time, soon I will be able to be a supervisor. This would never have been possible if I had not learned that I can make decisions on my own, that I can detect, analyze, and solve problems. I now see why in Spanish we say that "we take decisions" [*tomamos decisiones*] instead of "I make decisions" [*hacemos decisiones*] ... as if we were taking them from someone. Now I "make" them myself and know it is my right to do so. Also I make sure that if I make a mistake I accept it and fix it.
> —Genaro, middle-aged male participant in "I Want to, I Can ... Prevent Violence," Mexico City, Mexico

Leonor in Oaxaca learned that she could buy wheat by the ton and that it would last a long time in a dry place as long as it was far from other seeds:

> Before I would have been afraid of buying so much wheat; what if I could not pay for it or if it got ruined? With the program I learned that I can be organized, that I can take care of the wheat so it lasts. When I saw that I could do it ... the fear went away. [T]he next time I will buy double or maybe even a little more than that.

These ideas and processes on the development of personal agency have been addressed in psychology and development studies in ways that overlap heavily.[2] Examples include autonomy (Abrams, 1999), control (Nachshen, 2004; Rotter, 1966); self-efficacy (Bandura, 1997), self-esteem (Baumeister, 1999), and self-determination (Ryan & Deci, 2000). We recognize that these additional concepts add depth to the term "personal agency". In the following pages, we introduce some of these to offer a theoretical foundation from which FrEE originates.

AUTONOMY

Kagitcibasi defines agency and autonomy as overlapping concepts. In her view, agency develops throughout the lifespan and cumulatively leads to autonomy, or the state of being a "self-governing agent" (Kagitcibasi, 2005, p. 404). Autonomy is difficult to realize for those accustomed to external control or for those who rely on external criteria or influence to sustain their self-worth. When autonomy is low, people are very likely to be at the mercy of external demands, standards, rules, and expectations (Bekker & Belt, 2006; Lam, 2003; McCloskey, 1990). Conversely, a feeling of autonomy is related to satisfying, authentic relationships with others (Hodgins, Koestner, & Duncan, 1996) and to well-being (Ryan, Stiller, & Lynch, 1994). Although choice can be difficult initially, the positive effects of autonomy ultimately apply cross-culturally (Bandura, 2000).

Susana displays a great sense of autonomy in the following excerpt, where she responds to questions about decision making:

Interviewer: For what kinds of things do you ask permission from your husband?

Susana: From my husband? No, I don't ask permission.

Interviewer: Since when?

Susana: Um, well at times I'll let him know "I bought this," or "I'm going to buy this." So that if he doesn't need the money, I can use it. I still take him into account, but I trust my way, too.

Interviewer: Before did you ask more permission than now?

Susana: Yes.

Interviewer: When did that change?

Susana: From the time I started working in [my business] in order to buy things.

Kagitcibasi notes that autonomy is not necessarily antithetical to relatedness or connectivity with others, nor is it synonymous with isolation or selfishness (Kagitcibasi, 2005). In other words, creating agency does not lead to destruction of the family or community. In fact, the opposite often occurs:

> As I became the owner of my decisions, I was able to say "yes" and say "no" more clearly. My kids realized I had a say and they respected me more for it. It was the opposite of what I had always thought … that if you like or love yourself you become arrogant and people will not like you and move away from you. Being independent and feeling good about myself made me and my kids become much closer.
> —Participant in "I Want to, I Can … Prevent Pregnancies,"
> Colima, Mexico

> People say that if you do things on your own you will not need your family and friends anymore. I think that is why parents don't want us to learn too much. But it is not like that. We all need to be independent and dependent at the same time. We need to make the decisions that we want to make and at the same time we need the love and support of others. It is old-fashioned to believe that you only need one or the other.
> —Taxi driver in Guatemala City in a conversation with one of the authors (SP)

Autonomy can exist alongside relatedness as well as occurring independently of it (Keller, 2007). Relatedness is sustained because humans naturally seek well-being (Kagitcibasi, 2003). In fact, improving both contextual and individual capabilities through increasing personal agency is integral to both community and individual development. As people develop personal agency, these ideas are conveyed to family and friends, simultaneously strengthening these individuals, their personal relationships, and reducing the threat these friends and family members may feel when another embraces autonomy. In this way, the autonomy is self-perpetuating.

CONTROL

> … People find it gratifying to exercise control—not just for the futures it buys them, but for the exercise itself. Being effective—changing things, influencing things, making things happen—is one of the fundamental needs with which human brains seem to be naturally endowed, and much of our behavior from infancy is simply an expression of this penchant for control. (Gilbert, 2007, p. 22)

Gilbert goes on to give examples of research that shows how humans find pleasure in controlling their actions, as can be observed in a toddler who delights in showing that he has thrown a ball or knocked over a stack of blocks. Likewise, when the opportunity of having control is lost, people become "unhappy, helpless, hopeless, and depressed" (Gilbert, 2007, p. 22). And when we cannot control our own lives, we are more likely to look for means of controlling the lives of others, creating a vicious cycle of externally imposed control. In fact, the feeling of control is a demonstrated source of mental health (Taylor & Brown, 1988).

The concept of control is often associated with Locus of Control (Rotter, 1966), a continuum that reflects an individual's generalized expectancies about what or who determines the rewards that she obtains in life (Ryan & Deci, 2000). Those with strong external control believe that their behavior holds less importance because rewards in life are dictated by luck, chance, or powerful others.

> How can I know when I will go to get the funds my cousin sent from the other side of the border (i.e. remittances sent to Guatemala from the USA). Who knows when someone can take me to the bank? I am ashamed to ask for a ride. And who knows how long the lines at the bank will be? They make people like me wait and wait outside even if it is raining. So maybe tomorrow ... maybe I will go another day ... maybe I just have to wait until he comes back and gets them for me.
> —Adolfo, a middle-aged man, Huehuetenango, Guatemala

In contrast, people with a strong internal locus of control believe that their own actions determine what happens to them; success or failure results from their own efforts.

> I know we cannot trust when the bus comes, so I went with my friend, who has a truck, to the city. We went a few days in advance because my brother had told me that he sent the money. I asked him how long it takes. He said, two days after he sends it. By going early with my friend, I could also buy the things I need to construct the roof of the room I am building.
> —Felipe, a middle-aged man, Michoacan, Mexico

At the political level, Mexican writer and politician José Woldenberg looks at the implications of an external locus of control on low levels of credibility: "... in our politics, one gets the impression that no one falls by accident and much less due to personal mistakes. All who fall do so due to the meanness of someone else or make as if they were run over, that is why credibility is a rare commodity"[3] (Woldenberg, 2008, p. 14). And few have put the broader contextual implications of the need for a reform of power more clearly than Rene Delgado, editor-in-chief of *Reforma*: "Without a reform of power, any other reform is reduced to a mere remedy... the problem is how to escape the constant reforms regarding giving out power and (instead) tackling the reform of power; of the sense that power has"[4] (Delgado, 2008, p. 12).

The Theory of Planned Behavior (Ajzen, 1991) refers to the determinants of behavioral control: *(1)* beliefs regarding resources and impediments affecting the behavioral performance, and *(2)* perceived power—that is, the impact of these resources and impediments. There is also consensus among authors like Rotter (1966) and Bandura (1997) that repeated experiences of control or lack thereof lead to a generalized orientation; a general perception of control or lack thereof. Common phrases in Mexico characterize a strong external locus of control: "Whatever my husband says, he is the one in command [*Lo que diga mi marido, él es el que manda*]"; "If God wills it [*Si Dios quiere*]"[5]; or, when women refer to having to tolerate domestic violence, "It is the cross that we must bear [*Es la cruz que nos toca cargar*]."

Control affects an individual's motivation to take responsibility or make personal decisions (Rotter, 1966). This is often lacking in Latin American communities, where there is pressure to obey rather than to analyze and decide (Palomar & Valdés, 2004). There is also little predictability in Latin America concerning issues such as job security, health insurance, public services, or who gets preferential treatment in the application of the law. Discussing Mexico in particular, Luis Rubio writes, "Whilst top down control and democracy are antithetical, democracy and market economy are complementary. Control favors impunity and guarantees underdevelopment"[6] (Rubio, 2006, p. 19). An important difference is that which exists between control and freedom: A person does not need to have control over everything to have freedom, but he does need the assurance that the individual or group in control is undertaking decisions in such a way that his freedoms are being expanded rather than constrained. Freedom, therefore, refers to "a person's ability to get systematically what he would choose no matter who actually controls the levers of operation" (Sen, 1992, p. 65). This is partly why it is so important for the people who do have control at the government level to be sensitized to the importance of enabling agency. It is through learning to consider solutions and creating interpersonal trust that an internal locus of control is developed (Rotter, 1978).

SELF-EFFICACY

In psychology literature, agency has been linked with the idea of self-efficacy, one's belief in his ability to succeed—that is, an aspect of psychological functioning enabling individuals to exercise a measure of control over their thoughts, feelings, and actions (Bandura, 2001). As such, self-efficacy serves a regulatory function through which individuals can alter their environment and influence their actions, which is key to behavior change (Wingood & DiClemente, 1999). Belief in control over personal performance determines how long individuals will persevere in the face of obstacles and failure and affect whether they make good or poor use of the skills and knowledge they possess. From this perspective, individual effort depends on the person's sense of self-efficacy.

There are many ideas regarding how to best develop individual self-efficacy. According to one school of thought, the most effective way to reach this goal is through mastering experiences. Success fosters a robust belief in one's personal efficacy. Much like autonomy and control, "performance accomplishments provide a source of self-efficacy expectancy information" (Bandura, 1998, p. 108). Failures, however, undermine self-efficacy, especially if these occur before a sense of self-assurance has been established (Rotter, 1966).

Another approach to creating and strengthening self-efficacy is through social modeling. Watching a peer's success after sustained effort raises the observer's beliefs that he also possesses the capacity to master comparable activities (Bandura, 1971). Such a social frame can be especially relevant in cultures where social acceptance is a key factor in the decision to go against, or change, deeply ingrained customs regarding individual initiative and action. In societies such as Mexico, where cultural norms and attitudes sometimes work against developing a strong sense of self-efficacy (Orpinas, 1999), this can be especially critical. It is important to note that social modeling can be realized through creating vicarious experiences and does not occur only through actual, spontaneous experiences in life. This is how, to a great extent, programs work for participants (we will return to this point in Chapter 6).

In summary, individuals who have developed a sense of personal agency are more likely to be active agents, and participatory citizens, take initiative and responsibility, act autonomously, generate their own feedback, and engage in their own lives and those of their families and communities. Personal agency is enabled through trust in one's skills and knowledge, in one's competencies, and in repeated success in chosen behaviors, constructive feedback, and opportunities to participate, including opportunities created by the individual. In communities where many individuals possess a strong sense of personal agency, other community members will find it easier and more natural to develop. As repeated successes occur, the individual's perspective of herself changes, and thus the sense of agency broadens beyond specific behaviors. The identity through which she defines herself is modified from an object-like into an agent-like person.

Extrinsic and Intrinsic Empowerment

[This formerly very subdued woman] came to the clinic one day to ask me about specific medical procedures for her son's surgery. For the first time ever, she asked questions, wanted clarification about the surgery, the time it and the recovery would take, wanted to know who she could go to once I left the village. She looked into my eyes, and with her hands on her waist, leaned her body toward me when she spoke. When I questioned her change in demeanor she exclaimed, "Well doctor, don't you know about *empoderamiento?*"
—Account by a medical doctor practicing in the highlands of Oaxaca, Mexico

In many Latin American countries, the term *empowerment* is becoming part of the vernacular. The statement above comes from a doctor who had worked for 14 years in the highlands of Oaxaca, Mexico; he was commenting on changes he had noticed recently in his female patients. Despite this, the word *empoderamiento* [empowerment] has only recently become an official word in the Spanish language. Its adoption among marginalized groups reflects the success of CSOs and can be said to indicate an important transformation in the development field: societal development from the bottom up.

The literature on empowerment defines the concept in various ways, describing it as a goal, a process, and sometimes a form of intervention. The World Bank, World Health Organization (WHO), and the United Nations all emphasize empowerment as a means to improve human development, health, and equality. A WHO report states, "It is clear from the range of literature that empowerment strategies are promising in their ability to produce both empowerment and health impacts ... in working with socially excluded populations"

(Wallerstein, 2006, p. 14). The 2005 Human Development Report by the United Nations Development Program adds, "Empowerment of the poor is both an instrument to reduce poverty and, because participation in society is a dimension of human development, an aspect of poverty reduction" (UNDP, 2005, p. 61).

These reports, along with development literature, often include elements of agency within discussions of empowerment—particularly regarding the interplay between choices, transforming lives, and various contextual factors (Alsop, 2004; Strandberg, 2001; WHO, 2006). A definition of empowerment appears in a World Bank policy paper, stating that "if a person or group is empowered, they possess the *capacity to make effective choices*" (emphasis added) (Alsop & Heinsohn, 2005, p. 6). The above-mentioned WHO report defines empowerment as integrating "*psychological empowerment* (emphasis added) within organization and community level changes, and within multiple spheres of peoples' lives" (Wallerstein, 2006, pp. 7–8). And more explicitly, Alkire (2005, p. 222) suggests that: "Empowerment is an increase in certain kinds of agency that are deemed particularly instrumental to the situation at hand."

While agreeing with these authors, we would like to add a distinction that is often not made explicit in references to empowerment. We argue that a distinction between the individual and contextual levels is important because promoting agency at the individual level and the community level are not only distinguishable conceptually; they also tend to be sequential. This is why we differentiate personal agency and empowerment as two distinct concepts. Personal agency is needed to undertake initiatives that influence the social environment, but possessing such agency is not the same as using it to promote communal goals. We have observed that many program participants first develop personal agency through a process of self-realization. They then begin to impact a particular sphere of their surrounding environment as they adopt a critical consciousness and start to question the social norms and practices they previously accepted without consideration.

> I learned that I can go up a step at a time, like in a staircase. At every step, I turn around to see who is watching. At first they watch because they want to pressure me to stop, but after a few steps they watch because they want to learn to do the same. They realize it is a way of growing, of being independent, of not letting others tell you what to do or when to do it. Once I see that they are starting to watch through this different filter I feel proud that they are watching, and I am not scared anymore.
> —Mauricio, young male program participant, "I Want to, I Can ...
> Prevent Pregnancies," Santiago, Chile

> I used to feel *agachada*; I always kept my head down. I had no right to look up or to ask questions. I was an *agachada*. Now I can look straight up, and I can ask. I am not ashamed of looking into anyone's eyes. I am just as valuable as anyone else. And many others have learned from me. My daughters' lives are very different from mine. I talked to them many times after the course and they talked to their friends. It was like a chain that helped change things.
> —Ximena, a middle-aged field worker in "I Want to, I Can ...
> Prevent Cancer," Nuevo Leon, Mexico

Maybe it's not so much that I am different, but rather that I take more initiative in certain areas, like [in] groups. I always say to the women that they have to learn to collaborate with the [local municipal government] committee, not to veto it. I explain that really we are going to change the committee. It has changed, and for this reason they don't want me to leave the committee. They want me to continue as treasurer, and so everything else has changed. And [as] I see things change I feel the change in me as well.

—Guadalupe, an elderly program participant, "I Want to, I Can ... Care for My Health and Exercise My Rights," Hidalgo, Mexico

The work laid out above by various thinkers serves to indicate how empowerment has been defined as a means of enhancing an individual or group's capacity to make choices and transform those choices into desired actions and outcomes (Alsop & Heinsohn, 2005). However, an important distinction must be made here between intrinsically—or agentically—driven change, and change brought about through external factors. This distinction is largely absent in existing literature and public policies and thus limits the understanding of the role of individual community members in promoting community and institutional development. We seek to promote this understanding with a term that extends beyond personal agency and empowerment: "intrinsic empowerment."

Our concepts of empowerment are based on Hartman's (1967) typology of values: extrinsic, systemic, and internal. Similarly, we define three distinct types of empowerment: *extrinsic* and *systemic* (both of which are externally driven) and *intrinsic* (which is internally driven). In our experience with various urban and rural communities in Latin America, we have found the distinction between these three types of empowerment to be critical for designing and evaluating development programs.

Extrinsic empowerment refers to forms of empowerment where behavior is motivated by external factors, usually those of a material kind. An elderly woman's response to a visit by Mexican President Felipe Calderon to the state of Campeche offers a prime example of external motivation: "I came [to this political rally] because you are going to give us money and because we love you ... We love you because you are going to help us, we are going to have electricity, we are going to drink, we are going to dance"[7] (recorded by Núñez, 2007, p. 6). This woman's remarks illustrate the form of empowerment that the poor have come to expect from public figures and many development organizations in the region. In this case, material elements such as money and rewards form the basis of empowering individuals to act.

Various social welfare programs in Latin America, such as *Oportunidades* in Mexico, aim to reduce poverty and empower people through the provision of funds (Adato et al., 2000). *Oportunidades* is a highly influential program, currently reaching approximately 25 million people in urban and rural localities all over the country (SEDESOL, 2007). The program seeks to advance human development by providing the poorest families with talks on health, nutritional support, preventative health services, and school supplies for children, all tied to monthly subsidies for mothers (Levy, 2006). Although the program undoubtedly addresses the social and political "unfreedoms" of recipients through the provisions of funds and information, its potential role in enabling individual choice and making sustainable community change may not be optimally achieved because of its foundation in extrinsic incentives.

Furthermore, critics have pointed to the ways in which *Oportunidades,* albeit unintentionally, reinforces traditional paternalistic practices (Villatoro, 2007). This is because the structure of the program encourages a dependency among beneficiaries on externally controlled material rewards (in this case from the government). "*Oportunidades* is still not a right, it is a government decision. ... This is not social policy but a series of programs that seem to have been put together with little planning"[8] (Rea, 2007a, p. 5). As long as services and goods are seen as privileges rather than as entitlements, poor people tend to feel unworthy and not entitled to basic social and political rights. Officials and academics from Argentina, Colombia, and Brazil, whose programs to combat poverty function similarly to *Oportunidades,* admit that the plan "makes beneficiaries dependent on the State"[9] (Rea, 2007b, p. 4).

In so far as these objections are valid, the program does not necessarily facilitate the development of a sense of autonomy and freedom. Participant testimonies from rural field workers in the highlands of Oaxaca, Mexico, reflect the extrinsic empowerment embodied in the program:

> I like getting funds from *Oportunidades* because it helps us get slightly better food, but I do not like that I am supposed to go to their talks that I have heard over and over again. They make me go; they don't respect that I can decide what I need. They decide that I have to go. *Oportunidades* treats me like a little child. If you do this, you get this; if not, you do not.
>
> —Ana Maria

> Once they stop the handouts, what do we have left? Nothing. They do not teach us to do anything, just give us money and make us go to these talks in exchange for the money. Yes, we now know a little more about our health and have money to buy some things, but then what? Once the money is gone, we have nothing.
>
> —Dulce

In our view, programs must develop personal agency to be able to foster a sense of empowerment that lasts beyond the duration of the programs themselves. Individuals must first understand their choices and rights and become responsible and participatory citizens in order for long-term change and improvement in well-being to occur.

Systemic empowerment refers to motivation of behavior rooted in the norms of the society; you do things because you feel they are expected from you (*see* Chapters 2 and 8).

> As long as the teacher checks on us, we behave very well. As soon as she leaves the class, the noise and fun begin.
>
> —Claudio, sixth-grade student, Campeche, Mexico

> As long as my mother-in-law keeps an eye on me I do what I am supposed to, just like when the police are watching you. Once she leaves the house, I do too. She goes left; I go right.
>
> —Alejandrina, a young woman, San Juan Sacatepequez, Guatemala

These statements reveal how norms, socialization, and the system all provide a form of external motivation; the teacher and his classroom rules, and the mother-in-law and her expectations of conformity to societal norms about family structure.

Systemic empowerment need not be rooted in a particular person or public authority but on more abstract grounds, such as through laws and customs. These can serve as important external motivators. However, in either case, once the external impetuses are removed, the individual's inclination to act often vanishes with them. Like extrinsic motivation, systemic motivation can be positive (e.g., respect for the laws of the country is part of the foundation of society). However the personal agency, that is lacking, is what drives individuals to understand or question existing rules and laws of the country and to advocate for change.

The limited reach of systemic empowerment, even when present as a motivator, is illustrated by the recently modified Mexican law on domestic violence, *Ley general de acceso de las mujeres a una vida libre de violencia* [*General law on women's access to a violence-free life*] (SEGOB, 2007). A young man at a Public Ministry office in Mexico City elucidated:

> Well, we hear there is a new law, but what good is it if we actually believe that men have the right to hit their wives, simply because they get exasperated with them? And anyway, we men need to get stuff out, and when we have the need to do so, we cannot control it.
> —June, 2007, when asked about the new law,
> Miguel Hidalgo locality, Mexico City

Similarly, a woman in another Public Ministry office, also in Mexico City, said:

> Well this law is supposed to be protecting women but the reality is we ourselves don't feel we have the right to enforce the new law. It would bring too many problems here in the office. Most of the bosses are men who don't really understand what it entails and who really think that women must do something to deserve it....[W]e don't know how to ask for change. We don't know how to do it and don't think we should.
> —June, 2007, when asked about the new law, Benito Juarez locality,
> Mexico City

In the midst of entrenched social inequalities, systemic changes can make little headway. Denise Maerker (2007) commented on the Mexican Senate's media campaign surrounding the introduction of the law. She expressed that although the law provides an important initial step, it will do little to actually resolve the problem of domestic violence:

> The law has been victim of the absurd expectations generated by the irresponsible campaign which the Senate has promoted ... in fact this law does not assure at all that Patricia's [the woman in the ad to promote the law] husband will never hit her again ... its object is actually to improve the image of the senators and, in fact, all the campaign does is propagate lies, which can have dangerous consequences. Pity any woman who now actually believes that a policeman will come to arrest her husband for having beaten her up![10] (p. 9)

In summary, the two forms of external empowerment do not alone suffice to create access to choice, especially in a sustained manner. As long as governments merely "pump" in help or offer opportunities without equipping people to help themselves, the resulting changes will rarely be sustainable. The concept is well-illustrated by the Lao Tzu proverb "Give a man a fish and you feed him for a day. Teach him how to fish and you feed him for a lifetime." In a slightly altered interpretation, an individual who has skills, knowledge, and contextual support will be more inclined to go fishing than to wait for food to be offered.

Intrinsic empowerment contrasts with the external forms of empowerment. The concept is based on Hartman's conceptualization of internal values—that is, those which are generated from within the person. Intrinsic empowerment derives from—and facilitates—informed and autonomous choice and a sense of freedom within the context. From these changes come the intentional application of the skills and capacity for making choices to achieve desired outcomes in the community context. Although this process usually occurs in conjunction with changes in the context, it also could begin independent of contextual changes.

As personal agency develops, so do the capabilities required for intrinsic empowerment. The initial manifestations may be modest, but over time actions increase and generalize across different domains of the context.

> I now realize that I used to feel like a donkey, being pulled from one side to another ... I do not feel like a donkey anymore; now I believe I can decide and I can influence others as well.
> —Inés, middle-aged woman who participated in "I Want to, I Can ... Care for My Health and Exercise My Rights," Hidalgo, Mexico

The story of a 17-year-old boy in Queretaro, Mexico, illustrates the movement from personal agency to intrinsic empowerment:

> I had been asked to leave (secondary) school because my eating disorder was considered contagious. They kept saying that I looked too skinny and should not participate in class or in sports, that they did not want other kids to get sick too. At the "I Want to, I Can ... Care for My Health and Exercise My Rights" workshop, I learned that anorexia was not contagious and developed skills to communicate assertively. It was not easy, but once I became a community promoter of the program, I went back to talk to the principal and the teachers so I could return to school. I am now studying in high school. I also went to the community clinic to look for help. I now give talks to the community regarding nutrition, psychological disorders and also about the importance of speaking up.

As this young man demonstrates, the road to empowerment often involves a struggle, a socially unacceptable imbalance in the relationship between the individual and his environment (Kar, Pascual, & Chickering, 1999).

The following testimony from a middle-aged woman selling blankets and woven bags in a market in the outskirts of Antigua, Guatemala, illustrates a transition from systemic motivation to an increase in personal agency, and finally, to the intrinsically motivated empowerment, which we refer to as intrinsic empowerment:

> [*Systemically motivated empowerment*]
> My mother kept asking when I would get married. I felt that she would like me more and that I would be able to do more things if I had a husband or at least a boyfriend. My grandmother often repeated that a woman without a man is like a broom without fibers. I felt very ugly. So when this man asked me to marry him, I immediately said yes. I thought I would be much more respected and would be able to do more things, be more liked and accepted.

> [*Agency*]
> The reality is that this [feeling more respected and able to do more things, be more liked and accepted] only happened when he left me for a prettier woman. Not because he left but because it was then that I was forced to make a living for myself. A friend took me to courses that showed me how to work. I also learned to value myself there and to value responsibility. I had to find a way to feed my kids. It was when I realized that I really was able to accomplish things that I realized I was beautiful ... from inside, because I had the strength to go out, to look for work, and to really care for my children.

> [*Intrinsically motivated empowerment: Intrinsic empowerment*]
> I learned to weave, and now look—I have taught weaving to all these girls. I have told them my stories, and that they should look at themselves from the inside, not only from the outside. I tell them not to do things just because others tell them to do it or because they have to please the older people. To respect, yes, but to please, no. I did not know the difference before. I tell them that they have to be happy from inside not from outside.

Intrinsic empowerment allows for the advancement of individual freedom and the acquisition of entitlements. It is based on the premise that the way people behave is a consequence of both their capabilities and the economic and socio-cultural context from which they come, and in which their actions are embedded. A further premise is that characteristics of an individual and a community can change if there are capabilities for considering alternative choices. The term embodies the understanding that learning to make choices in concrete situations results in the development of personal agency and the generalization of this agency. Personal agency is indispensable for bringing about sustainable change in the context, and this process of intrinsic empowerment in turn reinforces personal agency; the relationship is bidirectional.

The concept of intrinsic empowerment also translates into macrotheories about citizenship and productivity, which manifests at the community level. Program participants who have developed a more holistic sense of themselves (and their role within a larger entity) can exert a more sustained impact on their families, communities, or regional or national politics. Internally motivated community action creates socially responsible leaders, organizations, and citizens because they have a sense of obligation and accountability toward one another. An example of a woman who realized the advantages of having the community join to get an extension of the road follows:

> It was when it became clear that we all could join—instead of me doing things by myself—to get a road coming into the community...that I called all the

women who had taken the "I Want to, I Can" course, and their families, to go together to talk to the municipal president. After about a year of meetings and promises—not all of which came through—we have buses coming almost all the way to the village, only about 20 minutes walk.

—Lorenza, middle-aged woman who participated in "I Want to, I Can …
Prevent Cancer," Michoacan, Mexico

We argue that intrinsic empowerment is instrumental in producing significant and sustainable change at the contextual level. Because it is rooted in personal agency, this form of empowerment is more likely to have a profound impact on human and socio-economic development. Simultaneously, it contributes to the sustainability of development, empowering individuals to achieve greater access, appropriation, and control over resources, organizations, and institutions, which in turn leads to more sustainable *human* development. The lack of personal agency and intrinsic empowerment contributes to an explanation of the lack of long-term success in many aid and development programs (Alkire, 2005; Zimmerman & Cleary, 2006).

Ideally, empowerment will stem from a combination of external and internal sources (Hornik, 2002). Circumstances for sustainable community development are optimal when both externally derived and intrinsically motivated empowerment work in tandem. This interaction creates a supportive environment for personal growth and simultaneously facilitates the development of the skills necessary for individuals to take full advantage of their environment and, eventually, to improve it.[11] Freedoms are best realized under supportive contextual conditions. However, we argue that intrinsic empowerment increases the likelihood of sustainability, over and above extrinsic empowerment, because it occurs as a result of personal change and an internal motivation. Most developing countries do not emphasize this human factor as a fundamental aspect to achieving self-regulatory health, education and social behaviors, and specifically, democratic participation. This neglect reduces the ability of programs to sustainably bring about change. If the agent-oriented perspective were incorporated into social and educational policy as a central component, choice as an entitlement, personal agency, control, and inner responsibility would be more broadly developed within society.

The Framework for Enabling Empowerment

We present the Framework for Enabling Empowerment (FrEE) as a way of conceptualizing sustainable human development.[12] The framework is based on years of program experience during which we learned that the most successful programs target specific situations. Departing from an individual's concrete experience enables the first steps along the road to sustainable human (and therefore social, political, and economic) development. Programs should provide knowledge and skills relevant to a small set of targeted situations. Addressing them one-by-one in an interactive process, facilitates the reduction of psychological barriers.

FrEE is based on the following principles:

People need to understand and experience the ways in which they can overcome psychological and social barriers. Through this awareness, they become contributors of their own growth process, as well as of the social, economic, and political development of their communities.

To exercise increased choice in various domains, people need to have, and feel they have, the competencies and knowledge not only to serve but also to demand rights and services.

Through the development of core competencies and the opportunities for reducing psychological barriers individual needs are connected to the newly acquired competencies and opportunities.

People first begin to change behaviors in a few concrete situations and can subsequently expand their learning into new domains. This expansion develops through success in specific situations and a growing sense of personal agency.

As people's competencies are enhanced, they are able to create new contexts where choices are more likely to be made, actualized, and sustained.

Maintenance of personal change is necessary for sustainability of development.

FrEE is designed to support CSOs, private companies, and government organizations by orienting their programs toward the development of personal agency and intrinsic empowerment. This framework can be at the base of education, health, politics as well as economic development programs.

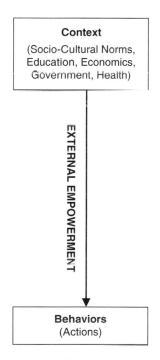

FIGURE 4–1A The Framework for Enabling Empowerment: External Empowerment

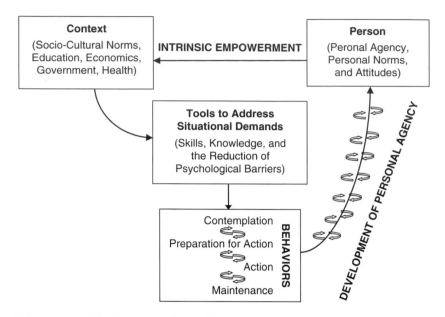

FIGURE 4–1B The Framework for Enabling Empowerment: Instrinsic Empowerment

In Figure 4–1b there are four frames: *Context, Person, Behaviors*, and *Tools to Address Situational Demands* (*see also* Pick & Poortinga, 2005; Pick, Poortinga, & Givaudan, 2003).

Context refers to the circumstances in which people are living. As we argue in Chapter 8, economics is among the key factors shaping the context (e.g., Berry et al., 2002). Members of an affluent group or society have easy access to all kinds of material and nonmaterial resources that are less available in a poor society. Unequal distribution of resources between different social groups or classes in a society compounds the contextual problems for the poor. Another aspect of context is education. The educational context cannot only provide factual knowledge, but needs to also impart know-how, skills, and a sense of identity that can ultimately enhance control over wider areas of life. Other aspects of external context that we mention are health and political systems. In this regard, Dréze and Sen (2002) state:

> The crucial role of social opportunities is to expand the realm of human agency and freedom, both as an end in itself and as a means of further expansion of freedom. The word 'social' in the expression 'social opportunity' … is a useful reminder not to view individuals and their opportunities in isolated terms. The options that a person has depend greatly on relations with others and on what the state and other institutions do (p. 6).

Consonant with this view of the individual as inseparable from his context, the concept of empowerment has been analyzed in relation to agency. *Context* also refers to socio-cultural variables that are, when shared within a society, largely norms and beliefs. Chapter 2 discussed how restrictive norms can be an impediment to behavior choice. For example, pervasive traditional gender role expectations have an effect on sexual behavior among both adolescents and adults (Pick, Givaudan, & Aldaz, 1996). To grasp the possible constraints on behavior changes that may be addressed by a program, one has to understand the rules that govern behavior, especially those with a normative character (Marín, 1993).

Person, the second frame in Figure 4–1b, refers to characteristics that provide stability to the traits of the individual. As we have seen earlier in this chapter, social–cognitive traditions in psychology have formulated concepts including autonomy, control, and agency. Included in this frame are also personal norms and attitudes. These tend to be stable but are potentially influenced by external factors. In Chapter 2, we argued that, especially in cohesive or "tight" societies (Pelto, 1968), one's personal norms tend to be consistent with those of important groups, such as a village community or church.

Tools to Address Situational Demands refers to the situations an individual faces as well as the means she has to react to those situations. This is the core of the enabling process that the framework aims to illustrate. A natural reaction of most individuals is to avoid the potential challenge and embarrassment initiating difficult confrontations that may defy social norms. Chapter 6 explains how appropriate skills allow one to react optimally according to her standards and desired outcomes. Skills include decision making; the use of direct, open, and assertive communication; and the expression of feelings, all of which contribute to overcoming the psychological barriers of fear, shame, and guilt. Also included is individual knowledge, or factually correct information, which stands in contrast to beliefs that may not be factually correct yet can shape an individual's decisions (*see* Chapter 6).

Behaviors (the second frame in Fig. 4–1a and fourth frame in Fig. 4–1b) refers to an action. The behaviors frame in Figure 4–1b is a component of the broader process that the diagram depicts of making choices operational, resulting from the application of tools to address situational demands and reduction in psychological barriers (as described previously). Figure 4–1a represents an alternative process of encouraging behaviors through external empowerment; we argue in Chapter 7 that this process leads to less sustainable change in behaviors because they are not internally motivated. An example of a change in behaviors as a result of external empowerment (Fig. 4–1a) would be to send one's child to school in exchange for a financial incentive. Alternatively, behavior change as a consequence of Programming for Choice (i.e., the behaviors frame in Fig. 4–1b) would be a decrease in reported substance abuse due to the acquisition of life skills and psychological support as part of the program.

In addition to the frames in Figures 4–1a and 4–1b, there are also five arrows, respectively, that describe the various processes of change. We start with Figure 4–1b:

The first arrow in Figure 4–1b represents the influence that the context can have on the development of tools to address situational demands, such as a nearby school or the presence of health clinics with quality services or roads that facilitate access to programs; these represent contextual factors that enable the practice of healthy behaviors when combined with the proper psychological support (e.g., Programming for Choice, quality education, familial support). The second arrow goes from *Tools to Address Situational Demands* to *Behaviors*. Chapter 7 demonstrates the importance of control, skills, and knowledge as precursors to behavior change. It then draws from the work of Prochaska and DiClemente (1982; Prochaska, DiClemente, & Norcross, 1992) to emphasize that once skills and knowledge have been obtained, behavior changes occur in steps—from contemplating change, to preparing for change, to making the change, and, finally, to maintaining the new behavior. Each step serves to reinforce the previous one. This view is compatible with the recommendations of the World Bank (Cabañero-Verzosa, 1999; World Bank, 2007) on how to provide essential health, nutrition, and population services.

Following from changes in behavior is the "Development of Personal Agency." In Figure 4–1b, this arrow between the *Behaviors* frame and the *Person* frame is intended to illustrate how the (repeated) practice of a behavior(s)—acting on the situation through skills, knowledge, and reduced psychological barriers gained in the previous frame—leads to experiences of mastery. As we explained earlier in this chapter, with mastery comes feelings of autonomy and personal agency, which extend beyond the specific behavior into different types of behaviors and develops into broad personal agency. This occurs differently depending on the specific actions a person takes, which are contingent on her personal needs, interests, and opportunities. Personal agency broadens its effect as it develops within the person, supporting further behaviors to address other challenging situations. This dynamic process is represented with the two-directional arrow and the smaller, circular arrows.

The process of developing personal agency contrasts with that of "external empowerment," a process depicted by the arrow between the *Context* and the *Behaviors* frame in Figure 4–1a. This is the pathway of externally motivated change. Extrinsic and systemic factors (e.g., payment and laws, as exemplified previously) may impact an individual's behaviors by creating opportunities at the contextual level. Similarly, behaviors impact the context, from the family level to the institutional level. Note that in the diagram, the arrow representing external empowerment excludes the *Person* frame. Although it is still the individual conducting the behavior, this depiction of the external empowerment process represents how changes along this pathway tend to involve the person less as an agent. Our argument is that changes along this pathway tend to be less sustainable than those in the "Development of Personal Agency" pathway as people are acting on an external impetus.

The final arrow in Figure 4–1b, from the *Person* frame to the *Context* frame, comes after the development of personal agency and reflects the individual's role in realizing contextual change and development. It represents the process by which the individual applies the newly acquired competencies and self-confidence to actively promote changes in his social environment. When this happens it can be said that empowerment is intrinsically motivated because it originates from an agentic individual. This final arrow represents how public policy can be "influenced by the effective use of participatory capabilities by the public" (Sen, 1999, p. 18).

The main empirical evidence for the approach outlined here is threefold. The first source of evidence is formed by the numerous testimonies scattered throughout the book. We only report a small percentage of the similar accounts that we hear repeatedly. More recently, we have begun to conduct quasi-experimental studies with control groups and pre- and post-program measurements where this has been demonstrated[13]. In recent years, we have also started to pursue a third kind of evidence, in the form of psychometric scales that contain items reflecting the key concepts of FrEE. In Pick et al., (2007) we have reported the first results obtained with such a questionnaire on personal agency and agentic (intrinsic) empowerment applied to over 1,000 high school and university students from both urban and rural areas in Mexico. The key result relevant for the present chapter is that the distinction between personal agency and intrinsic empowerment (termed *agentic empowerment* in the article) was reproduced. Factor analysis showed that the items could be characterized into these two groups, demonstrating that the theoretical concepts of personal agency and intrinsic empowerment were grouped into two distinct factors.[14] In the concluding chapter of this book, we refer to additional data that was collected while the book was in progress and had not yet been published. We appreciate that further research is necessary to validate the distinctions that are embedded in FrEE. In our opinion, the currently available evidence shows that there is sufficient empirical support to legitimize the need for a conceptual framework.

Conclusions

This chapter culminates in the description of a conceptual framework, called the FrEE. It is presented in a diagram (Fig. 4–1a and Fig. 4–1b) that outlines key elements (frames) and processes (arrows) that contribute to the development of external empowerment versus personal agency and intrinsic empowerment. The framework provides the theoretical foundation for the approach to development programs set forth by this book. We have argued in this chapter that the term *personal agency* describes changes at an individual psychosocial level as the person gains more control over his life. For changes in behavior patterns to be sustainable, they need to arise from internal motivation rather than as a reaction to external incentives or constraints. This process requires an intrinsically motivated and autonomous person: an agentic identity.

We have introduced a second term, *intrinsic empowerment*, to reflect the process of extending personal agency beyond the individual level to impact the context. Responsibility initially expands to the micro-environment (generally the family), and gradually expands to others in the community. In this way, a more comprehensive and sustainable realization of individual capabilities, personal entitlements, and human rights comes within reach. FrEE emphasizes the need for this historically neglected type of empowerment while also acknowledging the role that external empowerment can play. The following chapters describe in detail how each of the frames and processes of FrEE result in contextual change.

Notes

1. "Una sociedad que busca democracia no puede darse el lujo de abandonarse al conformismo y renunciar a la verdad."
2. One of the ways in which overlap between the concepts can be appreciated is in the similarities in item content between the scales that have been developed to assess these various conceptual terms: many use indicators such as planning skills, problem solving, quality and frequency of social interactions, and causality between one's decisions and its consequences or between perceived control over one's actions and the results (Deci & Ryan, 1985; Rotter, 1966; Sherer et al., 1982).
3. "...en nuestra política, da la impresión de que nadie cae por accidente y menos por errores propios. Todos caen por la maldad del otro o fingen haber sido atropellados, y por ello la credibilidad es un bien escaso."
4. "Sin la reforma del poder, cualquier otra reforma se reduce a un remedio ... El problema es cómo salir de la constante reforma del reparto del poder y cómo entrar a la reforma del poder, del sentido del poder."
5. There is an important difference between *Si Dios quiere* [If God wants] or *Si Dios me da licencia* [If God allows me] both of which indicate that God's active intervention is needed for something to happen, and *Dios mediante* (which is more similar to the English "God willing"), acknowledging God's omnipotence without direct consequences for human responsibility.
6. "Mientras que el control desde arriba y la democracia son antitéticos, la democracia y el mercado en la economía son complementarios. El control favorece la impunidad y garantiza el subdesarrollo."
7. "Vengo...porque nos va a dar dinero y, si no, también lo queremos [...] Lo queremos porque nos va a ayudar, vamos a tener luz, vamos a beber, vamos a bailar."
8. "Oportunidades ... todavía no es un derecho, es una decisión del Gobierno [...] No hay política social, hay una serie de programas que me parecen montados sobre las rodillas."
9. "convierte a los beneficiarios en dependientes del Estado"
10. "la ley ha sido víctima de las absurdas expectativas que generó la irresponsable campaña sobre el tema que promueve el Senado de la República. ... por cierto, a Patricia esta ley no le garantiza en absoluto que su marido no la siga golpeando. ... El objetivo es mejorar la imagen de los senadores y, sin embargo, la campaña lo único que hace es propagar mentiras que pueden tener consecuencias peligrosas. ¡Ay de aquella mujer que se crea que un policía va a venir a arrestar a su marido por haberla golpeado!
11. Personal agency and intrinsic empowerment presume an ethical orientation toward improving the well-being of the person and the community. Of course, they also can be used for socially negative purposes (e.g., an individual taking initiative to manufacture chemical drugs in the home and distribute them within the community, or a government official feeling empowered to practice nepotism and corruption).
12. In earlier publications we referred to the "Framework for Enabling Choice" (FECH) because of the focus on facilitating choices in concrete situations (Pick,

Poortinga, & Givaudan, 2003). More recently, there has been shift in emphasis toward more generalized behavior tendencies, in the form of personal agency and intrinsic empowerment. Hence, the name of the framework has been changed to the Framework for Enabling Empowerment.

13. *see* Beltrán, Elizalde, & Givaudan, 2009; Givaudan et al., 2009; Givaudan, Barriga, & Pick, 2008; Givaudan, García, & Pick, 2007; Givaudan, Leenen, & Pick, submitted; Givaudan & Osorio, 2009; Givaudan, Vitela, & Osorio, 2008; IMIFAP, 2008; Leenen et al., 2008; Osorio & Givaudan, 2008; Pick, Givaudan, & Poortinga, 2003; Pick et al., in press; Pick, Poortinga, & Givaudan, 2003; Pick et al., 2008; Universidad Autónoma de Aguascalientes, 2008a, 2008b, 2008c, 2009; Venguer, Pick, & Fishbein, 2007

14. The first factor was exemplified with items such as (with negative loading) "It is hard for me to publicly express my opinion" [*Me es difícil expresar mi opinión públicamente*], "I feel unsure of my decisions" [*Me siento inseguro de mis decisiones*], and (with positive loading) "I have the initiative to do things" [*Tengo iniciativa para hacer las cosas*] clearly reflected personal agency. The second factor with items like "In my community I help solve the conflicts that arise" [*En mi colonia/comunidad ayudo a resolver los conflictos que se presentan*], and "In my community I participate in the local assemblies or neighbor meetings" [*En mi colonia/comunidad participo en las asambleas o juntas vecinales*] fit the notion of intrinsic empowerment.

References

Adato, M., de la Brière, B., Mindek, D., & Quisumbing, A. (2000). *The impact of PROGRESA on women's status and intrahousehold relations: A final report*. Washington, DC: International Food Policy Research Institute, Food Consumption and Nutrition Division.

Ajzen, I. (1991). The theory of planned behavior. *Organizational Behavior and Human Decision Processes*, 50(2), 179–211.

Alkire, S. (2005). Subjective quantitative studies of human agency. *Social Indicators Research*, 74(1), 217–260.

Allport, G. W. (1966). Traits revisited. *American Psychologist*, 21(1), 1–10.

Alsop, R. (Ed.). (2004) *Power, rights, and poverty: Concepts and connections*. Washington, DC: World Bank and Department for International Development.

Alsop, R., & Heinsohn, N. (2005). *Measuring empowerment in practice: Structuring analysis and framing indicators* (Policy Research Working Paper No. 3510). Washington DC: World Bank Poverty Reduction and Economic Management Network [PREM Network], Poverty Reduction Group.

Aristegui, C. (2008, June 20). Acta por acta [Tally by Tally]. *Reforma*, p. 17.

Bandura, A. (1971). Vicarious and self-reinforcement processes. In R. Glaser (Ed.), *The nature of reinforcement* (pp. 228–278). New York: Academic Press.

Bandura, A. (1997). *Self-efficacy: The exercise of control*. New York: W.H. Freeman & Co.

Bandura, A. (1998). Health promotion from the perspective of social cognitive theory. *Psychology and Health*, 13(4), 623–649.

Bandura, A. (2000). Exercise of human agency through collective efficacy. *Current Directions in Psychological Science*, 9(3), 75–78.

Bandura, A. (2001). Social cognitive theory: An agentic perspective. *Annual Review of Psychology,* 52, 1–26.

Baumeister, R. F. (Ed.). (1999). *The self in social psychology: Essential readings.* Ann Arbor, MI: Taylor & Francis.

Bekker, M., & Belt, U. (2006). The role of autonomy-connectedness in depression and anxiety. *Depression and Anxiety,* 23(5), 274–280.

Beltrán, M., Elizalde, L., & Givaudan, M. (2009). Formación en habilidades para la vida y metodología participativa para personal de salud [Life skills training and participatory methodology for health workers], *Report presented to Public Health Services of Mexico City.* Mexico City: IMIFAP.

Berry, J. W., Segall, M. H., Dasen, P. R., & Poortinga, Y. H. (2002). Social behavior *Cross-cultural psychology* (2nd ed., pp. 52-85). Cambridge: Cambridge University Press.

Beyers, W., Goossens, L., Vansant, I., & Moors, E. (2003). Structural model of autonomy in middle and late adolescence: Connectedness, separation, detachment, and agency. *Journal of Youth and Adolescence,* 32(5), 351–365.

Cabañero-Verzosa, C. (1999). *Comunicación estratégica para proyectos de desarrollo. [Strategic communication for development projects].* Washington, DC: World Bank.

Comim, F. (2001). *Operationalizing Sen's Capability Approach.* Paper presented at the Conference on Justice and Poverty: Examining Sen's Capability Approach. Cambridge. Retrieved April 30, 2006, from www.uia.mx/humanismocristiano/seminario_capability/pdf/7.pdf.

Deci, E. L., & Ryan, R. M. (1985). The general causality orientations scale: Self-determination in personality. *Journal of Research in Personality,* 19(2), 109–134.

Delgado, R. (2008, June 21). Adiós al presidencialismo [Goodbye to presidentialism]. *Reforma,* p. 12.

Dréze, J., & Sen, A. (1995). *India: Economic development and social opportunity.* Oxford: Clarendon Press.

Dréze, J., & Sen, A. (2002). *India: Development and participation.* Delhi: Oxford University Press.

Frank, S. J., Avery, C. B., & Laman, M. S. (1988). Young adults' perceptions of their relationships with their parents: Individual differences in connectedness, competence, and emotional autonomy. *Developmental Psychology,* 24(5), 729–737.

Freire, P. (1970). *Pedagogy of the oppressed.* New York: Seabury Press.

Gilbert, D. T. (2007). *Stumbling on happiness.* New York: Vintage Books.

Givaudan, M., Barriga, M., Pick, S., Leenen, I., & Martinez, R. (2009). Desarrollo integral comunitario en México, en los estados de Hidalgo y Chiapas, con énfasis en salud sexual y reproductiva y derechos de mujeres, reporte final [Comprehensive community development in the Mexican states of Hidalgo and Chiapas, with emphasis on sexual and reproductive health and women's rights, final report], *Report presented to the United Nations Fund for Population Activities.* Mexico City: IMIFAP.

Givaudan, M., Barriga, M. A., & Pick, S. (2008). The children left behind: Researching the impact of migration on the development of children and developing, piloting and evaluating a program that answers their special needs, *Report presented to the Bernard van Leer Foundation.* Mexico City: IMIFAP.

Givaudan, M., García, A., & Pick, S. (2007). Programa de prevención de cáncer cérvico uterino en áreas de extrema pobreza rural de Michoacán [Cervical cancer prevention program in areas of extreme rural poverty in Michoacán state], *Report presented to the Inter-American Development Bank.* Mexico City: IMIFAP.

Givaudan, M., Pick, S., Leenen, I., & DuBois, L. (submitted). Health education and life skills: Building life skills and knowledge in rural children in Mexico.

Givaudan, M., & Osorio, P. (2009). Yo quiero, yo puedo ... prevenir y controlar obesidad, diabetes y enfermedades cardiovasculares. Reporte final [I want to, I can ... prevent and control obesity, diabetes and cardiovascular diseases. Final report], *Report presented to the Pfizer Foundation*. Mexico City: IMIFAP.

Givaudan, M., Vitela, A., & Osorio, P. (2008). Estrategia fronteriza de promoción y prevención para una mejor salud [Border strategy of promotion and prevention for improving health], *Report presented to the Pfizer Foundation*. Mexico City: IMIFAP.

Greenwald, A. G., Banaji, M. R., Rudman, L. A., Farnham, S. D., Nosek, B. A., & Mellott, D. S. (2002). A unified theory of implicit attitudes, stereotypes, self-esteem, and self-concept. *Psychological Review, 109*(1), 3–25.

Hartman, R. S. (1967). *The structure of value: Foundations of scientific axiology.* Carbondale, Illinois: Southern Illinois University Press.

Hodgins, H. S., Koestner, R., & Duncan, N. (1996). On the compatibility of autonomy and relatedness. *Personality and Social Psychology Bulletin, 22*(3), 227–237.

Holland, J. (2007). *Tools for institutional, political, and social analysis of policy reform: A sourcebook for development practitioners.* Washington, DC: World Bank.

Hornik, R. C. (2002). *Public health communication: Evidence for behavior change.* Mahwah, N.J.: Lawrence Erlbaum Associates.

Instituto Mexicano de Investigación de Familia y Población [IMIFAP] (2008). México-Centroamerica: Educación en sexualidad, salud y habilidades para la vida. Fase III: Reporte Final [Mexico-Central America: Education on sexuality, health and life skills. Phase III: Final Report], *Report presented to the World Bank*. Mexico City: IMIFAP.

Kabeer, N. (1999). Resources, agency, achievements: Reflections on the measurement of women's empowerment. *Development and Change, 30*, 435–464.

Kagitcibasi, C. (2003). Autonomy, embeddedness and adaptability in immigration contexts. *Human Development 46*(2-3), 145–150.

Kagitcibasi, C. (2005). Autonomy and relatedness in cultural context: Implications for self and family. *Journal of Cross-Cultural Psychology, 36*(4), 403–422.

Kar, S. B., Pascual, C. A., & Chickering, K. L. (1999). Empowerment of women for health promotion: A meta-analysis. *Social Science & Medicine, 49*(11), 1431–1460.

Karni, E. (2008). Agency theory: Choice-based foundations of the parametrized distribution formulation. *Economic Theory, 36*(3), 337–351.

Keller, H. (2007). *Cultures of infancy.* Mahwah, NJ: Lawrence Erlbaum Associates, Inc.

Lam, S. F. (2003). Chinese parenting and adolescents' susceptibility to peer pressure: A multi-dimensional approach. *Journal of Psychology in Chinese Societies, 3*(2), 183–204.

Leenen, I., Venguer, T., Vera, J., Givaudan, M., Pick, S., & Poortinga, Y. H. (2008). Effectiveness of a comprehensive health education program in a poverty-stricken rural area of Guatemala. *Journal of Cross-Cultural Psychology, 39*(2), 198–214.

Levy, S. (2006). *Progress against poverty: Sustaining Mexico's Progresa-Oportunidades program.* Washington, DC: Brookings Institution Press.

Maerker, D. (2007, March 13). Una ley víctima de la publicidad [A law victim to publicity]. *Excelsior*, p. 9.

Marín, G. (1993). Defining culturally appropriate community interventions: Hispanics as a case study. *Journal of Community Psychology,* 21(2), 149–161.

Martin, J. (2007). Interpreting and extending G. H. Mead's "Metaphysics" of selfhood and agency. *Philosophical Psychology,* 20(4), 441–456.

McCloskey, J. C. (1990). Two requirements for job contentment: Autonomy and social integration. *IMAGE: Journal of Nursing Scholarship,* 22(3), 140–143.

McGeer, V. (2008). The moral development of first-person authority. *European Journal of Philosophy,* 16(1), 81–108.

Mischel, W. (1968). *Personality and assessment.* Hoboken, NJ: John Wiley & Sons, Inc.

Nachshen, J. S. (2004). Empowerment and families: Building bridges between parents and professionals, theory and research. *Journal on Developmental Disabilities,* 11(1), 67–73.

Nation, M., Crusto, C., Wandersman, A., Kumpfer, K. L., Seybolt, D., Morrissey-Kane, E., & Davino, K. (2003). What works in prevention: Principles of effective prevention programs. *American Psychologist,* 58(6–7), 449–456.

Noom, M. J., Dekovic, M., & Meeus, W. (2001). Conceptual analysis and measurement of adolescent autonomy. *Journal of Youth and Adolescence,* 30(5), 577–595.

Núñez, E. (2007, May 3). Vengo porque da dinero [I come because he gives money out]. *Reforma,* p. 6.

Orpinas, P. (1999). Who is violent?: Factors associated with aggressive behaviors in Latin America and Spain. *Revista Panamericana de Salud Pública,* 5(4–5), 232–244.

Osorio, P., & Givaudan, M. (2008). Formación en microcréditos para mujeres indígenas y rurales en Oaxaca [Training in microfinance for rural indigenous women in Oaxaca State, Mexico], *Report presented to the Finnish Embassy in Mexico, Fund for Local Cooperation.* Mexico City: IMIFAP.

Palomar, J., & Valdés, L. M. (2004). Pobreza y locus de control [Poverty and locus of control]. *Interamerican Journal of Psychology,* 38(2), 225–240.

Pelto, J. P. (1968). The difference between "tight" and "loose" societies. *Transaction,* 5, 37–40.

Pick, S., Givaudan, M., & Aldaz, E. (1996). Adolescent sexuality: A qualitative study in Mexico City, *Report presented to the Rockefeller Foundation.* Mexico City: IMIFAP.

Pick, S., Givaudan, M., & Poortinga, Y. H. (2003). Sexuality and life skills education: A multistrategy intervention in Mexico. *American Psychologist,* 58(3), 230–234.

Pick, S., Leenen, I., Givaudan, M., & Prado, A. (in press). I want to, I can … prevent violence: Raising awareness of dating violence through a brief intervention. *Salud Mental.*

Pick, S., & Poortinga, Y. H. (2005). Marco conceptual y estrategia para el diseño e instrumentación de programas para el desarrollo: Una visión científica, política y psicosocial [Conceptual framework and strategy for the design and implementation of development programs: A scientific, political and psycho-social vision]. *Revista Latinoamericana de Psicología,* 37(3), 445–459.

Pick, S., Poortinga, Y. H., & Givaudan, M. (2003). Integrating intervention theory and strategy in culture-sensitive health promotion programs. *Professional Psychology: Research & Practice,* 34(4), 422–429.

Pick, S., Romero, A., Arana, D., & Givaudan, M. (2008). Programa formativo para prevenir la violencia a nivel primaria y secundaria [Training program for the prevention of violence at the primary and secondary school levels], *Report presented to the Chamber of Deputies of the Congress of the Union, 60th Legislature*. Mexico City: IMIFAP.

Pick, S., Sirkin, J., Ortega, I., Osorio, P., Martínez, R., Xocolotzin, U., & Givaudan, M. (2007). Escala para medir las capacidades de agencia personal y empoderamiento (ESAGE) [Scale for the measurement of personal agency and empowerment]. *Revista Interamericana de Psicología, 41*(3), 295–304.

Prochaska, J. O., & DiClemente, C. C. (1982). Transtheoretical therapy: Toward a more integrative model of change. *Psychotherapy: Theory, Research & Practice, 19*(3), 276–288.

Prochaska, J. O., DiClemente, C. C., & Norcross, J. C. (1992). In search of how people change. *American Psychologist, 47*(9), 1102–1114.

Rea, D. (2007a, April 29). Critican especialistas política social de FCH [Specialists criticize the social policy of Felipe Calderón Hinojosa]. *Reforma*, p. 5.

Rea, D. (2007b, April 29). Cuestionan en AL [America Latina] el modelo antipobreza [The antipoverty model is questioned in Latin America]. *Reforma*, p. 4.

Rotter, J. B. (1966). Generalized expectancies for internal versus external control of reinforcement. *Psychological Monographs, 80*(1), 1–28.

Rotter, J. B. (1978). Generalized expectancies for problem solving and psychotherapy. *Cognitive Therapy and Research, 2*(1), 1–10.

Rubio, L. (2006, June 18). Control. *Reforma*, p. 19.

Ryan, R. M., & Deci, E. L. (2000). Self-determination theory and the facilitation of intrinsic motivation, social development, and well-being. *American Psychologist, 55*(1), 68–78.

Ryan, R. M., Stiller, J. D., & Lynch, J. H. (1994). Representations of relationships to teachers, parents and friends as predictor of academic motivation and self-esteem. *Journal of Early Adolescence, 14*(2), 226–249.

Schwab, J. J. (2003). Health and behavior: The interplay of biological, behavioral, and societal influences. *American Journal of Psychiatry, 160*, 603–605.

Secretaría de Desarrollo Social [SEDESOL] [Ministry of Social Development] (2007). *Oportunidades. Un programa de resultados [Oportunidades. A program with results]*. Mexico City: Secretaría de Desarrollo Social.

Secretaría de Gobernación [SEGOB] [Ministry of Administration] (2007). *Ley general de acceso de las mujeres a una vida libre de violencia [General law of access of women to lives free from violence]*. Retrieved November 2, 2008, from www.cddhcu.gob.mx/LeyesBiblio/pdf/LGAMVLV.pdf.

Sen, A. (1985). Well-being, agency and freedom: The Dewey Lectures 1984. *The Journal of Philosophy, 82*(4), 169–221.

Sen, A. (1992). *Inequality reexamined*. Oxford: Oxford University Press.

Sen, A. (1999). *Development as freedom*. New York: Anchor.

Shavelson, R. J., & Bolus, R. (1982). Self-concept: The interplay of theory and methods. *Journal of Educational Psychology, 74*(1), 3–17.

Sherer, M., Maddux, J. E., Mercadante, B., Prentice-Dunn, S., Jacobs, B., & Rogers, R. W. (1982). The self-efficacy scale: Construction and validation. *Psychological Reports, 51*(2), 663–671.

Strandberg, N. (2001). *Empowerment of women throughout the life cycle as a transformative strategy for poverty eradication*. Paper presented at the United Nations Division for the Advancement of Women [DAW], Expert Group Meeting on "Empowerment of women throughout the life cycle as a transformative strategy for poverty eradication". New Delhi. Retrieved July 29, 2008, from www.un.org/womenwatch/daw/csw/empower/documents/Strandberg-EP6.pdf.

Taylor, S. E., & Brown, J. D. (1988). Illusion and well-being: A social-psychological perspective on mental health. *Psychological Bulletin,* 103(2), 193–210.

United Nations Development Program [UNDP] (2005). *Human development report 2005: International cooperation at a crossroads; aid, trade, and security in an unequal world.* New York: United Nations Development Program.

Universidad Autónoma de Aguascalientes (2008a). Implementación del Modelo de transmisión de conocimientos para el desarrollo de capacidades entre el personal de Diconsa, los Consejos Comunitarios y los Comités Rurales de Abasto. Primer reporte parcial: Sensibilización [Implementation of a knowledge transmission model for capacity development of Diconsa, Community Council and Rural Supply Committee personnel. First partial report: Developing awareness], *Report presented to Diconsa.* Mexico City: IMIFAP.

Universidad Autónoma de Aguascalientes (2008b). Implementación del Modelo de transmisión de conocimientos para el desarrollo de capacidades entre el personal de Diconsa, los Consejos Comunitarios y los Comités Rurales de Abasto. Segundo reporte parcial: Formación [Implementation of a knowledge transmission model for capacity development of Diconsa, Community Council and Rural Supply Committee personnel. Second partial report: Training], *Report presented to Diconsa.* Mexico City: IMIFAP.

Universidad Autónoma de Aguascalientes (2008c). Implementación del Modelo de transmisión de conocimientos para el desarrollo de capacidades entre el personal de Diconsa, los Consejos Comunitarios y los Comités Rurales de Abasto. Tercer reporte parcial: Réplica y Acompañamiento [Implementation of a knowledge transmission model for capacity development of Diconsa, Community Council and Rural Supply Committee personnel. Third partial report: Replication and follow-up], *Report presented to Diconsa.* Mexico City: IMIFAP.

Universidad Autónoma de Aguascalientes (2009). Implementación del Modelo de transmisión de conocimientos para el desarrollo de capacidades entre el personal de Diconsa, los Consejos Comunitarios y los Comités Rurales de Abasto. Informe ejecutivo final. [Implementation of a knowledge transmission model for capacity development of Diconsa, Community Council and Rural Supply Committee personnel. Final executive report], *Report presented to Diconsa.* Mexico City: IMIFAP.

Venguer, T., Pick, S., & Fishbein, M. (2007). Health education and agency: A comprehensive program for young women in the Mixteca region of Mexico. *Psychology, Health & Medicine,* 12(4), 389–406.

Villatoro, P. (2007). *Las transferencias condicionadas en América Latina: Luces y sombras [The conditioned transfers in Latin America: Lights and shadows].* Paper presented at the CEPAL Conference: Evolución y desafios de los programas de transferencias condicionadas [Evolution and challenges of the programs of conditioned transfers]. Brasilia, Brazil.

Wallerstein, N. (2006). *What is the evidence on effectiveness of empowerment to improve health?* Copenhagen, Denmark: World Health Organization Regional Office for Europe [Health Evidence Network Report].

Wingood, G. M., & DiClemente, R. J. (Eds.). (1999). *The use of psychosocial models for guiding design and implementation of HIV prevention interventions: Translating theory into practice.* New York: Plenum Press.

Woldenberg, J. (2008, January 24). Caer [Falling]. *Reforma,* p. 14.

World Bank (2007). *Healthy development. The World Bank strategy for health, nutrition, and population results.* Washington, DC: World Bank.

World Health Organization [WHO] (2006). What is the evidence on effectiveness of empowerment to improve health? Retrieved July 29, 2008, from Health Evidence Network [HEN]: www.euro.who.int/Document/E88086.pdf.

Zimmerman, B. J., & Cleary, T. J. (2006). Adolescents' development of agency. The role of self-efficacy beliefs and self-regulatory skill. In F. Pajares & T. Urdan (Eds.), *Self-Efficacy Beliefs of Adolescents* (pp. 45-69). Charlotte, NC: Information Age Publishing.

SECTION II

Sustainable Human Development

CHAPTER 5

Development as Enhancing Capabilities

*People are the real wealth of a nation. The basic objective of develop-
ment is to create an enabling environment for people to enjoy long,
healthy, and creative lives. This may appear to be a simple truth. But it
is often forgotten in the immediate concern with the accumulation of
commodities and financial wealth*

—United Nations Development Program, (1990, p. 9).

The freedom-centered approach,[1] defined by the conceptual work of Amartya
Sen, provides the groundwork for this chapter. Sen argues that development is
about "expanding the real freedoms that people enjoy" and "a process of
removing unfreedoms" (1999, p. 3; 86).

Freedoms and capabilities—terms often used interchangeably—are the
clear objective and the core of Sen's approach. The Capability Approach
broadens traditional notions about poverty, looking at it as capability deprivation, and "offers an alternative development objective which can be used to
inform a wide range of issues, from markets to gender, democracy to poverty"
(Stewart & Deneulin, 2002, p. 61).

> Sen argues for a more nuanced view of the determinants of poverty, enhancing
> ... the understanding of the nature and causes of poverty and deprivation
> by shifting attention away from *means* (and one particular means that is
> usually given exclusive attention, viz., income) to *ends* that people have reason
> to pursue, and, correspondingly, to the *freedoms* to be able to satisfy these ends.
> (1999, p. 90)

Sen emphasizes that by seeing development from a freedom-centered perspective, we can concentrate on the objective of individual freedom rather than on
proximate means such as the growth of gross national product (GNP). We can

focus on the way in which freedoms can enhance further freedoms of other kinds; freedoms do not occur in isolation, but have an instrumental value in enhancing development (Sen, 2001). Expansion of freedom is both the primary end and the principal means of development (Sen, 1999). Therefore, human factors have both intrinsic and instrumental importance to development policy: valuing both individual capabilities and community development can positively impact well-being, expand human potential, and, in so doing, make implementation of decisions more likely.

Sen believes that individuals should be able to make autonomous choices to lead the sort of life they inherently value. The Capability Approach relies on individuals to play an active role:

> The freedom-centered view captures the constructive role of free human agency as an engine of change. It differs from seeing people as passive beneficiaries of cunning development programs. (Sen, 2001, p. 3)

Furthermore, Saith outlines how the Capability Approach argues that "the possession of commodities may not necessarily translate into well-being," but personal characteristics must be taken into account. It is for "the 'conversion' of commodities to particular ends" that the personal characteristics are key (2001, p. 6). An individual's ability to exercise freedoms depends on her particular capabilities, which depend on actual and perceived opportunities, as well as on the socio-economic and cultural context. The interplay between personal and contextual constraints—along with the individual's ability to utilize his capabilities—are essential components of personal and community development. If personal skills, knowledge, and psychological access are absent, then the possession of commodities may not represent an opportunity and, therefore, may not translate into any improvement in well-being. Personal resources are of instrumental importance to individuals' conversion of resources and opportunities to particular ends (Saith, 2001).

Capabilities can thus be seen as substantive freedoms that involve both the development of human capacity and the reduction of socio-economic constraints. Expanding capabilities is the most effective and sustainable means of creating opportunities for autonomous choice and developing agency. Free of constraints and "unfreedoms", individuals cultivate the capabilities necessary to access choices and opportunities. "Once they effectively have these substantive opportunities, they can choose those options that they value most" (Robeyns, 2005, p. 95). This approach places an emphasis on individuals as the basic building block and on human development as the key to poverty reduction. In many ways, Sen's work represents a reconceptualization of development.

Since its introduction to the international community in the late 1980s, the Capability Approach has gained wide recognition and has evolved to embody the notion of sustainable development. Not only did its introduction broaden the conceptualization of development, but it has also expanded the potential for policy (and program) design and evaluation in terms of human capabilities (Robeyns, 2005). The transition toward this comprehensive view of development and the establishment of a consensus about the best means to achieve such development are far from complete in either the intellectual or policy-making arenas. A World Bank report illustrates how the international community is adapting its formulations to encompass a broader view of development than that previously held:

> "Development" is really much more than simple economic growth. The understanding of development can differ among countries and even among individuals, but it usually goes far beyond the objectives of increased average income to include things like freedom, equity, health, education, safe environment, and much more. (Soubbotina, 2004, p. 1)

Conceptually, the major international institutions all subscribe to the idea of sustainable development and to the fact that for it to be attainable, it must have a "human" component. But the practical implementation presents formidable challenges.

Development policy and programs have inadequately enabled human capabilities in the past as a result of a lack of political will and the challenges of creating cost-effective programs that are self-sustaining. Little clarity exists in translating theories into practice in a way that makes the short- and long-term gains visible to the stakeholders (e.g., policy designers, program implementers, funders, and politicians). The Capability Approach is often encumbered at the policy and implementation levels because short-term fixes, which are often easier to agree on and implement, trump investment in long-term goals or program sustainability initiatives. Policies and development programs could aim to enhance the capacity of the individual agent through supporting: participatory and reflection-based programming, an education system that promotes critical thought, and a democratic political system that allows individuals to exercise their freedoms. This chapter explores the Capability Approach as a model for increasing the sustainability of development programs that will more effectively meet the needs of the individuals and communities they intend to serve.

The Historical Context of Development Economics

The origins of modern development economics are often traced to the end of World War II; the field emerged as the study of "backward" economics or disadvantaged sectors of society within a given country.[2] Emphasizing similar goals as that of mainstream economics, development economics initially focused on economic growth, industrialization, and modernization.[3] Academics and practitioners alike focused on how less-developed economies could grow more rapidly than developed economies allowing for poor and rich countries to "converge" in living standards over time (Sachs & Warner, 1995).[4] It was the subsequent lack of convergence between poor and rich countries—and the increasing inequality that occurred as a byproduct of the emphasis on growth— that then contributed to the emergence of several alternative schools of thought to explain the persistent global inequality (Milanovic, 2005). These consisted of structuralism and Marxism, neo-colonialism, dependency, center-periphery and world-systems theories. The new ideas led toward inward-looking, state-controlled development models (Taylor, 1998) in Latin American and Soviet bloc countries between the 1930s and 1980s, although the emphasis on growth still held.

The intellectual counter-offensive to this movement in development economics was neo-liberalism, which rests on concepts of classical liberalism and laissez-faire economics. The scope of study broadened slightly when the idea of "human capital accumulation" entered the scene in the 1960s (Schultz, 1961, 1963). The underlying concept was simple: an educated and healthy population creates a productive labor force and, in turn, enhances economic growth. Although the emphasis remained centered on growth, there was a general understanding that education, health, and fertility were important factors behind economic growth and could potentially enhance or undermine the development process. A focus on the role of institutions was later incorporated into the dominant logic. It is a version of this school of thought, embodied by the "Washington Consensus,"[5] which seems to have gained adherence around the world (Rodrik, 2006; Rodrik & Rodriguez, 2001). Yet, neo-liberalism is often criticized for its almost exclusive emphasis on a market-driven approach to issues and its concomitant lack of attention to inequality, a social justice concepts of rights, and human agency. Although the evidence of success varies (Rodrik, 2006), it is clear that this one-size-fits-all approach is ultimately ineffective. Indeed, it has led to another round of ideological shifting in Latin America: "One key root in the region's shift to the left in political preferences is certainly the disappointing results of the economic reforms—inspired by the Washington Consensus—implemented by previous governments" (Moreno Brid & Paunovic, 2006, p. 44). Once again, the development paradigm in Latin America is changing.

Today, the study of development economics focuses on distributional issues—especially income distribution—with empirical studies in the field also finding variables such as human capital (educational attainment and health), financial development (ratio of investment to GDP), and political stability (maintenance of rule of law and ratio of government consumption spending) to be significantly correlated with economic growth (Barro, 1997; Barro & Sala-i-Martin, 2004). Some thinkers have broadly emphasized the human aspect in development, and some, such as with the Millennium Development Goals, have looked to measure development factors other than economic (Moreno Brid & Ros, 2009; Stiglitz, 2002; UN Millenium Project, 2005). These ideas generally operate within the greater framework of classical economic theory: the rational individual will act to enhance his utility. Policies that aim to enhance capabilities remain limited to particular organizations or institutions and often disregard the individual mechanisms of change. The (naive) assumption that people will grab opportunities as they come along still persists.

Developed in the early 1990s, the foremost indicator of development among policy circles is the Human Development Index (HDI). A composite of literacy, life expectancy, and command over resources needed for a decent living, the HDI is considered a standard measure of well-being with a human development focus. Various researchers have linked Sen's concepts with well-being and quality of life research: quality of life is determined by the possibility to use resources (capabilities) and by what the individual can achieve (functionings) with those resources (Verkerk, Busschbach, & Karssing, 2001). But the HDI and other quality-of-life measurements are limited in their ability to incorporate concepts such as freedoms or to understand how the means they are measuring translate into a particular end.

The emerging focus of development research has yielded positive results in terms of health and education, and a new generation of policies would be well-informed to encompass a broader perspective of development. Neither state nor market absolutism will address the multifaceted determinants of poverty or resolve the socio-economic disparities between and within nations. Pure market approaches (whether isolationist or liberal) share a common flaw: they try to resolve comprehensive problems utilizing macro-economic tools, rather than embracing a broader view that also recognizes the importance of investing in people so that they may realize their potential. The Capability Approach argues that empowering individuals needs to be involved not only in spirit but also in the foundation of policies and their implementation. Although psychological factors, philosophy, and social justice have long been discussed in economics, Sen's conceptualization of development represents a paradigmatic shift in the history of development studies. The Capability Approach distinguishes itself from its predecessors because of the emphasis it places on justice and for its recognition of human factors as both means and ends of development.

Development is at the heart of the issues that economics intends to address; after all, economics as a discipline began with an inquiry into the "nature and causes of the wealth of nations" (Smith, 1776/1982). Resources will be more effectively utilized and dynamically expanded as the focus of development economics transitions from its historical dependency on utilitarian and instrumental mechanisms to a multidisciplinary and multilevel approach.

Behavioral Economics and Development

Whereas the traditional economic model assumes that the rational actor[6] will make decisions in a predicted way that seeks to maximize utility, the study of human behavior has brought about new understandings of the psychology of such decision making (Lambert, 2006). From this research, the subfield of behavioral economics has emerged over the last 50 years as a hybrid of economics and psychology. Behavioral economists look to economics to understand aggregate actions and to psychology to understand individual decision making, departing from the standard economic model's assumption of rationality (Lambert, 2006).

Tversky and Kahneman[7] began the inquiry in this field by taking a simple, common-sense idea—that people do not always behave rationally—and designed studies to test their hypothesis, based on a comingling of psychology and economic theory. Their research showed that questions involving simple calculations may be answered differently depending on how they are framed, and thus people may not necessarily behave "rationally" in the neoclassical economic sense (1981). The introduction to one of their early articles describes this new approach:

> Explanations and predictions of people's choices, in everyday life as well as in the social sciences, are often founded on the assumption of human rationality. The definition of rationality has been much debated, but there is general agreement that rational choices could satisfy some elementary requirements of consistency and coherence. In this article we describe decision problems in which people systematically violate the requirements of consistency and coherence, and we trace these violations to the psychological principles that govern the perception of decision problems and the evaluation of options. (1981, p. 453)

The last clause of this statement is particularly illuminating. The authors did not simply want to demonstrate that people do not (always) behave rationally; they were determined to show that people's innate "irrationality" was, in fact, a direct result of already established psychological principles. In this and later articles examining decision theory, risk perceptions, and the psychology of choice, the authors go on to describe the innate error in theories of human behavior based on a purely rational model. This new way of thinking about human decision making has been a paradigm-shifting approach that has had important ramifications for economics and psychology alike and is very useful in looking at development.

The field of behavioral economics has accumulated a mass of empirical research, and although based in the work of psychologists (e.g., Becker, 1987; Camerer, Loewenstein, & Rabin, 2004; Tversky & Kahneman, 1979; Tversky & Kahneman, 1981), it has become an increasingly popular sector of mainstream economics. Behavioral processes have been integrated into economics in several ways, including through the idea of risk perceptions (Tversky & Kahneman, 1979), rational choice assumptions in relation to poverty reduction, the impact of self-efficacy on work efficacy (MacLachlan & Carr, 1999), and micro-enterprise development (Frese, Brantjes, & Hoorn, 2002).

The non- or underutilization of available opportunities demonstrates "irrational" economic behavior. This has been observed, for example, in the health field where available, and often free health services in low-resource settings are not used[8]—for example, cervical cancer screening in Bolivia, Peru, Kenya, South Africa, and Mexico (Bingham et al., 2003), mental health services in Chile (Saldivia et al., 2004), school-based parasite treatment in Kenya (Miguel & Kremer, 2004), and free health services in Mexico (Randall, 2006). Work in Cote d'Ivore also showed that men treat income deriving from different sources distinctly and will not use money from one source for expenses usually covered by the other source, even if the income from each source changes (Duflo, 2006). Immediate considerations often outweigh long-term benefits, unless incentives exist to save or to make an investment that will be rewarded in the future. In the case of deciding whether to send a child to school, the absence of children from school so that they can go to work outweighs both the instrumental value of education (i.e., education as a foundation for a future with a better job or a larger income) and the value of education as capability (a freedom in and of itself).

The behavioral approach suggests that psychological elements in the individual are closely correlated with poverty:

> Being poor almost certainly affects the way people think and decide ... What is needed is a theory of how poverty influences decision-making, not only by affecting the constraints, but by changing the decision-making process itself. That theory can then guide a new round of empirical research, both observational and experimental. (Duflo, 2006, p. 378)

The work of Banerjee and Newman (1994) has suggested that the behavioral differences among the poor—such as low savings or few entrepreneurial initiatives—do not arise from differences in preferences and abilities but rather from differences in economic environment. A poor peasant may not choose the optimal technology to cultivate the land because this would involve risking a considerable proportion of his scarce life savings; the poor may be so risk averse that they decline otherwise reasonable investment opportunities, thus perpetuating the poverty cycle (Banerjee, 2004). It is evident that a lack of income restricts, and in many cases totally negates choice. However, joint liability initiatives, which make a group responsible rather than a single individual, have shown to be successful models in lending to the poor (Chowdhury, 2005). When a financial institution lends to a group, repayment rates are quite good (Morduch, 1999a). Joint liability alleviates problems of asymmetric information between the borrowers and lender through many channels, including peer selection, peer monitoring, and dynamic incentives (Morduch, 1999a). Put simply, joint liability works because people do not like letting others down—clearly a behavioral insight. Although this reasoning has been centered primarily on credit market utilization, it may be extended to other economic disciplines.

The integration of psychology and development is relatively new. Thus far, psychological factors have been explored in public health (Ewart, 2004), family planning (Fishbein, 1972), nutrition (Cavalcanti, Dias, & Costa, 2005), conflict resolution (Daniel, 2000), rehabilitation (Brown et al., 2008) and microfinance (Morduch, 1999b). Models are needed that integrate (not just acknowledge) the individual and group psychological, economic, and social factors of development. The inclusion of behavioral factors within the field of development economics admittedly remains in its infancy. The poor in developing countries often fail to behave "rationally" (as traditional economics would predict); therefore, policies may be designed and implemented more effectively if the norms, culture, and behavioral factors of the targeted groups are taken into account. Understanding the behavioral processes and other psychosocial factors in communities where development policies are going to be implemented can have significant welfare-enhancing results. Research demonstrates that when it comes to the design of development policies, small behavioral details may have large welfare implications (Bertrand, Mullainathan, & Shafir, 2004).

The Capability Approach

The Capability Approach (Sen 1999; 2003; 2004) can be seen as part of this much wider movement in behavioral economics. It takes behavioral and developmental economics beyond their conceptual limitations, valuing human capabilities as a worthwhile goal rather than as the mere instrumental benefits of human capital formation. The approach provides an alternative to the traditional utilitarian views of investing in human capital as the *means* to economic development. In this model, the focus shifts toward enhancing the "freedoms" of individuals as the *goal* of development. In fact, in this way of looking at development, freedoms serve in both roles. As Sen explains it: "Expansion of freedom is viewed, in this approach, both as the primary end and as the principal means of development" (Sen, 1999, p. xii). The approach also emphasizes that norms and behaviors should become more closely integrated in economic theory and provides a systematic means of doing so, supplying a "framework for evaluating and assessing social arrangements, standards of living, inequality, poverty, justice, quality of life, or well-being" (Comim, 2001, p. 4). Such an approach will provide greater sustainability through the establishment of policies and programs that enlarge capabilities.

The foundational concepts of the Capability Approach provide the core for the paradigm. There are three key concepts:

1. *Entitlements* are the commodities over which a person has the potential to establish ownership and command (Sen, 1999). Entitlements can be political, economic, or otherwise. Sen argues that entitlements are not the ends but are important precisely as the *means* to the well-being of people (1997a).
2. *Functionings* are the diverse aspects of life that people value doing or being; achieved functionings, sometimes called realized functionings, are those that have been pursued and realized (Sen, 1999). Functionings represent the outcomes and depend on a variety of factors. "What a person actually succeeds in doing with the commodity, given its characteristics, his or her own personal characteristics, and external circumstances [context]. This achievement is referred to as the functioning" (Saith, 2001, p. 3). Sen categorizes functionings into both "doings and beings" (Nussbaum & Sen, 1993, p. 3). Doing functions are behaviors; being functionings are the more stable characteristics.
3. *Capabilities (or freedoms)* refer to the freedom to achieve valuable functionings (Sen, 1999); it can be seen as the "menu" from which people are able to choose (Sen, 1997b). A person's capability set has been described as "alternative combinations of functionings that are feasible for her to achieve" (Sen, 1999, p. 75) and "the range of life-options that people have" (Gasper, 2000, p. 991).[9] Sen asserts that certain capabilities are basic; they are necessary for a person to achieve a minimum level of well-being (Sen, 1999).

Thus, capabilities are the possibilities—or realizable opportunities—and functionings are constitutive of an individual (e.g., being healthy or being able to vote). The transition from capabilities to achieved functionings implies a process of enabling individuals to access opportunities and to make choices based on their needs and interests. Gasper (2000) highlights the value that Sen places on capability as the central component of choice in his approach:

> In assessing a person's situation Sen gives priority to capability, potential functionings, above achieved functionings. Sometimes he writes as if capability is the sole criterion ... The definition of development can become: more choice. No other aspects of life are specified, rather they are left for: choice. (p. 999)

Perceived access to options may be as essential as the physical presence of those opportunities. For example, it is not enough to have schools or health clinics available; people must have the capabilities to access those services. Otherwise, underutilization of available opportunities will occur. This is also true of access to intangible functionings, such as the choice of one's identity. The freedom to choose, and to freely express, one's identity erases the shame and fear caused by identity suppression, allowing the individual to more fully take advantage of other opportunities available to him (Flores-Crespo, 2007). These fundamental concepts provide the approach to training programs presented in this book, amounting to a possible means of making Sen's ideas operational.

One of the strengths of Sen's approach is its broad conceptual foundation, rooted in political and economic philosophers such as Aristotle and Smith "whose concern with actual human living has been lost in dominant contemporary approaches in liberal philosophy and politics" (Srinivasan, 2007, p. 459). Sen references Aristotle's point that "wealth is evidently not the good we are seeking; for it is merely useful and for the sake of something else" (Sen, 1988, p. 1). The Capability Approach also contributes sophisticated assumptions about human behavior operating within a framework of social justice:

> Given the Capability Approach's view of persons as agents who have diverse valued goals and commitments on behalf both of themselves and of their society, and who contribute to public discussion about social goals, the approach cannot coherently employ an entirely self-interested model of human motivation. A complex of other motivations, perhaps including identity, cooperation, altruism, habit, and sympathy, must also enter. (Alkire, 2005, p. 125)

These concepts have important implications for the conceptualization of development, which is now defined within the capability space as expanding individual opportunities and is assessed through realized individual achievement (i.e., functionings). The focus of the Capability Approach is not on utility maximization but on expanding the freedom of individuals to actively enhance opportunities. The approach looks to individuals to play an active role in their own development and their community's development: "Achievement of development is thoroughly dependent on the free agency of people" (Sen, 1999, p. 4).

Because a capability must be realizable (and not lie beyond the individual's reach) to be considered a freedom (Alkire, 2005), the role of the context in providing entitlements is integral to the success of this approach (*see* Chapter 8). The context can be a constraining or enhancing factor when it comes to the acquisition of freedoms. If an individual lives in a context that is constraining (be it economically, culturally, socially, or politically, or a combination of these) then her achieved functionings do not necessarily represent her capabilities, which may be much broader but simply cannot be achieved because of contextual limitations. "Unfreedoms" arise when people lack either the opportunities or the capabilities to achieve what they value. Thus, in practice, "capable individuals" may be restrained in a context that presents insurmountable barriers to action or when basic needs are not met. A woman may possess the skills and knowledge (the capacity) to act, but the context within which she lives may be so impoverished or repressive that she is unable to overcome the logistical and psychological barriers to action (Agarwal & Panda, 2007). Thus, her "capability set" can only be partially developed because of the extent of "unfreedoms" present in her environment. It is not only absolute measures of capabilities and functionings that matter but also relative measures, as this can lead to perverse effects. Agarwal and Panda (2007) explain it as: "A man married to a woman better employed than himself, for instance, may be irked by her higher achievement and physically abuse her, thus reducing her well-being achievement (e.g. by undermining her health) and her well-being freedom (e.g. by reducing her work mobility or social interaction)" (p. 359).

The context can also enhance capabilities in a productive fashion, although they are still dependent on personal factors:

> Observed functionings are only a good proxy for capability if people can be assumed to have the skills, knowledge and attitudes to perceive and take their best (or at least a steady proportion of their) opportunities. (Gasper, 2000, p. 999)

Strategically targeted policies and programs that simultaneously cover political, economic, and social components of the macrolevel will most effectively enhance the capacity of individuals. According to Sen, the mutually reinforcing nature of various freedoms

> … can be based on empirical analysis of the consequences of—and interconnections between—freedoms of distinct kinds, and on the evidence that freedoms of different types typically help to sustain each other. What a person has the actual capability to achieve is influenced by economic opportunities, political liberties, social facilities, and the enabling conditions of good health, basic education, and the encouragement and cultivation of initiatives. These opportunities are, to a great extent, mutually complementary, and tend to reinforce the reach and use of one another. (Sen, 2001, p. 2)

Thus, investing in the health, political, or education system and the individual's capability to access and utilize such systems will result in positive capabilities for both the individual and societal development.

The Capability Approach Operationalized

The Capability Approach is a conceptualization, not a formula for change. "There are many different ways through which any theory can be used or applied and it does not seem correct to limit the 'processes of putting these theories into operation' to one or two particular modes" (Comim, 2001, p. 1).[10]

Even Sen claims that "the Capability Approach can be used at different levels of sophistication" (Sen, 1992, p. 53); he does not see the approach as providing a single route for change. However, this has not been an obstacle to efforts to operationalize and institutionalize its approach to development. Proponents of the Capability Approach have put significant effort into doing just that, beginning with Sen himself. Making Sen's Capability Approach operative has important implications for policy design, as it suggests shifting some of the focus of development programs away from economic measures and instead looking at ways to enhance individual well-being. Sustainable approaches must alter the context to incorporate a vision of individual freedom, which improves well-being and encourages participation. Human development of this kind leads to schools with effective teachers, the enforcement of laws, operational democracies, and fully exercised freedom of press. This kind of development is about choice—about individuals having the capacity to decide and to act on their decisions.

Sen's recognition that an individual's ability to carry out her objectives depends as much on her personal characteristics as on her access to commodities paves the way for a psychosocial approach to development (Sen, 1999). The framework that we present in Chapter 4 of this book makes the Capability Approach operational in such a way, assigning and enhancing the active role of the individual in converting commodities into realized achievements (functionings). Chapter 8 will show that enhancing personal agency allows people to not only augment their achievements and personal characteristics but also to make a greater contribution to their community. This process of developing intrinsic empowerment eventually impacts social factors so that the context can become supportive and even a determinant of further capabilities. In other words, the person is directly involved in creating new opportunities that respond to her needs rather than just utilizing those that are provided. In our view, it is through the development of competencies (i.e., acquiring knowledge and uncovering and consolidating skills and putting them into practice) that the Capability Approach can most effectively be made operational in the developing world.

Figure 5–1 illustrates the relationship between Sen's approach and the FrEE framework presented in Chapter 4.

FrEE aims to translate Sen's abstract terminology used in the Capability Approach into specific psychosocial terms that can be practically implemented in development programs. Each of the components—knowledge, skills, behavior change, personal agency, and intrinsic empowerment—are part of the individual's capability set (as depicted by the circle in the figure). The capability set has implications for the expansion of the well-being, capabilities, and freedoms of individuals, and the relationship of the individuals to the context. The broader context within which FrEE has been conceptualized is through opportunities and constraints, which operate across all levels of the framework (psychological and contextual); in the language of Sen's Capability Approach,

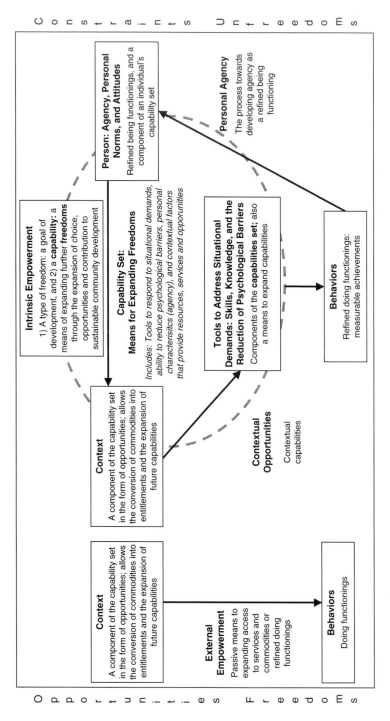

Person: Agency, Personal Norms, and Attitudes
Refined being functionings, and a component of an individual's capability set

Personal Agency
The process towards developing agency as a refined being functioning

Intrinsic Empowerment
1) A type of freedom: a goal of development, and 2) a **capability**: a means of expanding further **freedoms** through the expansion of choice, opportunities and contribution to sustainable community development

Capability Set:
Means for Expanding Freedoms
Includes: Tools to respond to situational demands, ability to reduce psychological barriers, personal characterisitcs (agency), and contextual factors that provide resources, services and opporunities

Context
A component of the capability set in the form of opportunities; allows the conversion of commodities into entitlements and the expansion of future capabilities

Contextual Opportunities
Contextual capabilities

Tools to Address Situational Demands: Skills, Knowledge, and the Reduction of Psychological Barriers
Components of the **capabilities set**; also a means to expand capabilities

Behaviors
Refined doing functionings: measurable achievements

Context
A component of the capability set in the form of opportunities; allows the conversion of commodities into entitlements and the expansion of future capabilities

External Empowerment
Passive means to expanding access to services and commodities or refined doing functionings

Behaviors
Doing functionings

FIGURE 5–1 Making the Capability Approach Operative through FrEE

these are termed freedoms and unfreedoms. Programming for Choice seeks to expand opportunities and to reduce constraints (or the "unfreedoms") that limit them.

Sen's doing functionings are operationalized as behaviors, which result from the application of an external stimulus that the context facilitates. When contextual change works to empower individuals internally by addressing situational demands, behaviors can be described as refined doing functionings. Doing functionings are "refined" when behaviors are operationalized through a process involving skills and knowledge-building as well as opportunities for reducing psychological barriers. Thus, in the latter case, behaviors are a product of applying personal capabilities and represent an aspect of individual achievement. As the individual realizes that she is successful in bringing about changes in her behaviors, the refined doing functionings evolve into more stable characteristics (i.e., being functionings), which is described in FrEE as personal agency and changes in personal norms and attitudes. These psychosocial changes occur as repeated behavior changes (i.e., doing functionings) successfully take place and the individual perceives the positive implications of her new behaviors. Because the development of personal agency is both an achieved functioning and a potential to realize future functionings (in Sen's terms), the concept represents a being functioning as well as a capability. The being functionings—in this case, personal agency and changes in personal norms and attitudes—represent stable long-term changes in individual characteristics (*see* Chapters 4 and 6). These individual characteristics become components of the capability set once the individual has adopted them as a result of successful behavioral experience.

As the sense of personal agency evolves, the process of intrinsic empowerment occurs. In Sen's terms, intrinsic empowerment can be understood as the ability to convert commodities from the context into entitlements, as their sense of personal agency (a capability) allows them to view these commodities as opportunities for making their rights a reality. Thus, intrinsic empowerment is both an individual freedom, which is a goal of development, and a capability, in the sense of a means toward achieving additional freedoms. Intrinsic empowerment is the instrument we propose to expand human capabilities and entitlements in the context; however, it is not only an instrument but should also be a goal in and of itself of development programs.

In our view, FrEE addresses what is probably the most important criticism raised against Sen's conceptualization. Gasper (2000) argues:

> Possible criticisms of Sen's conception of people can be stated as a series of over- and under-emphases: too much on people as choosers, rather than as actors in a fuller sense; too little on skills and on functionings, compared with opportunities; too little on meanings, and in fact too much on freedoms.

FrEE focuses precisely on how the mindset necessary to achieve personal agency is a natural manifestation when individuals have choices and opportunities as well as on life skills and behavior change as the points of departure.

It explains how socio-cultural roles and expectations create meaning and have the potential to shape or restrict choice. The importance of expanding freedoms is contextualized within our framework through not only economic and social restrictions but *also* psychological barriers. In this way, FrEE goes beyond the abstract notion of freedoms to address concrete actions in economic, legal, educational, and social contexts.

Some Practical Implications

One of the criticisms of the Capability Approach has been that there is not a list of specific capabilities and functionings that can be applied universally, making evaluation and assessment of change difficult and varied according to particular circumstances.[11] Proponents of the Capability Approach argue that having a list would reduce the approach to a formula, thereby taking away one of its main contributions as a framework of thought (Robeyns, 2000). Pointing to the impracticality of creating a list that accounts for all cultural variations, Sen explains: "There are diversities of many different kinds. It is not unreasonable to think that if we try to take note of all the diversities, we might end up in a total mess of empirical confusion" (1992, p. 117). The capabilities and functionings that would make up a list inherently vary among communities, individuals, and stages in life. Many, in fact, view context-based specification as a strength because this makes it possible to adapt the approach to the "challenges that poor people and countries face, rather than imposing a rigid orthodoxy with a set of policy prescriptions" (Fukuda-Parr, 2003, p. 302). The approach also avoids potential paternalism by not judging what a community's priorities should be, but instead encouraging democratic decisions on the issue. At the same time, international organizations tend to assert that some capabilities are so basic and universally valued that "their lack would foreclose many other capabilities" (Fukuda-Parr, 2003, p. 306). This view is further supported by the fact that values tend to be universally shared (Fontaine et al., 2008; Schwartz, 1992; Schwartz & Boehnke, 2004).

Although human capabilities provide the most comprehensive depiction of a person's potential, functionings (or outcomes) are generally easier to measure. Sen argues that the possession of commodities may not necessarily translate into well-being, but it is the ability to convert those commodities to achieve particular ends that is important (Saith, 2001). Yet, the majority of attempts to make the Capability Approach operative, for both programming and evaluation, have occurred at the level of functionings because they are easier to observe than capabilities (Saith, 2001, p. 20). Various approaches have been offered on how to address this difficulty. Sen (1999) himself posits that the assessment of capabilities has to be carried out based on observed functionings, supplemented by other information. Chiappero-Martinetti (1996) highlights the importance of measuring both capabilities and functionings, which is possible if available resources are compared. In this way, one could deduce whether outcomes were based on free choice or whether they were the direct consequence of available resources. The complication with this proposal is that the concept of capabilities is so broad that it is difficult to measure and may have different meanings depending on the context. In this regard, Nussbaum (2000) refers to the importance of a qualitative approach of testimonies, interviews, and other biographical methods, that would help to more accurately map out capabilities. Such methods, although a necessary step, are limited in their ability to provide comparison of findings between studies. Other researchers assert the importance of initial attempts:

> It is far more important to measure the correct thing imperfectly than to measure precisely that which is merely convenient (or standard). This message is particularly important in an era that seems to place great weight on off-the-shelf-measurements. (Hurley, 2001, p. 57)

So far, IMIFAP has relied on observation and testimony to map out *how* change is being realized (i.e., to map out the operation of the Capability Approach, *see especially* Chapter 4). At the same time, controlled studies of program outcomes have been conducted to establish whether programs indeed lead to change, as we presented in the introductory chapter.

Conclusions

This chapter has shown how Sen's Capability Approach places development in a much broader scheme than traditional economics or development theory has done. The view centers on choice and freedom, where economic aspects are key as a *means* more than as a final goal. The transition from capabilities to achieved functionings implies a process of enabling individuals to access opportunities and to make choices based on their needs and interests. Individuals will not simply grab opportunities as they come along. To do so requires that people and communities understand they have the right and the means to choose among possibilities and to create opportunities for themselves. This requires an expansion of capabilities both at the individual and contextual levels. These changes have both intrinsic and instrumental importance to development.

The ideas behind FrEE have derived from more than 25 years of fieldwork; its formulation is the crystallization of the Capability Approach into an operative scheme from a psychosocial perspective. Unlike propositions that aim at making a list of capabilities, FrEE allows programs to be adapted to the needs of target populations, although we have found underlying commonalities among these needs. It is through the common need to expand one's choices, and the common means through which this can be achieved, that FrEE can be widely applied. FrEE provides a plausible basis for putting the Capability Approach into practice in a relatively accessible manner that makes sense to the academic, the policymaker, and, foremost, to the individuals and communities whose needs development programs seek to address.

Notes

1. Sen has also called the Capability Approach an "agent-oriented approach." (Sen, 1999, p. 191)

2. At first, the field was mainly concerned with the reconstruction of Europe and the industrialization of the Eastern part of the continent. However, pivotal world events soon altered the international balance of power, and provided the thrust for development economics to emerge as a field: the process of decolonization in Asia and Africa established newly independent economies; the formation of international organizations such as the United Nations, the International Monetary Fund and the World Bank provided central international institutions through which funding and policy could be channeled; and perhaps most important, the Cold War with its two well-defined blocks and its residual "third world" clarified the need to better understand the non-aligned countries of Asia, Africa, and Latin America to gain their allegiance.

3. The focus under this intellectual tradition was on capital formation and the best measure of the extent of such progress was simply GNP.

4. The convergence debate is indeed very much alive to this day, although the empirical evidence for it is weak or nonrobust.

5. The Washington consensus was a list of ten US-Latin American policy guidelines to remedy the economic depression of the 1980s. The guidelines were the following: Fiscal policy discipline; Redirection of public spending from subsidies toward broad-based provision of key pro-growth, pro-poor services; Tax reform; Interest rates that are market determined and positive (but moderate) in real terms; Adjustment of exchange rates to reflect the conditions of the market; Trade liberalization; Liberalization of inward foreign direct investment; Privatization of state enterprises; Deregulation; Legal security for property rights. The term was coined by John Williamson (1990).

6. Behavioral economists have nicknamed this actor Economic Man, "… [he] makes logical, rational, self-interested decisions that weigh costs against benefits and maximize value and profit to himself. Economic Man is an intelligent, analytic, selfish creature who has perfect self-regulation in pursuit of his future goals and is unswayed by bodily states and feelings. And Economic Man is a marvelously convenient pawn for building academic theories. But Economic Man has one fatal flaw: he does not exist." (Lambert, 2006, p. 50)

7. Kahneman & Tversky are psychologists who conducted the seminal research in the field of behavioral economics; they are famous for the introduction of Prospect Theory (Kahneman & Tversky, 1979) (for which Kahneman received the Nobel Prize in 2002), and their study of decision-theory, risk-perceptions, and the psychology of choice.

8. This is also discussed in Chapter I.

9. None of these should be thought of in terms of exchangeable for money or income as that would restrict the Capability Approach to an economic approach. Robeyns (2005) gives the example that one is not interested in a bicycle because of the materials it is made of and its shape as much as because it can take us places in a faster way than walking.

10. A number of academics have presented or are working on ways of operationalizing the Capability Approach. They include Bina Agarwal, Sabina Alkire, Alexandre Apsan Frediani, Enrica Chiappero-Martinetti, David Clark, Flavio Comim, Severine Deneulin, Jean Dreze, Sakiko Fukuda-Parr, Des Gasper, Mozaffar Qizilbash, and Ingrid Robeyns, among others.

11. Nussbaum has developed a version of the Capability Approach intended for political purposes, and has created, "as a basis for constitutional thought," a list of 10 "Central Human Capabilities." These capabilities are "Life, Bodily Health, Bodily Integrity, the Development and Expression of Senses, Imagination and Thought, Emotional Health, Practical Reason, Affiliation (both personal and political), Relationships with Other Species and the World of Nature, Play, and Control over One's Environment (both material and social)." (Nussbaum, 2007, p. 21)

References

Agarwal, B., & Panda, P. (2007). Toward freedom from domestic violence: The neglected obvious. *Journal of Human Development,* 8(3), 359–388.

Alkire, S. (2005). Why the Capability Approach? *Journal of Human Development,* 6(1), 115–133.

Banerjee, A. V. (2004). The two poverties. *Nordic Journal of Political Economy,* 26(2), 129–141.

Banerjee, A. V., & Newman, A. F. (1994). Poverty, incentives, and development. *American Economic Review,* 84(2), 211–215.

Barro, R. J. (1997). *Determinants of economic growth: A cross-country empirical study.* Cambridge, MA: MIT Press.

Barro, R. J., & Sala-i-Martin, X. (2004). *Economic growth.* Cambridge, MA: MIT Press.

Becker, G. (1987). Economic analysis and human behavior. In L.Green & J. H. Kagel (Eds.), *Advances in behavioral economics* (Vol. 1, pp. 3–17). Norwood, NJ: Ablex.

Bertrand, M., Mullainathan, S., & Shafir, E. (2004). A behavioral-economics view of poverty. *American Economic Review,* 94(2), 419–423.

Bingham, A., Bishop, A., Coffey, P., Winkler, J., Bradley, J., Dzuba, I., & Agurto, I. (2003). Factors affecting utilization of cervical cancer prevention services in low-resource settings. *Salud Pública de México,* 45(Supplement 3), S408–S416.

Brown, K. S., Deleon, P. H., Loftis, C. W., & Scherer, M. J. (2008). Rehabilitation psychology: Realizing the true potential. *Rehabilitation Psychology,* 53(2), 111–121.

Camerer, C. F., Loewenstein, G., & Rabin, M. (2004). *Advances in behavioral economics.* Princeton, NJ: Princeton University Press.

Cavalcanti, A. P. R., Dias, M. R., & Costa, M. J. d. C. (2005). Psicologia e nutrição: Predizendo a intenção comportamental de aderir a dietas de redução de peso entre obesos de baixa renda [Psychology and nutrition: Predicting behavioral intention to follow weight reduction diets among low-income obese patients]. *Estudos de Psicologia,* 10(1), 121–129.

Chiappero-Martinetti, E. (1996). A new approach to evaluation of well-being and poverty by fuzzy set theory. *Giornale degli Economisti Annali di Economia,* pp. 367–388.

Chowdhury, P. R. (2005). Group-lending: Sequential financing, lender monitoring and joint liability. *Journal of Development Economics,* 77(2), 415–439.

Comim, F. (2001). *Operationalizing Sen's Capability Approach.* Paper presented at the Conference on Justice and Poverty: Examining Sen's Capability Approach. Cambridge. from www.uia.mx/humanismocristiano/seminario_capability/pdf/7.pdf.

Daniel, B.-T. (2000). From intractable conflict through conflict resolution to reconciliation: Psychological analysis. *Political Psychology,* 21(2), 351–365.

Duflo, E. (2006). Poor but rational? In A. Banerjee, R. Benabou & D. Mookherjee (Eds.), *Understanding poverty* (pp. 367–378). New York: Oxford University Press.

Ewart, C. K. (Ed.). (2004). *How integrative behavioral theory can improve health promotion and disease prevention.* Washington, DC: American Psychological Association.

Fishbein, M. (1972). Toward an understanding of family planning behaviors. *Journal of Applied Social Psychology,* 2(3), 214–227.

Flores-Crespo, P. (2007). Ethnicity, identity, and educational achievement in Mexico. *International Journal of Educational Development,* 27, 331–339.

Fontaine, J. R. J., Poortinga, Y. H., Delbeke, L., & Schwartz, S. H. (2008). Structural equivalence of the values domain across cultures: Distinguishing sampling fluctuations from meaningful variation. *Journal of Cross-Cultural Psychology,* 39(4), 345–365.

Frese, M., Brantjes, A., & Hoorn, R. (2002). Psychological success factors of small scale businesses in Namibia: The roles of strategy process, entrepreneurial orientation and the environment. *Journal of Developmental Entrepreneurship,* 7(3), 259–282.

Fukuda-Parr, S. (2003). New threats to human security in the era of globalization. *Journal of Human Development,* 4(2), 167–179.

Gasper, D. (2000). Development as freedom: Taking economics beyond commodities - the cautions boldness of Amartya Sen. *Journal of International Development,* 12, 989–1001.

Hurley, J. (2001). Commentary on "Health-related quality-of-life research and the Capability Approach of Amartya Sen". *Quality of Life Research: An International Journal of Quality of Life Aspects of Treatment, Care & Rehabilitation,* 10(1), 57–58.

Kahneman, D., & Tyersky, A. (1979). Prospect theory: An analysis of decision under risk. *Econometrica,* 47(2), 263–292.

Lambert, C. (2006, March-April). The marketplace of perceptions. *Harvard Magazine,* 50–57, 93–95.

MacLachlan, M., & Carr, S. C. (1999). The selection of international assignees for development work. *The Irish Journal of Psychology,* 20, 39–57.

Miguel, E., & Kremer, M. (2004). Worms: Identifying impacts on education and health in the presence of treatment externalities. *Econometrica,* 72(1), 159–217.

Milanovic, B. (2005). *Worlds apart: Measuring international and global inequality.* Princeton, NJ: Princeton University Press.

Morduch, J. (1999a). The microfinance promise. *Journal of Economic Literature,* 37(4), 1569–1614.

Morduch, J. (1999b). The role of subsidies in microfinance: Evidence from Grameen Bank. *Journal of Development Economics,* 60(1), 229–248.

Moreno Brid, J. C., & Paunovic, I. (2006). Old wine in new bottles?: Economic policy-making by left-of-center governments in Latin America. *ReVista: Harvard Review of Latin America* (Spring), 44–47.

Moreno Brid, J. C., & Ros, J. (2009). *Development and growth in the Mexican economy: A historical perspective.* Lima, Peru: Oxford University Press.

Nussbaum, M. C. (2000). *Women and human development.* New York: Cambridge University Press.

Nussbaum, M. C. (2007). Human rights and human capabilities: Twentieth century reflections. *Harvard Human Rights Journal,* 20, 21–24.

Nussbaum, M. C., & Sen, A. (1993). Introduction. In M. C. Nussbaum & A. Sen (Eds.), *The quality of life*. New York: Oxford University Press.

Randall, L. (2006). *Changing structure of Mexico: Political, social, and economic prospects*. Armonk, NY: M. E. Sharpe.

Robeyns, I. (2000). *Contesting choice: What's wrong with the gender division of labor?* Paper presented at the APSA Meetings. Washington, DC.

Robeyns, I. (2005). The Capability Approach: A theoretical survey. *Journal of Human Development*, 6(1), 93–114.

Rodrik, D. (2006). Goodbye Washington consensus, hello Washington confusion? A review of the World Bank's economic growth in the 1990s: Learning from a decade of reform. *Journal of Economic Literature*, 44(4), 973–987.

Rodrik, D., & Rodriguez, F. (2001). Trade policy and economic growth: A skeptic's guide to the cross-national evidence. In B. Bernanke & K. S. Rogoff (Eds.), *NBER Macroeconomics Annual 2000* (Vol. 15, pp. 261–338). Cambridge, MA: MIT Press.

Sachs, J. D., & Warner, A. M. (1995). *Economic convergence and economic policies* (NBER Working Paper No. 5039). Cambridge, MA: National Bureau of Economic Research [NBER].

Saith, R. (2001). *Capabilities: The concept and its operationalisation* (Queen Elizabeth House Working Paper, No. 66). Oxford: University of Oxford.

Saldivia, S., Vicente, B., Kohn, R., Rioseco, P., & Torres, S. (2004). Use of mental health services in Chile. *Psychiatric Services*, 55(1), 71–76.

Schultz, T. W. (1961). Investment in human capital. *The American Economic Review*, 51(1), 1–17.

Schultz, T. W. (1963). *The economic value of education*. New York: Columbia University Press.

Schwartz, S. H. (1992). Universals in the content and structure of values: Theoretical advances and empirical tests in 20 countries. *Advances in Experimental Social Psychology*, 25, 1–65.

Schwartz, S. H., & Boehnke, K. (2004). Evaluating the structure of human values with confirmatory factor analysis. *Journal of Research in Personality*, 38(3), 230–255.

Sen, A. (1988). Freedom of choice: Concept and content. *European Economic Review*, 32(2–3), 269–294.

Sen, A. (1992). *Inequality reexamined*. Oxford: Oxford University Press.

Sen, A. (1997a). *Entitlement perspectives of hunger*. Rome: World Food Programme.

Sen, A. (1997b). Maximization and the act of choice. *Econometrica*, 65(4), 745–779.

Sen, A. (1999). *Development as freedom*. New York: Anchor.

Sen, A. (2001). *Development as freedom: An approach*. Paper presented at the Boston Research Center: Amartya Sen on Freedom Lecture. Boston. Retrieved December 10, 2007, from http://69.36.178.127/thinkers/sen_article.htm.

Sen, A. (2003). Development as capability expansion. In S. Fukuda-Parr & A. K. Shiva Kumar (Eds.), *Readings in human development*. New York: Oxford University Press.

Sen, A. (2004). Gender equity and the population problem. In V. Navarro & C. Muntaner (Eds.), *Political and economic determinants of population health and well-being: Controversies and developments* (pp. 27–33). Amityville, NY: Baywood Publishing Company, Inc.

Smith, A. (1776/1982). *An inquiry into the nature and causes of the wealth of nations*. London: Penguin Classics.

Soubbotina, T. (2004). *Beyond economic growth, second edition: An introduction to sustainable development*. Washington, DC: World Bank.

Srinivasan, S. (2007). No democracy without justice: Political freedom in Amartya Sen's Capability Approach. *Journal of Human Development,* 8(3), 457–480.

Stewart, F., & Deneulin, S. (2002). Amartya Sen's contribution to development thinking. *Studies in Comparative International Development,* 37(2), 61–70.

Stiglitz, J. (2002). *Globalization and its discontents.* New York: W.W. Norton & Company.

Taylor, A. M. (1998). On the costs of inward-looking development: Historical perspectives on price distortions, growth, and divergence in Latin America from 1930s-1980s. *Journal of Economic History,* 58(1), 1–28.

Tversky, A., & Kahneman, D. (1979). Prospect theory: An analysis of decision under risk. *Econometrica,* 47(2), 263–292.

Tversky, A., & Kahneman, D. (1981). The framing of decisions and the psychology of choice. *Science,* 211(4481), 453–458.

UN Millenium Project (2005). *Investing in development: A practical plan to achieve the Millennium Development Goals.* New York: United Nations Development Program.

United Nations Development Program [UNDP] (1990). *Human development report 1990: Concept and measurement of human development.* New York: Oxford University Press.

Verkerk, M. A., Busschbach, J. J. V., & Karssing, E. D. (2001). Health-related quality of life research and the Capability Approach of Amartya Sen. *Quality of Life Research: An International Journal of Quality of Life Aspects of Treatment, Care & Rehabilitation,* 10(1), 49–55.

Williamson, J. (1990). What Washington means by policy reform. In J. Williamson (Ed.), *Latin American adjustment: How much has happened?* (November 2002 ed., pp. 7–20). Washington, DC: Institute for International Economics.

CHAPTER 6

The Elements of FrEE

*Enhancing Opportunities and Reducing Barriers to
Development by Addressing Situational Demands*

> *Opportunities can be missed if the capabilities to grasp them are blunted or
> misdirected*
>
> —World Bank, (2007, p. 46)

Programming for Choice is the name we use to emphasize that programs are
geared toward promoting choice of action in situations where the range of
actions tends to be constrained by restrictive norms or other kinds of unfreedoms. From the start, IMIFAP's Programming for Choice aimed to bring about
changes in targeted behaviors. To do so, programming had to focus on the
determinants of behavior. This chapter introduces the Theory of Reasoned
Action (Fishbein & Ajzen, 1975) from which IMIFAP developed its understanding of these determinants. Thereafter we focus on our experience, which
is captured in the central Tools for Addressing Situational Demands frame of
the FrEE diagram (Fig. 4–1b). The frame charts the way that limited knowledge can result in beliefs that restrict choices. We make explicit how the provision of knowledge and the development of particularly fundamental skills can
bring about increased access to choice by allowing people to address situational demands.[1] This results in a process of conduct change leading to healthier behaviors and, with time, greater personal agency and competencies.
Finally, the chapter discusses how programming can target the knowledge and
skill components for addressing situational demands. Chapter 7 will address
the resulting process of behavior change and personal agency development.

Attitudes and Intentions as Concepts Focusing on Behaviors

In developing programs, a strong theoretical basis provides a guideline. Creating a program without an underlying framework is akin to going on a trip without a map. Most significantly, programs aimed at bringing about changes must be based on an understanding of how change comes about. Programs at IMIFAP were first based on the Theory of Reasoned Action (TRA; Fishbein & Ajzen, 1975),[2] the leading theory for explaining behavior outcomes for over a quarter century, and later, on the complementary Theory of Planned Behavior (Ajzen, 1991).

In TRA, an individual's intention to undertake a particular behavior is the central determinant of the behavioral outcome. This intention amounts to having a clear and concrete plan of action. It is built of two major factors: subjective norms and attitudes. Subjective norms refer to the perception the individual has of what most people important to him think regarding conducting or not conducting a behavior. Attitudes refer to positive or negative feelings toward performing the behavior (Ajzen, 1991). They are a consequence of what she thinks can be the outcome of performing the behavior and the value of these outcomes for her; attitudes are formed on such informational sources as beliefs, factual knowledge (Fishbein & Ajzen, 1975; 2010), and practical experiences (Pick, 2007). Previously unfavorable attitudes toward a specific behavior may be modified as she acquires new information. The TRA delineates intentions as the central precursor to behaviors and sees attitudes and subjective norms as the key antecedents to intentions.

The TRA served as a base for both IMIFAP's initial research and its program development, providing a clear definition of each of the components that were, at the time, understood to be antecedents of behavior. During a period when behavior change theory was grouping specific behaviors and their antecedents together as "behaviors," the TRA's distinction of antecedents as separate from behaviors enabled more precision in measurement and programming. Proving critical to the application of this theory by IMIFAP, however, was that the research behind the TRA focused on a literate and educated population and on behavior outcomes that were within the control of the participants. We found that among populations with low education—particularly in societies with tight social norms—intentions are not necessarily the immediate precursors to behavior. The formation of intentions, which by definition go beyond general desires, implies certain levels of both knowledge and control over the situation. In a situation of limited control or certainty, it makes little sense to form intentions, for they will almost certainly not come to fruition. Furthermore, people with few alternatives are lacking in articulate ideas about even their desired outcomes, hindering their ability to develop intentions. Attitudes are not articulated and people act according to the existing norms, neglecting choice because this is simply beyond the possibilities that can be imagined by an individual with a mindset of futility or helplessness.

In the late 1970s, an exploratory study was conducted (Pick de Weiss, 1978) to examine intentions among young men and women in marginalized areas of Mexico City. The sample was composed of about 150 individuals, all with low levels of schooling. In interviews, participants were asked about their intentions to engage in specific behaviors, such as using contraceptives the next time they had sex, drinking less the next time they went out with friends, vaccinating their children in the upcoming vaccination campaign, and going out to look for a job during the coming month. Phrases used included: "Do you have the plan to …?" "Will you do …?" "In what time period do you think you will be doing …?" "If all goes well would you carry out this plan?" Many reactions did not amount to a concrete answer. Phrases such as the following tended to be used: "I am ashamed," "It is not for me to decide," "It depends if my man allows me," "If God wants," "How can I know, it is not in my hands?" "Yes a person can have intentions, but then what? It is not a thing of his own." Smiles and laughter pointed to feelings of discomfort. People simply did not feel it was up to them to decide. They felt strongly limited by factors outside their control. Nélida, a teacher in greater Mexico City, explains how the context may create uncertain outcomes:

> If once I arrive at the clinic I do not know whether or not the doctor will take the time to see me, whether or not I will be attended to by the same physician I saw the last time, who seemed to understand my problem—after having seen several who did not and made me feel not too good … all of this leads to a feeling of not being able to anticipate, not being able to control anything regarding what I want; being no more than a wish—my life, my decisions, my choices are out of my hands.

In the same late 1970s study, a series of questions were designed to understand whether feeling control over time was a condition for having intentions. This was done in an indirect fashion. Participants were asked how long they would wait for a person they were expecting before they considered him to be late, and the reason for their answers. Many answered something like: "Well if the day is over and the person has not come I guess he is late," or "How can I know if he is coming; it does not depend on him wanting to. So I cannot say he is late, that would make him feel bad," or "Well, if he does not come I guess it is because it did not depend on him; who can know?" Such answers make sense in light of the numerous uncertainties for people with a minimal sense of control over their life. Conditions creating uncertainty—such as poor physical infrastructure, variable income, and pressing needs that take precedence over existing plans—limit the plausibility of someone actually arriving, let alone arriving on time. The study found that with control of time being so diffuse within these communities, members had difficulty developing and carrying out intentions.

Many testimonies specifically point to the importance of control in intention formation. An individual stated, "A person cannot know if he really wants something … it does not depend on him; it is decided 'there' by them, or who knows by whom." The relationship is thus conditional: intentions can exist only if basic control exists (Pick, 2007). Subjective norms were the aspect of the original TRA, which made most sense as an antecedent to behavior among these populations; social norms were the main guide for decision making and, therefore, for behavior in those groups living in tightly socially controlled circumstances.[3]

In summary, in communities where people are likely to have limited social support for taking initiative as well as a limited sense of control over their actions, the context becomes an inhibiting force to intention formation. Those intentions that are formed have a limited role in determining behaviors because they are often impeded by contextual factors; an individual is more an object than an agent of change.[4] Then, for behaviors to change in these communities, individuals need to gain both a sense of entitlement and an ability to take control over their actions. In this way, the context is no longer merely an inhibiting factor. Making choices becomes a common mode of functioning.

Thus, the foundations for this process are having both knowledge and an ability to reduce the psychological barriers that hinder individuals from seeing decision-making rights and opportunities. Practicing life skills hand-in-hand with specific knowledge and opportunities for reduced psychological barriers prepares participants for specific scenarios, such as responding to high-risk situations, deciding on a course of action, and realizing goals or specific behaviors. What follows is a focus on the way in which these foundations are missing in many communities that have limited social support for autonomous decision making, choice, and taking initiative.

Beliefs, Action, and the Need for Knowledge

In communities with low levels of education and limited access to a diversity of information resources, beliefs tend to be uniform and shared; established beliefs are seldom challenged (Halloran, Dunt, & Young, 1993; Kiefer, 1992; Waller, McCaffery, & Wardle, 2004). There is also a strong tendency for beliefs to be based on "myths" as opposed to "facts" (Pick, Poortinga, & Givaudan, 2003). Within the communities where IMIFAP implements its programs, we have come across a number of myths, including:

- A woman exists to serve her family and, therefore, her own health is secondary to that of the rest of the family.
- Taking birth control pills will lead to prospective babies piling up in the abdomen.
- Use of contraceptives leads to unfaithfulness and increased risk of illness.
- Putting crickets under a child's tongue will accelerate his speech development.
- Cancer can be transmitted through the air from the corpse of the deceased, thus being particularly easily transmitted to others during wakes.
- Looking at a man for too long will make you unable to think of anything else.
- The boiling of water will remove its vitamin content.
- Growing vegetables can lead to contagion with fertilizer.
- Clean-looking people cannot be a source of sexually transmitted infections.
- Using helmets for bike riding is promoted by the Americans to sell more helmets; it is foolish to wear them.

Myths surrounding behaviors can result in serious consequences. Gender role inequality myths have led to agriculture being divided into a "female/subsistence" sector and a "male/commercial" sector, putting money only into the hands of the men and thereby giving explicit value to the work of men. At the micro level, Adams (2004) refers to subjective beliefs playing a central role in producing objective realities regarding one's body. In a similar fashion, it is unlikely that a mother will boil the drinking water for her children if she believes that boiled water has fewer vitamins; that a woman will ask her husband to use condoms if she believes these have a high likelihood of breaking; that a man will begin to express his feelings if he thinks real men should not express any emotion except anger; or that a woman will expect her husband to stop hitting her if the same thing happened to her mother and her neighbors. With low levels of knowledge, often closely related to tight social norms and external control, choice is reduced. In fact, one of the myths often encountered in these contexts is that individuals should simply obey what is socially expected of them and not try to make autonomous decisions; they ought to accept external control as the basis for individual and social survival. This is a reason why situational demands often cannot be met.

Beliefs not only function at the individual level but also impact the societal norms of a community (Albarracín et al., 2001). Sexuality education, a controversial topic in Mexico, is often not included in school curricula because of pressure from conservative minority groups who believe that certain preventative sexual behaviors are a sin. The pressure leads to the development of a normative environment where such behaviors are socially unacceptable (Albarracín et al., 2001). In a community with low education and limited information resources, people are likely to base their decisions and actions almost exclusively on social norms. This leads to a self-reinforcing cycle in which beliefs feed norms, and these in turn serve to further limit possibilities for expanding choice, personal agency and having more control over one's life.

Beliefs are malleable and influenced by information, experience, and debate (Gasper, 2000). An important element of successful development programs is the provision of knowledge to counter factually incorrect beliefs, the social norms linked to them, and the resulting psychological barriers. Overcoming psychological barriers necessitates that knowledge provided in health-oriented programs go beyond the facts of a disease and include a focus on methods to prevent infection or to cure the disease (Mangrulkar, Whitman, & Posner, 2001; Wallerstein, 2006) and how to access them. Messages to enable a supportive social context for accessing knowledge and making use of it also need to be integrated. Concretely, a program that aims to disseminate knowledge about HIV as a sexually transmitted infection would teach not only how HIV is passed from one person to the next but also the options for prevention (using condoms, abstinence) and the means to treat the disease (antiretroviral drugs and their side effects). It would bring conscious awareness regarding the prevailing social norms and attitudes about the disease (e.g., societal stigmas against those with HIV and the reasons for these). Ideally, this provision of knowledge within a community would result in the reduction of stigma toward those who already have the disease and would impact social norms regarding protected sex.

Women's health and life-skills programs[5] do exactly this: aiming to help women develop the necessary tools to confront the beliefs and social norms that limit their capability set, through the provision of knowledge that is specific to each theme and to the reduction of psychological barriers. Patricia, a middle-aged female program participant from Oaxaca, explains how such provision of knowledge led to changes in behaviors among the women in her community:

> They give many courses about prevention. [Before the course] most fell sick from diarrhea and the flu. Then, they gave the training about preventing diarrhea … to wash food well, boiling water, putting bleach in water [for washing], peeling fruits and vegetables, taking out the trash, etc … we had all of these discussions about prevention.

She went on to explain how she now has more control over her health:

> I have more control because [there is] more information … I didn't know what could happen to us, if we didn't have a pap smear, a mammogram … or boil water. And now we do these things and we have more control over prevention and more chances to go to the doctor.

Her cousin Angelina further expanded on this idea to discuss control over her decisions and actions in the midst of social norms and expectations:

> Before we were afraid to go to the doctor … no one went. It was simply not done. We were ashamed of what people would think and of what the doctor would say. That was our way of doing things. If a woman would have gone to the doctor, for example because of a simple cold or knee pain, the others would have looked at it as bad. Also our husbands and mothers-in-law do not allow it. We are not supposed to take any initiative. Now that many of us have learned about [expectations and personal control in the workshops], it is easier to decide to go see the doctor for a problem even if it is not a really, really serious one. We have the support of others, and if someone says "Don't go," we know that it is better to go before the problem gets too big. And also [we know] how to say that it is our right and that it is okay to see a doctor and also to invite others to go too.

Going Beyond Knowledge: Skills and Competencies

Knowledge will only have an effect on behaviors in combination with appropriate skills. Research has shown that development programs that only focus on the provision of knowledge will not sufficiently lead to adoptions of new behaviors (Nation et al., 2003; Pick de Weiss & Andrade Palos, 1989; UNICEF, 2005; World Health Organization [WHO], 1999). Purely knowledge-based health promotion programs have done little to change attitudes, beliefs, and behaviors (Bartlett, 1981; Oberst, 1989; Smith, Zhang, & Colwell, 1996; Uchoa et al., 2000). For example, studies examining knowledge-based health education programs found that although the programs were effective in increasing knowledge, they were only somewhat effective in changing attitudes and were largely ineffective in changing health behaviors and practices (Bartlett, 1981; Daghio, Fattori, & Ciardullo, 2008; Evans, 1998; Parcel, Kelder, & Basen-Enquist, 2000). Other programs have produced even more dismal results (Cox et al., 2007; Elders, 1997; Perrucci & Wysong, 2007). For example, one knowledge-based middle-school smoking prevention program in Texas had no effect on students' knowledge, perceptions, or behavioral intent for smoking (Smith, Zhang, & Colwell, 1996).

Traditional education is based on transmitting information—that is, memorization. This methodology is effective at providing the student with new knowledge. When the goal is transformation of the knowledge into behaviors, however, the chance of this occurring as a result of traditional education is limited because the student may not have the skills or feelings of entitlement to utilize the information. In addition, when the prevailing social and psychological barriers are such that they limit the expansion of choice, utilizing new knowledge is simply not part of the psychological or social makeup. One is just not accustomed to looking for information or to postponing decision making until all the necessary information is gathered.

Although an individual may already possess certain skills because they are simply part of the human psychological makeup, they may not be employed because the social context does not encourage it. The context may even limit the use of particular skills as those in power see the outcomes as unfavorable to their interests. And other skills may need to be fully learned. The specific skills included from the start of IMIFAP's programming were derived from the adolescent focus groups held in the 1980s (Pick, Díaz-Loving, & Atkin, 1988). A decade later, when the WHO developed its list of most essential skills and termed them "life skills," it became clear that there were strong similarities between the approaches developed by the two organizations (Mangrulkar, Whitman, & Posner, 2001; WHO, 1999). The life skills that were identified by the WHO in conjunction with CSOs and governments were based on their cumulative research and programming experience, when they came together in the early 1990s to develop the concept of life skills. In recent years, the "Life Skills Approach" has become a prominent international strategy (Mangrulkar, Whitman, & Posner, 2001; Pick, Givaudan, & Poortinga, 2003; WHO, 1999).

The United Nations Children's Fund defines life skills as "a large group of psycho-social and interpersonal skills which can help people make informed decisions, communicate effectively, and develop coping and self-management skills that may help them lead a healthy and productive life" (UNICEF, 2004). The Pan American Health Organization sees life skills as consisting of social skills, cognitive skills, and emotional coping skills (Mangrulkar, Whitman, & Posner, 2001). In effect, they are "abilities for adaptive and positive behavior that enable individuals to deal effectively with the demands and challenges of everyday life" (WHO, 1996, p. 72). A "Life Skills Approach" teaches this subset of basic skills that are most essential for adopting positive behaviors.

Key elements of life skills programs that successfully lead to behavior change include: informational content, skills development, the use of interactive teaching methods, and the opportunity to practice skills newly realized during instruction (WHO, 1996). When we discuss "skills" in Programming for Choice, we are referring precisely to life skills. Life skills education enables children from very early ages to employ their capabilities for their personal development; in turn, they use skills to influence others and their social context. This makes Sen's Capability Approach operative at the most basic level.

The end target is not only to address the specific demands but also to have the foundation upon which to expand individual choice in a range of situations. Recently, the Organization for Economic Co-Operation and Development (OECD) built on the WHO's concept of life skills to address in a comprehensive fashion both specific situational demands and the varying aspects of the broader context. For this, the OECD has employed the term *competencies*, defined as "the ability to successfully meet complex demands in a particular context" (Rychen & Salganik, 2003, p. 43). A competency is a complex action system that implies the mobilization of knowledge, cognitive and practical skills, and social and behavioral components such as attitudes, emotions, and values and motivations (Rychen, 2003). A competency allows an individual to address multidimensional challenges. The list of OECD competencies was developed from a multicountry/multisectoral study aimed at identifying those relevant in OECD countries (Salganik & Stephens, 2003).[6] Competencies are crucial because within our complex, diverse, and interconnected world, they are prerequisites for a successful life and a well-functioning society. They permit individuals to not only cope with but also to shape the world (Rychen, 2003). As stated by the OECD Education Ministers, "sustainable development and social cohesion depend critically on the competencies of all of our population" (OECD, 2001, p. 6).

In Sen's terms, just as having freedoms is both a means and an end in itself, the same is true with competency building. Competencies are useful to achieve functionings and to expand freedoms; they facilitate the development of new tools and choice. Just having them provides a sense of security— she knows that she possesses the elements necessary to approach a variety of situations, even with little planning. Having competencies allows a woman to trust her own judgment and capacity for problem-solving. Considering that education centers around the human being, it is clear that schooling should go beyond reading, math, and writing. In a very direct way, "I Want to, I Can" is a means of operationalizing the Capability Approach within the classroom.

Programs are ultimately intended to enhance competencies, not only specific skills. Ideally, government policies and education systems would support this. Governments hold a central role in the process, as they manage the public education system, and it is through education that skills and competencies can be taught. Local governments can train teachers in skill and competency building, and can work to ensure that the educational system is structured so as to support such integral learning.

Developing Competencies: The Foundation for Behavior Change

IMIFAP sees skills as the foundation for competencies and thus as the point of departure for programs that aim to expand choice. Skills are formed in relation to specific situational demands and are put into action through behaviors, which—as will be explained in detail in Chapter 7—come about as a result of a gradual process. Skills are enhanced as opportunities in the context arise, and as the individuals become adept and confident at utilizing them in increasingly complex situations, skills slowly transform into competencies. The IMIFAP approach to developing competencies through programming mimics the way in which the process occurs naturally. This is grounded in Bandura's Social Learning Theory (1997), which explains that children learn to behave through both instruction and observation as well as through the results and the responses of others to their behaviors. The theory concludes that real-life teaching methods, meaning those involving social interaction, are a fundamental means of replicating the natural processes by which individuals learn behavior (Ladd & Mize, 1983).

Life skills, such as effective communication and negotiation, are thus taught in the context of specific thematic knowledge and situations, such as planting vegetables, using latrines, or having a pap smear. Participants are encouraged and provided with the opportunities to broaden the application of these skills through repetition under circumstances of increasing complexity and diversity. Reflection is supported to identify how to extend the skills to other spheres. As individuals strengthen their abilities to adapt skills to those necessary for the particular context or situation, competencies will be enhanced, and their application will increasingly become routine. With these competencies, possibilities of new behaviors—that is, choice—are expanded (this point will be made clear in the examples of exercises provided in this chapter). From there, competencies enable personal agency and intrinsic empowerment.

A conscious focus on this broadened application of skills is particularly important for work within traditional societies, as numerous studies have shown that learning in these societies may be generalized and transferred less than in societies with extensive formal education (Segall et al., 1999).

Life Skills in IMIFAP Programs

Life skills are taught as a foundation in all IMIFAP programs. When IMIFAP teaches these life skills (e.g., communication, decision making) in conjunction with information specific to the program's thematic content, we call them "specific life skills." Thus, general communication becomes communication about obtaining job training, substance abuse, and difficult topics with parents, or asking a question in the classroom. By utilizing exercises geared specifically toward the development of particular skills, the skills become competencies that can be applied across situations. Workshops are based in participatory and reflective methodology to facilitate social learning: hearing an explanation of the skill in question, observation of the skill (modeling), practice of the skill within selected situations in a supportive learning environment, and feedback about individual performance of skills. These methods provide participants with the opportunity for reflection, social support, reinforcement of behaviors, and clarification of doubts.

To ensure that the skills extend beyond the workshop, programs aim to facilitate comfort with and application of the skills in daily life (Sheridan, Hungelmann, & Maughan, 1999). Participants are assigned to practice specific skills outside of workshops to achieve the sense of comfort needed for using the skills in the real world. Such assignments are particularly useful when they involve participants' families and communities in the programming. As participants start to apply their new skills in natural settings, they will be reinforced by others who find them socially desirable because they respond to *their* needs as well.

The following section outlines the basic skills taught in IMIFAP programs: decision making; communication; negotiation; self-knowledge; identifying and managing emotions; empathy and perspective-taking; and reflection. The skills addressed in greatest detail are decision making and communication. These are the most basic and central for enabling choice across existing opportunities. The skills we present here are not the totality of those being taught in IMIFAP programs; these were selected especially for this discussion because of the opposition, or at least lack of support, that we have often found among conservative groups for enhancing them. Definitions are based on existing literature, as well as on experiences and observations from IMIFAP programs. The description of each skill includes specific exercises and testimonies about how IMIFAP participants experienced these skills in the workshops. With a similar practical basis, we also facilitate problem solving, understanding the consequences of an individual's actions, and value clarification.

Decision Making

IMIFAP defines decision making as choosing between two or more options after analyzing each option's advantages and disadvantages (Pick et al., 1995). Decision-making processes are influenced by: others (e.g., family and peers), accessible information, and personal experience. In IMIFAP programs, the role of each of these factors is discussed as well as the difference between making uninvolved and involved decisions (Pick, Givaudan, & Martinez, 1997).

Uninvolved decisions are those decisions that include any of the following components: others making the decision; not making the decision; deciding impulsively; postponing decision making; allowing luck or destiny to decide. The concept of "magic thought" (as exemplified by the practice of writing requests for favors or thanks for those that occurred, onto pieces of tin), and typical sayings such as "If God wants," "If it so happens," "If by a miracle," reflect the norm in Mexico of making uninvolved decisions. There are many consequences from this reliance on external forces. Most centrally, it allows people to avoid making decisions and taking responsibility for the consequences, be they related to work, health, or participation in the community.

Involved decisions, on the other hand, include any of the following components: evaluating different options before deciding; obtaining information before deciding; evaluating the consequences of decisions; and planning the desired outcome and acting accordingly to achieve that outcome. In conditions of uncertainty, such as in remote rural and indigenous communities and in many urban communities in developing countries, it is much harder to make involved decisions; there simply is not the necessary predictability, control, or social support in place for this to be part of the way things are done. Therefore, getting involved and planning is initially only minimally relevant. It is through opportunities to participate that participation becomes part of the scheme of things and in that way, little by little, brings about involved decision making.

Typical in Mexico is the practice of *el acarreo* (being pulled in), where politicians provide a payoff, such as food, in exchange for a vote or support. A relationship then results where politicians make large demands of communities but concurrently provide a payoff so the people will perform. This occurs because so many individuals in power are accustomed to asserting their control in this way, and because so many people are accustomed to responding to external demands instead of their own. They simply are not accustomed to making decisions autonomously, but rather are used to doing so in an uninvolved manner. Similarly, the practice of controlling what others read is a way of limiting autonomous decision making. Juan Manuel, a student from a private, conservative university in Mexico City, commented:

> I was reading Nietzsche and a few weeks earlier I had gone onto the Web looking for Octavio Paz. I was called into the office of the coordinator of student affairs and asked why I had an interest in such damaging books.

A mother of a student at a private Catholic elementary school, also in Mexico City, refers to her experience:

> We ask for permission from the school to read any materials, because they "take care of our minds." A woman I recently met gave me some books to read that dealt with gender equality and how to make decisions—someone who saw me reading the book ratted on me. I was told if it happened again I would have to leave the group of mothers that were teaching values to the students.

IMIFAP's "I Want to, I Can" programs repeatedly stress that this life skill is both socially acceptable and beneficial, and workshops support participants in following a multistep process of involved decision making:

1. Obtain information about the decision.
2. Analyze your own values and needs so that your final decision will be in accordance with them.
3. Make a list of advantages and disadvantages of each option.
4. Estimate the probability of each option's success, as more probable options are more likely to bring about the desired goal.

5. Analyze the consequences in the short, medium, and long term.
6. Make your decision.
7. Evaluate the results—Are they what you had hoped for? If they are not, think about what you should do next time to obtain the results you want.

This approach is similar to those components more recently highlighted by the WHO as important in decision making: information gathering, evaluating future consequences of present actions for oneself and others, analyzing the influence of values on one's motivations to act, and determining alternative solutions to problems (2003).

IMIFAP programs also emphasize a number of principles regarding decision making. These principles have been detected by IMIFAP as absent among its target populations and have been identified as necessary for the acceptance of and ability to make choices. They are: everyone has the right to make decisions regarding his personal life, everyone takes risks all the time and every decision implies a risk, analysis of advantages and disadvantages is necessary, and making decisions means we are responsible for the consequences (e.g., deciding to not be clean has consequences for our health).

The following (*see* Figure 6–1) is an exercise used in programs for developing decision-making skills that focuses on making involved decisions.

La Mano en la Bolsa (The Hand in the Bag)

- The facilitator divides the group into four teams.

- The facilitator asks a member of each team to come to the front of the room and pull a slip of paper from a bag. Each slip of paper has one decision written on it, for example: "Take care of my health," "That the village dump gets cleaned up," "That my daughter learns about menstruation," "Go to the clinic when there is knee pain," and so forth. The facilitator or participant reads what is written.

- The facilitator next explains what decision making entails and its importance, especially in the sense of having control over outcomes rather than attributing or leaving them to luck, destiny, etc.

- Participants must then decide if the decision read by the teammate has been left to luck or is an active decision made by the individual.

- Next, the facilitator solicits examples of behaviors that come about through uninvolved decision making as well as examples of those behaviors that come from involved decision making.

- The facilitator asks questions that include: "What advantages lie in leaving decisions up to luck/fate/others?" "Why shouldn't belief in luck/fate influence decisions?" The facilitator emphasizes that by not making a decision, we allow something or someone else to make the decision for us.

- A discussion follows around questions such as: How did you feel when group members said they could or could not do something, in that they could decide whether or not to do it? What reasons exist for not making your own decisions?

FIGURE 6–1 Decision Making Exercise

Overcoming the view that decisions are outside of the individual's control is a necessary precursor to the decision-making process, particularly because many individuals in IMIFAP's target populations—especially women—often blindly accept what fate brings, as well as others' ideas, wishes, and decisions. These attitudes result from perceived lack of control over one's decisions as well as from fear of appearing unknowledgeable, opinionated or insulting someone; they feel others are probably more knowledgeable, and they are unaccustomed to expressing their thoughts and opinions. It is important to note that there are different exercises for each step of the decision-making process.

This and other decision-making exercises emphasize that everyone can learn how to effectively make decisions by following certain steps and undertaking practice (Venguer, Pick, & Fishbein, 2007). This realization can be monumental for participants, as is expressed in the following testimonies:

> My favorite exercise was the one on how to analyze the advantages and disadvantages of making a decision. It made me realize that I can make decisions and how to do it. I used to think that decisions were something out there … that things somehow happened … now I see that it is something I can hold in my hands, look at, caress, carry around with me and do … and if I take the wrong one, *I* took it and *I* can change that, and if *I* took the right one, *I* did it and *I* can be proud *I* did it.
>
> —Female participant in "I Want to, I Can … Care for My Health and Exercise My Rights," Quetzaltenango, Guatemala

> It was amazing to learn that everyone can learn to make decisions … not only the important people … I can look at all the good and bad aspects of a decision and I can make it … it should not make anyone feel bad that I make decisions … we all have that right, and it is not easy to make decisions but we can all learn.
>
> —Teenage boy after the "I Want to, I Can … Care for My Health and Exercise My Rights" program in secondary school, Lima, Peru

Communication

For the purpose of IMIFAP programs, communication is defined as a process through which we give and receive information, it is an exchange of ideas, feelings, and experiences, allowing us to express our wishes and needs, among other things. Communication consists of both verbal and nonverbal components and is seen as a key skill for interpersonal relationships. Under circumstances of strong social opposition to using direct and transparent communication, programs must address not only the skill itself but also the underlying reasons why it is not used. In this way, people will recognize their rights and the importance of open communication. Sen (1999) discusses the instrumental freedom of transparency. He highlights its relevance in prevention of corrupt business and political practices, occurrences at the macrolevel or contextual level. At the microlevel, social acceptance of transparency in social interactions is equally central to developing clear and direct communication and facilitating negotiation, in lieu of circular, indirect modes of communication.

Important in this regard is the reduction of psychological barriers, such as shame and fear, which impede engagement in effective communication. Building of skills is a means to simultaneously develop competencies and address an individual's context; it is a direct way to enhance intrinsic empowerment, which is more likely to be sustainable.

IMIFAP programming on effective communication includes the components detected by exploratory research and workshops as missing among the target populations: verbal/nonverbal communication, active listening, expressing feelings, and giving and receiving feedback (Pick, 1991; Pick, Díaz-Loving, & Atkin, 1988). Organizations ranging from the Pan American Health Organization and the WHO to UNICEF additionally highlight these specific components and have an understanding of them similar to that of IMIFAP (Mangrulkar, Whitman, & Posner, 2001; UNICEF, 2008; WHO, 2003). The WHO has identified communication as one of its five basic areas of life skills that are relevant across cultures (1999).

NONVERBAL COMMUNICATION

Within Latin America, cultural norms and gender issues combine with lack of communication skills to bring about general timidity, shame, and fear at expressing oneself. This often brings a speaker to keep her head down to avoid looking into the recipient's eyes and engage in talk that is more circular than direct, or not to engage in speech at all. What is said verbally often does not correspond to nonverbal messages displaying submissiveness and a lack of confidence. This is one of the specific communication topics addressed in workshops.

Constructive nonverbal skills include:

- Maintaining eye contact—which helps undertake sincere, confident, and emphatic communication.
- Body posture—standing and facing the other delivers a stronger message than other postures.
- Distance and physical contact—which can affect factors such as intimidation and provocation.
- Gestures—which can emphasize a message, but which often depend on the culture and individual.
- Facial expression—which should agree with the verbal messages.
- Tone, volume, inflection of voice—gives emphasis and clarity of expression.
- Fluidity—referring to the ability to speak calmly, directly, and without interruptions.
- Prolonged silences—which give the impression that the individual knows what he is talking about and is responsible for his words.
- The right moment—this refers to understanding when and when not to say something so as not to provoke an argument that will not resolve any issues.
- Listening—which is important for validating what another person is saying and appearing respectful, and is also critical for negotiation and expressing empathy.

Sin Palabras (Without Words)

- The group is divided into pairs.

- The facilitator asks the pairs to identify one person as "A" and the other as "B".

- The facilitator then asks person A to communicate to person B what he/she did the day before—but without using any words, only gestures.

- After 2 minutes, the partners switch roles.

- After another 2 minutes, the facilitator asks both members to discuss (with words) what they were trying to say and determine if the other was able to understand.

- Next, the facilitator asks three pairs to share their experiences: whether it was easy or difficult and whether they understood each other and why.

- Upon completion, the facilitator discusses communication and explains what it is, why it is necessary, the differences between verbal and nonverbal language, and the importance of consistency between the two.

- Afterward the facilitator asks for a few volunteers to provide examples of instances in which they said certain things while their body language said something different.

FIGURE 6–2 Nonverbal Communication Exercise

The following (*see* Figure 6–2) is an exercise focused on nonverbal communication. It is aimed at illustrating the importance of body language and other nonverbal communication and also provides a chance to practice such communication.

A young participant, Joel, described how recognition of his nonverbal communication changed his approach:

> I used to not ask anything, never question anyone … whatever they said I would just say yes with my head … now I say yes or no with words and with my eyes … and it is okay.
>
> —Joel, fourth-grade student, "I Want to, I Can … Prevent Drug Use," Chiapas, Mexico

ASSERTIVE COMMUNICATION

Assertive communication is clear, direct, and expressive without insulting others and is a critical component of effective communication. Assertive communication may also take place nonverbally, as was visible in the following example. In Chilpancingo, Guerrero, Mexico:

> Nahuatl indigenous people blocked access to the local congress in order to ask the congressmen to require the … mayor of the town of Xalpatlahuac … to work from his municipal office. For more than two years the mayor has worked from the town of Igualita [located further away].[7] ("Piden retorno," 2007)

In Latin America, assertive communication is seldom used and is often confused with aggression. Children are taught to be nice to others by not saying what they think; "nice" people are largely more socially accepted than those who openly voice disagreements or contrary opinions. Many women, in particular, do not want to appear aggressive by pushing for changes. As a result, rather than using confrontation and proactive attempts to address situations, interpersonal disputes often result in gossip and complaints to others, or excuses and appeasement are preferred over concrete answers as seen below. The occurrence of scenes such as the following is not unusual:

> *Client*: We have been asking when the computer system will be working as it should.
>
> *Computer specialist*: Sir, we are doing everything we can and are here to give you the best service possible.

Based on such norms and individual needs detected by IMIFAP, elements of assertive communication stressed within workshops generally include:

- Making wise decisions (e.g., including friendships and relationships, how many children to have, money allocation).
- Taking initiative for well-being (e.g., starting conversations, planning activities).
- Confidence in actions (e.g., not depending on others to make things to happen).
- Defending rights without guilt or anxiety (e.g., being able to calmly confront others).
- Knowing when and how to say "no" (e.g., putting limits to work, time).
- Not allowing others to criticize or belittle when expressing one's opinions.
- Honestly expressing emotions without feeling bad for the other person (e.g., expressing disagreement, anger, fear, sadness).
- Not denying the rights of others (e.g., not criticizing unjustly, intentionally hurting others, insulting, manipulating, controlling, intimidating).

These components are developed and expanded as new needs are detected. IMIFAP programs further teach communication together with responsibility. Focus is placed on how communicating directly and clearly is a way of being responsible while it is also stressed that communication should be utilized to respond appropriately for the consequences of one's actions.

The following (*see* Figure 6–3) is an exercise designed to foster assertive communication skills. Coming at the start of the thematic module, the exercise largely teaches the skills for and addresses hindrances to such communication.

The exercise above and others similar to it allow individuals to experience first-hand how clarity and directness in communication reduce misunderstandings, are not necessarily aggressive or incompatible with kindness, and can be socially acceptable.

As has been mentioned repeatedly, the opportunity to practice what one has learned is key for skills development and utilization. The following case illustrates this specifically for communication skills: In Santiago, Chile, IMIFAP invited to a radio program a teacher who had extensive training in the "Planning your Life" program. Her response was, "There is no way I can do that. I work

Yo Siento, Yo Pienso, y Yo Digo (I Feel, I Think, and I Speak)

- The facilitator describes assertiveness and assertive communication and explains that all people have the right to say what they think and feel and that it is important to learn how to do so in a clear, direct, and respectful manner.

- The importance of speaking in the first person, using "I," is also emphasized to stress taking responsibility for one's words. For example, instead of a statement such as "That kid is so rude!" it is clearer and less insulting to use statements such as "I really don't like the way that girl speaks," or " I feel badly when children talk that way to their elders."

- Next, the group divides into two teams and chooses a name for their team. The facilitator announces the team names loudly and with applause (this supports participants' identity).

- Each person, alternating teams, takes their turn coming to the front of the room and pulling a slip of paper with a statement on it out of a bag. The facilitator asks if the participant wants to read it or if he/she wants the facilitator to read it (supporting participants' decision making).

- Next, the group member has to change the statement to one beginning with "I".

- The teams receive a point for each sentence that is successfully transformed. The facilitator determines if the group earns this point by comparing the newly transformed sentence with the list of possible assertive statements. In the case that a participant cannot transform the sentence, someone from the other team can take his/her place but must choose a new sentence.

- The exercise continues until all the sentences have been picked.

- The team with the most points is the winner and gets a huge round of applause.

- A discussion follows around questions such as: Why is it sometimes difficult to clearly and effectively express yourself? What happens when a person does not clearly express his rights? How can unassertiveness affect a person? What makes certain communication aggressive? Is it due to shame and fear that we are not more assertive? What makes us feel ashamed or scared of being assertive? Is this way of communicating a means to reduce misunderstandings? What can we do to overcome these barriers?

- As in all exercises in the "I Want to, I Can" workshops, participation of each member in the group is encouraged and facilitated. In this way social participation, experience with the issue at hand, and social supports, are all built up in parallel.

FIGURE 6–3 Assertive Communication Exercise

in this very poor area. I also live there. Take someone who can speak better than I can. [It is one thing] to talk in the workshop, another on the radio." An IMIFAP staff member responded by asking her "How about coming with me just to watch so that one day you can do it?" and she responded, "Well, I will come along just to go into the city." Once on the radio program the announcer asked her some questions, and she started answering and answering, until she actually started making spontaneous comments as well. As she came out and the announcer congratulated her, she said, "Well, once I saw I could talk and that neither the microphone nor you would bite ... once I heard myself doing it, what I had learned came together and I believed in it, and it just kept going."

Comments made by program participants on effective communication illustrate its undervalued importance. Participants build the skill to effectively communicate their feelings and thoughts as well as a sense of their right and ability to do so:

> In respect to the skills they taught us, I can say now that the most important thing is communication, to be able to express what you're truly thinking without feeling bad about it. I feel that I can talk to my kids more....The same goes with my husband ... Also for negotiating ... Now when they hire me or ask me for a sweater or for empanadas, I can negotiate. And when I want something that my husband doesn't want, I know how to negotiate and how to convince him, because I've realized that I'm important too. He now tells me that he needs me whereas before he never did that.
>
> —63-year-old female participant in "I Want to, I Can ...
> Start My Own Business" and "I Want to, I Can ...
> Prevent Violence," Iztacalco, Mexico City

> I have always been ashamed of asking for things. In "I Want to, I Can ... Prevent Cancer," I learned that I can ask the doctor to explain things to me. I went to the clinic the other day and asked him, "Can you please speak slower? I do not understand what you are saying."
>
> —Sonia, middle-aged female participant, Michoacan, Mexico

> I like that now I can talk about different matters with the women in the community. ... In the courses we talk about what we feel, what we need, we say what we think. I learned that it is okay to say what I think and not only what others want to hear.
>
> —Eugenia, female health promoter, "I Want to, I Can ...
> Provide Better Health Services" participant, Bogota, Colombia

When individuals dare to be open and assertive, community censorship often becomes severe, not only in small or marginalized communities but in the society at large. External control over decision making and the use of shame, fear, and guilt as means of control are prevalent in many developing countries. A student was scheduled to talk at the inauguration of a program called Safe Schools, at which the Minister of Education would be present. The program focused on checking students' backpacks for drugs and weapons. She was told to be spontaneous and say whatever she thought was relevant to the issue of having a safe school, but nothing "negative." Because it was discovered beforehand (when an authority asked to see what she had written) that the talk would include reference to the fact that in her school drugs and weapons were being exchanged, she was asked to take out the "negative" parts (Hernández, 2007). IMIFAP programs address censorship while discussing communication. Because community censorship is likely to arise initially when individuals adopt a more assertive communication style, these individuals need to exercise the skills enabling them to manage this censorship. Exercises include role-plays in which program participants negotiate with local and federal authorities.

Effective communication is a basic skill upon which competencies can be built to engage in different kinds of communication under different circumstances. In addition, it is important to point out that through effectively communicating needs, interests, and desires, it broadens the potential for communicating one's choices and in this way expands his capabilities. Together with decision making, effective communication is at the most basic level of skills required to further facilitate freedoms.

Negotiation

IMIFAP sees negotiation in interpersonal relationships as seeking a solution together, with the understanding that to do so, all parties must view it as being not about one individual winning but rather about searching for a middle ground. It is a life skill based on effective communication and may be limited by those same social norms that limit effective communication. These foci are in line with the guidelines of the WHO, where effective negotiation is said to include conflict management, assertiveness skills, and refusal skills. IMIFAP programming places further importance on being able to stay calm, rational, and objective, rather than resorting to lies, deception, and power struggles.

The following (*see* Figure 6–4) is an exercise designed to foster negotiation skills. It takes as its point of contention whether or not to attend a training program. Because this is ultimately an individual choice, the exercise is equally about making an informed choice by considering the pros and cons of a decision as it is about negotiation skills:

Taken together, negotiation exercises emphasize the role of clear, rational communication in defending rights and achieving desires. This skill can be successfully fostered in anyone with practice. The outcomes are discussed by participants:

> My father wanted me to be a lawyer. For some reason, he had it in his head that I—or one of my sisters—had to be a lawyer. Before the IMIFAP program I told him that I would be one ... but afterwards I realized that this was a mistake. The program helped me to grow according to my own criteria; before I only did what my father wanted in order not to disappoint him. Later in the program, I learned how to negotiate with him because he didn't want me to go into town for work, he said it was dangerous and a waste of time. But seeing as I wanted to do it, I did, and he just had to resign himself to that fact. So, when I decided that I didn't want to continue studies to be a lawyer either because it wasn't what I wanted, well, it didn't come as much of a surprise to him and I could negotiate it with him. Well, I told him that I was going to study management and not law, but that he wasn't going to have to pay a penny because I was going to pay myself, because I was going to try to get a scholarship—because in the workshop they told me there are scholarships. That way, my father wouldn't have to pay. And so I got the scholarship and he had no other option except to let me study what I wanted. The scholarship is for all of university studies where you have to maintain an average of 9.9 or 10 [out of 10]—if not they take it away. As a result, I have to study a lot. In this way, I get 10,000 pesos [approximately 800 USD] per month from the government.
>
> —Ricarda, 23-year-old female participant in "I Want to, I Can ...
> Prevent Cancer," Oaxaca, Mexico

El Debate (The Debate)

- After discussing key points about effective communication and negotiation skills, the facilitator explains that in a debate, two or more people argue different points of view, and each tries to convince the opponent that in his or her opinion, his or her own view is correct.

- Next, the facilitator states that there will be a debate in which some program participants will debate and the rest will observe and give feedback.

- The facilitator asks for 8 volunteers, half of whom will hold the "yes" position and the other half the "no" position. A drawing is held to determine the two sides; those individuals who draw colored slips of paper are the "yes" side.

- The point of debate is why one would or would not want to attend a human development training program, such as the one in which they are currently participating. Debaters then have 10 minutes to come up with at least 10 reasons that support their opinions.

- The non-debaters are instructed to attentively observe and be prepared to comment on the following techniques at the end of the debate: use of nonverbal communication skills, whether or not they were able to hear the debaters, use of the first person and collective tenses such as "I" and "we," speaking at the right moment, and clarity in defending views.

- The debate then takes place, with teams facing one another. Each team has 5 minutes to explain its reasons.

- After both teams have stated their views and rationales, the debaters have 10 minutes to discuss (negotiate) and come to an agreement about whether or not an individual should attend the human development training program to ensure his or her greatest benefit.

- Next, the observing individuals are given 5 minutes to organize their ideas and present their observations of the debating teams.

- As the observers present, the debaters are encouraged to defend themselves when they feel the observers are incorrect about something, as well as to accept their mistakes.

- After a round of applause and congratulations, a discussion takes place around the following questions: Why do you think it is important to participate in exercises about effective communication? How did it feel to see that you are able to defend your point of view? What is the difference between defending a group's rights versus defending your own rights?

FIGURE 6–4 Negotiation Exercise

A while ago I was a victim of fraud and I didn't know how to fight for my rights; instead I just got depressed, not knowing what to do. See, when I bought land to build on they told me the land was on the edge of a freeway with lots of services nearby, and as it turns out, when we saw it, they were doing our building on a piece of land very far from the freeway in an area without a single service nearby. So, we had to organize. There were things from the workshop that helped me a lot, like how to deal with people and how to organize among women. I learned how to listen, to speak, and [to] speak clearly without overwhelming the other person. Because of the program "I Want to, I Can ... Prevent Cancer," I learned that I have rights and that I can fight for them.

—Sofia, middle-aged female program participant in "I Want to, I Can ...
Prevent Cancer," Michoacan, Mexico

Self-Knowledge

Facilitators inquire about the feelings that emerge as a consequence of defending one's rights and standing up for oneself. The responses are generally in terms of more self-confidence and higher self-esteem. These opportunities for building self-knowledge encourage the formation of personal agency as the person realizes that she can be in possession of and enjoy the new ways of being and the mindset that comes with them.

IMIFAP defines self-knowledge as "our ability to know who we are, what we want, and what we like or dislike. To know ourselves is to see ourselves as a whole: with a physical body, our own inner world of thoughts and feelings, an ability to connect with others, and an ability to care for and protect ourselves" (Pick et al., 2006, p. 25). Self-knowledge is also emphasized by the WHO (2003); the WHO's Skills for Increasing Personal Confidence and Abilities to Assume Control, Take Responsibility, Make a Difference, or Bring About Change include "creating self-awareness skills, including awareness of rights, influences, values, attitudes, rights, strengths, and weaknesses" and "self-evaluation/self-assessment/self-monitoring skills."

The importance of self-knowledge is highlighted in workshops; people with extensive self-knowledge are more:

- Prepared to face difficult situations, like an unwanted pregnancy, as they have experienced that they have the ability to resolve problems.
- Creative when following their own life paths. They are able to seek various alternatives for each situation that arises and do not simply do what is expected of them
- Confident in finding and creating new opportunities.
- Ambitious with regard to what they expect from life, because they know their worth and will not settle for less than a full life, a good job, great friends, etc.
- Capable of establishing deeper, richer relationships with others and seeking a supportive companion. Also open to surrounding themselves with people who will help them grow.
- Respectful of diversity, because they accept themselves and can therefore accept others even when they are different.

These are all goals of human development programming because they reflect personal development.

As with most programmatic exercises, the following "My Labels" exercise (*see* Figure 6–5) includes discussions of socio-cultural norms. As mentioned before, Latin American education—both formal and informal—often employs tools such as threats, shame, pride for the sake of appearance, and denying or not recognizing one's defects and virtues. Through their use they are transmitted to the students as values. As an individual tries to understand herself, these ways of educating (for educators) and their effect on personal traits (for students) can be overcome. Workshops emphasize that the discovery of self-knowledge should be an awareness-building process occurring with openness to feelings, assessment, and thought. Therefore, self-knowledge is broached gradually across many exercises, especially in the later workshops of a program when people feel more at ease with reflective processes. The process is neither simple nor brief.

The importance of self-knowledge and its transformative ability are expressed in the following testimonies:

> [T]here is a saying that goes: "I change myself, I change the world." We have to start with ourselves. We have to learn to love ourselves. When we arrived at the workshop, we were all of the opinion that it would be a workshop like any other, but we soon were able to see that this one was different. This one is like a chain that continues from the teacher to the student, from the student to the community, and from the community to society.
>
> —Alberto, teacher and Academic Coordinator, "I Want to, I Can …
> Care for My Health and Exercise My Rights," Chiapas, Mexico

> I realized that with these workshops, the children can develop skills and attitudes that will help them to have social relationships that are more beneficial to their well-being. Each activity in the training workshop made me think about myself and about my role as an educator. It made me face up to my emotions, my strengths, and [my] weaknesses. We didn't keep our noses in the texts but learned interactively. They didn't teach us methods to memorize, but we learned through experience; we built a new image of what it means to be a teacher.
>
> —Miguel Angel, teacher who participated in "I Want to, I Can …
> Be a Better Parent (of Children Under 12)," Chiapas, Mexico

---

Mis Etiquetas (My Labels)

- The facilitator gives participants four name tags and asks participants to remember how they were labeled as children.

- Participants are given 5 minutes to write a label on each name tag and put the name tag on.

- Next, they form a circle. A box is placed in the center. For the next 5 minutes participants are asked to think about the following questions: How did you acquire these labels? Who reinforced them? What labels limit you in your personal, emotional, and social development?

- Each participant then is invited to approach the box in the middle and to remove any labels they do not want or they wish to modify. The facilitator states, "Right now we all have the opportunity to leave behind or modify those attributes or labels we do not want for our personal growth."

- A discussion follows regarding topics such as: How did you feel when recalling those labels and placing them on yourself? How do labels affect people's lives?

FIGURE 6–5 Self-Knowledge Exercise

It is through the active process of building the individual's self-knowledge that he can become more open to identifying his needs, engaging in new experiences, and accepting and giving constructive criticism with others.

Identifying and Managing Emotions

Emotion identification and management refer to understanding one's emotions and communicating them in a manner that allows one to indicate internal states, motivations, wishes, and needs (Mangrulkar, Whitman, & Posner, 2001). Each person expresses his emotions in different ways, depending on previous experiences, learning, character, and the current situation. For example, it is commonly accepted in Latin America, as well as in the United States and other countries, that males do not and should not express certain emotions, specifically those that are believed to be a sign of weakness. If these are to be demonstrated, it should be through anger—verbally or physically aggressive behaviors.

Workshops teach about these sources of an individual's emotion identification and management. Facilitators emphasize that everyone has a right to express what he feels and needs and bring to light how failing to do so increases stress levels, anxiety, and interpersonal problems. Program concepts include naming emotions and communicating them, not letting emotions control us, and knowing how to effectively channel emotions, and from there move on to foster participants' abilities to recognize emotions in others. For practical reasons, this is done with focus on the most common emotions, including fear, surprise, aversion, anger, happiness, sadness, and love. Like most other life skills, the skill is presented across varying thematic exercises as a means of reinforcing its development.

In the following exercise (*see* Figure 6–6), emphasis is placed on allowing oneself to feel and positively express emotions rather than repressing them.

The following testimonies demonstrate the outcomes of successful emotion management:

> Now that both my husband and I express our anger and sadness in a clear way and without crazy acts, we both grow. My husband is committed to the relationship because he now understands that I also have power. I am no longer afraid of also getting angry. I now understand that I too can get angry and that he can cry.
> —Middle-aged female participant in "I Want to, I Can …
> Care for My Health and Exercise My Rights," Hidalgo, Mexico

> I used to think that if I was sad, I could not say so because she would look down at me, so I would yell. Men are supposed to be strong. Also in that way I would keep her under my boot, so to say. Now I understand that I can say that I am worried or sad, and it is okay, and I can ask her to do things for me without threatening her.
> —Trinidad, middle-aged male participant in "I Want to, I Can …
> Prevent Violence," Mexico City, Mexico

Like the other life skills, knowing one's emotions and understanding different ways of expressing them and the impact this can have on interpersonal

Alegría y Tristeza (Happiness and Sadness)

- The facilitator gives each participant a blank sheet of paper and asks them to fold it inhalf.

- Markers are placed in the middle of the room and accompanied by music that suggests sadness. The facilitator then says, "Please close your eyes and think of a sad moment in your life. Who was there? What was it like? Give yourself time to remember this moment."

- After 3 minutes, the facilitator asks the participants to open their eyes and on one half of the paper, draw the sad moment they thought of.

- After finishing this drawing, the facilitator plays music that suggests happiness and, says, "Now close your eyes again and think of the happiest moment of your life. Who was there? What was it like? Give yourself time to remember."

- After 3 minutes, the facilitator asks them to open their eyes and draw the happy moment on the other half of the paper.

- Next, the facilitator requests that the participants observe both drawings and ask themselves: If they had a chance to undo one of those moments, which would they choose?

- After placing a trash can in the middle of the room, the facilitator asks them to cut the drawing that represents the moment they want to undo and throw it into the trash.

- The participants are then instructed to take a piece of tape and stick the remaining drawing to another sheet of paper.

- The exercise is followed by a discussion allowing for reflection. Questions presented include: "How did you feel during the exercise?" "Why did you decide to throw away that particular drawing?" "When you feel sad or happy, what do you do to express or positively manage these emotions in your personal life or, for facilitators, in the classroom?"

- The concluding discussion is based on the role of identifying and managing expression of emotions in supporting self knowledge, personal development, and interpersonal relationships.

FIGURE 6–6 Managing Emotions Exercise

relationships is fundamental for well-being and for expanding access to opportunities. Adequate expression of emotions can be conducive to the expansion of capabilities.

Empathy and Perspective-Taking

The capacity to feel empathy is the ability to imagine what life is like for another person in a very different situation. Empathy incorporates the "ability to listen, understand another's needs and circumstances, and express that understanding" (WHO, 2003, p. 13). It helps students to understand and accept diversity, and it improves interpersonal relations between diverse individuals (PAHO, 2005). It also facilitates strong interpersonal relationships on the whole, as it allows for greater cooperation and acceptance.

There is often confusion between showing empathy and sympathy. Whereas the former implies support and understanding on an equal one-to-one basis, the latter is associated with pity and reflects top-down interaction. Clarification of this difference is essential in life skills programming in Latin America, because showing sympathy rather than empathy is frequent and indicative of the paternalistic social, political, and educational systems. Program participants also encounter difficulty in expressing empathy because of their inability to distance themselves from the situation to the degree necessary to have such feelings. A Mexican Jungian psychologist describes how this situation derives from the strong limitations in the individual's interpersonal relationships:

> When one's own limitations are big, one must focus only on oneself; there simply is no space to incorporate others' needs and perspectives. When the father is so distinctly outside the family relationship, so devalued, and therefore so limited in his possibility of bringing balance in the triad, the bond ends up being composed of the mother and the child. Yet also because this relationship is based on fear, anger, and guilt on the part of the kid, it is hard to grow up being able to see beyond himself; he simply is too immersed in himself, in his own situation, limiting his possibility for becoming strong enough to be able to express empathy toward others. (Julieta Besquin, personal communication)

To develop and enhance healthy interpersonal relationships, showing empathy is necessary. This does not imply giving advice but, rather, sending a message that you are listening, accompanying, and trying to understand the feelings and experiences of the other. Both cognitive and emotional empathy, as well as nonverbal communication skills and body language are therefore heavily emphasized in the "I Want to, I Can" programs. The impact of empathy on self-knowledge is discussed in workshops, given that exercises such as the one below (*see* Figure 6–7) also allow participants to reflect on their own emotional needs:

Empathy enables individuals to listen more openly to others:

> [The workshops] helped me listen to constructive criticism because it's difficult to accept criticism and to change. To listen to your colleagues saying you did this and that wrong and listen to them saying we can do it better is hard, but it's good. Each time I'm about to make the same mistake I remember their words and I try to do it differently. I think it's very important to know how to listen and criticize in a positive manner.
>
> —Socorro, teacher, participant in "I Want to, I Can …
> Be a Better Citizen," Coahuila, Mexico

Workshops also encourage participants to motivate and teach others to have this same interest in people, allowing for the possibility of radical changes in the social environment in which they live.

Validando/No Validando (Validating/Not Validating)

- The participants form two groups, with one of the groups leaving the room.

- The facilitator asks the group outside to think of an important event in each of their lives and to choose a group member to go into the room and share his or her event.

- To the group inside the room, the facilitator explains that half of them must listen to the person from outside who will be sharing her experience with them and they must try to make her feel that the experience is validated. This should be accomplished through respect, silence, and body language. The other half of the group is to do the opposite, through verbal and nonverbal communication that indicates they are not listening or validating what the person is saying.

- After doing this, the teams switch roles and repeat the activity.

- After 10 minutes, all participants form a circle for discussion. Those who shared their experiences are asked: "Did you feel validated and respected by the others?" "How did you feel when the others expressed these attitudes?" The rest of the participants discuss questions such as: "How did you validate or not validate what the person experienced?"

FIGURE 6–7 Empathy Exercise

Reflection

Reflection provides an opportunity for assessment and deeper processing, attributing outcomes to a particular cause and providing a chance to modify future behaviors. Archer has described how this takes place in the form of internal conversations (2003). Reflection therefore serves the inherent purpose of allowing the individual to think, feel, and consider. It precedes behavior change but also occurs as a result of such change. People make conclusions about their capacities and capabilities based on observing what they can and cannot do. Recognizing what they or fellow workshop participants have achieved also brings them to recognize the achievement that they may be able to reach.

Reflection is a skill that, like so many others taught in the "I Want to, I Can" programs, is part of human makeup. Most of what the programs do is simply open the space for the application of these skills by presenting the opportunity to put them into practice or, in other words, creating the "feeling there is permission" to do so. In an educational system that focuses on memorization and obedience and a work structure that focuses on the latter, having opportunities for reflection is a new experience.

For this reason, reflection is a key part of the methodology of many exercises (*see* Figure 6–8). The skill itself is realized through practice in specific exercises geared toward its development and in the question-and-answer and

Pasado y Presente (Past and Present)

- The facilitator instructs participants to close their eyes and focus on their breathing. The facilitator then asks them to bring to mind their interpersonal relationships 10 years ago. "What were your attitudes?" "Which people were important to you?" "What did you achieve by being the person you were at that point in time?"

- Participants then open their eyes, and the facilitator distributes a pencil and piece of paper to each individual. They are instructed to draw the person they were 10 years ago, including the characteristics they just remembered.

- After 10 minutes, the facilitator once again asks participants to close their eyes and focus on their breathing. Participants are instructed to reflect on the person they are today. They are asked to think about: "What are your attitudes now?" "What are your relationships like with the people with whom you live?" "Which people are important to you today?"

- Participants are instructed to again open their eyes and take up pencil and paper, this time to draw the person they are today, including the characteristics they thought about.

- After 10 minutes, the facilitator asks participants to pair with a partner and share their drawings, describing how their life experience has affected their personal growth.

- A reflection period follows in which various questions are put forward by the facilitator: "What differences do you see between the two drawings?" "What is your main reflection from this exercise?" "How has your life experience affected your personal growth, in all senses (relationships with friends, family, partner, etc.)?"

- The concluding discussion addresses how getting in touch with who we used to be and who we are now allows us to understand how we have changed over time, appreciate how we have grown through our life experiences, and examine who we are today.

FIGURE 6–8 Self-Reflection Exercise

discussion sections of all exercises; as such, it is targeted to become a competency that can be applied across situations.

> As I attended that [workshop] and started reflecting on the different possibilities I actually had for doing things, I realized how being able to choose among them could open new doors.
>
> —Miguel, male adolescent participant in "I Want to, I Can …
> Prevent Violence," Texas, United States

> When I saw that the other women were asking questions and saying what they thought, and reflected on their doing so, I came to the realization that it was okay to do so, I felt I could then also say what I felt.
>
> —Dolores, middle-aged woman participant in "I Want to, I Can …
> Take My Life in My Own Hands (Program for Domestic
> Workers)," Morelos, Mexico

What was the worst that could happen? I thought about the fact that it would be perhaps that my mother would stop talking to me, but in exchange I would have a better life with at least a few more chances of success.

—Ariela, adolescent participant in "I Want to, I Can … Care for My Health and Exercise My Rights," Chimaltenango, Guatemala

Reflection is a key skill for understanding what one's values are and understanding the basis on which they have been developed and the priority each one has for the individual. Personal agency and intrinsic empowerment are continued growth processes in which reflection plays a central role. Questioning of the context, reflecting on alternatives that are more in accordance with his real needs and those of the community, reduction of psychological barriers in accessing those alternatives, achieving new functionings, and thus expanding his capabilities are results of putting this skill into practice.

Conclusions: From the Antecedents of Choice to the Actual Expansion of Freedoms

Life skills education has been shown to have a positive effect on essential aspects of development: basic education; gender equality; democracy; good citizenship; disease prevention; healthy child and adolescent development; childcare protection; quality and efficiency of the education system; the promotion of life-long learning; quality of life; predictability; preparing young people for changing social circumstances; and the promotion of peace (WHO, 1999). The reason for this is that hand-in-hand, life skills and knowledge are the most basic components of making informative choices and addressing individual needs. They function at a more basic level than technical or work skills, serving as the point of departure from which other skills can be built and complemented. Life skills may even open the door to acquiring the more technical skills and competencies.

As noted earlier, people generally possess these skills; they are very much part of the human psychological make-up. Yet many individuals in Latin America have been socialized to emphasize modes of behavior that are socially constrained, such as "blindly sticking to the rules." Once such models of behavior become dominant and are perceived as the only option, the *modus vivendi* itself is limiting to personal and community development. The use of basic skills is truncated. As the common saying goes, "What one does not use, dies."

In Programming for Choice, people are provided with knowledge and given the opportunity to practice the skills that they tend to underuse. They become comfortable using them and so begin to see the potential to apply them in a variety of situations of varying degrees of difficulty. This enhances not only their functionings but also their capabilities. The new behaviors that result (deriving from choices that were made) may be ones that the individual was unaware he could undertake. The change from passively waiting for something to happen to making it happen is the beginning of a life that can go from helplessness and hopelessness to actively shaping one's own future; from lack of control over the context and unpredictability to internal control; from passive expectation to active participation.

As with many new experiences, realizing one has choices and making them a reality can be both a pleasant and a scary experience. After all, making choices (understood by Sen as expanding freedoms) implies a responsibility as well as a risk and, therefore, a reorientation in the way the individual looks at himself and his own development. Sen states clearly the bi-directional relationship:

> The linkage between freedom and responsibility works both ways. Without the substantive freedom and capability to do something, a person cannot be responsible for doing it. But actually having the freedom and capability to do something does impose on the person the duty to consider whether to do it or not, and this does involve individual responsibility. (1999, p. 284)

Growth and development never come easily and, as is so often the case with choice, they tend to be accompanied by mixed feelings. The process of change is not a magic wand, neither for the individual nor for society. As Carmen Aristegui has said, "It takes longer ... but that is what democracy is like"[8] (2005). Life skills programming is about building citizenship and responsibility and opening the doors for a thriving democracy. When individuals have skills and knowledge to access and respond to their needs and to expand their choices and opportunities, society will be strengthened. Moreover, investing in individuals will augment the impact of governmental and nongovernmental programs and policies. The result is a cycle of positive and productive reinforcement between individuals and their communities that facilitates the *human* basis required for breaking the poverty cycle in a way that can be sustainable.

Notes

1. Situational demands are the tasks demanded by the situation in order to address or solve it

2. A more recent version of this theory is the Theory of Planned Behavior (Ajzen, 1991). When IMIFAP started its work, the Theory of Planned Behavior had not been developed and we used the Theory of Reasoned Action (Fishbein & Ajzen, 1975) as a base for developing our first programs. We wanted a theoretical foundation and this theory was the clearest and most systematic at the time. The Theory of Planned Behavior was later developed as a complement to the Theory of Reasoned Action and it adds control as a precursor. In our practical experience, this newer theory is closer to explaining behavior change among populations with little control over their lives, as it considers the central role that externalities play in decision-making and ultimately behavior change.

3. More recent versions of the TRA are in line with FrEE insofar as they confirm that an intention to engage in a behavior will be achieved only once a person feels that he or she can successfully implement a behavior (Fishbein et al., 2003); intentions by themselves are not sufficient.

4. Although the TRA did not broach these issues, later modifications, such as the Integrative Model of Behavioral Prediction (Fishbein, 2000), a further extension of the

Theory of Reasoned Action and the Theory of Planned Behavior, have attempted to do so. This later model suggested that impediments to behavior change, especially among underprivileged groups, can reside in attitudes, norms and psychological barriers in the social context. Although this later model fails to address specifically shame, guilt, fear, and the issue of low skill levels among populations with low education, it was a welcome advancement at the time and supported IMIFAP's further understanding of the relationship among context, intention formation and behavior change.

   5. For example, "I Want to, I Can ... Care for My Health and Exercise My Rights,", "I Want to, I Can ... Prevent Violence," "I Want to, I Can ... Prevent Cancer," "I Want to, I Can ... Start My Own Business."

   6. Although the study was conducted within the developed OECD countries, the competencies identified coincide with those targeted by IMIFAP programs historically. This correspondence could be an indication that competencies address general human needs.

   7. "Indígenas nahuas bloquearon los accesos del Congreso local para pedir a los diputados que obliguen al alcalde ... de Xalpatláhuac ... a que regrese a despachar los asuntos de gobierno en la cabecera municipal. El edil despacha desde hace más de dos años en Igualita."

   8. "Es más tardado, pero así es la democracia."

References

Adams, V. (2004). Equity of the ineffable: Cultural and political constraints on ethnomedicine as a health problem in contemporary Tibet. In P. Anand & A. Sen (Eds.), *Public health, ethics and equity* (pp. 283-94). Oxford: Oxford University Press.

Ajzen, I. (1991). The theory of planned behavior. *Organizational Behavior and Human Decision Processes,* 50(2), 179–211.

Albarracín, D., Johnson, B. T., Fishbein, M., & Muellerleile, P. A. (2001). Theories of reasoned action and planned behavior as models of condom use: A meta-analysis. *Psychological Bulletin,* 127(1), 142–161.

Archer, M. (2003). *Structure, agency and the internal conversation.* Cambridge: Cambridge University Press.

Aristegui, C. (2005, September 30). Acuerdo nacional [National agreement]. *Reforma,* Retrieved January 15, 2008, from www.reforma.com.mx

Bandura, A. (1997). *Self-efficacy: The exercise of control.* New York: W.H. Freeman & Co.

Bartlett, E. E. (1981). The contribution of school health education to community health promotion: What can we reasonably expect? *American Journal of Public Health,* 71(12), 1384–1391.

Cox, S. M., Allen, J. M., Hanser, R. D., & Conrad, J. J. (2007). *Juvenile justice: A guide to theory, policy and practice* (6th ed.). Thousand Oaks/Newbury Park, CA: Sage Publications.

Daghio, M. M., Fattori, G., & Ciardullo, A. V. (2008). Health education 'at the cross-roads'. In L. V. Sebeki (Ed.), *Leading-edge health education issues* (pp. 83–108). Hauppauge, NY: Nova Science Publishers.

Elders, M. J. (1997). *Preventing tobacco use among young people: A report of the Surgeon General.* Atlanta, GA: Centers for Disease Control.

Evans, V. (1998). Training the drugs educators: Quality assurance for schools. In L. O'Connor, D. O'Connor & R. Best (Eds.), *Drugs: Partnerships for policy, prevention and education. A practical approach for working together* (pp. 8693). Herndon, VA: Cassell.

Fishbein, M. (2000). The role of theory in HIV prevention. *AIDS Care,* 12(3), 273–278.

Fishbein, M., & Ajzen, I. (1975). *Belief, attitude, intention, and behavior: An introduction to theory and research.* Reading, MA: Addison-Wesley.

Fishbein, M., & Ajzen, I. (2010). *Predicting and changing behavior: The reasoned action approach.* New York: Psychology Press (Taylor & Francis).

Fishbein, M., Hennessy, M., Yzer, M., & Douglas, J. (2003). Can we explain why some people do and some people do not act on their intentions? *Psychology, Health & Medicine,* 8(1), 3–18.

Gasper, D. (2000). Development as freedom: Taking economics beyond commodities - the cautions boldness of Amartya Sen. *Journal of International Development,* 12, 989–1001.

Halloran, J., Dunt, D. R., & Young, D. (1993). Coronary risk factors, knowledge and beliefs in "blue collar" men attending general practice. *Australian Family Physician,* 22(3), 351–355, 358.

Hernández, M. (2007, Febrary 22). Promete SEP atención de 3 dependencias. Inicia el blindaje en secundarias. [SEP promises the attention of 3 dependencies. It initiates the shield in junior high school]. *Reforma,* p. 6.

Kiefer, R. (1992). El SIDA y la infección VIH pediátrica: El problema de la madre infectada y de su recién nacido [AIDS and pediatric HIV infection: The problem of the infected mother and her newborn]. *Revista Latinoamericana de Psicología,* 24(1–2), 157–167.

Ladd, G. W., & Mize, J. (1983). A cognitive-social learning model of social-skill training. *Psychological Review,* 90(2), 127–157.

Mangrulkar, L., Whitman, C., & Posner, M. (2001). *Life skills approach to child and adolescent human development.* Washington, DC: Pan American Health Organization.

Nation, M., Crusto, C., Wandersman, A., Kumpfer, K. L., Seybolt, D., Morrissey-Kane, E., & Davino, K. (2003). What works in prevention: Principles of effective prevention programs. *American Psychologist,* 58(6–7), 449–456.

Oberst, M. T. (1989). Perspectives on research in patient teaching. *Nursing Clinics of North America,* 24(3), 621–628.

Organisation for Economic Co-operation and Development [OECD] (2001). *Investing in competencies for all.* Paper presented at the Meeting of the OECD Education Ministers: Investing in Competencies for All. Paris.

Pan American Health Organization [PAHO] (2005, February 25). Life skills Retrieved October 19, 2007, from www.paho.org/English/DD/PUB/SP579_04.pdf

Parcel, G. S., Kelder, S. H., & Basen-Enquist, K. (2000). The school as a setting for health promotion. In B. D. Poland, L. W. Green & I. Rootman (Eds.), *Settings for health promotion: Linking theory and practice* (pp. 86–119). Thousand Oaks/ Newbury Park, CA: Sage Publications.

Perrucci, R., & Wysong, E. (2007). *The new class society: Goodbye American dream?* Lanham, MD: Rowman & Littlefield.

Pick de Weiss, S. (1978). *A social psychological study of family planning in Mexico City.* Unpublished Thesis, University of London, London.

Pick de Weiss, S., & Andrade Palos, P. (1989). Development and longitudinal evaluation of comparative sexuality education courses, *Report presented to the United States Agency for International Development.* Mexico City: IMIFAP.

Pick, S. (1991). Training of instructors for the implementation of "Planeando tu Vida" in public high schools in the State of Mexico, *Report presented to the United States Agency for International Development.* Mexico City: IMIFAP.

Pick, S. (2007). Extension of theory of reasoned action: Principles for health promotion programs with marginalized populations in Latin America. In I. Ajzen, D. Albarracín & R. Hornik (Eds.), *Prediction and change of health behavior: Applying the reasoned action approach* (pp. 223–41). Mahwah, NJ: Lawrence Erlbaum Associates.

Pick, S., Aguilar, J. A., Rodriguez, G., Reyes, J., Collado, M. E., Pier, D., Acevedo, M. P., & Vargas, E. (1995). *Planeando tu vida [Planning your life]* (6th ed.). Mexico City: Editorial Limusa.

Pick, S., Díaz-Loving, R., & Atkin, L. (1988). Adolescentes en la Ciudad de México: Estudio psicosocial de prácticas anticonceptivas y embarazo no deseado [Adolescents in Mexico City: Psychosocial study of contraceptive practices and unwanted pregnancy], *Report presented to the Pan American Health Organization and the United Nations Fund for Population Activities.* Mexico City: IMIFAP.

Pick, S., Givaudan, M., & Martínez, A. (1997). *Aprendiendo a ser papá y mamá [Learning to be dad and mom]* (2nd ed.). Mexico City: Editorial IDEAME.

Pick, S., Givaudan, M., Olicón, V., Beltrán, M., & Oka, S. (2006). *My voice, my life. A training program to prevent teen pregnancy.* Mexico City: Editorial IDEAME.

Pick, S., Givaudan, M., & Poortinga, Y. H. (2003). Sexuality and life skills education: A multistrategy intervention in Mexico. *American Psychologist,* 58(3), 230–234.

Pick, S., Poortinga, Y. H., & Givaudan, M. (2003). Integrating intervention theory and strategy in culture-sensitive health promotion programs. *Professional Psychology: Research & Practice,* 34(4), 422–429.

Piden retorno de alcalde [The mayor is asked to return] (2007, January 24). *Reforma,* Retrieved January 24, 2007, from www.reforma.com.mx

Rychen, D. S. (2003). *Definition and selection of competencies: Theoretical and conceptual foundations (DeSeCo): Summary of the final report "Key competencies for a successful life and a well-functioning society".* Neuchâtel, Switzerland: OECD.

Rychen, D. S., & Salganik, L. H. (2003). *Key competencies for a successful life and a well-functioning society.* Göttingen, Germany: Hogrefe & Huber Publishers.

Salganik, L. H., & Stephens, M. (2003). Competence priorities in policy and practice. In D. S. Rychen & L. H. Salganik (Eds.), *Key competencies for a successful life and well-functioning society* Cambridge, MA: Hogrefe & Huber Publishers.

Segall, M. H., Dasen, P. R., Berry, J. W., & Poortinga, Y. H. (1999). *Human behavior in global perspective: An introduction to cross-cultural psychology.* Boston: Allyn and Bacon.

Sen, A. (1999). *Development as freedom.* New York: Anchor.

Sheridan, S. M., Hungelmann, A., & Maughan, D. P. (1999). A contextualized framework for social skills assessment, intervention, and generalization. *School Psychology Review,* 28(1), 84–103.

Smith, D. W., Zhang, J. J., & Colwell, B. (1996). Pro-innovation bias: The case of the Giant Texas SmokeScream. *Journal of School Health,* 66(6), 210–213.

Uchoa, E., Barreto, S. M., Firmo, J. O., Guerra, H. L., Pimenta, F. G., & Lima e Costa, M. F. (2000). The control of schistosomiasis in Brazil: An ethnoepidemiological study of the effectiveness of a community mobilization program for health education. *Social Science & Medicine,* 51(10), 1529–1541.

United Nations Children's Fund [UNICEF] (2004). Definition of terms. Life skills Retrieved October 4, 2007, from www.unicef.org/lifeskills/index_7308.html.

United Nations Children's Fund [UNICEF] (2005). Life skills-based education in South Asia. A regional overview prepared for the South Asia Life Skills-Based Education Forum. Kathmandu, Nepal: United Nations Children's Fund.

United Nations Children's Fund [UNICEF] (2008). Life skills: Which skills are life skills? Retrieved June 11, 2008, from www.unicef.org/lifeskills/index_whichskills. html.

Venguer, T., Pick, S., & Fishbein, M. (2007). Health education and agency: A comprehensive program for young women in the Mixteca region of Mexico. *Psychology, Health & Medicine, 12*(4), 389–406.

Waller, J., McCaffery, K., & Wardle, J. (2004). Beliefs about the risk factors for cervical cancer in a British population sample. *Preventive Medicine, 38*(6), 745–753.

Wallerstein, N. (2006). *What is the evidence on effectiveness of empowerment to improve health?* Copenhagen, Denmark: World Health Organization Regional Office for Europe [Health Evidence Network Report].

World Bank (2007). *World development report: Development and the next generation.* Washington, DC: World Bank.

World Health Organization [WHO] (1996). *Life skills education: Planning for research.* Geneva: World Health Organization.

World Health Organization [WHO] (1999). *Partners in life skills education: Conclusions from a United Nations inter-agency meeting,* Geneva.

World Health Organization [WHO] (2003). *Skills for health: Skills-based health education, including life skills: An important component of a child-friendly/health-promoting school.* Geneva: World Health Organization, United Nations Children's Fund, United Nations Educational, Scientific and Cultural Organization, United Nations Fund for Population Activities, World Bank, Education Development Center, and Partnership for Child Development.

CHAPTER 7

Behavior as Choice

Mexico urgently needs to escape from its predators [of poor democratic governance and corruption], and it will only be achieved through... building a citizenry capable of writing letters and challenging elites and starting independent organizations and fomenting civic norms and shaking consciences and scrutinizing authorities and advocating in favor of the public interest[1].

—Denise Dresser (2008)

As the previous chapter illustrated, the provision of skills and knowledge facilitates the development of autonomous choice. Exercising this choice translates into concrete behaviors or, in Sen's terminology, the development of new "doing functionings." Dresser's quote refers precisely to the kinds of behaviors required for social development. Focusing here on the Behavior frame of the FrEE diagram (*see* Fig. 4–1b), we move from the cognitive foundations presented in the previous chapter to concentrate on behavior formation.

Behavioral outcomes are not present immediately after an individual uncovers skills and acquires knowledge; they occur as part of a longer process. This view is compatible with World Bank recommendations for facilitating behavior change in preventive programs offering essential health and nutrition services (Cabañero-Verzosa, 1999; World Bank, 2006, 2007). the difficulty of moving directly to behaviors from skills and competency building, attainment of knowledge, and reduction of psychological barriers. The development of autonomous choice is an interactive process, at times irregular. Steps backward sometimes follow steps forward, so monitoring and feedback are important throughout the process. Literature asserts that the main outcomes of programs include changes in precursors to behavior, followed by new behaviors at the individual level.

Sen (1999) acknowledges that negative choices can be built in this process, and in fact these unintended consequences can be predicted. In discouraging the development of potentially negative choices, means of social control and a well-defined ethical framework are indispensable. Social regulation of this kind also increases overall sustainability.

In this brief chapter, we examine the behavior change theory, which provides the foundation for FrEE. We then investigate how changes in concrete behaviors can impact more stable aspects of the person, or being functionings. Adjustments at this level are represented in the "Person" frame of the FrEE diagram (*see* Fig. 4–1b).

Behavior Change As an Outcome

The Stages of Change Model, developed by Prochaska and DiClemente (1982; Prochaska, DiClemente, & Norcross, 1992) some years after the Theory of Reasoned Action discussed in Chapter 6, has made an important contribution to the study of behavior change. It illustrates how a behavior does not emerge in a single step, but rather in a sequence of steps. It complements the Theory of Reasoned Action, asserting that predecessors of behavior exist, but goes further by looking specifically at these predecessors as part of a series of stages in behavioral development. The specificity of this model lends itself to developing and assessing program strategy.

Stages of Behavior Change

The introduction of stages is valuable in modeling the mechanism of behavior change (Fawcett et al., 1999). The development of choice and the recognition of alternative worldviews entails a process, which vacillates between new and old forms of action. The stages of change are:

- Stage 1. *Precontemplation*—A person may not be happy with a certain state of affairs or may feel it is wrong, but the possibilities for change are not (yet) recognized and articulated.
- Stage 2. *Contemplation*—There is acknowledgment of a need that can be addressed. The individual begins to deliberately increase his awareness and knowledge related to the problem and its solution.
- Stage 3. *Preparation for Action*—At this stage, the individual begins to reevaluate his needs. He commits to change and develops an intention and a plan to conduct the behavior.
- Stage 4. *Action*—The person undertakes the change in behavior.
- Stage 5. *Maintenance*—Vigilance is required to avoid relapse to previous stages or older behaviors. Once the change is part of the person and has become so automatic that there is little or no possibility of reverting to a previous stage or undesired former behavior, maintenance has been achieved and behavior is stable.

The early stages of behavior change are cognitive. People first contemplate the possibility of taking action, then what to do and how to do it. In the later

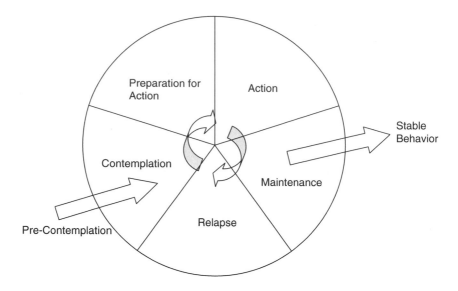

FIGURE 7–1 Stages of Change Model

stages, they recognize the possibility and make it a reality. Juana, a middle-aged woman in Michoacan, Mexico, explains her process of deciding to participate in the program "I Want to, I Can … Prevent Violence":

> At first I thought there was no way I would go to those meetings with the other women. I had learned that being scolded and beaten is part of life … that it is one's cross to bear. I asked my friends what they did and learned in those meetings. I had to ask my mother to take care of my daughter so I could attend. I was not very convinced, but at the same time, I wanted to hear what they did there, so I went once. I got very scared of what they were saying; they even talked about leaving one's husband because no one should be subjected to violence. I thought it over some more and started going more regularly, though not every Tuesday because sometimes my mother could not take care of my child. It was not easy, but I went because a part of me knew that it was not fair to get treated like that.

The Stages of Change Model (SCM) (*see* Fig. 7–1) describes this process, which was also noted in field observations of Programming for Choice. We rely here on the model to propose this dynamic understanding of behavior change, and we have integrated the model into our "Behavior" frame. FrEE strengthens the SCM as a template for behavior change because it elucidates for programmers and policy makers the reason that behaviors take time to change and provides a concrete strategy for planning programs and budgets.

The SCM sees stable, long-term changes as contingent on changes within a person—on a mental and emotional progression. For this internal process to occur, change cannot be externally imposed. Nor do external factors such as new laws or economic incentives lead directly to change. Such factors may provide support or open opportunities, but ultimately it is the person who will make the change; the individual is an active and key participant in the process. The elements of FrEE are in accordance with this view and further stress that if the context is the only source of support, then changes in the person and mindset—and thus sustainable change—are less likely to occur.

> I never thought I would end up daring to go to the doctor for a check-up of my woman parts, much less talking to other women about it. Many of us in the community have had cancer—many have died, even younger ones. And we saw it as normal, as part of being a woman. It was as we started getting involved in the "I Want to, I Can ... Prevent Cancer" program that I began to consider for the first time the possibility of talking with my husband and getting a check-up. Once I realized that I had the right to live a life without being accused, beaten, and threatened and made to feel like I was worthless and I learned how to say things more directly, I started thinking of ways to talk to him. I went to speak with friends, also with my mother. I also spoke with the health promoter [who was the "'I Want to, I Can" facilitator] several times and practiced with her how to say it and how to negotiate. Then one day I told my husband about what I had learned in the workshop; he did not believe me that one could get a test for [cancer]. He kept saying it was just because I wanted pleasure with the doctor that I wanted to do it, so I asked him to come along to talk to the doctor. Finally he accepted and stayed with me during the test. I did not like that, but it helped me be able to have it every year. I have now had the Pap test every year for 3 years and have helped organize groups of women and their husbands to convince them that it is important and that it can save lives. Many women have followed in my steps and I am proud of that.
> —Ana María, middle-aged woman, Michoacan, Mexico

The SCM assumes that people are accustomed to weighing the pros and cons of specific behaviors. Among groups with low educational levels or tight normative systems, where decisions tend to be driven by others, the process of decision making and recognizing an individual's choices cannot be taken for granted. It is, however, a necessary cognitive skill that must be accepted as an entitlement. For this reason, the SCM cannot be directly employed in a program for individuals with low education levels, but must be modified to support them in moving from the contemplation stage to the action and maintenance stages.

IMIFAP has found that when introducing the SCM in these communities, it is important to foster a realistic perspective on the process, knowledge, and skills it will involve before encouraging behavior change. FrEE provides a means to instill individual understanding of what the acquisition and maintenance of a behavior entails. Having and being able to use the skills necessary for maintenance is similar to identifying the tools required for a carpenter's job. The role-playing techniques of "'I Want to, I Can" programs (see Chapter 6) address this aspect of the SCM sequence by allowing participants to acquire a sense of the prerequisite behavior, skills, and methods. For example, they may notice the need to communicate their decision in a clearer manner or learn more about the behavior in question. At this point, they may experience what Malotte et al. (2000) describe as "self-liberation," a new way of self-understanding. Role-playing facilitates the development of the skills and knowledge necessary to support intentions by repeatedly putting them to small tests.

One of the biggest challenges in program development and implementation is maintenance of the new behaviors. It is difficult to ensure that people continue new behaviors once the facilitators are no longer present. Along with an individual's developed sense of self and ability, which is a natural result of Programming for Choice, supportive social and structural environments with continuous assessment and feedback ease the progress of behavior maintenance (Nation et al., 2003). Ideally, actions undertaken by program participants at the behavior stage must also work to expand community support networks, which support participants to continue healthy behaviors after the termination of the training sessions.

The behaviors that emerge from an internal process of building skills and knowledge constitute "refined functionings." As explained by Sen (1987), the individual here possesses not only "achieved functionings" but also potential "alternative functionings." These differ from functionings that merely arise as the result of increased access to one commodity. Such functionings attained through external means are achievements that are not necessarily accompanied by a capability; these will not lead to further achievement.

Generalization from Concrete Behaviors to Nontargeted Outcomes

Recent reviews of the literature and meta-analyses have shown that programs to promote health can have effects beyond the behaviors that were targeted (Flay, 2002). This extension of learning to a broader array of situations is generalization (Flay, 2002), or "expansive learning" (Engeström, 2000). As skills are applied to a broader and more complex array of situations, the individual is able to generalize these skills in such a way that they become competencies applicable across a range of behaviors. With the development of competencies and the internalization of behavior change successes, the individual comes to understand that both change and choice enhance freedoms. It is this understanding and acceptance of choice that leads to changes beyond those originally targeted in a program.

There has been extensive debate over the best strategy for bringing about the attainment of key competencies. Programs that focus on a single thematic area, such as drugs and substance abuse (Botvin & Griffin, 2002), sexual risk behaviors, sexually transmitted infection and HIV prevention (Kirby, 2002; Magnani et al., 2005), mental health (Dwivedi & Harper, 2004), or violence reduction (Farrell & Meyer, 1997; Fawcett et al., 1999; Flannery et al., 2003) have impacted targeted behaviors, as have comprehensive life skills programs (Flay, 2002; Pick & Givaudan, 2007; Venguer, Pick, & Fishbein, 2007). The distinction is that the purely monothematic programs bring about change less frequently beyond their particular areas of focus, whereas comprehensive programs, such as Programming for Choice, more consistently drive change in multiple areas. The latter engender a mindset of personal agency more immediately and across a wider range of behaviors, increasing prospects for generalization of personal agency. In Sen's terms, freedoms expand to new domains; he explicitly points to the connections between different kinds of freedoms as integral to development (1999).

Flay (2002) shows that comprehensive programs are valuable because of the foundation of common skills and personal agency that develop through targeting multiple behaviors, thus providing diverse opportunities for generalization. He explains that the process of generalization requires cross-sectional opportunities, which allow individuals to make connections between the base skills used to address different opportunities and constraints. The more comprehensive the program, and the greater the incorporation of base skills, the more generalized the changes will be. This is also the case with programs that focus on a single theme but also provide a base of common skills and personal agency. This foundational approach is also more cost-effective.

Ramiro, a secondary school student in Guatemala City, Guatemala, described the transferability of skill sets that evolved through programmatic support when he recalled his experience in the comprehensive "'I Want to, I Can ... Care for My Health and Exercise My Rights" program:

> At first we learned to apply decision making, communication, and problem solving to issues of being clean, eating healthfully, and also to certain aspects of civics; then we used this basis to talk about more complicated things. It was great to see how the same skills could be applied to different problems in life. By sixth grade, workshops were much more focused on sexuality and drugs, and other more difficult aspects of life. I learned to analyze before taking action, I can make decisions, say what I feel, defend my position on different issues (some very controversial), understand my values, and compare them to those of others. ... It is as if I have a bigger lens through which I see the world...and now I not only speak, but I look fully and I am an active part of my world ... [the program] taught me to think big, to take into account many more things, and [to] decide which ones I take and which ones I leave.

Maria de los Angeles, a mother of three in Lempira, Honduras recalled a similar experience in the "'I Want to, I Can ... Care for My Health and Exercise My Rights" program:

> At first I was really happy to have learned about the importance of not only getting wet to get clean but of also really washing, scrubbing each part of my body. Then I started bathing my kids really well too and talking to others about this. And then we learned about what vegetables to eat and how to keep them clean; [and] about the importance of boiling water. All this made me think about other things I did not know, and I started looking for more information. I even started organizing groups in the community to plant things that were healthier and I got us organized to go to the municipal president to get running water in the community. We had asked him many times before, but now we had the information and courage to insist.

Although evaluations reveal that comprehensive programs are highly effective, the reality of providing life skills education as a Latin American CSO is that the intervention structure is sometimes compromised by time, availability of personnel, funding specifications, financial constraints, and political issues. With this in mind, we have integrated monothematic modules, all focusing on a common skills base, into comprehensive programs that can be provided in a modular fashion, such as the "'I Want to, I Can" programs described in Appendix A.

The effectiveness of IMIFAP's modular programs in changing multiple target behaviors has been demonstrated in evaluation studies of our programs (e.g., Givaudan et al., 2005; Pick, 2007; Pick & Givaudan, 2007). For example, through building specific knowledge on top of common skills and reducing psychological barriers at the school level, we have been able to promote changes in nutrition, in understanding, norms, and behaviors regarding sexual abuse, and in physical activity (Pick & Givaudan, 2007). Through programs for women, we have been able to bring about targeted changes in practices related to nutrition, prevention of cervical cancer and unwanted pregnancies, personal hygiene, and household and environmental sanitation (Venguer, Pick, & Fishbein, 2007). In the latter project, new nontargeted behaviors that emerged included organizing to ask the municipal president for electricity and water services, demanding that women be part of the local assembly, encouraging pap smears, obtaining government funding for breakfasts for young children and the elderly, and starting small businesses.

It would be difficult to explicitly promote behavior generalizations through a change in mindset because they would have to be taught as abstract concepts. Rather, it is the integration of learning into daily life that allows for application in different settings and eventually in more complex situations (Kolb, Boyatzis, & Mainemelis, 2000). As behaviors and skills are integrated and the individual engages in new behaviors, opportunities for reducing psychological barriers develop and a sense of accomplishment and internal control expands. "Knowing a general rule by itself in no way assures any generality it may carry is enabled in the specific circumstances in which it is relevant. In this sense, any 'power of abstraction' is thoroughly situated, in the lives of persons and in the culture that makes it possible" (Lave & Wegner, 1991, p. 34).

As individuals further engage in more diverse and complex situations, they develop new competencies, which represent the possibility of change beyond the behaviors specifically targeted in programs. With time, they become incorporated into an individual's repertoire of common behaviors. As we saw in the prologue, with the example of women standing outside the IMIFAP office asking for support to start their bakery, such behaviors emerge after demonstrated success in several instances. In this case, the petition came after progress in other domains: using contraception, vaccinating their children, and forming support groups for victims of violence.

Consequences of Behavior Change: Extension of Impact to the Person Frame of FrEE

Personal agency is a consequence of successfully choosing and executing behavioral changes (*see* Chapter 4) and, in turn, increases one's opportunities for making further autonomous choices. The resulting sense of entitlement becomes an inherent part of the individual's self-perception, enabling the individual to go beyond the specific targeted behaviors and concrete situations of the workshops. A conscientious focus on developing personal agency is central to human and social development. The process underlying this development, like the stages of behavior change and maintenance, is nonlinear and often involves periods of conflict and uncertainty. In fact, the processes of behavior change and development of personal agency are intertwined.[2] As people begin to make autonomous choices, changes also occur at the more stable level of the person. A classic example of this nonlinear process is the case of victims of domestic violence, who waver between leaving their partners and remaining in an abusive relationship. Marcela, a middle-aged mother of four in Mexico City, explains:

> I attended the workshop for women who are victims of violence. It helped me start talking with other women and seeing that I was not the only one, and that no one should be yelled at or hit. It made me think that I really had to get out of my house before my husband hurt me and my kids even more. I also finally talked to my mother about the problem. One day I even talked to my husband, and he promised it would never happen again, but a few days later he came home angry and it all started again. I really wanted to stay in my marriage, so I really wanted to believe that he would change. This happened so many times: "I promise, I promise that I won't ever hit you again, that will change," he would say. And one day I talked to other friends who came to visit from Morelos. One of them had offered to help me look for a job some years back and I had not accepted. But now she offered again, and that made it easier to finally decide to leave him. I now work as an assistant in a preschool. When I go visit my mother, who still lives in the same place, I sometimes see him and he still tries to convince me to come back. I would like to, but now the voice inside of me that says "Don't" is stronger than the one that says "Go back."

By understanding the necessity of personal agency for behavior maintenance and the extensive and layered process through which it is constructed, programmers and policymakers can improve development programs—particularly regarding questions of duration and budget.

Impact on Personal Norms

As individuals succeed in acquiring new behaviors, they see that their refined doing functionings, and therefore their freedoms, can be expanded. With this realization, changes occur at the level of refined *being* functionings as well, initiating the development of personal norms. one of the most important consequences of repeated behavioral success. The experience of control, and its subsequent effect on personal agency and personal norms, facilitates more sustainable change; these experiences also impact attitudes and intentions regarding choice, rights, and engaging in new behaviors (Pick, 2007).

Maria, a domestic housekeeper in Mexico City, discussed her experience in the program "I Want to, I Can ... Care for My Health and Exercise My Rights (Version for Household Help)":

> When I came to work at this house, I did not know how to tell her ... Finally I said, "But I have a boyfriend." I had learned that a maid was not supposed to have a boyfriend. I had lost two jobs already because of it. The woman answered

that she was happy I had a boyfriend. "That way you will be happier and will carry out your work better," she said. I did not understand what she meant, but I was glad. After the workshop for maids where I learned that we could ask for our rights and not just always obey, I accepted that it really is okay for a maid to have a boyfriend. I even talked to other maids about it and to my sister in the village, so that she could learn about boyfriends and how to deal with them. The strange thing is that in the village they say, "Don't have a boyfriend," but then if you don't, they say, "You will be an old maid." With these courses, we can argue better with people who say these things.

A Mexican-American adolescent girl told us a similar story after having participated in "I Want to, I Can ... Prevent Pregnancies," in Tacoma, WA:

No one is supposed to talk about drugs; we all act as if they don't exist. My parents think that if we do not talk about things that are difficult for them to discuss, we will not become interested in them. I believed that was the best way to go about things until I started to understand that not only is it okay but it is necessary to talk with your kids in an open and clear manner. It made me change my whole view about education. With information, people can make better decisions than by repressing the issue. After the program, I went out to look for information about sex, which is another topic [that is] hard for parents to talk about. And I have talked about it with my mother, and we now read books about it together.

These testimonies exemplify the impact of newly acquired knowledge, skills and, ultimately, behaviors on the formation of personal norms—that is, modifications in personal standards of what is "wrong," "right," and "proper." Personal norms do not necessarily need to depart from a person's perception of others' opinions concerning her behavior (subjective norms). As a woman observes that certain socially desirable norms simply do not fit with her new approach to situations, she is very likely to modify her personal norms. She can accomplish this by developing her own standards or by adopting the standards of groups with which she identifies. Newly adopted personal norms will support her continued development of self-efficacy and motivate her to put her enhanced set of capabilities to use. Norms derived from personal choice enhance the perception of oneself as an agent. In these particular cases, personal norms are not adopted because they represent the only possibility, but rather because they represent a capability.

Consequences of Changes in the Person: Extension of Impact to the Context Frame of FrEE

As the individual applies these newly acquired capabilities to actively promote change in her social environment, she exercises intrinsic empowerment: enhancing her own capabilities and contributing to a more facilitative context. Akin to developing new behaviors and agency, the road to intrinsic empowerment often involves a struggle, a socially unacceptable imbalance in the relationship between the individual and her environment. Throughout the process of change, the realization of individual capabilities and human rights comes within reach. The individual holds a central role in realizing sustainable contextual change at the family, community, and institutional levels. Clearly, as far as there is social support, this process is much easier and can advance at a faster rate.

A Note on Behavior Change

An emphasis on children can make a great deal of difference to individual and community prevention and development at relatively low costs (Mangrulkar, Whitman, & Posner, 2001). A child's early environment predicts future outcomes, including cognitive and noncognitive abilities (Carneiro & Heckman, 2003; Cunha et al., 2006; Heckman, 2006) and behaviors (Hetherington, Lerner, & Perlmutter, 1988). Within communities at risk for various negative outcomes, such as poor school achievement, risky social behaviors, and unfavorable health patterns, it is likely that children's development opportunities will be reduced, negatively affecting their personal identities (Woodhead & Oates, 2008).

Alejandra, a young, female preschool teacher in Hidalgo, Mexico, expresses this clearly:

> It is very hard to go back to traditional methods once one has been involved in "I Want to, I Can" preschool programs. The kids open up like buds. Taking them back to the old system folds them down and makes them, and us, sad.

Indicating the need for such programs that open children up "like buds," the World Bank writes:

> Broadening the opportunities available to young people for services and the start of a sustainable livelihood and helping them choose wisely among them are the priorities. Many young people cannot take advantage of these opportunities, however, because they were ill-prepared during younger ages. (2007, p. 59)

Group activities that develop problem-solving skills, a secure environment, and a sense of belonging will favor resiliency, enabling children to move into new stages of life with a sense of self-awareness.

In recognition of this key developmental window, it is important to begin programs early (Capuzzi, 1998; Gammage, 2008; Givaudan, Barriga, & Pick, 2008; Gomby et al., 1995; Reynolds & Crane, 1998), especially for disadvantaged populations. Numerous studies have revealed that early education life skills programs yield the best results in terms of improving cognitive abilities, which in turn affect school progress and achievement, language development, planning and organization, as well as thinking and reasoning skills (Capuzzi, 1998; Dwivedi & Harper, 2004; Gomby et al., 1995). Early intervention also has the capacity to improve social and emotional qualities, including emotional well-being, interpersonal communication, self-management and self-control, confidence, and coping with stress (Dwivedi & Harper, 2004; Gomby et al., 1995; Mangrulkar, Whitman, & Posner, 2001; Spoth et al., 2002). Children who have participated in these programs also exhibit fewer negative health and behavior patterns such as alcohol and substance abuse, HIV/AIDS, eating disorders, aggressive behavior, unintended pregnancies, contact with the juvenile justice system, and dependence on social service systems (Palfrey et al., 2005). Higher levels of educational attainment, income, health, and well-being demonstrate that program outcomes extend well into these children's futures (Heckman, 2006).

Behavior change at an earlier age will have significant economic outcomes as well. James J. Heckman, Nobel Laureate in Economics, states, "On a purely economic basis, it makes a lot of sense to invest in the young … early learning begets later learning and early success breeds later success" (2000, p. 2). Economic gains increase as the age of investment decreases. Returns are highest in preschool years, whereas starting later, even in the primary grades, can yield results below opportunity cost of funds. One program conducted in an inner-city setting in the United States showed that participating children ages 3 to 4 years demonstrated economic returns at the rate of 15% to 17% with a benefit-to-cost ratio over 8-to-1 (Gomby et al., 1995; Heckman, 2006; Schweinhart, Barnes, & Weikart, 1993).

Early intervention life skills programs are able to achieve remarkable results for a variety of reasons. First, the young are much more flexible and learn at a faster rate; it is more practical to instill new behaviors than to try to change established patterns. Second, the early application and repeated practice of such healthy behaviors and skills improves chances for beneficial results in the future. Finally, the acquisition of basic reasoning skills benefits children's development—psychologically, socially, and in specifically targeted behaviors (Botvin & Griffin, 2002). In Sen's terms, the earlier we start acquiring healthy and productive refined doing functionings, the more choices we will be able to develop.

This also explains why programs must address not only children but all socializing agents, including teachers. Successful development of new functionings in each of the agents can raise their motivational energy, encourage participation, and boost both students' and teachers' confidence and self-efficacy (Gomby et al., 1995; Heckman, 2006; Woodhead, 1988), thus enhancing their refined being functionings. The following testimonies demonstrate these improved refined functionings as a result of programming:

> We need training workshops such as the one we recently participated in that are different from the other classes provided for the teachers. This workshop was motivational, sensitizing, and supportive to the teacher so that she can look within herself and give as much of herself as possible to the school and community in which she works, without being afraid of making mistakes—understanding that it is part of being human, to err.
>
> —Andres, elementary school director and teacher, participant in
> "'I Want to, I Can … Integral Human Development Program,"
> Chiapas, Mexico

> I realized that with the ["'I Want to, I Can"] workshops the children can develop skills and attitudes that will help them have social relationships which are more humane. There is no need to threaten the students with taking away recess or lots

of homework or going to the director or getting beaten. Each activity in the training workshop made me think about myself and about my role as an educator. It made me face up to my emotions, my strengths, and [my] weaknesses. We didn't keep our noses in the texts but learned interactively and were not afraid of saying things. We built a new image of what it means to be a teacher.

—Leticia, teacher, participant in "'I Want to, I Can ... Integral Human Development Program" in Santiago, Chile

Conclusions

Societal development is not exclusively a matter of economics. It has a central psychological component, which is receiving more attention in recent years from economists, among others. We have referred repeatedly to the work of Amartya Sen (1987, 1995, 1999, 2004), who emphasizes a broader view of development, as outlined in the Capability Approach. He does not, however, propose a particular method for bringing these changes about. In the set of chapters on FrEE (Chapters 4, 6 and 7), we described how changes in the individual's behavior repertoire can be realized through programs and how the psychological processes underlying these changes can be understood.

In this chapter, we have emphasized that because a new behavior may contradict community norms and beliefs or provoke uncertainty in individuals, undertaking a new behavior cannot be compared to simply flicking a switch. Realizing a new and unfamiliar course of action is a process, often a non linear one—intending to change or implement a new behavior is not enough. To engage in decision making, the individual must first acquire a feeling of control over the situation and a sense of entitlement to choice. We have distinguished the various stages of this process following DiClemente and Prochaska's model. Initially, a person may only think about a behavior in vague terms. Gradually, however, she will determine a means of carrying out the contemplated action. But in IMIFAP's programs completing and maintaining the action does not conclude the process of change. Specific behavior changes may generalize, enabling their application in a broader range of situations. The processes of generalization and internalization are among the central consequences of skills-based behavior change; these processes result from the growth in competencies and the reduction of psychological barriers and can be enhanced through a supportive context. Modifications to personal norms are also a function of this process. Working at the personal level not only helps maintain new behaviors but also enhances capabilities and a sense of personal agency. The process occurs gradually, as program participants gain a greater sense of control over their affairs.

Notes

1. "A México le urge escapar de los depredadores y sólo lo logrará mediante reglas rigurosas e instituciones imparciales. . . . Se trata -en esencia- de cambiar cómo

funciona la política y cómo funciona la sociedad. Y ello también requerirá construir ciudadanos capaces de escribir cartas y retar a las élites y fundar organizaciones independientes y fomentar normas cívicas y sacudir conciencias y escrutinar a los funcionarios y cabildear en nombre del interés público."

2. The concept of personal agency is closely tied to ideas of self-efficacy but goes beyond this to include a broader spectrum of characteristics. According to Bandura (1997), "Perceived self-efficacy refers to beliefs in one's capabilities to organize and execute the courses of action required to produce given attainments" (p. 3). In contrast, personal agency measures one's ability to enact personal behavioral change to affect the situations in life and guide their outcomes. Personal agency is not a belief in itself; rather, it is a process by which individual beliefs and behaviors can be moved toward an arrangement, which allows the agent more freedom and greater control over his own life.

References

Bandura, A. (1997). *Self-efficacy: The exercise of control.* New York: W.H. Freeman & Co.

Botvin, G. J., & Griffin, K. W. (2002). Life skills training as a primary prevention approach for adolescent drug abuse and other problem behaviors. *International Journal of Emergency Mental Health, 4*(1), 41–48.

Cabañero-Verzosa, C. (1999). *Comunicación estratégica para proyectos de desarrollo. [Strategic communication for development projects].* Washington, DC: World Bank.

Capuzzi, D. (1998). Addressing the needs of at-risk youth: Early prevention and systemic intervention. In C. C. Lee & G. R. Walz (Eds.), *Social action: A mandate for counselors* (pp. 99-116). Alexandria, VA: American Counseling Association.

Carneiro, P., & Heckman, J. J. (2003). Human capital policy. In J. J. Heckman, A. B. Krueger & B. Friedman (Eds.), *Inequality in America: What role for human capital policies?* (pp. 77-237). Cambridge, MA: MIT Press.

Cunha, F., Heckman, J. J., Lochner, L., & Masterov, D. V. (2006). Interpreting the evidence on life cycle skill formation. In F. Welch & E. Hanushek (Eds.), *Handbook on the economics of education* (Vol. I, pp. 697–812). Amsterdam: Elsevier.

Dresser, D. (2008, June 2). Ausencia doble [Double absence]. *Reforma*, Retrieved June 3, 2008 from www.reforma.com.mx

Dwivedi, K. N., & Harper, P. B. (2004). *Promoting the emotional well-being of children and adolescents and preventing their mental ill health: A handbook.* London: Jessica Kingsley Publishers.

Engeström, Y. (2000). Activity theory as a framework for analyzing and redesigning work. *Ergonomics, 43*(7), 960–974.

Farrell, A., & Meyer, A. (1997). The effectiveness of a school-based curriculum for reducing violence among urban sixth-grade students. *American Journal of Public Health, 87*(6), 979–984.

Fawcett, G., Heise, L. L., Isita-Espejel, L., & Pick, S. (1999). Changing community responses to wife abuse. A research and demonstration project in Iztacalco, Mexico. *American Psychologist, 54*(1), 41–49.

Flannery, D. J., Vazsonyi, A. T., Liau, A. K., Guo, S., Powell, K. E., Atha, H., Vesterdal, W., & Embry, D. (2003). Initial behavior outcomes for the PeaceBuilders universal school-based violence prevention program. *Developmental Psychology, 39*(2), 292–308.

Flay, B. R. (2002). Positive youth development requires comprehensive health promotion programs. *American Journal of Health Behavior,* 26(6), 407–424.

Gammage, P. (2008). The social agenda and early childhood care and education: Can we really help create a better world? *Online Outreach Paper 4,* from http://es.bernardvanleer.org.

Givaudan, M., Barriga, M. A., & Pick, S. (2008). The children left behind: Researching the impact of migration on the development of children and developing, piloting and evaluating a program that answers their special needs, *Report presented to the Bernard van Leer Foundation.* Mexico City: IMIFAP.

Givaudan, M., Pick, S., Poortinga, Y. H., Fuertes, C., & Gold, L. (2005). A cervical cancer prevention program in rural Mexico: Addressing women and their context. *Journal of Community & Applied Social Psychology,* 15(5), 338–352.

Gomby, D. S., Larner, M. B., Stevenson, C. S., Lewit, E. M., & Behrman, R. E. (1995). Long-term outcomes of early childhood programs: Analysis and recommendations. *The Future of Children,* 5(3), 6–24.

Heckman, J. J. (2000). *Invest in the very young.* Chicago: Ounce of Prevention Fund and the University of Chicago Harris School of Public Policy Studies.

Heckman, J. J. (2006). Skill formation and the economics of investing in disadvantaged children. *Science,* 312(5782), 1900–1902.

Hetherington, E. M., Lerner, R. M., & Perlmutter, M. (Eds.). (1988). *Child psychology and life-span development.* Hillsdale, NJ: Lawrence Erlbaum Associates.

Kirby, D. (2002). Effective approaches to reducing adolescent unprotected sex, pregnancy, and childbearing. *Journal of Sex Research,* 39(1), 51–57.

Kolb, D. A., Boyatzis, R. E., & Mainemelis, C. (2000). Experiential learning theory: Previous research and new directions. In R. J. Sternberg & L. F. Zhang (Eds.), *Perspectives on cognitive, learning, and thinking styles.* Mahwah, NJ: Lawrence Erlbaum Associates.

Lave, J., & Wegner, E. (1991). *Situated learning: Legitimate peripheral participation.* Cambridge: Cambridge University Press.

Magnani, R., Karim, A. M., Brown, L., & Hutchinson, P. (2005). The impact of life skills education on adolescent sexual risk behaviors in KwaZulu-Natal, South Africa. *Journal of Adolescent Health,* 36(4), 289–304.

Malotte, C. K., Jarvis, B., Fishbein, M., Kamb, M., Iatesta, M., Hoxworth, T., Zenilman, J., & Bolan, G. (2000). Stage of change versus an integrated psychosocial theory as a basis for developing effective behavior change interventions. *AIDS Care,* 12(3), 357–364.

Mangrulkar, L., Whitman, C., & Posner, M. (2001). *Life skills approach to child and adolescent human development.* Washington, DC: Pan American Health Organization.

Nation, M., Crusto, C., Wandersman, A., Kumpfer, K. L., Seybolt, D., Morrissey-Kane, E., & Davino, K. (2003). What works in prevention: Principles of effective prevention programs. *American Psychologist,* 58(6–7), 449–456.

Palfrey, J. S., Hauser-Cram, P., Bronson, M. B., Warfield, M. E., Sirin, S., & Chan, E. (2005). The Brookline Early Education Project: A 25-year follow-up study of a family-centered early health and development intervention. *Pediatrics,* 116(1), 144–152.

Pick, S. (2007). Extension of theory of reasoned action: Principles for health promotion programs with marginalized populations in Latin America. In I. Ajzen, D. Albarracín & R. Hornik (Eds.), *Prediction and change of health behavior: Applying the reasoned action approach* (pp. 223-241). Mahwah, NJ: Lawrence Erlbaum Associates, Inc.

Pick, S., & Givaudan, M. (1994). *Yo, mi familia y mi medio ambiente: Un libro de educación para la vida. Tercero de primaria [Me, my family and my environment: A life skills book. Third grade]*. Mexico City: Editorial Planeta.

Pick, S., & Givaudan, M. (2007). Yo quiero, yo puedo: Estrategia para el desarrollo de habilidades y competencias en el sistema escolar ["I Want to, I Can: Strategy for the development of skills and competencies within the school system]. *Psicologia da Educação: Revista do Programa de Estudos Pós-Graduados em Psicologia da Educação/Pontifícia Universidade Católica de São Paulo, 23,* 203–221.

Prochaska, J. O., & DiClemente, C. C. (1982). Transtheoretical therapy: Toward a more integrative model of change. *Psychotherapy: Theory, Research & Practice,* 19(3), 276–288.

Prochaska, J. O., DiClemente, C. C., & Norcross, J. C. (1992). In search of how people change. *American Psychologist,* 47(9), 1102–1114.

Reynolds, A. J., & Crane, J. (1998). The Chicago child-parent center and expansion program: A study of extended early childhood intervention. In J. Crane (Ed.), *Social Programs That Work* (pp. 110–147). New York: Russell Sage Foundation.

Schweinhart, L. J., Barnes, H. V., & Weikart, D. P. (1993). *Significant benefits: The HighScope Perry Preschool study through age 27 (Monographs of the HighScope Educational Research Foundation, No. 10)*. Ypsilanti, MI: High/Scope Press.

Sen, A. (1987). *The standard of living.* Cambridge: Cambridge University Press.

Sen, A. (1995). *Inequality reexamined.* Boston: Harvard University Press.

Sen, A. (1999). *Development as freedom.* New York: Anchor.

Sen, A. (2004). Gender equity and the population problem. In V. Navarro & C. Muntaner (Eds.), *Political and economic determinants of population health and well-being: Controversies and developments* (pp. 27-33). Amityville, NY: Baywood Publishing Company.

Spoth, R. L., Redmond, C., Trudeau, L., & Shin, C. (2002). Longitudinal substance initiation outcomes for a universal preventive intervention combining family and school programs. *Psychology of Addictive Behaviors,* 16(2), 129–134.

Venguer, T., Pick, S., & Fishbein, M. (2007). Health education and agency: A comprehensive program for young women in the Mixteca region of Mexico. *Psychology, Health & Medicine,* 12(4), 389–406.

Woodhead, M. (1988). When psychology informs public policy: The case of early childhood intervention. *American Psychologist,* 43(6), 443–454.

Woodhead, M., & Oates, J. (2008). *Developing positive identities.* Milton Keynes, United Kingdom: Open University Press.

World Bank (2006). *Repositioning nutrition as central to development. A strategy for large-scale action.* Washington, DC: World Bank.

World Bank (2007). *World development report: Development and the next generation.* Washington, DC: World Bank.

CHAPTER 8

Context

Humans are born with a biologically endowed potential, but what is made of that potential is the workings of their lifetime experiences with their environments . . .

—Cigdem Kagitcibasi (2002, p. 38)

Local and national organizations, government systems, and institutions are an integral part of the development process. However, they depend on the personal agency and intrinsic empowerment of individuals to engineer and implement sustainable change. Individuals, in turn, rely on the opportunities and freedoms that institutions create to promote personal agency, enhance capabilities, and build vibrant communities. Institutions also have the potential to promote "unfreedoms" and barriers to development through poorly designed and implemented public policies, insufficient law enforcement, lack of good governance, and social responsibility. We have argued that changes in individual behavior patterns are the foundation for sustainable social change. This chapter frames the personal agency argument within a broader context, pointing to the interdependence between a person and his environment; as Sen asserts, ". . . no one is truly independent of the influences of the society in which she or he lives" (1999, p. 67). Acknowledging that people are more likely to realize their potential in favorable circumstances, we focus on both opportunities and constraints within the context for individual development.

Ideally, the interaction between an individual and his context results in a positive change for both parties: people can "push" institutions to change (as demonstrated in the previous discussion of intrinsic empowerment), and institutions can foster change in people. Sen's concept of "entitlements" illustrates the potential synergy between people and the environment (Buttel, 2000, Malenbaum, 1988; Nestle, 1998). *Entitlements* are bundles of commodities

167

over which a person can establish command (Malenbaum, 1988). The term not only encompasses the physical commodity itself but also the concept of ownership rights to such a commodity, or "the set of all those goods vectors to which one could acquire title" (Gasper, 2000, p. 996). Included in this definition is "attention to security of achievement" (Gasper, 2008, p. 11); individuals should be able to achieve the behaviors they desire with relative stability. Thus, an entitlement implies that an individual has "a normative claim to title" or ownership rights to a commodity (Gasper, 2000, p. 996).[1] Sen (1999) argues that the focus of development programs should not only be the commodities themselves (the fish) but also the freedoms that those commodities generate and the sustainability of these commodities (e.g., nutrition, employment, technical skills). The various domains of the context have the potential to foster (or inhibit) those individual freedoms that are invaluable for sustainable development.[2]

To facilitate clarity, we discuss the context in terms of separate domains, which we categorize according to the freedoms Sen has identified as advancing a person's capability set[3]: social opportunities (e.g., education, health), economic facilities, political freedoms, transparency guarantees, and protective security (1999). These domains are all part of the unified experience of an individual and are interrelated. There is a "remarkable empirical connection that links freedoms of different kinds with one another" (Sen, 1999, p. 11). For example, good health is both limited or facilitated by economic resources and protective security, whereas political freedoms are limited or enhanced by education and transparency guarantees.[4] In this way, freedoms are more than the goal of development—they are also a principal means because they serve to "strengthen one another" (Sen, 1999, p. 11). Given the common base and the mutually reinforcing quality of many behavioral changes, programs and policies should, from the psychosocial perspective, aim to be multithematic. In addition, such policies may prove to be more cost- and time-effective than traditional single-theme or single-sector programs. To form a basis for the practical analysis of different policies, institutions, and interactions, this chapter focuses on each individual domain, acknowledging their interactions.

Within each domain, many current institutional practices constitute impediments to development—here, we focus on examples from Mexico that are common in many developing countries. The ideal conditions for development occur when governments and institutions create opportunities rather than exercise their power only to establish constraints or facilitate assistance-based aid. As Sen argues, "Individuals live and operate in a world of institutions. Our opportunities and prospects depend crucially on what institutions contribute to our freedoms, their roles can be sensibly evaluated in the light of their contributions to freedoms" (1999, p. 142). Such entities have the potential to utilize available resources and the power to directly develop individual capabilities (e.g., through the education system), provide spaces for people to operate and exercise their rights (e.g., as often occurs in a democratic political system), and ensure that people have logistical and psychological access to basic services. The latter responsibility applies mainly to health services, financial institutions, legal institutions, and service-providing professions.

The context is not a nebulous entity but is made up of the individuals who direct and work in these institutions. These agents have the potential to perpetuate or modify an organizational culture, promote or limit incentive structures, and transform the human rights perspective into an operative framework within the context. Actors representing such institutions and geographical areas may be administrative officials and politicians who design and control national policies or local policies and programs. Another layer of actors consists of the professionals and bureacrats who are functionaries and service providers in each of the social institutions (e.g., teachers, police, medical doctors, and municipal civil servants). A third layer of agents are the policy and program beneficiaries: healthcare consumers, citizens, parents, and children.

This chapter should not be seen as a treatise on economics, government, education, health, or the theory of organizations. We focus on four domains of context to illustrate the potential synergy (and barriers) for people to flourish in their environment. Each of the domains addressed in the following sections touches on the issues brought up throughout this book.

Educational Context

Essential education ... (is) crucial for the formation and use of human capabilities. (Sen, 1999, p. 42)

A substantial body of research has highlighted the association between education and other social indicators, such as poverty reduction, improved income distribution, crisis prevention, and democracy (USAID, 2005). School achievement has been linked to an individual's economic success—particularly for those who traditionally complete only low levels of schooling (Krueger & Lindahl, 2001)—and social capital later in life (Glaeser, Laibson, & Sacerdote, 2002). Both the quantity and quality of education have been associated with a country's economic growth rate (Hanushek, 2005). Education can be an ideal means for providing people with the personal knowledge and skills to successfully respond to their needs and environmental demands. Conversely, lack of education presents a formidable barrier to individual and community achievement.

The degree to which education actually supports skills development and generates knowledge depends on how it is realized. Often, a broad distinction is made between two educational processes: one that is dictatorial (external) and one that is facilitative (internal) (Ellerman, 2001). The dictatorial method is hierarchical, where the teacher dictates (literally and figuratively speaking) the lessons to the pupil. Paulo Freire has written extensively on the method. In *Pedagogy of the Oppressed*, he described it as the banking model of education, where the teacher aims to deposit information and skills in students: "The more completely she fills the receptacles, the better a teacher she is. The more meekly the receptacles permit themselves to be filled, the better students they are" (p. 72). Freire rejects this model because the possibility for the individual to develop understanding and have a voice is strongly curtailed. On the other hand, facilitative education focuses on building autonomy, self-control, and internally motivated student action. Freire writes: "Knowledge emerges only through invention and re-invention, through the restless, impatient, continuing, hopeful inquiry human beings pursue" (1970, p. 72). Facilitative education creates mentor–pupil relationships in which the mentor (or teacher) is a facilitator of the student's learning process.

This section will briefly describe how Freire's understanding has not been realized in Mexico and the factors that tend to impede the implementation of an educational style conducive to the development of personal agency and intrinsic empowerment. It distinguishes three main actors and, on occasion, their interactions: the government, teachers, and parents. The policy and structure surrounding education are important enabling factors, but the training, attitudes, and support that teachers and parents provide at the microlevel are also critical determinants of children's success.

Education Administration

The recent reforms instituted by the Mexican government to make quality education more accessible to its citizens have produced varying results. The Ministry of Education has made significant investments in education over the past decade, with a 47% increase in investment between 1995 and 2004 (OECD, 2007a).[5] Consequently, Mexico now ranks above the OECD average for percentage of gross domestic product (GDP) invested in education (OECD, 2007a).[6] Nevertheless, indicators still reflect poor outcomes,[7] and school attrition rates are a major concern. Although over a recent period, 30 million Mexican students remained registered in the primary and secondary school systems or completed their studies through high school, over the same period, 53 million Mexican students dropped out early (Díaz de Cossío, 2005). In secondary education, Mexico, in particular, has fallen behind, showing less progress in raising attainment than most other countries (OECD, 2007a). [8]

The Mexican government has attempted to remedy some of the school attendance and attrition problems through the national implementation of *Oportunidades* (formerly known as *Progresa*), a program that provides cash transfers to families as an incentive to keep children in school and to alleviate some of the economic barriers to children's education (Levy, 2006).[9] Program evaluations (Fernald, Gertler, & Neufeld, 2008; Molyneux, 2008) and OECD studies (2007a) have demonstrated significant improvements in school attendance.[10] However, the program does not address the quality of the schools, teachers, and the national curriculum, a critical weakness also raised by the OECD educational data.

> Without diminishing the social feat of our country of nearing universalization of basic education, it is important to recognize that the evaluation of the school, given the group of social and political relationships which underlie its work, is far from responding to the demands of social democratization and the forming of

a new citizenship participatory, critical, and competent in the economy. [11] (Barba Casilla & Zorrilla Fierro, 2009, p. 42)

This weakness is very much grounded in the system's structure.

Mexico's education system is a product of its historical hierarchical structure (Gershberg, 1999), which in the early 20th century may have served the labor needs of the manufacturing and extracting economy. However, in the 1990s, Mexico began to decentralize within the context of an education decentralization movement in Latin America (Gajardo, 1999)[12]; the aim of this movement was to address inequalities, meet local needs, and respect local values and traditions (Guevara & González, 2004). Although policy has begun to change as a result, and there is more control at the local level over schools, decentralization has had little impact (Homedes & Ugalde, 2005; Trillo, Cayeros, & González, 2002; Wilder & Romero Lankao, 2006).

One of the barriers to reform is the administrative system, which supports mainly the idea of reform and building the public image of authorities, rather than broad structural changes. Local adminstrators come from a punitive norms system in which taking action entails taking responsibility, and hence, inaction is preferable (*see* Chapter 2). Many officials lack the technical and personal skills to optimize the beneficial effects of decentralization. Maintaining the autocratic structures, local government officials have tended to use their newly acquired authority for personal gain (*see* Chapter 2).[13] There are few incentives to alter the status quo of a paternalistic orientation to one where individuals take personal responsibility for their obligations. Decentralization has failed to be accompanied by changes in curricula, teacher training, and teaching methodology that drive quality of education. These arguments have been developed in a recent study of Mexican civil servants, which concludes with suggestions about how training programs for civil servants may lead to a change in orientation (Pick, Givaudan, & Reich, 2008).

Mexico's education system is also a product of the power of the national teachers union. With more than 1.4 million members, the National Union of Education Workers is the largest labor union in Latin America (de la Madrid, 2007). Since 1989, it has been directed by Elba Esther Gordillo, nicknamed *"La Maestra"* [The Teacher]. She is considered by many to be the second most powerful politician in Mexico, after the president ("The Teacher," 2007). Allegedly, she has negotiated favors for dozens of senators' votes, and when the time comes for the Union to negotiate with the federal government, Gordillo bypasses the Ministry of Education and sits down directly with the president ("Mexico's Politics," 2007). The relationship between The Ministry of Education and the teachers' labor union has been described as symbiotic, based on exchange of favors (Rodriguez, 2010). In appropriating educational resources, the union responds to union and political incentives, in place of academic and professional incentives necessary for an effective education system (Romero, 2009).

The pure size of the union makes school reform slow, and the union can hardly be expected to have an interest in a new order in which the autonomy and independence of the union members is emphasized. As a student in the teacher training school (Escuela Normal) put it during a training course in Mexico City:

> It is better to close one's eyes to what happens in the Union and know one's job is assured, even if the students do not turn out that well, than to have to think and decide by oneself. In this way you get up, have breakfast, take the bus, teach, get your paycheck, and everything else is taken care of by the Union.

Teachers

Teachers are an important determinant of school performance (Fuchs & Wößmann, 2007)—they implement educational programs and set the tone for social interaction and intellectual curiosity in the classroom. Rote memorization and lack of independent engagement with texts preserves the classroom as a site of indoctrination, thus preventing critical thinking and analytical skills (Corral Jurado, 2009). The authoritarian teaching style in many of Mexico's public schools helps to explain why students scored far below most other OECD countries in international comparisons of educational performance, especially the Programme for International Student Assessment (PISA) (OECD, 2007c). A cycle of autocratic behavior among teachers feeds disinterest and a negative attitude among pupils. Compounding this, a lack of commitment, preparation, motivation, and perpetual absenteeism of teachers has been noted (Gajardo, 1999). For many years this has been a concern of parents:

> Parents are particularly scandalized by what they see as teachers' instrumental attitudes to their work—going absent when it suits them, swapping classes for their own convenience, trading leaves of absence for the mutual advantage of those involved. Meanwhile the children suffer. (Martin, 1993, p. 171)

The outcome is disinterested students who fail to participate and become involved in their learning. The quality of instruction is a critical social reform that has the potential to expand individual opportunities (as discussed in Chapter 2).

Teachers and administrators often do not consider the long-term benefits of a system that encourages independent and analytical thinking. A survey by the National Institute for Education Evaluation illustrated the prevailing mentality about teaching style in Mexico: two of every three teachers used memorization as a key means of teaching reading comprehension, and 52% dedicated less than 30 minutes per week to individual reading (Treviño et al., 2007). Approximately 80% of schools spend 3 hours or longer each school day on the following activities: dictating texts to the students, asking students to answer questions about identifying explicit information in the text, and asking students to copy the parts of the texts with the most important information (Treviño et al., 2007). A PISA report cited Mexican students' difficulty analyzing scientific data and experiments as evidence that: "Students who learn just to memorize and reproduce scientific knowledge and skills may find themselves ill-prepared for tomorrow's job market" (OECD, 2007b, p. 2). In other words, the dominant approach to teaching in Mexico has not provided students with the compctencies and skills to help them succeed in the real world; this has negative implications not only for individuals but also for society.[14]

Facilitative approaches that emphasize development of skills, personal agency, and intrinsic empowerment are needed to increase feelings of responsibility and motivation. In turn, this should increase teachers' enthusiasm for their own work, stimulate student initiative and participation (Stefanou et al., 2004), and introduce new teaching methods. When teachers are approached individually or by their school system, we have found that they generally react positively to training programs that enhance their skills and provide them with the tools to motivate their students. They demonstrate a willingness for change and motivation to effect that change in their classrooms. For example, we have seen that when teachers are trained to provide sexuality education, they not only provide the appropriate information, but also foster responsible behaviors in their students (Givaudan, 2003; Pick et al., 2007). A study by Givaudan (2003) found that the results imparted by these participatory methods were long-term and palpable. Teachers can be important facilitators of personal agency and intrinsic empowerment and, thus, of expanding freedoms for themselves and for their students.

> It's a very substantial program for us as human beings. It helps us get balanced, to know how to overcome different situations that we go through personally as well as in groups. They also taught us . . . that we should set up the rules before the class begins but that we not talk as much about discipline but about responsibility, and that's something that really pleases me.
> —Fifth-grade teacher, Hidalgo, Mexico

> I learned how to talk to kids, how to motivate them, the importance of giving them challenges and not only memorizing . . . If the kids are interested, they do things because they want to, not because I force them ... it makes everything more fun and more interesting . . . What good is it to tell kids you have all these rights over and over again if they cannot live them, feel them, put them into practice?
> —Fifth-grade teacher, Campeche, Mexico

Economic incentives and other logistical aspects of teachers' jobs are essential for recruitment and retention of quality teachers. Low wages, delays in payment, poor benefits, and corruption in the workplace can combine to cause dissatisfaction among teachers. These factors can lead to an increase in unionization and strikes, as occurred throughout southern Mexico in 1979 to 1980 (Foweraker & Craig, 1990). In recent years, teachers' wages have increased significantly in Mexico, more than in any other OECD country between 1996 and 2002. This improvement points to the dependence of systemic components on administrators; contemporary teacher salaries are now unlikely to hinder recruitment and retention. However, quality of education remains an issue, particularly among older teachers (Guichard, 2005).

Parents

Strictly speaking, parents are not part of the formal education system. Yet they are the primary agents of socialization and the formal education system can support their efforts. In turn, parents can make a difference when they apply practices that enhance their children's performance and participation in school. It is at home that children are encouraged to take initiative and responsibility or conversely, are taught that obedience and following the norms are most important if they want to be "good" children. It is within the family that the development of capabilities must begin to take place for children to be successful once they enter school. However, as demonstrated in Chapter 2, there can be strong socio-cultural pressure to undertake an obedience-oriented upbringing of children based on punishment, guilt, and fear, rather than informed, autonomous decision making and concomitant internally developed responsibility. An adolescent in Oaxaca, Mexico, expressed it well:

> My father is afraid that he will lose control if he plays with us, cries, or says nice things. Everything has to be done yelling and threatening, that is how he feels he is a true man and an authority in the house. And my mother gives in, she does whatever he says and then wants us to do whatever she wants. They don't understand that even if we are young, we can think and see what happens and decide. The mere sound of us [children] saying the word "decide" makes them bark. My grandmother once yelled at us: "Children obey; adults do the thinking and deciding."

At school, children will develop relationships with their teachers similar to those they have with their parents and other adults. When the teacher serves as an authoritarian figure rather than an emotional anchor, this impacts the child's feelings of protection, security, and sense of belonging within the classroom, hampering the emotional well-being and stability of the student (Ranganathan, 2000).

Once children have entered school, parents play an important role interacting with teachers and school administrators and staying up to date on their children's progess. Yet attempts at parental involvement in the school system are limited within Mexico. If parents make inquiries, teachers tend to see such approaches as meddling in their affairs and undermining their authority; hence, they respond negatively. A mother's testimony in Arequipa, Peru, provides an illustration:

> I asked the teacher to not ever hit my kid again and to find other ways of disciplining kids, and her answer was, "So how do you expect them to obey then? Kids must obey what adults say and the best way is by making them show respect to us. If you would see how quiet they are in my class...you can hear a fly go by. That's how I want to keep it. I talk, they obey."

There is little history of grassroots mobilization of stakeholders in the education sector, and the recent attempt by the Mexican government to write parental participation into the federal reform legislation has shown little or no positive effect (Gershberg, 1999). Although economic barriers to parental involvement represent a tangible obstacle, parents often fail to use the freedoms they do possess, especially within such a constrained context. Parents generally do not realize the powers they have to transform schools; with concerted effort over time, a parents' committee can encourage change. An increased willingness by the central government to give such councils substantive control over school personnel, budgets, and local curricula would encourage these efforts (Gershberg, 1999). It is understandable that parents are scared to organize and find it difficult, but they should not feel submissive to teachers.

The reorientation toward personal agency and intrinsic empowerment argued for in this book provides a new perspective on the potential for parental involvement in education. A mother's testimony in Campeche, Mexico, after having participated in a Programming for Choice workshop targeting parenting skills, illustrates what is possible:

> The facilitators explained things to us and had us role-play behaviors that many years back we all had a gut feeling were needed but had never thought were possible, nor knew how to put in words. For example, that we can have a voice, that we don't have to just wait to see what the government wants and follow like little sheep. After going to the program, we organized a group that went to the school director and then to the Ministry of Education [of the state] to ask that teachers come to give their classes everyday, that they don't ask for "cooperations" [money] all the time. ... And we formed a group of parents that meets every month to oversee things, and we don't allow the school to see us as the enemy but rather as a group that supports them. We even set up a raffle to buy a computer for the fifth grade—only one, but something is better than nothing.

Educational reforms exist in many Latin American countries that aim to promote human development (Gajardo, 1999). These are conceived not only for expanding educational coverage but also for promoting social rights, ensuring participation in other programs, and opening access to new opportunities. Although the teacher may be described as the main protagonist, the results of the teaching–learning process are not entirely dependent on the teacher or the student but, rather, are a product of an integrated system (Cox, Jaramillo, & Reimers, 2005). Changes are needed both at the political level and at the microlevel that will have a positive behavorial impact on the personal agency of administrators, teachers, children, and parents. This will only be successful as part of a multifaceted process that involves all relevant actors, restructures the curriculum and teacher training, and, as a result, changes attitudes about the role of education.

Economic Context

The economic entitlements that a person has will depend on the resources owned or available for use as well as on conditions of exchange. (Sen, 1999, p. 39)

The interaction between the economic context and personal agency is, in some respects, obvious: economic poverty restricts the range of opportunities to those that individuals can afford, whether it is access to educational opportunities or healthcare. Poverty is a constraint on individual capabilities (Sen, 1999). However, the relationship extends beyond access to commodities, because even if provided with access, deeply rooted psychological barriers, social norms, and attitudes often limit the ways in which marginalized groups perceive and access opportunity (Estrada-Lopez, 1999). As discussed in Chapter 5, Sen rejects mainstream economics' concentration on growth of commodity production because an increase in freedoms depends on many factors besides income and commodities (Gasper, 2000).[15] Economist Jeffrey Sachs points to some of these other factors:

> Although economic growth has shown a remarkable capacity to lift vast numbers of people out of extreme poverty, progress is neither automatic nor inevitable. Market forces and free trade are not enough. Many of the poorest regions are ensnared in a poverty trap: they lack the financial means to make the necessary investments in infrastructure, education, healthcare systems, and other vital needs. (Sachs, 2005, p. 57)

Efforts toward enabling access to economic assets should be measured in terms of the various outcomes and utility that these assets generate for people, rather than seeing them as goods in and of themselves (Sen, 1999). Of course, economic growth is crucial, but mainly as a means to well-being more than as an end in itself. For example, Osmani (2008) discusses some of the positive social and economic implications of increasing women's employment opportunities in particular: Employment opportunities empower women (often leading to improved health, education, and nutrition for women and children), extra income enables families to send their children to school, and the environment is positively impacted because as people become less desperate, there is less abuse of the environment and individuals are more able to care for it. The point is that it is these outcomes—these freedoms—on which we need to focus when assessing the economic context.

In Mexico, the economy has been characterized by instability, oscillations in economic policy, devaluations of the peso, deficits in foreign trade, lack of fiscal discipline, inflation, and, as a result, recurrent crises (Goldstein, Kaminsky, & Reinhart, 2000; Lopez Gallardo, Moreno-Brid, & Puchet Anyul, 2006; Villegas Hernandez & Ortega Ochoa, 2002). Crises plunge more people into extreme poverty, restrict access to jobs, cut off essential services, force people to sell assets, and deprive individuals of the opportunites to enhance their human capital (especially as children suffer from malnutrition and drop out of school). These losses set the stage for transgenerational, chronic poverty (Blomquist et al., 2001). Today, Mexico has a GDP per capita (adjusted for purchasing power parity) of about $13,200 USD (CIA, 2010). We focus here on the roles of the financial, employment, and security sectors in providing individuals with opportunities.

Financial Institutions, the Poor, and Government Intervention

Sen writes: "The availability and access to finance can be a crucial influence on the economic entitlements that economic agents are practically able to secure" (1999, p. 39). Results of a World Bank study on banking in Mexico's formal sector have concluded that very few people utilize the formal banking system—only 30% of the adult population has access to formal financial services (CGAP, 2009). Limited participation in the formal sector defines the scope of the economic landscape for many of Mexico's poorest.

Many Mexicans avoid formal financial systems because of both structural and psycho-social barriers. On the one hand, they are discouraged by high transaction fees and initial deposits, minimum balances, and documentation requirements (Solo, 2005, 2008) as well as limited physical access resulting from the fact that in many rural areas the nearest bank can be a considerable distance away (Taber & Cuevas, 2005). Those insitutions that do exist in these rural settings are often unreliable and insecure, described as "small, community-based organizations… with no links to the national payment system, limited product offerings, and low levels of technology and efficiency" (Taber & Cuevas, 2005, p. 4). On the other hand, many Mexicans "do not like dealing with banks" (World Bank, 2005b, p. 62) and carry a general mistrust of the banking system. This lack of trust in formal financial institutions has a strong foundation in attitudes and discrimination between socio-economic sectors. A poor woman in Puebla, Mexico, recounts her negative experiences with a banking institution that promotes itself as a socially responsible enterprise for the poor:

> I stopped going to them for loans because they made me feel bad every time … they would threaten us with delays for hours. I understand they have to make their money, but they also should understand that we have to travel long distances, look for a place to leave our small kids to be able to come to the weekly meetings, get the payments from the people to whom we sell … those guys who loan us the money do not understand those things, and on top of it, they charge us 7% a month (they say it is 4%, but when one adds up the fees, the reality is much higher). We may be poor, but not stupid. Like anyone else, we deserve to be treated like people, not like grass that one just steps on.

Inferior treatment in banks because of physical appearance or socio-economic status is sufficient rationale to avoid the formal banking system (Villegas Hernandez & Ortega Ochoa, 2002), particularly when one lacks the voice to change it. Diagnostic research shows that the poorest sectors of the population prefer to pay higher prices for informal services than to use formal banking institutions, because of the rejection and distrust that is manifested by the latter (Solo, 2005).

Individuals are equally drawn to informal financial institutions for structural and psycho-social reasons. Structural barriers may be logistical or economic, such as the lack of documentation or assets to serve as collateral, which is required by formal financial institutions for the granting of a loan. The poor operate in a mini-economy, where economic transactions—for example, production, consumption, trade and exchange, saving, borrowing, and income-earning—occur on a small scale. Therefore, the transaction costs (both direct and indirect) tend to be high. This has important implications for the use of formal sector institutions, as the charging of administrative costs tends to make transactions unattractive to the poor (Matin, Hulme, & Rutherford, 2002). Informal markets provide easier cash liquidity, and savings associations provide social capital unattainable through formal institutions. Additionally, abstaining from the use of formal financial institutions may result from personal preferences as much as it may be based on logistical or psychological barriers that constrain utilization of the formal systems (World Bank, 2005b).

Despite the benefits of remaining outside the formal financial system, those who conduct economic exchanges informally face greater risk, often pay higher interest, and generally have lower rates of economic growth. Informal financial markets tend to have higher transaction costs to cash paychecks, higher interest rates on loans or credit, and more barriers to save money (World Bank, 2005b). Informal lenders (*aboneros*[16]) conduct predatory or usury lending at very high interest rates and with arbitrary rules for repayment. Otherwise, acquiring funds to cover emergency expenses or start a business may require loans from family or friends, which necessitates a certain level of social capital. Informal solutions fail to protect against economic shocks that affect an entire community or social network (Dercon, 2002). Exclusion of large swaths of society from formal institutions perpetuates cycles of poverty and disempowerment, and thus complicates the promotion of economic agency. Increasing access (economic, logisitical, and psychological) can contribute to poverty alleviation (World Bank, 2005b) and increase individuals' real and perceived entitlements and opportunities.

Governments have a responsibility to create economic policy and to regulate financial institutions that may support or impede the functioning of markets. To its credit, the Mexican government has undertaken what has been called the "most ambitious effort to massively scale-up access to financial services for poor and marginalized people in the world" with the 2001 Popular Savings and Credit Act (Taber & Cuevas, 2005, p. 5). Coming partially in response to widespread fraud and failure of many formal and informal cooperatives, credit unions, and savings and loan associations between 1998 and 2000 (Taber & Cuevas, 2005), the Act addresses the structural barriers to formal sector usage. Through the Act, the federal government created a national bank, BANSEFI. By providing a variety of second-tier central banking services to existing banks, as well as opening new branches in some of the most financially marginalized areas of the country, BANSEFI seeks to develop a culture of saving in Mexico and develop a well-integrated, nationwide system of banks that can support the growing financial needs of the Mexican population. The bank currently connects more than 2,000 formal small financial institutions to build capacity, improve reliability, and create greater security within them (Taber & Cuevas, 2005). Furthermore, BANSEFI's branches provide significantly more coverage throughout the country than the private banks, which do not have branches in 74% of Mexican municipalities; these municipalities contain 22% of the population and can be understood as largely rural (World Bank, 2005a). The psycho-social barriers to formal sector usage are more difficult to address. Although we expect that the decreased socio-economic inequality expected from BANSEFI's involvement may have some effect on low income users' attitudes toward banks, we see this as a longer process that also requires changes in the attitudes of banks and bank employees toward low-income users.

Employment, the Poor, and the Governmental Factor

Promoting human development and reducing poverty will require redirecting the economic focus toward growth processes that increase and improve employment (Osmani, 2008). "The country needs a deep labor reform that allows for greater productivity, which will give workers and the country increased prosperity"[17] (Sarmiento, 2010). Researchers and politicians need to address work conditions, barriers to entering the formal sector, and the important link between "labor market conditions" and "household outcomes" (Osmani, 2008). Most countries lack data about the progression of employment quality for poor workers, yet this information is critical for "understanding the problematic and designing instruments to remedy it" (Osmani, 2008, p. 10).

Attention to the informal sector is particularly important for understanding these characteristics. In Mexico, 57% of the employed population works in the informal sector (Tokman, 2007). That amounts to approximately 24.6 million Mexican workers in the informal sector.[18] Impoverished individuals often work informally because this sector requires less financial capital investment and relatively small amounts of human capital and allows for the use of local technology and resources. As with the informal financial system, this may be something that an individual is not only pushed toward but also pulled to. However, employment in the informal labor market not only prevents workers from earning a regular source of income but also excludes them from several other benefits connected with formal work, such as job security, social security protection, and medical insurance (van Ginneken, 1999).

Yet given an unsteady and unpredictable economic context, impoverished individuals have neither much incentive nor many opportunities to take initiative in creating significant sources of income. This consequence of context is particularly problematic for those lacking skills and knowledge dependent on formal education. The risk of suffering a negative shock to income, health, or physical assets further defines the context in which impoverished individuals have to manage their assets; those with few assets are often (and rationally) averse to taking on the additional risks that accompany entrepreneurial activities (Matin, Hulme, & Rutherford, 2002). Policies addressing the determinants of impoverished people's (lack of) participation in the economy—a culture of risk-taking, objective and perceived access to formal sectors—are critical for efforts to involve impoverished individuals in entrepreneurial activities.

In sum, the Mexican economic context points to a high level of insecurity, vulnerability, and structural and psycho-social barriers that many individuals face in achieving their economic potential. These aspects of the economic context manifest themselves in the experiences of poor people in several ways, including a "lack of access to basic infrastructure, rural roads, transportation, and water" and psychological consequences such as "powerlessness, voicelessness, dependency, shame, and humiliation." Societal growth necessitates simultaneous progress on multiple levels: macro-economic reform, combined with psychosocial education and training for employment, can prepare individuals to grasp economic opportunities. This book serves to address the issues associated with the latter level, micro-growth factors. Economic opportunities may generate the greatest impact on welfare when they co-exist with personal agency because individuals actively utilizing their commodities will create additional economic opportunities. But this does not deny that there is also a need for policy and implementation of macro- and micro-economic objectives, which address the needs of disadvantaged social sectors and assure distribution of economic benefits at the microlevel.

Government Context

Political and civil rights, especially those related to the guaranteeing of open discussion, debate, criticism, and dissent, are central to the processes of generating informed and reflected choices. (Sen, 1999, p. 153)

Democracy is an international standard for free and fair political systems. It is the only system that maximizes opportunities for self-determination and choice while still providing the best means for people to protect and advance their personal and community interests (Siegle, 2007). Democracy is an ideal system for an enabling context because leaders must be elected, and therefore, the public can hold officials accountable for developing and implementing policies that serve their constituents. This serves as a political incentive, preventing widespread disasters. For example: "It is not surprising that no famine has ever taken place in the history of the world in a functioning democracy—be it economically rich... or relatively poor" (Sen, 1999, p. 16). The democratic system provides political and legal protection to the country's citizens.

Despite these universal benefits of democratic governance, ensuring political freedoms for those who are traditionally excluded involves more than just allowing these individuals political rights; it requires their integration into the system, so individuals can exercise choice and have the necessary elements to access their political entitlements.[19] It is important to note that democratic governance does not necessarily result in equity. Although minority groups in the United States and European countries are members of a democratic society, they still suffer political, economic, and social inequalities. Therefore, political (macrolevel) democracy must be supplemented with the social structures and microlevel implementation to enhance freedoms and opportunities for all citizens. This section addresses how democratic political regimes and practices might enhance political freedoms and provide entitlements to historically powerless individuals.

To promote the participation of various actors, a political system must recognize individuals' agency and power to make choices (by law and in practice). Emphasis on personal agency and community empowerment is, at the national level, important for increased participation and for a stronger democracy, whereas at the microlevel it changes the way people conceive of and understand resources, relations, and power structures. As democratic structures and processes contribute to a skilled and willful citizenry, they strengthen democracy; and similar to the relationship between personal agency and the context, the two positively reinforce each other. Too often, however, the formal institutional arrangement of democracy exists without the day-to-day practice of democratic governance.

Mexico provides a relevant example of a country that has been technically a democracy for nearly 100 years yet has a history of one-party leadership in violation of democratic norms. Mexico's experience under what prolific Latin American writer Mario Vargas Llosa nicknamed "the perfect dictatorship" of the semi-democratic *Partido Revolucionario Institucional* (PRI) illustrates this point:

> It looked like a democracy, headed by a president who could not be re-elected, and equipped with all the institutional bells and whistles usually found in democracies. But since the PRI was everywhere, and since the president could choose all party candidates, including his successor, he enjoyed near-absolute power. (Lichfield, 2000, p. 4)

The party maintained its 71-year stronghold by lavishing money and power on trade union leaders, newspapers and artists to acquire their support and even funding opposition parties to keep opponents divided (Lichfield, 2000).

Neither the socio-cultural norms nor the individual provide support for participatory citizenship or open governance in Mexico (World Bank, 2006). Schedler (2005) describes Mexico as an "electoral autocracy" (p. 12), citing macro- and microlevel political corruption (e.g., voter fraud, registration restrictions against certain parties and candidates, violations of civil and political liberties, and unequal access to media and campaign resources) and the hierarchical structure of government. Such a political context has led to the continuation of a democracy characterized by "low-intensity citizenship" that, in practice, violates certain fundamental elements of a democratic society:

> In a democracy of low intensity citizenship, such as Mexico, there are pockets where rights and institutions exist only on paper. Individuals in these areas are not quite citizens making these regimes, not quite democracies, even if they are legally defined as such. (Ochoa Espejo, 2004, p. 1)

Pointing to the individual component, one political analyst in particular argued that the fundamental problem of the Mexican political system, as in many other "democracies," is that "this country does not obey law, it obeys authority" (Guillermoprieto, 2001, p. 182). As mentioned in Chapter 2, this authoritarianism was particularly problematic within the political system itself when the country underwent major reforms to decentralize the administration in the 1990s and was key to the lack of facilities for expanding capabilities and enabling personal agency and intrinsic empowerment both at the individual and institutional levels. At a more general level and reflecting on the longer term, at the time of the 2009 influenza epidemic in Mexico, calls were made for a State that could adequately respond to people's needs:

> Protection of our health is the best reason for us to respect the State's attributions. But this will only be seriously reflected if our representatives and government

during and after this experience, take it upon themselves to rebuild the State as an instrument of good … of wellbeing. (Lajous, 2009, p. A18)[20]

This extends to security challenges as well (O'Neil, 2009).

Public Officials and Street-Level Bureaucrats

Like any large organization, governments need a hierarchy of people to make policies and to implement them on all levels: from top officials to street-level bureaucrats that deal directly with the everyday citizen. High-ranking officials "act as critical links between the political will of ministers and the long-term public interest as understood by the public service", and are therefore positioned "at the crossroads between political power and public administration" (Larson & Coe, 1999, p. 1).

> They are the power brokers, the managing directors in the government hierachy. At the other end of the spectrum are the legions of lower-level bureaucrats and public servants. These men and women serve as the vital link between the policy direction of head office and the actual delivery of services. (Carroll & Siegel, 1998, p. 4)

This position makes bureaucrats the face of government in the average person's life, and thereby, places them in a public relations role even more important than that of the top-level officials and their spokespersons. Public officials and street-level bureaucrats represent a particularly essential role in the realization of national policies at a local level, having a salient impact on individual freedoms and opportunities.

Mexico's decentralization experience over the past 25 years represents a promising shift toward increased development and strengthened democracy (Rodriguez, 1997). However, during the decentralization process, many responsibilities were reissued to midlevel public officials who had never been given much responsibility before and were unprepared to take on their new roles (Pick, Givaudan, & Reich, 2008). There is extensive anecdotal evidence that these public servants are lacking, particularly in the areas of technical expertise and entrepreneurial skills.

An analysis of local welfare reform in the United States found that the strongest indicators for successful local implementation were program managers' experience, expertise, and entrepreneurial skills, enabling them to "exercise leadership in bringing about dramatic changes in their organizational mission(s), cultures, structures, procedures" (Cho, Kelleher, Wright, & Yackee, 2005, p. 49). Exacerbating widespread weaknesses in expertise, public servants in Mexico have cited envy, power struggles, hidden violence, and lack of trust as the main factors contributing to failure in decentralization processes (Pick, Xocolotzin, & Ruesga, 2007). That same study also showed a lack of competencies and personal agency among Mexican government officials, including fear of decision making and low self-confidence. Limited political expertise compounded by restricted personal agency and the absence of legal or social pressure to face the consequences of one's decisions, represents a particularly grave fault line in the realization of national policies to support freedoms and opportunities. To reach their potential, public officials need more training and support in the context of the decentralization reforms and the expansion of municipal autonomy in Mexico.

Lichfield's description of public servant behavior reflects the larger political practices in Mexico within which the decentralization and daily activities of public officials and street level bureaucrats have taken place:

> Corruption on the outrageous scale of the oil-mad 1970s is mostly gone, but petty corruption is still endemic. The police no longer collaborate with criminals the way they used to, but nor have they learned to fight them effectively. (2000, p. 4)

A recent U.S. State Department report confirmed that "Corruption throughout Mexico's public insitutions remains a key impediment" (Agence-France Press, 2009). Corruption is often related to extant political structures, in which structural contradictions exist among the norms and goals of social institutions; the inability of the individual to fulfill institutional norms and simultaneously reach goals results in delinquent behavior on the part of the individual (Doig, Watt, & Williams, 2005). Furthermore, institutions that are formally democratic still often lack mechanisms to ensure accountability and transparency. Yet it is exactly this—creating transparency in decision-making processes—that will limit selfish behaviors by policymakers (Smith, 2006). Such mechanisms should be embedded within laws and, once in existence, should be upheld through monitoring by auditors and citizens (e.g., municipality councils).

The 2007 Mexican Constitutional Amendment to Article 6, securing transparency in the public sector, has bolstered democratic citizen rights and agency by providing institutional oversight bodies and electronic access to information (Lujambio, 2008). Despite this promising shift toward increased governmental accountability, transparency is not yet guaranteed in Mexico, as evidenced by breaches of the Constitutional provision in several different states (Article 19, 2008). These breaches point to a need for continued focus on accountability in the public sector and better monitoring by auditors and citizens. The bureaucrats at the street level need incentives to reduce corruption and to implement policies and programs as they were intended. Furthermore, to achieve the full benefits of the new legislation upholding transparency, more emphasis must be placed on empowering citizens to use their democratic rights and hold their government accountable.

Public officials and bureaucrats could benefit from psychosocial training to support more productive behaviors and fortify their attitudes associated with building social capital: social trust, equality, tolerance, and civic participation. Such psycho-social support can derive from the kinds of programs laid out in this book. Increased focus on public servants, who comprise the fabric of Mexico's newly decentralized government, will serve to bolster the democracy of the country and, in doing so, will empower its citizens. People can begin to shift their view of their rights from "What power does (or doesn't) the governance structure have over me?" to "What do the powers that the governance structure does (or doesn't) give me allow me to do?"—a shift from "power over" to "power to."

Participation of Citizens

Contextual factors are of key importance in addressing the lack of citizen involvement that may impede full realization of a democracy. The public must be enabled and encouraged to take an active role in change. Encouraging active citizenship promotes "positive forms of life for communities, individuals and governments" (Marinetto, 2003, p. 109). Yet studies indicate that a majority of people do not feel empowered by their political context. In survey results from 2005, 65% of the population perceived politics to be complicated or very complicated, and 27% believed that politics did not contribute to bettering their lives (SEGOB, 2005).[21] Nine of every 10 Mexicans says they are not interested in politics (Casar, 2009). And politicians play a central role in generating this disinterest (Curzio, 2009).

The World Bank study *Voices of the Poor* highlights that although politicians, state officials, and public servants may be deemed important by a large proportion of impoverished individuals, they are rarely perceived as effective, trustworthy, or participatory by these same people (Narayan et al., 2000).[22] In an opinion piece in the newspaper *El Universal*, Curzio writes that politics "is boring because, first of all, the actors don't care what the people think. They do as they please... without consideration for the people"[23] (2009, p. A23). Rakodi (2003) illustrates how those with political power organize their interaction with society. Powerful political figures tend to develop influence not only through the formal political structure but also through an informal network of obligations and favors. As such, social leadership and the way it relates to the formal government structure may be a determinant of both people's real and perceived political status and benefits, affecting their choices. Curzio describes the Mexican democracy, writing:

> Citizens act like minors who, bothered by watching their parents fight, leave the trenches to seek refuge in personal matters. It is the worst possible situation because politicians who do not represent their constituents will continue to administer a country in which, due to laziness or immaturity, society refuses to assume its role in demanding change.[24] (2009, p. A23)

In a functional and free democracy, power lies in the hands of the citizens, in addition to their social leaders. As Gasper points out, "Democracy provides both for free circulation and testing of vital information, and for incentives to decision-makers to anticipate or respond to the informed pressures from their electorate" (2000, p. 993). The freedom of information characterized by successful democracies facilitates the distribution of power and agency to empower the substituent members of a society.

Despite the compelling benefits offered by democratic governance, the United Nations Development Program's report *Democracy in Latin America* concluded that preference of citizens for democracy is relatively low and that many Latin-Americans value development over democracy (2004). In 2004,

57%[25] believed or were ambivalent to the idea that "it is more important to develop a country than to preserve democracy and they would not object if a non-democratic government came to power if it managed to resolve the country's economic problems" (p. 134). This view reflects citizens' overall lack of information regarding the importance of democracy for development. In a comparative review of development performance, Siegle (2007) has shown that no trade-off exists between democracy and development. The high percentage of citizens who prioritize development over democracy also serves as evidence of limited understanding of individuals' potential role in a democratic government. We refer here again to the work of Sen, who has argued for the value of individual participation. There is an apparent need for people to understand how democracy benefits them at the local level and how they themselves can operationalize democracy.

For the political embodiment of personal agency to take place, democratic structures and attitudes must exist. These are ideal when combined with opportunities for citizens to develop the necessary knowledge, skills, and psychological preparedness for accessing a functioning democracy's freedoms. A government system can provide such opportunities through various mechanisms: encouraging a civil society (Diop & Léautier, 2007); facilitating fuller public discussion (Sen, 1999); improving transparency of government institutions, policies, and spending (Piccone, 2007); and enhancing the quality of media coverage, administration functioning, and regulations governing finance of political parties (McMahon, 2007). Other societal institutions also must contribute to the realization of such goals. For example, as argued, schools must promote autonomous decision making for citizens to fully participate in democracy.

The role of the individual as a policymaker and active citizen is at the core of a democracy that provides citizens with political entitlements. The individual is at the center of policy development, institutional action, decision making, and change implementation. Democracy can play an important role in bolstering agency in many areas of society. Further progress requires that individuals not only acquire personal agency themselves but that they also empower others within their community. As Luis Rubio noted in a 2004 article in the Mexican newspaper *Reforma*, "Democracy, when it operates adequately, has the virtue of promoting the active participation of the different political forces and interest groups in the decision making process"[26] (p. 17a). It is important to foster a culture of informed decision-making among leaders in addition to focusing on citizens' active participation and political entitlements. Individuals in government positions may change structural components, but ordinary citizens must continuously push for accountability from their local leaders.

Health Context

There is a difference between someone who is not well nourished because he/she fasts and a person who does not have the capability to be well nourished. ... The

difference between the two is that the person who fasts has the opportunity to be
better nourished. The notion of capability distinguishes between the achievement
of functionings of a healthy person and a person with a disease. ... The capabil-
ity of the patient is less than the capability of the healthy person. (Verkerk,
Busschbach, & Karssing, 2001, p. 53)

In 1978, at a conference in Alma-Ata (now Almaty), Kazakhstan, the World
Health Organization (WHO) declared that health "is a state of complete physical, mental and social well-being, and not merely the absence of disease or
infirmity" (WHO, 1978, p. 1). Although it was more than 30 years ago that
these basic public health goals and tenets of care were outlined, they still
remain unresolved in the healthcare policy and design of many countries.

Primary healthcare is at the forefront of the health system and plays an
important role in prevention and the provision of holistic care. It is the first
level of contact of individuals, the family, and the community with the national
health system (WHO, 1978). Yet deeply rooted social and economic inequality
in developing countries has created persistent mistrust (Uslaner & Brown,
2002), and tied with other psychological barriers has led to suboptimal use of
health services (Moseley et al., 2007). The empirical literature on social development reveals that such instances are not unusual,[27] and in fact are quite rational
(Mullainathan, 2005).

Those who lack access to primary healthcare are more likely to suffer from
ill health. Poor health has been shown to negatively impact the individual's
capacity to work toward personal development through education and employment and limits broader social development; it constrains the use of human
capital (Shepard, 2001). Poor health during childhood has been associated with
lower economic status and educational attainment later in life, even when controlling for factors such as parents' income and social class (Case, Fertig, &
Paxson, 2005). Absence of good health presents a barrier to exercising capabilities; and ironically, one's perceived capabilities may impact how an individual views his own right to healthcare.

Attending to the diverse health needs of a nation requires a well-developed
and well-executed healthcare system, in addition to participation of social and
economic sectors of society (WHO, 1978). Health policies begin with a national
strategy laid out at the federal and state level, which is filtered through implementing institutions, and, ideally, is molded to fit the local context. Practitioners
and officials (i.e., local bureaucrats) translate the policy so that healthcare
facilities become available to the individual user. Doctors, nurses, and health
promoters in this ideal schema have the communication and empathy skills as
well as the knowledge that allow them to respond to patients' needs. Patients
themselves possess the capacity to access and demand opportunities to care for
their health.

National Health Policies

In a country like Mexico, the constitution protects the individual right
to healthcare, but it is widely understood that the structure of the health

system has long kept many from accessing quality care (Barraza-Lloréns et al., 2002; Knaul & Frenk, 2005; Mexican Ministry of Health, 2004; OECD, 2005). Structural variations within the system—in terms of access, quality, coverage, and funding—still translate into massive inequalities. The health status of the affluent communities in Mexico often mirrors the developed OECD countries, whereas the poorer and rural areas have epidemiological profiles closer to those of less developed countries; communicable diseases like diarrhea, influenza, and pneumonia are still important causes of death ("Fallecidos por gripe porcina" [Swine flu deaths], 2009; OECD, 2005). For example, in the Sierra Mixteca in the State of Oaxaca, the average number of available doctors per 1,000 inhabitants hovered around 0.13 in 2001, while the national average was 1.34 (INI, 2001). Within the country, regional infant mortality rates vary by a factor of 2 and maternal mortality by a factor of 5 (OECD, 2005). These wide variations—linked to socio-economic status and degree of marginalization—remain even after accounting for disparate per capita spending on health (Frenk, Knaul, & Gómez-Dantés, 2004).

These inequalities are partly rooted in the design of the Mexican health system, which has remained relatively inelastic since 1943, when various institutional structures were established to serve different population groups. The Mexican Institute of Social Security was set up to manage the social security schemes of formal labor groups, and included healthcare as a component, while the Ministry of Health was established to provide care to the poor (who were largely informally employed) (OECD, 2005). This division in services had salient consequences. The Mexican Institute of Social Security coverage included access to a broad range of services at its health centers, including maternal healthcare. These were more complete than the services afforded by the Ministry of Health at its health centers (OECD, 2005). The funding mechanism involved led to further inequality because Ministry of Health services were funded solely by the government and were perpetually underfunded, whereas the Mexican Institute of Social Security was funded through arrangements generating money from employees and employers beyond that provided by the government (OECD, 2005). Thus, the quality of care depended on one's labor status, effectively discriminating against the 57% of the population working in the informal sector (Tokman, 2007). Additional disparities grew out of the geographical distribution of salaried, formal work. The best care provision was highly concentrated in major urban centers or in rural areas with industry; dispersed rural populations had very little access to care (OECD, 2005). This healthcare system maintained inequity and prohibited healthcare from being an effective entitlement (Barraza-Lloréns et al., 2002). Despite subsequent and significant health system reforms, one of the strongest layovers from this system today is the absence of a competitive environment in the healthcare delivery network to provide increased quality and consumer choice (Frenk et al., 2006).

Partial decentralization of the healthcare system undertaken during the 1970s aimed to move some services to the state level, intended to make the health system more responsive to local needs. This laudable goal was not met, largely because the state-by-state funding of health services exacerbated inequalities between the wealthy states and poor states (Birn, 1999). Furthermore, insufficient training for state-level administrators on how to manage the programs now under their guidance led to deterioration in program management (Ugalde & Homedes, 2005).

In 2004, Mexico undertook a massive reform of the healthcare system with the aim of making it more democratic (Mexican Ministry of Health, 2004). The goals of the System for Social Protection in Health were "reducing the prevalence of catastrophic expenditures by families, lowering the proportion of health spending that comes from out-of-pocket payments, and increasing access to insurance coverage" (Mexican Ministry of Health, 2004, p. 7). Underlying these aims, the Mexican Ministry of Health laid out the following five values: equal opportunity, social inclusion, financial justice, coresponsibility, and personal autonomy. As a result, the functions of the national health system were horizontally integrated, with stewardship under the Ministry of Health and tripartite financing from the federal government, state government, and families. National funding is now linked to the number of individuals enrolled, meaning that the money is directed to those states with the lowest levels of insurance coverage, typically those with the fewest resources.

Unveiled between 2004 and 2010, the full results of the reform are not yet clear at the time of the writing of this book. Intermediate results, however, show significant positive changes. As a result of the 2004 reform, the budget of the Ministry of Health grew by 69% in real terms between 2002 and 2006 as public resources were mobilized (Frenk et al., 2006). Equity of public health expenditure across states has improved (Gakidou et al., 2007). Catastrophic and impoverishing health expenditures have fallen steadily, attributable to economic growth and the poverty alleviation of the *Oportunidades* program, in conjunction with the changes in healthcare delivery (Frenk et al., 2006). Reports document that a challenge continuing to face the system is its poor client orientation and responsiveness (Frenk et al., 2006; Mexican Ministry of Health, 2004). An initiative accompanying the reform, entitled the National Crusade for Quality of Health Care, was launched in 2001 to improve technical quality and interpersonal responsiveness.

Testimonies by program participants have demonstrated to us that language and cultural barriers persist for the indigenous, and penetration into rural areas has been slow (Palacio-Mejía & Rangel-Gómez, 2003). The reform goals of social responsibility and correspondibility have not, at least not yet, translated from institutional restructuring to a more diffused organizational culture of service. One of the depressing aspects of the reform is the use of substantial program funds for image building—notably, through excessive advertising—to create a positive impression of the system. After exposure to flashy advertisements on citizens' right to healthcare, it is not at all uncommon for individuals to find a scarcity of basic medical supplies and health personnel with very little availability at their nearby clinic. Much progress is still needed to improve quality of care and heighten the trust of citizens in their healthcare system.

Health policies are often developed at the national level for local institutions to implement and are finally translated by practitioners to reach intended beneficiaries. As previously discussed in relation to the other sectors, policy development is driven by the politicians and implementation by the relevant bureaucrats. The building blocks of healthcare, such as quality, equality, access, and financial protection, must make sense to these individual decision makers. In the health context, the focus should be on the quality and extent of patient-centered orientation and responsiveness; key actors are the healthcare administrators and providers in the public health sector.

The Healthcare Administrators and Providers

Despite the frequent lack of even elementary resources in some regions, it is our impression that the main weakness of Mexican healthcare lies in the sphere of human resources. Health services are person-to-person services, meaning that the primary factor determining quality of care is individual characteristics, from availability to attitude and knowledge (Haddad, Clasen, & Davini, 1994). Practices at hospitals and clinics tend to be extremely rigid and unsupportive of patients and their elementary human rights. Personnel frequently fail to provide care-seekers with adequate, and respectful, attention. Perhaps the most convincing observations are the long rows of patients that collect in the early morning at many public hospitals. They are made to wait for a good portion of the day, sometimes to be turned away when services halt at the end of office hours. This is a simple illustration of the lack of individual control over healthcare; it is absent even at the most fundamental level of obtaining basic attention. In many institutions, few attempts are made to reduce waiting times through regulation of appointments, a step that would signal respect for the patient and improve access. In Sen's terminology, these practices are unsupportive of expanding the freedoms of patients.

Although there are many concerned and hard-working doctors and nurses, the system as such is not geared toward treating the patient as an autonomous and agentic human being capable of making decisions regarding his health. Explanations are not necessarily given in a way that the patient can make sense of, questions are largely unwelcome, interruptions during consultations are frequent, and empathy is not commonly expressed as part of the practice. We have seen that marginalized communities often face particular difficulties accessing quality care because of distance, language issues, and the relatively poor quality of care available in rural communities. An integral component of indigenous peoples' experiences in accessing healthcare is the divide between traditional and "modern" medicine. When modern clinicians and practitioners see traditional medicine only as an impediment to proper care, their attempts at both preventative and curative care can be hamstrung because of a fundamental clash with their patients' views.

Generally neither the individual patient nor the individual staff member can, on his own, overcome unfriendly patient practices that have long been considered acceptable. A psychosocial study undertaken with health personnel in Mexico's public health sector revealed that over one-third of those surveyed demonstrated high levels of emotional stress, and over one-fourth expressed feeling unfulfilled by their work, manifesting in high levels of tension, low efficiency and effectiveness, and excessive absenteeism (Beltrán, Elizalde, & Givaudan, 2009). During a training session for health promoters, a physician approached the program staff and expressed how the healthcare system and clinic morale was affecting doctors' work:

> How come it is health promoters that are getting all this training? You guys think we, the doctors, know how to talk to patients, how to value ourselves? We don't. All we do is try to comply with rules and with the expectations of our bosses, we can say we go through the motions of what it is we have to do, just so we get our lousy paycheck every 2 weeks. We just comply with the system but we cannot really do too much for the patients…not only because the most basic medicines and equipment are missing but because we don't really care much anymore. We are so fed up with how things work that we lose motivation and will.

For healthcare quality and access to be solidified in the clinical setting, policies must make sense to the administrators setting the tone and the clinics implementing the policies. In accordance with our suggestion to enhance teacher and public official training, both health providers and administrators deserve opportunities for personal and professional development.

In a recent study, Huichol[28] women in the state of Nayarit, Mexico, also shed light on barriers to healthcare, beyond those stemming from institutional practices. They not only cited language as hindering the quality of healthcare they receive but expressed a desire to be treated more humanely (Bingham et al., 2003). Testimonies from program participants have expressed similar sentiments:

> I do not understand anything the doctor says, he just scolds me, and I feel like he barks at me, so I prefer not to go see him.
>
> —Woman, Chichicastenango, Guatemala

> We don't understand what the doctor tells us; he does not speak our language and he does not make sense to us. He comes to the clinic whenever he wants to and does not really care about our health. All he wants is to report to the big bosses that he complied with his schedule.
>
> —Tarahumara woman in Northern Mexico

Overcoming barriers to service utilization requires that people are given support and respect, and made to feel comfortable. Practitioners can improve care by taking account of the values, traditions, and beliefs of their patients to frame programs and treatments in a way that better fits their worldview (Venguer et al., 2002). For this reason, attending to individuals in a way that is culturally and psychologically appropriate is central to enhancing well-being.

Several years ago, a screening program for otitis media (inflamation in the middle ear) was implemented in Australia with Aboriginal infants (Verkerk, Busschbach, & Karssing, 2001). An Aboriginal health worker entered the patients' homes, screened the infants, and provided their mothers with training in certain health concepts. An evaluation of the program determined that the greatest benefit to the community was not in terms of the individual screenings of infants; rather, the training of an Aboriginal health worker and the health training of mothers empowered the entire community to become more proactive about its healthcare. Not only had healthcare been provided in a culturally sensitive way by someone community members felt they could inherently trust, but those skills had been diffused throughout the population as an integral part of the program. The community had found new confidence in the health sector, a fact that would increase future health visits, and was also better educated to deal with health issues as they arose. The two key empowering acts—training a culturally sensitive health worker to do this job and imparting health knowledge to members of the community—changed the entire attitude toward the healthcare system in the community. This serious social change has important and permanent positive ramifications for the entire community.

Efforts to improve the exchange of communication between traditional and institutional practitioners have been shown to lead to more collaborative efforts between the two groups and improved practices by both (Venguer et al., 1998). One woman explained:

> The doctor now is more patient with me, listens, and even shows he cares. It used to be "Come in, get out."

Health professionals who are close to the community, such as community health workers (i.e., *promotores*), are in a unique position to mediate between community members and doctors and to facilitate understanding and trust.

Recent development efforts have worked with both doctors and patients to focus on bridging some of the misconceptions surrounding medical visits and interactions with medical personnel. Looking specifically at domestic violence initiatives, Pick et al. (1998) reported that a majority of doctors and community promoters working with women experiencing domestic violence encouraged women to press charges against the spouse and expressed certain prejudices against those women who continued in the abusive relationship (Fawcett et al., 1998). The study's results led to the development of initiatives to support providers in more effectively communicating risks to individuals in situations of domestic violence (Pick et al., 1998; Venguer et al., 1998). Medical providers afterward explained to program evaluators that they now understood the violence problem as a whole, rather than just knowing a specific action that should be taken that might or might not produce results (Fawcett et al., 1998). Behaviors could now be chosen from an array of alternatives, allowing women to exercise greater personal agency over their lives.

Lack of personal agency and intrinsic empowerment among the individual providers may also impede the success and sustainability of programs and policy (Greene & Yedidia, 2005). For example, an evaluation of training programs for HIV/AIDS prevention workers across Asia, Africa, and the Caribbean conducted by the United Nations Fund for Population Activities (UNFPA) found that the "high level of discomfort the trained service providers had with STI/HIV/AIDS issues... greatly compromised their effectiveness in dealing with STI/HIV/AIDS and reduced the benefit of training. The tendency was...

to stay in safe and familiar territory," relying on didactic rather than proven participatory methodologies (Office of Oversight and Evaluation, 1999, p. 2). Sensitizing and strengthening psycho-social capabilities in doctors and nurses improves their relationships with their patients, affecting care (Barnhart et al., 2006; Office of Oversight and Evaluation, 1999; Venguer & Givaudan, 1999).

The Healthcare Users

The collaboration of community members in healthcare planning and operation is particularly important to the system's effectiveness. The Declaration of Alma-Ata declared that healthcare:

> … requires and promotes maximum community and individual self-reliance and participation in the planning, organization, operation, and control of primary health care…and to this end develops through appropriate education the ability of communities to participate. (WHO, 1978, pp. 1–2)

However, historically in Mexico, the public sector has been top-heavy and has taken very little interest in citizens' participation (Barraza-Lloréns, Bertozzi, González-Pier, & Gutiérrez, 2002). In the private sector, on the other hand, communities have tended to have a great degree of autonomy as those health institutions have been more grounded in local needs (Barraza-Lloréns et al., 2002).

The intention of the Mexican government to facilitate community participation in public health services was clear even before the health system reforms of 2004, when the Ministry of Health explicitly included "social participation" as a strategy for health promotion, particularly looking to "the organized participation of society in defining priorities and executing local programs that deal with health promotion" (Pan American Health Organization). Since the reforms were passed, this intention has been reflected in recent trends, although the Comisión Intersecretarial para la Transparencia y el Combate a la Corrupción [Interministry Commission for Transparency and Fighting Corruption] recognizes that this movement is still young and gaining momentum.

According to the Comisión Intersecretarial para la Transparencia y el Combate a la Corrupción (2008), the federal government is seeking ways to include more provisions for community participation by changing the way governing bodies function and building community participation initiatives into its budgets. Specifically, it will fund programs that seek to build positive attitudes regarding community participation, both in government institutions and in the larger society; it will find ways to clear the path toward more direct citizens' participation by training government employees to receive citizens in a more productive way; and it will help citizens understand how the government works so that it is clearer to them what routes should be pursued to influence their governments.

The dimension of the individual (administrator, provider and patient) is often ignored or undervalued in nations' health policies. Policymakers, administrators, and doctors must possess the personal agency and intrinsic empowerment to translate policy and provide appropriate care. Patients must be treated in such a way that they are empowered to care for their health. Refocusing the vision of primary healthcare delivery within a broader context of individual and social development will be necessary to achieve true reform. As changes are implemented, they must be evaluated in the scope of their impact on expanding freedoms and capabilities.

Conclusions

The aim of this chapter has been to elucidate the context frame in FrEE. We only touched on certain aspects of the broader context—namely, education, economics, government, and health. Sen (1999) includes further domains in his list of freedoms, such as transparency guarantees and protective security. Even this list is not comprehensive, omitting important domains, such as the environment, which is finally and increasingly becoming an area of concern. The socio-cultural domain is also part of the context, but given its centrality in limiting or enhancing personal agency and intrinsic empowerment, it has been given its own chapter (*see* Chapter 2).

In our opinion, the four domains discussed illustrate how societal institutions can stand in the way of or can facilitate the development of personal agency and intrinsic empowerment. The self-interest of incumbents in certain roles and positions, beliefs in time-honored traditions, and resistance to change all play a role in promoting unfreedoms. However, the inability to see beyond current practices and the lack of skills and confidence to seek out and promote new strategies may be even more detrimental to development. Therefore, initiatives must work from both the top and bottom to overcome these considerable structural barriers to achieving development. The leadership and bureaucrats must be trained, children must be educated, and active citizenship must be built from the grassroots.

Strong leaders can challenge and change practices in societal institutions. Moreover, institutions can also be conducive to the promotion and maintenance of well-being, personal agency, and intrinsic empowerment. They can expand people's doing functionings and eventually their being functionings. The provision of these freedoms—democratic rights, health and healthcare, quality education, economic security—need not wait until after economic development is achieved, "but are positive factors in or even preconditions of development" (Fleurbaey, 2002, p. 71).

Notes

1. In the case of food entitlements, for example, "Sen means people's ownership rights to food (because they produce it) or to resources for obtaining it (through labor, barter, wages, inheritance, and social and other relationships)....increasing food production is only one way to increase entitlements; other approaches are to improve social

security through wage increases, education, low-cost health care, epidemic control, and community action" (Nestle, 1998, p. 372).

2. Sen emphasizes the fundamental role of the context in the expansion of individual freedoms, "Social arrangements may be decisively important in securing and expanding the freedom of the individual". (1999, p. 41)

3. Other authors have identified similar lists of domains. Bronfrenbrenner (1979) characterized "the context" as a series of systems contributing to personal psychological development, which he entitled micro-, meso-, exo-, and macro-systems. Moser (1998), identified the factors that are most valuable to people in their efforts to react and survive in situations of vulnerability, like the loss of a job, macro-economic crises, social conflict; these can be grouped under: work, education, health, productive activities, family relations and social capital. Finally, the sustainable livelihoods approach frames understandings of context by formulating a model based on a web of influences affecting the individual that include livelihood assets, vulnerability context, and livelihood context (International Fund for Agricultural Development, 2007).

4. Sen (1999) illustrates some of the important linkages between types of freedoms: "Political freedoms (in the form of free speech and elections) help to promote economic security. Social opportunities (in the form of education and health facilities) facilitate economic participation. Economic facilities (in the form of opportunities for participation in trade and production) can help to generate personal abundance as well as public resources for social facilities" (p. 11).

5. "Spending per student increased by 30%, at a somewhat lower rate, because enrolment also rose by 14%. Both the change in expenditure and the change in the number of students in Mexico are above the OECD average" (OECD, 2007a).

6. In 2003, the most recent data available, the OECD average was 5.9% of GDP, whereas Mexico spent 6.8%.

7. In reading, Mexico's score average was 410, whereas the OECD average was 492 ("The teacher," 2007, p. 225). In math, Mexico's score average was 406, whereas the OECD average was 498 ("The teacher," 2007, p. 230).

8. Seventy-five percent of 25- to 34-year-olds have not completed high school education in Mexico (grades 10–12), which is by far the lowest rate of all OECD members (OECD, 2007b).

9. The educational component of *Oportunidades* provides monthly scholarships for children who regularly attend school (over 85% attendance and do not repeat a grade more than twice) (Nigenda & González-Robledo, 2005). The stipends are intended to increase children's transition to higher grades and secondary school, and are slightly higher for girls beginning in secondary school because of their higher dropout rates. The amounts of the monthly grants range from about $7.50 (105 pesos) in the third grade of primary school to about $41 (580 pesos) for boys and $47 (660 pesos) for girls in the third year of high school (Levy, 2006).

10. "[R]ecently upper secondary completion rates have picked up.... The proportion of students graduating at upper secondary level has risen from 33% in 2000 to 40% in 2005, thus reducing the upper secondary attainment gap between Mexico and other OECD countries" (OECD, 2007a, p. 12).

11. "Sin desmerecer la hazaña social de nuestro pais de acercarse a la universalización de la educación básica, es importante reconocer que la evaluación de la escuela, debido al conjunto de relaciones sociales y políticas que estructuran su labor está lejos de responder a las exigencias de la democratización social y a la formación de una nueva ciudadania participativa, crítica y competente en la economía."

12. Countries that have taken part in this shift include Argentina, Colombia, Brazil, the Dominican Republic, and El Salvador.

13. Often this is seen as plain corruption, but officials and those around them will have a different perspective. Although such behavior is self-serving, the encumbents are inclined to see their personal privileges as entitlements which come with their position.

14. Pointing to the inability of dictatorial education to train students for today's world, Concepción Briseño, the Director of Psychopedagogy at the *Instituto para el Desarrollo de los Niños con Alto Potencial* [Institute for the Development of Children with High Potential] in Mexico, noted that: "The world is changing faster and faster, for this reason today's children need to acquire new forms of learning that will permit them to resolve problems in the best possible way, in the shortest time possible.... The traditional educational techniques are being left behind to give way to new visions that will allow skills to be developed, rather than making student memorize facts" (Gutiérrez, 2007).

15. The example of Kerala in southern India, where the level of health and education is much higher than in other places in India such as Uttar Pradesh and Haryana, is an excellent example of economic wealth being more as a means to wellbeing and of how often other variables such as social policies are much more relevant. If one looks at standard economic measures there is less poverty in Haryana, but in Kerala people live 10 years longer and everyone can read. This is related to public policies and so with a much lower economic wealth Kerala's citizens have reached a much higher level of functionings and well-being. (Dréze & Sen, 2002)

16. *Aboneros* are informal lenders who sell largely clothes, home appliances and jewlery, on credit. *Aboneros* lend over long periods of time on credit, and charge high interest rates.

17. "El país necesita.... una reforma laboral de fondo que permita una mayor productividad, la cual dará más prosperidad a los trabajadores y al país."

18. This number is calculated from the 2006 statistic on the total Mexican workforce, obtained from The World Bank Group's Genderstats, available online at http://genderstats.worldbank.org/.

19. Sen describes political freedoms as "the opportunities that people have to determine who should govern and on what principles... They include the political entitlements associated with democracies in the broadest sense (encompassing opportunities of political dialogue, dissent and critique as well as voting rights and participatory selection of legislators and executives)" (1999, p. 38).

20. "La protección de la salud es la mejor razón para que decidamos respetar las atribuciones del Estado. Pero esto sólo será reflejado con seriedad si nuestros representantes y gobiernos se toman como tarea, durante y tras esta experiencia, reconstruir al Estado como un instrumento de bien.....de bienestar."

21. "En general, ¿Qué tan complicada es o no es para usted la política? 1 Muy complicada 30.42%; 2 Complicada 34.45%; 3 Poco complicada 23.00%; 4 Nada complicada 7.65%". [In general, how complicated or not complicated are politics for you? 1 Very complicated: 30.42%; 2 Complicated: 34.45%; 3 Slightly complicated: 23.00%; 4 Not complicated: 7.65%"]. "En su opinión, ¿la política contribuye o no contribuye a mejorar el nivel de vida de todos los mexicanos? 1 Sí contribuye 39.43%; 2 Sí contribuye, en parte 26.54%; 3 No contribuye 27.01%". [In your opinion, do politics contribute or not to improving the quality of life for all mexicans? 1 Yes, it contributes: 39.43%; 2 Yes, it contributes somewhat: 26.54%; 3 No, it does not contribute: 27.01%].

22. "From the perspective of poor people, the state is largely ineffective. To a surprising extent, although the government's role in providing infrastructure and health and education services is recognized by poor people, their lives remain unchanged by

government interventions. Poor people report that their interactions with state representatives are marred by rudeness, humiliation, harassment, and stonewalling. Poor people also report vast experience with corruption as they attempt to seek health care, educate their children, claim social assistance or relief assistance, get paid, or receive protection from the police and justice from local authorities." (Narayan, Patel, Schafft, Rademacher, & Koch-Schulte, 2000, p. 8)

23. "aburre porque en primera instancia a los actores no les importa lo que piense la gente. Hacen y deshacen … sin considerar a la gente."

24. "Los ciudadanos se comportan como menores de edad que, fastidiados de ver a sus padres pelear, dejan la trinchera para refugiarse en asuntos personales. Es el peor de los mundos porque politicos con poca representatividad seguirán administrando un pais en el cual por pereza o inmadurez, la sociedad se niega a ocupar el papel que le corresponde para exigir un cambio."

25. The report does not break out Mexico separately, though it does provide that the Central America and Mexico region has a combined score of 53.5% on this indicator.

26. "La democracia, cuando opera adecuadamente, tiene la virtud de promover la activa participación de las distintas fuerzas políticas y grupos de interés en el proceso de toma de decisiones."

27. For an example of under usage of medical services applied to ethnic minorities in the United States, *see* Zambrana et al. (Zambrana, Ell, Dorrington, Wachsman, & Hodge, 1994). Evidence from developing countries on sub-utilization of free public assistance services is more scant but there exist anecdotal evidence from field practitioners (Venguer et al., 2002) .

28. One of Mexico's Indian groups, the Huichol primarily live in the Huichol Sierra in western Mexico.

References

Agence-France Press (2009, February 28). Corruption impedes Mexico drug fight. *Sydney Morning Herald*, from http://news.smh.com.au/breaking-news-world/corruption-impedes-mexico-drug-fight-20090228-8krm.html.

The Americas: "The teacher" holds back the pupils (2007, July 19). *The Economist*, 384(8538), 48.

Article 19 (2008). Mexico: Legislative power breaches the constitutional provision on transparency and access to information. *UNHCR Refworld*. Retrieved March 14, 2009 from www.unhcr.org/refworld/docid/4891d9532.html

Barba Casilla, B., & Zorrilla Fierro, M. (2009). La formación inicial de docentes en México ¿tiene salida? [The initial training of teachers in Mexico, will it lead to anything?]. *Megapolítica*, 13(63), 64.

Barnhart, J. M., Cohen, O., Wright, N., & Wylie-Rosett, J. (2006). Can non-medical factors contribute to disparities in coronary heart disease treatments? *Journal of Health Care for the Poor and Underserved*, 17(3), 559–574.

Barraza-Lloréns, M., Bertozzi, S., González-Pier, E., & Gutiérrez, J. (2002). Addressing inequity in health and health care in Mexico. *Health Affairs*, 21(3), 47–56.

Beltrán, M., Elizalde, L., & Givaudan, M. (2009). Formación en habilidades para la vida y metodología participativa para personal de salud [Life skills training and participatory methodology for health workers], *Report presented to Public Health Services of Mexico City*. Mexico City: IMIFAP.

Bingham, A., Bishop, A., Coffey, P., Winkler, J., Bradley, J., Dzuba, I., & Agurto, I. (2003). Factors affecting utilization of cervical cancer prevention services in low-resource settings. *Salud Pública de México, 45*(Supplement 3), S408–S416.

Birn, A.-E. (1999). Federalist flirtations: The politics and execution of health services decentralization for the uninsured population in Mexico. *Journal of Public Health Policy,* 20(1), 81–108.

Blomquist, J., Cordoba, J. P., Verhoeven, M., Moser, P., & Bouillon, C. (2001). Social safety nets in response to crisis: Lessons and guidelines from Asia and Latin America, *Paper submitted to the APEC Finance Ministers.* Washington DC: World Bank.

Bronfenbrenner, U. (1979). Contexts of child rearing: Problems and prospects. *American Psychologist,* 34(10), 844–850.

Buttel, F. (2000). Ending hunger in developing countries. *Contemporary Sociology,* 29(1), 13–27.

Carroll, B. W., & Siegel, D. (1998). *Service in the field: The world of front-line public servants.* Ithaca, NY: McGill-Queen's University Press.

Casar, A. M. (2009, March 23). Alertas [Alerts]. *Reforma,* from www.reforma.com.mx

Case, A., Fertig, A., & Paxson, C. (2005). The lasting impact of childhood health and circumstance. *Journal of Health Economics,* 24(2), 365–389.

Central Intelligence Agency [CIA] (2010, March). World factbook: Mexico Retrieved March 14, 2010, from www.cia.gov/library/publications/the-world-factbook/geos/mx.html#Econ

Cho, C.-L., Kelleher, C. A., Wright, D. S., & Yackee, S. W. (2005). Translating national policy objectives into local achievements across planes of governance and among multiple actors: Second-order devolution and welfare reform implementation. *Journal of Public Administration Research and Theory,* 15(1), 31–54.

Comisión Intersecretarial para la Transparencia y el Combate a la Corrupción [Interministry Commission for Transparency and Fighting Corruption] (2008). *Participación ciudadana... ¿Para qué? Hacia una política de participación ciudadana en el gobierno federal [Citizen participation... What for? Towards a politics of citizen participation in the federal government].* Mexico City: Secretaría de Salud.

Consultative Group to Assist the Poor [CGAP]. (2009). Notes on Branchless Banking Policy and Regulation in Mexico. Washington DC: CGAP, Technology Program. Retrieved March 7, 2010, from www.cgap.org/gm/document-1.1.1306/Mexico%20Branchless%20Banking%20Notes.pdf

Corral Jurado, J. (2009, April 14). Reforma educativa: ¿podrá Lujambio? [Educational reform: Can Lujambio do it?]. *El Universal,* p. A17, from www.el-universal.com.mx/noticias.html

Cox, C., Jaramillo, R., & Reimers, F. (2005). *Education and democratic citizenship in Latin America and the Caribbean.* Washington, DC: Inter-American Development Bank.

Curzio, L. (2009, April 20). La democracia anémica [Anemic democracy]. *El Universal,* p. A23, from www.el-universal.com.mx/noticias.html

de la Madrid, R. R. (2007). *Los socios de Elba Esther [The partners of Elba Esther].* Mexico City: Editorial Planeta.

Dercon, S. (2002). Income risk, coping strategies and safety nets. *World Bank Research Observer,* 17(2), 141–166.

Díaz de Cossío, R. (2005). Desigualdad en la educación [Inequality in education] In F. Solana & R. Díaz de Cossío (Eds.), *Educación y desigualdad [Education and inequality]* (pp. 21–25). Mexico City: Siglo XXI Editores.

Diop, A., & Léautier, F. (2007). Democracy: An adaptable system critical for development. *Development Outreach*. Retrieved January 13, 2008 from www1.worldbank. org/devoutreach/

Doig, A., Watt, D., & Williams, R. (2005). *Measuring "success" in five African anti-corruption commissions*. Bergen, Norway: U4 Anti-Corruption Resource Center.

Dréze, J., & Sen, A. (2002). *India: Development and participation*. Delhi: Oxford University Press.

Ellerman, D. (2001). *Helping people help themselves: Toward a theory of autonomy-compatible help* (Policy Research Working Paper No. 2693). Washington, DC: World Bank.

Estrada-Lopez, J. L. (1999). Poverty and economic reforms: Public policies in Mexico from a comparative perspective with Chile and South Korea *Project on Latin America and the Pacific Rim*. University of California, San Diego.

Fallecidos por gripe porcina en México suben a 89 [Swine flu deaths in Mexico rise to 89] (2009, May 26). *El Nuevo Herald*, from www.elnuevoherald.com/308/story/459458.html

Fawcett, G., Venguer, T., Vernon, R., & Pick, S. (1998). *Detección y manejo de mujeres víctimas de violencia domestica: desarrollo y evaluación de un programa dirigido al personal de salud [Detection and handling of women who are victims of domestic violence: Development and evaluation of a program directed to health personnel]* (Population Council Working Paper No. 26). Mexico City: Population Council/INOPAL III.

Fernald, L. C. H., Gertler, P. J., & Neufeld, L. M. (2008). Role of cash in conditional cash transfer programs for child health, growth, and development: An analysis of Mexico's Oportunidades. *Lancet*, 371(9615), 828–837.

Fleurbaey, M. (2002). Development, capabilities, and freedom. *Studies in Comparative International Development*, 37(2), 71–77.

Foweraker, J., & Craig, A. L. (1990). *Popular movements and political change in Mexico*. Boulder, CO: Lynne Rienner Publishers.

Freire, P. (1970). *Pedagogy of the oppressed*. New York: Seabury Press.

Frenk, J., González-Pier, E., Gómez-Dantés, O., Lezana, M. A., & Knaul, F. M. (2006). Comprehensive reform to improve health system performance in Mexico. *Lancet*, 368, 1524–1534.

Frenk, J., Knaul, F., & Gómez-Dantés, O. (2004). *Fair financing and universal social protection: The structural reform of the Mexican health system*. Mexico City: Secretaria de Salud [Ministry of Health].

Fuchs, T., & Wößmann, L. (2007). What accounts for international differences in student performance? A re-examination using PISA data. *Empirical Economics*, 32 (2–3), 433–464.

Gajardo, M. (1999). *Reformas educativas en América Latina. Balance de una década [Educational reforms in Latin America. Balance of a decade]* (PREAL Working Paper No. 15). Santiago de Chile: Programa de Promoción de la Reforma Educativa en América Latina y el Caribe.

Gakidou, E., Lozano, R., González-Pier, E., Abbot-Klafter, J., Barofsky, J. T., & Bryson-Cahn, C. (2007). Evaluación del impacto de la Reforma Mexicana de Salud 2001-2006: un informe inicial [Evaluation of the impact of the Mexican health reforms of 2001-2006: An initial report]. *Salud Pública de México*, 49(Suppl. 1), S23–S36.

Gasper, D. (2000). Development as freedom: Taking economics beyond commodities - the cautious boldness of Amartya Sen. *Journal of International Development*, 12, 989–1001.

Gasper, D. (2008). From 'Hume's law' to policy analysis for human development - Sen after Dewey, Myrdal, Streeten, Stretton and Haq. *Review of Political Economy*, 20(2), 233–256.

Gershberg, A. I. (1999). Fostering effective parental participation in education: Lessons from a comparison of reform. *World Development*, 27(4), 753–771.

Givaudan, M. (2003). Precursors of protective sexual behavior in Mexican youth: Development and longitudal evaluation of an intervention, *Doctoral dissertation, Katholieke Universiteit Brabant, 2003*. Amsterdam: Dutch University Press.

Glaeser, E. L., Laibson, D., & Sacerdote, B. (2002). An economic approach to social capital. *Economic Journal*, 112(483), 437–458.

Goldstein, M., Kaminsky, G. L., & Reinhart, C. M. (2000). *Assessing financial vulnerability: An early warning system for emerging markets*. Washington, DC: Peterson Institute.

Greene, J., & Yedidia, M. (2005). Provider behaviors contributing to patient self-management of chronic illness among underserved populations. *Journal of Health Care for the Poor and Underserved*, 16(4), 808–824.

Guevara, M., & González, L. (2004). *Attracting, developing and retaining effective teachers. OECD activity: Country background report for Mexico*. Paris: OECD.

Guichard, S. (2005). *The education challenge in Mexico: Delivering good quality education to all* (OECD Economics Department Working Paper No. 447). Paris.

Guillermoprieto, A. (2001). *Looking for history: Dispatches from Latin America*. New York: Pantheon Books.

Gutiérrez, V. (2007, July 3). Innovan educación [Innovating education]. *Reforma*, from www.reforma.com.mx

Haddad, J., Clasen, M., & Davini, M. (1994). *Educación permanente del personal de salud*. Washington, DC: Pan American Health Organization.

Hanushek, E. A. (2005, June). Why quality matters in education. *Finance and Development*, 42(2), 15–19.

Homedes, N., & Ugalde, A. (2005). Why neoliberal health reforms have failed in Latin America. *Health Policy*, 71(1), 83–96.

Instituto Nacional Indigenista [INI] (2001). *Programa nacional para el desarrollo de los pueblos indígenas 2001-2006 [National program for the development of indigenous communities, 2001–2006]*. Mexico City: Instituto Nacional Indigenista.

International Fund for Agricultural Development (2007). Sustainable livelihoods approach Retrieved July 24, 2008, from www.ifad.org/sla/.

Romero, J. (2009, April 8). Los retorcidos incentivos del sistema educativo [The twisted incentives of the education system]. *El Universal*, p. A16, from www.el-universal.com.mx/noticias.html.

Kagitcibasi, C. (2002). Psychology and human competence development. *Applied Psychology: An International Review*, 51(1), 5–22.

Knaul, F., & Frenk, J. (2005). Health insurance in Mexico: Achieving universal coverage through structural reform. *Health Affairs*, 24(6), 1467–1476.

Krueger, A. B., & Lindahl, M. (2001). Education for growth: Why and for whom? *Journal of Economic Literature*, 39(4), 1101–1136.

Lajous, A. (2009, May 6). Salud pública: Actuar ahora [Public health: Act now]. *El Universal*, p. A18.

Larson, P. E., & Coe, A. (1999). *Managing change: The evolving role of top public servants*. London: Commonwealth Secretariat.

Levy, S. (2006). *Progress against poverty: Sustaining Mexico's Progresa-Oportunidades program*. Washington, DC: Brookings Institution Press.

Lichfield, G. (2000, October 28). Mexico: Revolution ends, change begins (Survey). *The Economist*, 357(8194), M3–M4.

Lopez Gallardo, J., Moreno-Brid, J. C., & Puchet Anyul, M. (2006). Financial fragility and financial crisis in Mexico. *Metroeconomica*, 57(3), 365–388.

Lujambio, A. (2008, July 13). Transparency, what's next. *Reforma, Enfoque Supplement*, from www.gwu.edu/nsarchiv/mexico/lujambio_eng.pdf

Malenbaum, W. (1988). Amartya Sen on future development policy and program. *Economic Development and Cultural Change*, 36(2), 401–409.

Marinetto, M. (2003). Who wants to be an active citizen?: The politics and practice of community involvement. *Sociology*, 37(1), 103–120.

Martin, C. (1993). The "shadow economy" of local school management in contemporary west Mexico. *Bulletin of Latin American Research*, 12(2), 171–188.

Matin, I., Hulme, D., & Rutherford, S. (2002). Finance for the poor: From microcredit to microfinancial services. *Journal of International Development*, 14(2), 273–294.

McMahon, E. R. (2007). Regional organizations, sustainable development and democratic governance. *Development Outreach*. Retrieved January 14, 2008 from www1.worldbank.org/devoutreach/

Mexican Ministry of Health (2004). *Financiamiento justo y protección social universal: La reforma estructural del sistema de salud en México [Fair financing and universal social protection: The structural reform of the Mexican health system]*. Paper presented at the International Conference on Innovations in Health Financing. Mexico City.

Mexico's politics. (2007). *The Economist*. Retrieved February 19, 2008 from www.economist.com/displayStory.cfm?Story_ID=9516526

Molyneux, M. (2008). Progress against poverty: Sustaining Mexico's Progresa-Oportunidades. *Journal of Latin American Studies*, 40(1), 175–177.

Moseley, K., Freed, G., Bullard, C., & Goold, S. (2007). Measuring African-American parents' cultural mistrust while in a healthcare setting: A pilot study. *Journal of the National Medical Association*, 99(1), 15–21.

Moser, C. (1998). Reassessing urban poverty reduction strategies: The asset vulnerability framework. *World Development*, 26(1), 1–19.

Mullainathan, S. (2005). Development economics through the lens of psychology. In F. Bourguignon & B. Pleskovic (Eds.), *Annual World Bank Conference on Development Economics: Lessons of experience* (pp. 45–88). Washington, DC: World Bank and Oxford University Press.

Narayan, D., Patel, R., Schafft, K., Rademacher, A., & Koch-Schulte, S. (2000). *Voices of the poor: Can anyone hear us?* (Vol. 1). New York: Oxford University Press.

Nestle, M. (1998). Review: World Hunger by E. M. Young. *Journal of Public Health Policy*, 19(3), 372–374.

Nigenda, G., & González-Robledo, L. M. (2005). *Lessons offered by Latin American cash transfer programs, Mexico's Oportunidades and Nicaragua's SPN. Implications for African countries*. London: DFID Health Systems Resource Centre.

O'Neil, S. (2009). The real war in Mexico: How democracy can defeat the drug cartels. *Foreign Affairs*, 88(4), 63–77.

Ochoa Espejo, P. (2004). *The problem of "low intensity citizenship" in Mexico: Popular sovereignty and the logic of progress*. Paper presented at the Annual Meeting of the Southern Political Science Association. New Orleans, LA. www.allacademic.com/meta/p67621_index.html.

Office of Oversight and Evaluation (1999). *UNFPA support to HIV/AIDS-related interventions Part II: HIV/AIDS-related training.* www.unfpa.org/monitoring/pdf/n-issue12.pdf.

Organisation for Economic Co-operation and Development [OECD] (2005). *OECD reviews of health systems: Mexico.* Paris: OECD.

Organisation for Economic Co-operation and Development [OECD] (2007a). Education at a glance 2007: OECD briefing note for Mexico Retrieved July 11, 2008, from www.oecd.org.

Organisation for Economic Co-operation and Development [OECD] (2007b). PISA 2006 science competencies for tomorrow's world (Vol. 2). Retrieved February 23, 2008 from www.oecd.org/document/2/0,3343,en_32252351_32236191_39718850_1_1_1_1,00.html

Organisation for Economic Co-operation and Development [OECD] (2007c). *Program for international student assessment [PISA 2006]: Country note on Mexico:* OECD.

Osmani, S. (2008, Feb.). The role of employment in promoting human development. *The Maitreyee: Human Development and Capability Association [HDCA]* (10), 2–9.

Palacio-Mejía, L. S., & Rangel-Gómez, G. (2003). Cervical cancer, a disease of poverty: Mortality differences between urban and rural areas in Mexico. *Salud Pública de México*, 45(Suppl. 3), S315–S325.

Pan American Health Organization (2001). Country health profile. Health situation analysis and trends summary. Country chapter summary from Health in the Americas, 1998. Mexico. Retrieved June 15, 2009, from www.paho.org/english/sha/prflmex.htm.

Piccone, T. J. (2007). Building institutional capacity for democratization. *Development Outreach.* Retrieved February 13, 2008 from www1.worldbank.org/devoutreach/

Pick, S., Fawcett, G., Venguer, T., & Gamboa, M. (1998). *Domestic violence and reproductive health: Training for assessment and intervention in health care settings.* New York: INOPAL/Population Council.

Pick, S., Givaudan, M., & Reich, M. (2008). NGO-government partnerships for scaling up: Sexuality education in Mexico. *Development in Practice*, 18(2), 164–175.

Pick, S., Givaudan, M., Sirkin, J., & Ortega, I. (2007). Communication as a protective factor: Evaluation of a life skills HIV/AIDS prevention program for Mexican elementary-school students. *AIDS Education and Prevention*, 19(5), 408–421.

Pick, S., Xocolotzin, U., & Ruesga, C. (2007). Capacity building for decentralisation in Mexico: A psychosocial approach. *International Journal of Public Sector Management*, 20(2), 157–166.

Rakodi, C. (2003). Politics and performance: The implications of emerging governance arrangements for urban management approaches and information systems. *Habitat International*, 27(4), 523–547.

Ranganathan, N. (2000). *The primary school child: Development and education.* New Delhi: Orient Longman.

Rodriguez, V. E. (1997). *Decentralization in Mexico: From Reforma Municipal to Solidaridad to Nuevo Federalismo.* Boulder, CO: Westview Press.

Rodriguez, G. (2010, February 26). SEP-SNTE: Simbiosis atípica [SEP-SNTE: Atypical simbiosis]. *La Jornada*, p. 21.

Rubio, L. (2004, November 21). La era de la responsabilidad [The era of responsibility]. *Reforma*, p. 17a, from www.reforma.com.mx

Sarmiento, S. (2010, February 26). Unionized mafia [Mafia sindical]. *Reforma*, p. 18.

Sachs, J. D. (2005). Can poverty be eliminated? *Scientific American*, *293*(3), 56-65.

Schedler, A. (2005). From electoral authoritarianism to democratic consolidation. In R. Crandall, G. Paz & R. Roett (Eds.), *Mexico's democracy at work: Political and economic dynamics* (pp. 9-38). Boulder, CO: Lynne Rienner Publishers.

Secretaría de Gobernación [SEGOB] [Ministry of Administration] (2005). Encuesta Nacional sobre cultura Política y Prácticas Ciudadanas (ENCUP) 2005 [National Survey of Political Culture and Civic Practice 2005]. Retrieved July 25, 2008: www.gobernacion.gob.mx/encup/.

Sen, A. (1999). *Development as freedom*. New York: Anchor.

Shepard, R. (2001). Perceptual-cognitive universals as reflections of the world. *Behavioral and Brain Sciences*, 24(4), 581–601.

Siegle, J. (2007). Overcoming autocratic legacies. Retrieved March 3, 2008 from www1.worldbank.org/devoutreach/article.asp?id=445

Smith, K. B. (2006). Representational altruism: The wary cooperator as authoritative decision maker. *American Journal of Political Science*, 50(4), 1013–1022.

Solo, T. (2005). The high cost of being unbanked: Data from Mexico, Colombia and Brazil shows urban poor pay large portion of income for basic financial services. *Access Finance*. Retrieved November 8, 2007 from www1.worldbank.org/finance/html/accessfinance/022005/index.htm

Solo, T. (2008). Financial exclusion in Latin America - or the social costs of not banking the urban poor. *Environment and Urbanization*, 20(1), 47–66.

Stefanou, C., Perencevich, K. C., DiCintio, M., & Turner, J. C. (2004). Supporting autonomy in the classroom: Ways teachers encourage student decision making and ownership. *Educational Psychologist*, 39(2), 97–110.

Taber, L., & Cuevas, C. (2005). Integrating the poor into the mainstream financial system: The BANSEFI and SAGARPA programs in Mexico. *National Community Reinvestment Coalition: Global Fair Banking Initiative - Mexico*. Retrieved November 16, 2007 from www.ncrc.org/global/americas/Mexico_Page.htm

Tokman, V. E. (2007). *Modernizing the informal sector* (UN Department of Economic and Social Affairs [DESA] Working Paper No. 42). New York: United Nations.

Treviño, E., Pedroza, H., Pérez, G., Ramírez, P., Ramos, G., & Treviño, G. (2007). *Prácticas docentes para el desarrollo de la comprensión lectora en primaria [Teaching practices for the development of reading comprehension in elementary school]*. Mexico City: Insituto Nacional para la Evaluación de la Educación [National Institute for Education Evaluation].

Trillo, F. H., Cayeros, A. D., & González, R. G. (2002). *Fiscal decentralization in Mexico: The bailout problem* (RES Working Paper No. 3143). Washington, DC: Inter-American Development Bank Research Department.

Ugalde, A., & Homedes, N. (2005). Neoliberal health sector reforms in Latin America: Unprepared managers and unhappy workers. *Revista Panamericana de Salud Pública*, 17(3), 202–209. Retrieved November 26, 2007 from www.scielosp.org/scielo.php?script=sci_arttext&pid=S1020-49892005000300011&lng=en&nrm=iso

United Nations Development Program [UNDP] (2004). Democracy in Latin America: Towards a citizens' democracy. Retrieved November 29, 2007 from http://democracia.undp.org/Informe/Default.asp?Menu=15&Idioma=2

United States Agency for International Development [USAID] (2005). *Education strategy: Improving lives through learning*. Washington, DC: United States Agency for International Development.

Universidad Autónoma de Aguascalientes (2009). Implementación del Modelo de capacitación para la orientación y promoción social. Descripción técnica y plan de trabajo [Implementation of a training model for orientation and social promotion. Technical description and work plan], *Report presented to Diconsa*. Mexico City: IMIFAP.

Uslaner, E., & Brown, M. (2002). *Inequality, trust, and civic engagement.* Paper presented at the Annual Meeting of the American Political Science Association. Boston. from http://siteresources.worldbank.org/EXTECAREGTOPSOCDEV/Resources/ Uslaner_Inequality_trust_political_engagement.pdf.

van Ginneken, W. (1999). Social security for the informal sector: A new challenge for the developing countries. *International Social Security Review,* 52(1), 49–69.

Venguer, T., Fawcett, G., Vernon, R., & Pick, S. (1998). *Violencia doméstica: un marco conceptual para la capacitación del personal de salud [Domestic violence: a conceptual framework for the training of health personnel]* (Population Council Working Paper No. 24). New York: Population Council/INOPAL III.

Venguer, T., & Givaudan, M. (1999). *El rol del personal de salud en la sociedad: un enfoque humanista. Manual para instructores [The role of health personnel in society: A humanist focus. Manual for instructors]*. Mexico City: Editorial IDEAME.

Venguer, T., Heinz, C., Givaudan, M., Morales, N., Morales, G., Barriga, M. A., & Pick, S. (2002). Programa para el desarrollo de un modelo de atención materno-infantil para poblaciones indígenas [Program for the development of a model of mother-child care for indigenous populations], *Report presented to the Special Japanese Fund and Inter-American Development Bank.* Mexico City: IMIFAP.

Verkerk, M. A., Busschbach, J. J. V., & Karssing, E. D. (2001). Health-related quality of life research and the Capability Approach of Amartya Sen. *Quality of Life Research: An International Journal of Quality of Life Aspects of Treatment, Care & Rehabilitation,* 10(1), 49–55.

Villegas Hernandez, E., & Ortega Ochoa, R. M. (2002). *Sistema financiero de Mexico [The Mexican financial system]*. Mexico City: McGraw-Hill/Interamericana Editores.

Wilder, M., & Romero Lankao, P. (2006). Paradoxes of decentralization: Water reform and social implications in Mexico. *World Development,* 34(11), 1977–1995.

World Bank (2005a). *Income generation and social protection for the poor.* Mexico City. World Bank.

World Bank (2005b). *Mexico. Broadening access to financial services among the urban population: Mexico City's unbanked* (Report No. 32418-MX): World Bank Group.

World Bank (2006). Open and participatory governance in Mexico. Retrieved July 17, 2007 from http://go.worldbank.org/6TLVPMZY10

World Health Organization [WHO] (1978). *Declaration of Alma-Ata Conference on Primary Health Care.* Paper presented at the Alma-Ata International Conference on Primary Health Care. Geneva. 17 July 2007, from www.who.int/hpr/NPH/docs/ declaration_almaata.pdf.

Zambrana, R. E., Ell, K., Dorrington, C., Wachsman, L., & Hodge, D. (1994). The relationship between psychosocial status of immigrant Latino mothers and use of emergency pediatric services. *Health & Social Work,* 19(2), 93–102.

SECTION III

Development Strategies

CHAPTER 9

Strategy for Program Development and Implementation

In the first part of this book, we discussed the Framework for Enabling Empowerment (FrEE): the conceptual underpinning for health promotion and poverty reduction programs aimed at expanding choice through enhancing the capabilities of individuals. We argued that FrEE offers a way of making Sen's Capability Approach operational, emphasizing that people expand freedoms by extending their range of choices. Programming for Choice is a means of bringing this idea to fruition. In the second part of the book, we addressed how programs can help realize desirable changes in individuals, contributing to personal agency and intrinsic empowerment in communities. This chapter discusses how to approach the development and implementation of such programs. We show how Programming for Choice can be constructed and implemented through a step-by-step process in line with the principles of FrEE.

As we have seen throughout the book, the idea is to have a sustainable, expandable, and scalable approach to development. It is precisely through the Programming for Choice strategy that these aims can be reached. Sustainability occurs on two levels: individual and community. It is through the repeated application of a person's newly acquired capabilities that he forms the habit of putting these into practice, acquiring new behaviors. As that happens in a successful manner it builds personal agency and intrinsic empowerment, facilitating sustainable human development. Second, sustainability occurs at the community level as individuals direct efforts toward enhancing other individuals' and the community's well-being. Expandability refers to the extent to which a program is thematically expandable. Such is the case in the programs developed under FrEE. With a base of common skills and opportunities for psychological barrier reduction, numerous thematic programs can be designed, implemented, and evaluated. Finally, scalability refers to the possibility of a

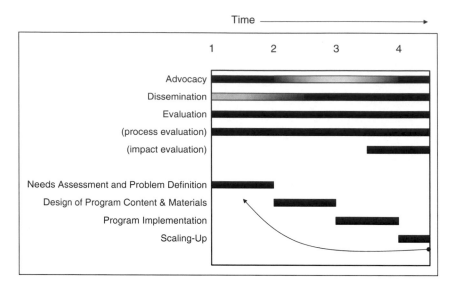

FIGURE 9–1 Program Development and Implementation Timeline

program being applied in greater magnitude. As demonstrated in this chapter, one of the objectives of the Programming for Choice strategy is precisely to scale-up a program once it has been implemented and tested.

The strategy outlined here distinguishes four stages in the development of a program that is sustainable, expandable, and scalable (*see* Fig. 9–1): *(1)* Needs Assessment & Problem Definition; *(2)* Design of Program Content & Materials; *(3)* Program Implementation; and *(4)* Scaling-Up. There is a series of supporting activities that are continuous throughout the entire process of program development and implementation—namely, advocacy, dissemination, and evaluation. Although introduced here, these supporting activities will be referenced throughout the discussions of each stage.

Advocacy & Dissemination

Advocacy and dissemination are directed toward program stakeholders, individuals, and organizations with an interest or a role in the program's financing, conceptualization, implementation, and/or results. Advocacy and dissemination allow for communication and coordination with these actors (Sohail, Maunder, & Cavill, 2006, p. 4). Stakeholder support enhances the probability that results obtained in the needs assessment and program pilot will be utilized (Segone, 2008b). Strong links with policymakers as well as the involvement of collaborating parties can be important determinants in an organization's success (Moynihan et al., 2008).

The notion of advocacy refers to the promotion of a cause. In Programming for Choice, advocacy is utilized to influence the environment in which a program is conducted, in the hopes of forming a context more supportive of the program and of individual and community development in general. To accomplish this, advocacy efforts should target a broad range of stakeholders, with approaches tailored to their diverse interests. Efforts should center on sensitization and negotiation (Ratne & Nguyen, 2005). Advocacy intended to sensitize broadens awareness of an issue to create a dialogue and rally support for addressing the problem. These efforts materialize in the form of meetings with funders and authorities in different sectors (e.g., education, social development, economic planning) and at various levels within these entities. Negotiation efforts aim to garner support—technical, financial, and institutional—for the implementation of a program.

The goal of dissemination is to diffuse program information. It also serves to spread word of program results and, in doing so, to muster continued support. An adequate flow of information regarding the program events is motivating; absence of information can result in reduced interest. For political reasons, politicians often prefer to support programs that have high visibility. They prefer programs wherein results are easily and broadly identifiable and that can show such results repeatedly at each stage of program implementation. These may be in the form of press and photo opportunities. Furthermore, dissemination encourages the diffusion of new ideas through informal channels (e.g., conversations at meals, in waiting rooms and community meetings) to new individuals who may themselves influence the context (Lazarsfeld & Katz, 1955). Dissemination is closely related to advocacy—the two facilitate one another. For example, when local authorities hear radio messages, they may reflect on their acceptance and understanding of the issues addressed by the program, furthering sensitization. Public campaigns not only educate the community but also increase social support for the program and the choices it advocates.

It is useful to distinguish between formal dissemination strategies, which mainly employ reports and publications, and public dissemination strategies, which focus on media and community events. Formal dissemination often targets donors and government officials with technical and financial investment in the program and typically involves presentations and reports on the progress of the initiative. Often dissemination of this kind is requested or even required by donors and government officials. For the most part, guidelines are already in place for both the format and the content.

Public dissemination can appear in a variety of forms, including opening and closing ceremonies (which can also be viewed as part of advocacy), press releases, radio and press interviews and general coverage, posters and promotional pamphlets, and presentations of diplomas to facilitators and participants. In contrast to the formal strategies, public and media events provide information to a significantly broader and more diverse audience. Public events represent a key dissemination strategy. The more people in the community—especially leaders or other influential individuals—are exposed to the issues and potential solutions, the more direct and indirect recipients of information will develop new attitudes and personal norms. The involvement of program participants in public dissemination initiatives contributes to their personal agency and intrinsic empowerment as well as to their investment in the particular issue or program to be implemented.

At the beginning of a program's implementation, advocacy and dissemination strategies serve to market an initiative, drive participation, and increase stakeholder support. At the later stage of program implementation, these activities create an environment receptive to the program and increase program sustainability. Widespread diffusion of program goals, advances, results, and impact promote support for continuation of the program in the future. In addition, dissemination serves as a means to increment transparency of program operations and accomplishments. Finally, as program participants take part in advocacy and dissemination (formally or informally), they become more open to change and supportive of personal agency and intrinsic empowerment among community members.

Evaluation

Historically, evidence-based policy decisions have not been widespread in the realm of public policy (Banks, 2009). For example, in the field of sexual health, only in the last decade have politicians begun to focus on scientific evidence as a basis for policy. Even so, recent statements from politicians demonstrate that this scientific approach has yet to become standard (de Anda, 2007). Segone[1] (2008a) echoes the near international consensus which stresses the importance of adopting such an approach, stating that "monitoring and evaluation should inform evidence-based policy options, to facilitate public argumentation among policy makers and societal stakeholders and facilitate the selection of policies" (p. 8). What policymakers have tended to value, and thus focus on, is cost-effectiveness analysis and cost–benefit analysis (Drummond et al., 2005; Fisher et al., 2002). However, many outcomes of social programs cannot be easily evaluated in such a cost-focused manner (Monk & King, 1993); psycho-social change is generally not as straightforward to measure as economic indicators.

Further complicating the use of evaluation is that some effects can only be appreciated after a long period of time—for example, when programs lead to higher educational achievement (Kagitcibasi, 1995). Often, diverging stakeholder interests drive the evaluation process and the stakeholder's perception of the results. For example, community-based facilitators may perceive an evaluation as "passing judgment" if it is not framed correctly and if they are not aware of the process from the beginning; in these cases, the findings may not be well-received within the community. Additionally, the study design, sophistication, speed of data collection, and various methods of data analysis often depend on the interested parties and requirements of the funding entity.

The potential to address these issues lies in the evaluation process. A democratic approach to evaluation can provide a forum for a number of interests. An additional evaluation approach to empowerment, which Fetterman et al. define as "the use of evaluation concepts, techniques, and findings to foster improvement and self-determination" (1996, p. 4), addresses the bias that has typically associated evaluation with contexts of institutional power (Segone, 2006). These approaches inherently further the mission of Programming for Choice.

Our program evaluation methodology aims to involve communities throughout the research process as a way to create awareness, improve outcomes, and reduce disparities; it is key to understanding people's needs and enhancing feelings of ownership.

Because a considerable volume of literature concerning evaluation methods is available already (Rossi, Lipsey, & Freeman, 2004; Shadish, Cook, & Campbell, 2002; Shadish, Cook, & Leviton, 1991; Weiss, 1998), here we simply aim to highlight some of the main components essential to Programming for Choice. It is an integral task of program coordinators to utilize evaluation procedures that are independent of their own enthusiasm for the program. To reduce this bias in evaluation and achieve a comprehensive assessment of the program, evaluation must be designed in conjunction with the planning of the program itself (Pick & Poortinga, 2005). Through this continuous and systematic process, it becomes possible to avoid the perception that the evaluation process is forced, a means of judging the program, or a "necessary evil." Rather, evaluation is more likely to be viewed as a standard learning tool and an instrument for improving program quality.

PROCESS AND IMPACT EVALUATION

There are two aspects of evaluation: impact (or outcome) evaluation and process evaluation (or monitoring). *Impact evaluation* measures the effectiveness of the program through documenting changes in target outcome variables. Selected variables in which change should occur are specified beforehand. They usually represent aspects of behavior that lend themselves to objective psychometric assessment and/or observation. They are a subset of all the behavior changes that may result from Programming for Choice. This evaluation data must be collected systematically both pre- and post-program, in intervals extending over a number of years. The program group ideally is compared with a control group to account for natural behavior changes. The most statistically rigorous method of evaluation is the randomized control trial, where the sample is randomized into experimental and control groups and the program is evaluated both before and after it is implemented (Shadish, Cook, & Campbell, 2002). Unfortunately, field conditions often make it impossible to execute such a rigorous approach because the program may already be in place or ethical considerations may preclude having a classic "control" group. Therefore, a carefully balanced decision must be made in determining the most appropriate evaluation design for a particular program.

Process evaluation refers to keeping tabs on the quality of each activity of the program from the conceptualization stage through final evaluation. It provides a record of activities and intermediate results, which are important for accountability to stakeholders, such as financial sponsors. It also provides insight into processes contributing to the observed program impact. Examples of evaluation components include attendance records as well as comments regarding acceptance and understanding of contents, type, and quality of experiential exercises. Process evaluation in social development programs can assess the various nontargeted changes that may have occurred in attitudes, knowledge, and actual behaviors and competencies. In addition, it is possible to use indicators of personal agency and intrinsic empowerment to measure interim success. Changes may also be observed at the contextual level—that is, in socio-cultural norms and economic, educational, political, and health opportunities and constraints. As changes at these levels are the emphasis of Programming for Choice, process evaluation plays a particularly valuable role. In fact, to facilitate replication and understanding of the program, having documentation of each of the program components is key.

In undertaking evaluation with these multiple foci, both quantitative and qualitative instruments can be utilized. Quantitative methods are modeled on the experimental paradigm of the natural and life sciences and the survey methodology of the social sciences. For example, impact studies based on survey instruments (e.g., questionnaires or standardized interviews) with a pre-post-design and a control group are the prime example of a quasi-experimental quantitative approach (Silow-Carroll & Alteras, 2005). Qualitative evaluation includes a variety of methods, including focus groups, semi-structured interviews, and observation guides. They tend to be more exploratory; general objectives may be formulated, and evidence is assessed as it emerges (Mittman, 2001). Given the complexities of programs and program implementation, sometimes a combination of these instruments (i.e., mixed methods) is the best means to assess program effectiveness.

Program developers and evaluators must decide on the percentage of program funds that should be directed toward each type of evaluation. Considerations may include: issues of budget allocation, evaluation goals, and research audience. Whereas funders, policymakers, and academic researchers are generally interested in the quantitative data, community representatives may be more convinced by qualitative data—examples of how individuals have experienced participation in a program and what impact it had on their lives. Moving evaluation results into the political sphere, so that they can inform policy options, necessitates not only technically sound but also politically relevant evaluation and presentation (Segone, 2008a).

Moreover, it should be understood that policymakers are often under pressure to show fast results, react to emergencies, and make headlines. Program evaluators may need to present findings in ways that address these needs, which often requires reporting outcomes at various stages instead of solely upon program completion. Rather than being a burden, evaluation and reporting are often perceived as constituting an opportunity to draw attention to the program. Handing over a report to a government official, for example, creates occasions for photographs and press appearances.

In summary, both impact and process evaluation can contribute to successful program evaluation, at various levels and time periods throughout the program. They must incorporate target variables and yet remain open to the inclusion of new variables that emerge throughout the evaluation process. Ideally, evaluation should cover all stages and core activities of program development and implementation, as well as the more peripheral activities of advocacy, dissemination, and evaluation itself. The amount of work may seem prohibitive, but once evaluation becomes routine, rewards from careful and critical (including self-critical) reporting minimize the burden. Additionally, involving stakeholders in the evaluation process elevates their sense of program ownership and, correspondingly, increases future support for program expansion.

Stages of Program Development and Implementation

This section describes the four stages of program development and implementation. Figure 9–1, entitled Program Development and Implementation Timeline, provides an overview. It lists the general objectives of each stage, gives examples of methods and activities, and indicates the form that continuous activities have taken. Each of the stages is illustrated with concrete examples taken from a program originally called *"Si yo estoy bien, mi familia tambien"* [If I Am OK, So Is My Family] and later renamed *"Yo quiero, yo puedo . . . cuidar mi salud y ejercer mis derechos"* [I Want to, I Can ... Care for My Health and Exercise My Rights]. Because the program discussion that follows focuses on the original version of the program, we refer to it by its original name: "If I Am OK."

In 1998, GlaxoSmithKline[2] asked various civil society and government institutions to present proposals for health promotion in Latin America. After submission of a proposal, IMIFAP teamed up with the Mexican Social Security Institute's Opportunities program (*IMSS-Oportunidades*) to turn their two proposals into a single program, named "If I Am OK," with funding from GlaxoSmithKline. The program was designed and implemented by IMIFAP by training *IMSS-Oportunidades* community promoters and was reviewed by *IMSS-Oportunidades* to ensure it was in accordance with government norms. It was conducted in the target area of Mixteca, an impoverished, rural, largely indigenous region in the Mexican state of Oaxaca. The impetus for this program was that women should not sacrifice their health and well-being for their husbands and children, as socio-cultural norms in Latin America encourage, but instead need to look after their own health to be able to act in the interests of their families. The goal was to reach 32,000 young women (up to age 20 years); ultimately, 39,000 women participated. The program has been documented in progress reports for the sponsor and in scientific publications describing the program rationale and results. (Venguer et al., 2002; Venguer, Pick, & Fishbein, 2007)

Despite the simplicity of this description, the development of a program does not begin as suddenly as it may appear. Implementation is preceded by a considerable amount of work, including brainstorming and protracted negotiations with financial sponsors to get a program off the ground.

These negotiations are followed by a decision to undertake an initiative and the establishment of a target population. Although early activities related to scope and funding tend to vary, the stages described in the remainder of this section are described in systematic steps (*see* Fig. 9–2).

Program Stages	Objectives	Methods and Activities	Advocacy and Dissemination	Evaluation
Needs Assessment & Problem Definition	Identify needs, both individual and community level Determine the issues (specifically behaviors) to be targeted for change Define the target population of the program	CONTEXTUAL LEVEL Government statistics, ethnographic reports INDIVIDUAL LEVEL Focus groups, interviews, questionnaires	Involve the various stakeholder groups Seek collaborators to conduct formative and exploratory research Seek financing Disseminate expressed needs, problem definition, and program goals to the target communities and other stakeholders	Clearly define the needs Ensure the necessary information has been collected. Assess the quality and quantity of basic information Ensure there is sufficient representation of the main stakeholders Assess whether sufficient exploratory and formative research exists (i.e., questionnaires, focus groups, interviews)
Design of Program Content & Materials	Develop program components and other materials Plan for advocacy and dissemination locally Conduct small small-scale field trials (piloting)	CONTEXTUAL LEVEL Advocacy meetings Building messages for mass media INDIVIDUAL LEVEL Select themes and contents Select educational methodology Develop manuals, textbooks and supporting materials	Focus on local stakeholders Pilot preliminary advocacy strategies Undertake local dissemination campaigns	Test program concepts, methods, and contents with program developers and through small-scale field trials Ensure the needs of the chief stakeholder groups have been addressed Ensure that the local contextual conditions for behavioral change have been facilitated
Program Implementation	Establish the effectiveness of the contents and methodology and undertake necessary revisions	CONTEXTUAL LEVEL Deliver community level program components (e.g., radio messages) INDIVIDUAL LEVEL Train program facilitators Deliver program to target individuals	Continue work from the previous stage (including advocacy to affect contextual conditions) Disseminate information on program advances to both donor(s) and the public Meet with funding agencies and government officials on scaling up	PROCESS EVALUATION Calculate the attendance rates Assess the overall acceptance of the program IMPACT EVALUATION Determine whether there are observable effects in experimental (versus the control) group Conduct qualitative assessments
Scaling-Up	Extend the reach of the program	Adapt program elements in accordance with contextual differences and local needs Develop specific systems for distribution of materials, for training of facilitators and for quality monitoring	Negotiate with funders, the media, and authorities (local, national, or regional) Undertake mass media campaigns Facilitate contextual conditions for behavior change (national or regional)	BEFORE SCALING-UP Determine how the needs of the target population will be addressed Make sure the key stakeholders are involved AFTER SCALING-UP Evaluate whether the program is effective in its large-scale application

FIGURE 9–2 Summary of Program Development and Implementation Stages

Stage 1: Needs Assessment & Problem Definition

OBJECTIVE

The main objective of the first stage is the identification of needs, accomplished through defining the problems the program will address, the scope of the program, and the specific target population. Program developers must have a fairly complete picture of the prospective program beneficiaries' lifestyles and be familiar with their levels of personal agency and intrinsic empowerment.

METHODS

Two modes of program development are to be distinguished: *(1)* a program can be developed from scratch, or *(2)* an existing program can be adapted. In the first situation, the needs of the target population and program possibilities need to be explored; in the second, a pre-existing program is presented to members of the new target group, who then decide whether the program objectives— specifically the targeted behaviors—suit their needs. If the program is deemed fitting, potential beneficiaries then assist in adjusting the program to fit its new environment.

> The development of the "If I Am OK" program provides a good example of the methodology described above. This particular program was developed based on previous experience at IMIFAP and principles of FrEE. IMIFAP and *IMSS-Oportunidades* jointly selected two municipalities in the Mixteca region to implement the program. An analysis of the municipalities most in need shaped this decision, pointing to high poverty rates, lack of infrastructure, and absent social services. The organizations then selected specific communities within each municipality for a total of 480 communities. Once the target population was defined, its members had a voice at every stage of the process of program development and implementation. Their input was incorporated either directly or through representatives (e.g., teachers, community leaders, health professionals).

ACTIVITIES

Various methods exist to examine local needs. A first distinction in needs is between contextual and individual needs. At the contextual level, economic, demographic, and epidemiological information is useful because it informs the incidence of events and the influence of macrolevel determinants. To understand the determinants of poverty in a given area, one may investigate income levels, means of subsistence, fertility rates, and frequency of particular health practices. Government statistics (when they exist) are also an important source for such information, as are ethnographic reports. Cultural anthropologists often provide careful descriptions of the way of life, the socio-cultural norms, and the practices of a group. A contextual analysis for Programming for Choice in Oaxaca combines these methods of research.

> The state of Oaxaca, one of the poorest in Mexico, has a population of approximately 3.5 million (INEGI, 2000b).[3] Forty-eight percent of homes had a water

distribution system; 39% had dirt floors (INEGI, 2000b).[4] In Oaxaca, the infant mortality rate was 3.17%, and the national rate was 2.49%, an excess of 728 infant deaths per year (CONAPO, 2009).

The situation of indigenous people in Oaxaca was, and remains, even worse. Oaxaca has one of the largest indigenous populations of all the Mexican states: 46% of all households in the state are indigenous, and 32% of the population speaks an indigenous language (INEGI, 2000a). According the Instituto Nacional de Estadística, Geografía e Informática (INEGI) census in 2000, 25% of this population earned less than the minimum wage (set by the Mexican government at around 2.60 USD/day that year), twice the percentage for the entire state. Only 2% earned more than five times that amount (INEGI, 2000b). As of 2005, 62% of all illiterate people in Oaxaca were indigenous, even though indigenous people made up less than one-third of the total population (INEGI, 2005). The situation of indigenous women is still worse; today, only slightly more than half of these women know how to read and write (INEGI, 2008).

Even though a problematic picture of Oaxaca emerges from these figures, they still underestimate the situation in the Mixteca, for which few separate demographic statistics are available. For example, in the Mixteca, much of the soil has been eroded, making it very hard to harvest anything (Altieri et al., 2006). In addition, both actual and perceived access to schooling and health services is exceptionally low (Pick, 2007; Venguer, Pick, & Fishbein, 2007).

To address the population's needs, this contextual information must be supplemented with individual data and reports. Focus groups, interviews, questionnaires, and talking with individuals and local authorities are some of the ways to gain an understanding of the range of factors driving the statistics. Research focusing on the individual level can highlight the underlying psychosocial and cultural factors that act as both constraints to and potential opportunities for improved utilization of the context. These methodologies and materials will serve for pre- and post-program evaluation as well as shape decisions regarding indicators and instruments of data collection for process and impact evaluation.

It is important to note that there is an inherently imperfect relationship between the way needs are expressed and the way in which needs must be translated into a curriculum. Often, questions posed to the community about their needs are met with short and diffuse responses such as "I am always sick," or "There is no chance to do anything in this community," and must be combined with the program developers' common sense and expertise—using information gleaned from contextual data—to achieve a more complete assessment. Responses of this nature must be analyzed in light of contextual research. Additionally, some people may be more communicative in individual interviews, whereas others may feel more at ease in a focus group. For these reasons, it is best to employ a variety of formative and exploratory research strategies.

Use of these strategies in Oaxaca brought about new understandings of the target community:

The program staff of the "If I Am OK" program conducted four focus groups, each with 6 to 12 women in attendance, as well as 60 individual interviews with teachers, students, traditional healers, local and federal authorities and health professionals, priests, and midwives, across 16 of the 480 total communities in order to understand needs. Questions addressed knowledge, beliefs, and practices regarding hygiene (e.g., not having animals inside the house, frequency of bathing, existence of trash cans, use of latrines), nutrition (e.g., the need to boil drinking water, eating of vegetables), sexual and reproductive health (e.g., use of and access to contraception), and personal agency (e.g., assertive communication and involved decision making). Follow-up questions were included in order to understand reasons for reported courses of action, advantages and disadvantages of engaging in those actions, and the role of family and community in the decisions. Examples of findings obtained through the focus groups and interviews include: reasons for not growing vegetables (e.g., fear of contagion with fertilizer, expense of seeds) and reasons for not boiling drinking water (e.g., believed loss of nutritional value, poor taste, lack of family approval of the practice).

In addition to providing program developers with an understanding of the poverty conditions and general atmosphere of the communities, the results demonstrated that unequal gender relationships, obligation, uninvolved decision making and adherence to norms often guided the action of community members. These results would eventually drive program development with an eye for multithematic contents and were used immediately to develop a questionnaire for systematic data collection.

An additional questionnaire was conducted to assess pre-program levels of all the target variables for impact evaluation. The items fell within various broad categories: knowledge, beliefs, attitudes, and practices related to nutrition, hygiene, sexual and reproductive health, and personal agency. Retired teachers and upper-level students from the local communities, who were specially trained, conducted the surveys in homes with 856 women and 360 men (ages 12–30 years) across a sample of 160 communities.

ADVOCACY & DISSEMINATION

Involving the various stakeholder groups—both those from the community (e.g., trusted community members) and those outside of the community (e.g., federal authorities)—as early as possible can be conducive to program support at initial and subsequent stages. When stakeholders are part of the problem identification and program planning process, they begin to understand the issues to be addressed, learn to value the methodology and program objectives, and support the concepts behind Programming for Choice. These stakeholders may also facilitate the formative or exploratory research. Not everyone can participate in each decision, so the reasoning for bringing different stakeholders to the table needs to be transparent. For each party involved, the expected level of commitment should be jointly determined. Furthermore, the open discussion and valuation of community participation inherent in this stage demonstrates an acceptance for voicing needs, which is itself a means of expanding capabilities.

A variety of such strategies were employed in Oaxaca to meet these ends:

In the case of "If I Am OK," expressed needs and program goals were disseminated in presentations to the general population at community gatherings, to which key local, state, and federal authorities and funders were also invited. In addition, individual meetings were conducted with key stakeholders, local authorities, and the media.

EVALUATION

The principal question at the end of the needs assessment and problem definition stage is whether needs have been clearly defined and the necessary information for program development and implementation has been collected. From here, program coordinators can begin to assess the quality and quantity of information-gathering procedures. It is important to determine whether the main stakeholders have been sufficiently represented, as well as whether an appropriate number of focus groups and interviews have been conducted. Without this pause for evaluation, the issues of potential interest for decisions regarding, for example, quality, feasibility, continuation, or institutionalization of a program may never be exposed. In the early stages of program implementation, it is also important to ensure that sufficient time is reserved for meetings with local administrators and that the agendas for these gatherings remain clear and precise. Assessing these factors contributes to the development value of process evaluation.

The initial evaluation activities should also involve an examination of the initial methods of process and impact assessment. At this stage, the stakeholders should agree on the program sites, methodology, materials, and quality of data explored. Adjustments to the program structure and evaluation methodology should be made before the principle intervention begins. Evaluation is most effective when all of the program stakeholders are on the same page from the beginning.

An initial evaluation in Oaxaca looked at the activities undertaken thus far:

> One of the strengths of the initial phase of "If I Am OK" program development was the extensive data collection, which involved the target communities and assessed their needs. Survey findings, in particular, not only provided baseline data for an impact evaluation but also helped to support and modify impressions gained from open-ended interviews and focus groups.
>
> It proved extremely helpful that the *IMSS-Oportunidades* health-care infrastructure could provide program staff with easy access to the local populations and to staff of rural hospitals and clinics. Although it is difficult to evaluate the extent to which all the critical issues facing these populations were identified, the findings did highlight the components needed to improve well-being of women in these areas of Mexico. Only a small part of the community was directly involved in this initial stage; nevertheless, comments received from community members showed that word spread of this involvement and aided in generating a sense of community ownership at later stages of the program.

We must point out that in the initial stage, it is not easy for stakeholders, coming from very different backgrounds and perspectives, to agree on a community's main needs and the best means of targeting a problem. For example, the politician is likely to be interested in gaining political support; men want to alleviate the economic and health problems of their families, but preserve the status quo in social relationships; and teachers may worry that parental involvement and active student participation will create more work for them. Program developers must account for these diverse interests and should determine how much they are willing to compromise their interest with stakeholder perspectives and proposals.

Stage 2: Design of Program Contents and Materials

OBJECTIVES

The purpose of Stage 2 is to develop all program components for implementation and use in Stage 3. These elements are not limited to the program as such but include materials needed for community level activities, such as advocacy and dissemination. The piloting of small-scale field trials with a preliminary version of the program materials is included in this stage (*see* Fig. 9–2).

Additionally, the recruitment of program facilitators is undertaken at this point. Based on geographical location and an interest in being part of the program, community-level *IMSS-Oportunidades* staff were identified to serve as program facilitators. Sustainability is enhanced when facilitators are from the community, especially when they are professionals whose job it is to train children, adolescents, and adults. Their positions of trust enable them to continuously facilitate development of personal agency, intrinsic empowerment, and accompanying changes in social norms within the community. They also enhance community ownership of the program.

METHODS

The development of the program is based on the information gathered in Stage 1 and on the programmers' professional expertise. A theoretical framework should guide program design efforts to facilitate evaluation and attain program coherence and success. Within FrEE, program contents and methods will be developed primarily to provide relevant knowledge, skills, and opportunities for reducing psychological barriers and changing behaviors. Given the common bases of many behaviors, we undertake this program development with the multithematic understanding gained in Stage 1. Many of the concerns of people living under conditions of poverty are similar, especially across a region. As such, the task of program developers is to merge components specific to the communities (as identified by the needs assessment) with knowledge about the success and failure of prior programs and psychological principles about instruction and learning.

ACTIVITIES

Once the content and methodology have been set, program developers design the manuals that facilitators will use, the textbooks for students (in the case of school-based programs), and other support materials. These may include question-and-answer books, flipcharts, games, videos, posters, brochures, various promotional items, and, more recently, interactive Web pages and blogs.[5] The data collected in the previous stage support selection of the most context-appropriate design, text, and illustrations. For all materials, designers create rough drafts and modify them according to community feedback and results of piloting (discussed later). This dialogue between program designers and the community should be constant throughout program development, implementation, and follow-up.

Supporting materials help reinforce the information provided in program sessions. They also serve as a primary means of sensitization for people who are not participants. Aesthetically pleasing and durable materials that are designed with participation and feedback from the target communities builds a positive image of the program among stakeholders. For facilitators and the target population alike, these materials foster feelings of trust and self-importance as well as a sense of ownership over the program.

Content, methodology, and a range of materials were developed from the program in Oaxaca:

For "If I Am OK," specific topics were chosen that were then organized by theme, and the themes grouped into modules (seen numbered below; each theme was emphasized in turn during a series of workshop sessions). Themes and modules included:

1) Women's personal development
   1. Health and agency (health rights; decision making; communication; assertiveness)
   2. Nutrition, health, and agency (women's and pregnant women's nutritional needs)
   3. Hygiene, sanitation, and agency (prevention of common infectious diseases; personal hygiene, negotiation)
   4. Sexuality, reproductive health, and agency (fertility, pregnancy, and breast-feeding processes; knowledge about sexually transmitted infections, cervical cancer, and contraceptive methods)
2) Children's development
   1. Supporting children's development and agency (the meaning of being a woman; socio-cultural norms regarding the role of maternity; early childhood stimulation; children's developmental stages)
   2. Children's health, nutrition, and agency (nutrition, malnutrition, and health; prevention of accidents; respiratory and gastrointestinal problems and how to prevent and cure them).

IMSS-Oportunidades ensured that the developed content was in line with government norms and standards, which would allow for any future institutionalization of the program.

The following provides an example of how an identified need was integrated into content and methodology.

In interviews conducted at the start of "If I Am OK," many women expressed that they were tired because they had so many children but that there was not much they could do about it, given their husbands' intolerance of family planning. Any contraceptive methods they used, which they were hesitant to discuss even in individual interviews, could not be referred to and did not always work. Through these interviews, it became clear that the women needed specific information on the topic. As such, the "If I Am OK" program included:

1. Knowledge about different kinds of contraceptives and where to obtain them, and exercises on how to ask for them (*see* Fig. 6–3),
2. Skill-building for deciding among methods (*see* Fig. 6–1),
3. Awareness raising on social role expectations (*see* Fig. 6–5), and

4. Skill-building on how to confront related social norms (*see* Fig. 6–3 and Fig. 6–5), including those imposed by one's spouse.

In addition, the opportunities to participate in role plays and other exercises allowed participants to express their concerns, listen to those of others, and practice the options which they desired to put into practice.

In creating the methodology of any Programming for Choice, a strong emphasis should be placed on incorporating interactive methods. Knowledge provision and skills practice in the safe and open environment of small-group workshops is an important learning strategy. When a secure environment is combined with a methodology that encourages the use of discussion and reflection this supports the internalization of the knowledge and skills that participants develop and helps reduce psychological barriers.

Knowledge provided in context rather than in the abstract is commonly known as embedded knowledge. Learning through embedded knowledge "makes sense" more than it could if acquired outside of its natural context. During the needs assessment stage, we discovered, for example, that popular wisdom dictates that boiling water affects its taste or reduces vitamin content. Wisdom may also posit that well-cooked vegetables taste better than those less cooked. Simply stating that water should be boiled to prevent diarrhea or that vegetables should not be overcooked to retain vitamins is less effective than offering new information within the framework of an exercise in which participants actually cook vegetables. In a hands-on, interactive setting, participants can share recipes and express doubts. They are free to share and discuss their opinions on the taste of boiled water and of vegetables that are cooked for shorter periods of time. The group facilitator is able ask questions about becoming accustomed to a new taste and why it is important to prioritize vitamin content. These methods engage participants, rather than lecturing at them. The experiences of program participants highlight for the group that the new knowledge is useful, and trust in the facilitator begins to grow. The social and personal connections formed increase the likelihood that new information will be spread among community members and adopted in the community, eventually replacing prior beliefs and practices.

ADVOCACY & DISSEMINATION

Advocacy occurs more or less as a continuation of earlier activities. In this second stage, rather than focusing on sponsors and authorities, the focus is primarily on local stakeholders (e.g., administrative and health authorities, headmasters of schools). The goal is to create a context favorable for forthcoming program implementation and expansion of opportunities. This work also supports the recruitment of local facilitators. Strategies for advocacy are continually tested and reviewed. For example, one-to-one negotiations may be preferable in some stages, whereas group meetings may work better at other phases of program development. There are many possibilities for advocacy and dissemination—some more successful than others—that are realized as the program evolves.

Discussions begin with local media in the geographic area of implementation for purposes of dissemination, and presentations are made at community meetings. In short, the basics of the upcoming program contents are widely shared to keep all stakeholders involved and knowledgeable. Program advocacy and dissemination efforts for the "If I Am OK" program in Oaxaca were undertaken in partnership with *IMSS-Oportunidades*:

> Activities entailed meetings with local and federal *IMSS-Oportunidades* staff and other health sector authorities to sensitize them to the philosophy behind the program and to gain their support. It was not easy for these individuals to support a comprehensive program developed with community participation as a central tenet. They were accustomed to programs that did not involve the community and that were based solely on sensitization and information provision strategies (under the misguided conception that they suffice to bring about behavior change). Aiming to provide local contextual support as well as community-wide dissemination of program ideas, "If I Am OK" dissemination strategies entailed the development of a radio jingle, pamphlets, and posters.

EVALUATION

The actual writing of the program and its supporting materials occurs in the office. Hence, much of the evaluation tends to be conducted by the program developers themselves. Critical reflection occurs at three levels:

1. *Concepts*: Refers to the testing of the concepts (e.g., choice, life skills, psychological barriers, knowledge) underlying the program and the level of difficulty and depth with which they are presented.
2. *Methods:* Refers to such aspects as use of interactive activities and types of materials.
3. *Contents*: Refers to physical design, figures, kinds and depictions of fruits, vegetables, landscapes, and clothing.

Evaluation of the program in Oaxaca occurred at the three levels:

> These levels were evaluated after small-group piloting. IMIFAP and *IMSS-Oportunidades* staff reviewed and discussed all program modules. Subsequently, a group of 25 women from the target population reviewed the first two program modules and were asked to make recommendations.
>
> Staff and women reviewers recommended changes both in the content and in the design of visual materials. Primarily, they felt the program needed to more effectively encourage a sense of program ownership among participants. The idea to develop a distinct program logo resulted from these discussions; the logo was printed on all program booklets, on bags, and on a program button given to all participants. In retrospect, the buttons—perhaps more than anything else—helped to create the atmosphere of program ownership and the sense of community that led to very high attendance rates (*see* Stage 3). These stakeholders' receptiveness toward the program reflected contextual conditions.
>
> The remaining modules were not tested because piloting of the first two modules addressed concerns relevant throughout the entire program. Program staff had also learned that the training workshops for facilitators served as a major review process in itself and that shortcomings could be identified at this point, before the program was implemented for the beneficiaries. Piloting thus served both a developmental and an evaluative role.

Activities undertaken at the contextual level continue to be evaluated during this time. Questions are repeatedly posed, including: "Have all chief stakeholders been addressed?" and "Have the local contextual conditions for behavior change been facilitated?"

Stage 3: Program Implementation at the Local Level

OBJECTIVES

This is the major testing phase of the newly constructed program. It is where one establishes the effectiveness of the contents and methodology. For the participants, it is an investment of time and effort, which can only be requested if the program developers are convinced they have something worthwhile to offer.

METHODS

The methods used to teach the program material to facilitators are crucial for replication among participants. Integrating both specific and general skills, knowledge, and opportunities for their application is an ideal way to encourage the development of life skills and to conduct facilitator training. Manuals provide guidelines for the facilitators, but they are encouraged to adapt their facilitation style based on their strengths and on the specific group dynamic. The following excerpt comes from the facilitators' training manual for the program "My Voice, My Life" (an abbreviated version of "I Want to, I Can ... Prevent Pregnancies" developed for Latino populations in the United States):

> A good facilitator needs to be constantly observing and reading the group in order to respond effectively to the group's needs. Try to look for body language that will tell you: if the energy of the group is low, there is tension, or there is positive momentum building. It is also important to be self-observant, asking yourself questions such as: How is my energy level? How much have I been talking versus the group? What am I feeling? Through observation, the facilitator can detect special "learning moments" for the group—either new relationships being formed between participants or new ways of understanding the topics

The key to successful program implementation is to provide facilitators with training both as individuals (for their own personal development) and for their role as facilitators. The reason for this is essentially the oft-heard phrase that "One cannot give what one does not have." Facilitators at any level have to be able to communicate and make decisions before they can teach the same skills, need to address taboos and myths about gender equality and sexuality, and must understand, experience, and value being agents of their own lives. Program implementation requires facilitators to agree with and be able to utilize teaching methods that promote critical thinking, creativity, reflection, and application of skills as well as cater to different learning styles.

Training of both facilitators and program beneficiaries involves interactive activities, reading materials, and open communication. Individual participation as well as teamwork is fostered. Various exercises are implemented to guide the group through the concepts and activities presented in the program. There is rarely a moment when facilitators give a long presentation or lecture on a topic. Rather, the facilitator is expected to guide the group, ensuring the information flows as part of the discussions and reflection periods. Interactive workshops of this nature empower participants to come up with solutions themselves; no recipes are provided. Only on a few rare occasions, which are always rooted in activities, are facilitators expected to deliver in-depth explanations directly to the beneficiaries.

It is important to give feedback to participants throughout the program activities to ensure that they get the most out of the workshop. Facilitators begin to empower participants to direct their own learning processes by asking them to reflect on their experiences, posing questions such as, "What strengths did you display as a participant in this activity? What would you like to improve?" The feedback process is an opportunity for the facilitator and the group to learn through the process of reflection (Pick et al., 2006).

We shall use the "If I Am OK" program to elucidate the means of training program facilitators—particularly a large number of them. Ideally, a system should be used that has the facilitator working directly with the target population. The reality is that this is rarely possible because of the short-term costs involved; rarely are the longer term costs of such an effort calculated. Therefore, varying kinds of cascade systems are generally employed. A cascade approach closely reflects the internal structure of many service organizations and has been used widely in programs. The benefit of the cascade training system is that it creates a team of facilitators that is much larger than the organizing institution's staff. Therefore, this allows a program to reach larger population than would otherwise be possible. If carried out with facilitator accompaniment and systematic feedback mechanisms, program sustainability increases significantly because locally trained community leaders and members may continue program replication once the program staff leaves. The shortcoming is that the more levels involved in the cascade, the higher the likelihood of information being diluted. Therefore, it is important to strike a balance between the number of levels and the projected number of beneficiaries.

Given the direct and extended access to target populations of school teachers and health workers, they are most widely recruited as facilitators, hence the extensive employment of *IMSS-Oportunidades* personnel in "If I Am OK." However, Programming for Choice does not necessitate reliance on trained professionals. Laypeople who receive training can act as program facilitators in their own communities. Needless to say, considerable advocacy and dissemination efforts are required to secure their involvement, especially if facilitators do not receive financial compensation. Details of the closely accompanied cascade training system used in the program in Oaxaca demonstrate how this can work (*see* Fig. 9–3).

To ultimately reach 39,000 participants, in the "If I Am OK" program, a closely monitored cascade system of training was followed. This was based in the structure of *IMSS-Oportunidades*. The cascade consisted of four levels: IMIFAP training personnel, *IMSS-Oportunidades* community action promoters,

IMSS-Oportunidades rural health assistants, and, finally, *IMSS-Oportunidades* social volunteer promoters who undertook the workshops directly with program participants (*see* Figure 9–3). The training plan was put together with the community and relevant authorities. Each group received an equal amount of training, whereas the scheduling of the training sessions was tailored to the requirements of the participants at that level.

For each pair of program modules IMIFAP personnel, making up the first level of the cascade, individually trained approximately 20 community action promoters. This was done through a 1-week training course of 40 hours. The training was directed both at achieving with the trainees the goals of the program itself (e.g., knowledge, psycho-social skills, reducing psychological barriers) and at developing their group management skills and ability to utilize the didactic materials within their own classrooms.

These community action promoters, working in pairs, then replicated the week-long training with groups of rural health assistants. Each pair conducted about 15 of these training courses. The pair structure facilitated mutual support and learning between the promoters. In total, they trained approximately 500 rural health assistants to be facilitators.

The 500 rural health assistants replicated the workshop individually with small groups of social volunteer promoters, totaling around 3,100. At this juncture, the week-long training course became a month-long course, taught less intensively in daily 2-hour sessions, as this schedule was more convenient for the trainees. It is worth mentioning here that conducting training as well as replications over longer periods of time is useful in that it allows space for further reflection.

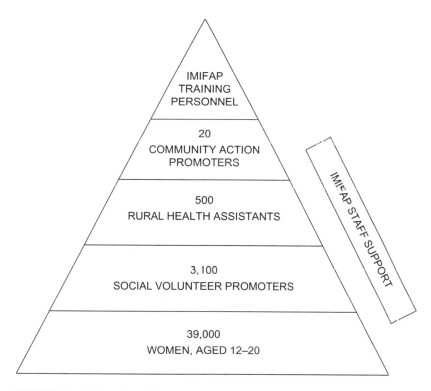

FIGURE 9–3 Training Pyramid

Longer time-frames, however, are not always feasible given the needs and interests of different groups. At each of the levels, IMIFAP personnel accompanied new facilitators, filled out observation guides, carried out interviews, answered questions, and provided feedback.

ACTIVITIES: ADMINISTERING THE PROGRAM

After the final level of facilitators has been trained, a program is ready for implementation. These facilitators will run the interactive workshops in the target population. The example of Programming for Choice demonstrates how this can occur:

> Within "If I Am OK," social volunteer promoters facilitated the workshops for women in their own communities, reaching 39,000 women in total. The workshops were given in weekly sessions that lasted around 2 hours each, an average of 4 months for a set of two modules. It was rare for workshop sessions to be held more often than once a week, as both promoters and participants were busy with their daily activities. Sometimes a session was postponed because the women had to attend to home responsibilities, harvesting, or care for a sick child. Group size ranged between 10 and 15 people.
>
> In this way, the implementation of a full cascade, beginning when IMIFAP personnel train community action promoters and concluding with the training of the target women, took approximately 7 months. This process was repeated three times, once for each set of two modules in the program. The entire program covered a period of 18 months and involved 120 hours of training for each facilitator. Although each round of module training sessions focused on new topics, they also expanded on facilitators' skills and their personal growth and development.

ADVOCACY & DISSEMINATION

Advocacy and dissemination work continues through the implementation stage of a program. Continued focus must be placed on the target population and their immediate environment. New efforts are geared toward diffusing information about program advances both to donors and to the public, intended to draw continued support for the program and ensure transparency.

The primary means of dissemination at this stage are presentations, reports, and public and media events. Presentations and reports particularly target donors and government officials who have made investments in the program; they often request data in forms according to their needs. Public and media events address the communities through different means, including executive summaries, press releases, radio and press interviews, television coverage, presentations of diplomas to facilitators and participants, and closing events.

Dissemination of program results feeds advocacy efforts. As politicians see progress being made, they increase their support for Programming for Choice. Positive results (*see next section on Evaluation*) also lead to new meetings with funding agencies and key government officials, jump-starting negotiations for program implementation on a wider scale. Public media campaigns can advocate for change in the local context and simultaneously demonstrate an interest in fostering institutional change, including new laws and regulations, or development of roads, schools, or clinics. This returns to a crucial point—that for any programming efforts to be scaled-up and maintained, government involvement is often necessary.

EVALUATION

Evaluation of the implementation stage has to determine whether Programming for Choice is leading to targeted changes in behavior or whether it is less effective than anticipated. Both process and impact evaluation are carried out at this stage. The population's acceptance of the program is evaluated as well as attendance rates and any other *ad hoc* observations that highlight positive or negative effects.

Fundamental to an effective program, and of particular importance within a cascade system, is the quality of program delivery. For this reason, much attention should be given to close monitoring and accompaniment of training at the various levels of the cascade. In the cascade, in particular, information passes through many eyes and ears over time, causing a high risk of distortion or misinterpretation of information. A method of addressing this challenge is presented with the program in Oaxaca:

> A monitoring system was built into the "If I Am OK" program to evaluate facilitators and their quality of program delivery. IMIFAP training personnel accompanied all first level of trainees (community action promoters) for a full 2 days of their replications. Quality of instruction, use of materials, and atmosphere in the groups were monitored, and the appropriate feedback provided.
>
> An impact evaluation was also conducted with the community action promoters following their first training. The assessment consisted of a close-ended questionnaire dealing with attitudes, beliefs, and knowledge that had been applied pre-training, as well as a similar but open-ended interview. The results, with almost no exception, showed a high level of knowledge paired with favorable attitudes and beliefs in accordance with programmatic objectives. With minor modifications in language, the same questionnaire was administered in the next two levels of the cascade. In the few instances where performance was deemed inadequate, trainees did not become facilitators.
>
> As a component of process evaluation, each social volunteer promoter kept track of attendance in a notebook provided by IMIFAP. A sample of 100 attendance records showed that the average attendance increased from 15.5 persons at the beginning of the program to 17.4 persons at the end. In fact, many women over 20 years of age, and even men, attended even though they were not the targeted population. There were a few dropouts because of harvesting seasons and emigration from the region. There were no reports of dropouts resulting from parental pressure or dislike of the program. Informal, qualitative indicators, such as comments from community leaders on changes they had witnessed within program recipients, also pointed to success of the program. This intricate evaluation of training at each level of the cascade shows that the monitored cascade method worked well and that the program was delivered to the target population in accordance with programmatic objectives.

The main criterion for program success is impact data—that is, evidence of changes in behavior repertoire in ways targeted by the program.

> The results of the impact evaluations—both questionnaire and interview—as compared to a control group, provided clear evidence of a positive impact of "If I Am OK." Changes were found in both the self-report questionnaire items and in standardized observations made by the interviewers when collecting data. For example, they found a lower frequency of animals being stabled inside the house, a higher number of patches with planted vegetables, a higher incidence of boiling drinking water, and cleaner houses. All evaluative methods indicated the success of the "If I Am OK" program, providing objective evidence of behavior change stimulated by the workshops. For more detailed information on findings, we refer the reader to Venguer et al. (2007).

The final question remaining concerning new evaluation data is whether any changes are necessary to improve the effectiveness of the program. If they are, the program must either be abandoned or retested in its new format. Stage 3 must then be repeated. Only when the effectiveness of a program has been demonstrated unambiguously does it make sense to proceed to the final stage.

Stage 4: Scaling-Up Toward Regional/National Implementation

OBJECTIVES

Once a program has been evaluated and shown to succeed, it can be considered for scaling-up. Implementation in larger target groups creates an opportunity to broaden the reach of a program. Scaling-up increases the number of final beneficiaries of a program, either by including more people within a given region or by incorporating more geographical locations. As Binswanger (2000) has argued, we cannot continue to have programs, which "like expensive boutiques" are only "available to a lucky few" (p. 2173). Scaling-up is a cost-effective method of reaching more individuals, but decisions about when and how to scale-up are not trivial.

Given that sustainable development comes about not only through initial change but also through maintenance of that change, it is important to strike a balance between starting new programs and using resources to follow up with previous program participants. Moreover, the ideal time for scaling-up may vary depending on the program and evaluation goals and the sophistication of research methods and measurement. Many psycho-social variables are difficult to properly measure and experimental designs are not always ideal, or attainable for field work, and thus quasi-experimental designs may be the best option in these circumstances. Finally, despite the fact that CSOs often deem collaboration with government unacceptable, it is primarily governments that can sustainably augment large-scale programs given their geographic reach, human and economic resources, and long-term presence. Achieving the proper balance requires a realistic assessment of the particular needs of the context, the organization, and stakeholders.

METHODS

Large-scale implementation is more successful when specific systems for distribution of materials, facilitator training, and for monitoring quality have already been established. The management of a large-scale program implementation requires key decisions, such as where activities should take place (e.g., from a centralized location, locally, or preferably, concurrently at both sites). These decisions depend on a variety of factors: the programmatic perspective, availability of resources, predicted impact on ownership, and capacity for program replication. Integral to this decision, however, must be confidence in the potential to enhance the freedoms of the individuals and communities involved.

The transfer of programs from one population to another can be an important and precarious step in the scaling-up process, particularly when the new target population differs in some respects from the original group. It can also be a controversial issue among professionals. Skepticism may arise concerning the implementation of a program in one community, which was initially developed based on another community's expressed needs. The overarching concern in these cases is whether scaling-up a program truly responds to the needs of the new target population. Strictly speaking, program transfer implies that this population does not define its own needs, because others have already accomplished this for them. When formulated in this way, the inalienable right to personal agency and intrinsic empowerment of the target population, central in FrEE, is limited. However, presenting the program and its goals to all stakeholders in the new community—and allowing them to decide whether the program meets their needs and to suggest changes—ensures that the rights and personal agency of the new program participants is respected.

If there are cultural differences between the original population for which a program was developed and the new target population, then it will be necessary to determine the extent to which the program must be adapted to fit its new context. In our experience (e.g., Leenen et al., 2008; Osorio & Givaudan, 2006; Pick & Reyes, 1994), literature on transfer of psychological tests from a source culture to a target culture (van de Vijver & Hambleton, 1996; van de Vijver & Leung, 1997; van de Vijver & Poortinga, 2005) can be applied to program development in so far as adaptations may be necessary at the following levels (applied also in the evaluation in Stage 2, *see above*):

1. *Concepts.* Program developers in collaboration with local consultants and members of the target population must decide whether or not equivalence of concepts can be assumed as a starting point in program transfer. The central question to be asked is: Do the concepts addressed in the program, like lack of control or psychological barriers, make sense in the target culture? In the case of Latin American countries, there is strong connection of historical, linguistic, economic, and religious backgrounds, which in many cases eases transfer even between countries. Transfer between developing countries outside of Latin America requires testing, but our previous experience, and given the social and economic similarities between countries, points to a likely positive answer in this regard as well.

2. *Methods*. It must be determined whether the same methodology is suited for use in the new target culture. For example, are participatory and reflective techniques acceptable in the new setting? Once again, we would side with an answer of yes to this question; people simply gain more from participating, asking, playing, interacting, analyzing, questioning, and reflecting than from patiently sitting and listening.

3. *Content*. At this level, adaptations are likely to be needed even if the cultural distance between the source culture and the target culture is small. For example, in the transfer of the "If I Am OK" program to a region in Guatemala, specific items like the types and names of nutritious plant species had to be changed (Leenen et al., 2008). What of the current program content will be used meaningfully in the new target population?

Across Mexico, programs that worked successfully in one region have been used with similar results elsewhere (Pick, 2007; Venguer, Pick, & Fishbein, 2007). Also, transfer across countries both within and outside of Latin America appears to be feasible (Anaya et al., 2008; Leenen et al., submitted; Leenen et al., 2008; Martínez, Givaudan, & Pick, 1995; Osorio, submitted; Osorio & Givaudan, 2006; Pick de Weiss et al., 1994; Pick et al., in press; Pick & Reyes, 1994; Ramón et al., 2000; Ramón et al., 2002; Tacher et al., 2008; Tacher et al., 2009; Vera et al., 2002). Our impression is that in most cases, conceptual and methodological equivalence exists, and modification is only required in the material content. Such changes in content may include the types of fruits and vegetables promoted or the dress depicted in visual materials. Sometimes transfer across regions also necessitates the utilization of different kinds of media. Nevertheless, there is a distinct possibility that when programs are transferred across national or regional borders, or to distinct cultures, equivalence will be lacking. For this reason, it is important to recognize the range and degree of difference involved before attempting to scale-up a program.

IMIFAP's largest transfer and scaling-up of a program is the recently completed "Comprehensive Community Development" funded by the United Nations and with the participation of more than 10 state and federal institutions. Its aim was to implement and evaluate a multistrategic model of empowerment, health, and economic productivity to improve the quality of life of marginalized families. The project was formed from the integrated application of three separate programs that targeted health and rights for women, men, and children, and a program on micro-enterprise—one of these programs being "If I Am OK." It reached nearly 150,000 parents, children, teachers, community promoters, and authorities in close to 1,000 communities across Hidalgo and Chiapas (Givaudan et al., 2009; Givaudan et al., submitted; Pick, Barriga, & Givaudan, submitted). The most recent effort of scaling-up, of IMIFAP's nutrition and empowerment program in the 300,000 poorest households of Mexico showed statistically significant increases in nutritious eating (Leenen et al., 2009). Likewise the hygiene, nutrition and empowerment program implemented in 11,000 communities served by Diconsa showed statistically significant increases in positive hygiene- and nutrition-related practices, as well as in assertiveness, personal agency, and intrinsic empowerment (Universidad Autónoma de Aguascalientes, 2009; García, Pick, & Romero, submitted). As this book goes to print, negotiations are underway for the application of this model to a program with Seguro Popular for supporting the extended adoptions of maternal lactancy and of early stimulation of babies.

Activities

The activities undertaken for scaling-up are in many ways a return to the beginning. Program developers conduct Stage 1 activities of needs assessment and problem definition among the new population, as they determine necessary adaptations of design, language, and methodology. This is also an opportunity to consider whether additional themes might fit well into the program for the new target population. From there, they move to redesigning the program content and materials (Stage 2) through to program implementation. Although equally important, these stages are much faster the second time around and conducted on a much larger scale.

Frequently, scaling-up involves program implementation by actors other than the original developers, and these new actors often attempt to create shortcuts to the original scheme. Not surprisingly, they also tend to contribute additional themes to a program. Inadequately shortening programs to save resources is a weakness of many projects at this stage. For example, new actors replicating the program sometimes focus only on training for replication and omit the training for facilitators' personal growth. If the program is in line with the FrEE model, training for one's personal growth and development is an integral part of facilitator training. Without this, activities are unlikely to make sense to recipients or to be sustainable, and the program is unlikely to see positive results.

The following basic principles for scaling-up are recommended:

1. *Incorporate all players.* Do not allow a single party to shape the program agenda in accordance with its political preferences. Following this principle will enable communities to set the agenda in accordance with their needs (Whitty, 2006).
2. *Negotiation with limits.* All parties will have to give somewhat in program negotiations, but each party should set clear limits about how much they are willing to concede and which program components are indispensable. Scaling-up entails changes, often related to reducing periods of training, application, and accompaniment. Yet to have a trustworthy replication of a program, incorporating the method and materials on which it was originally based is key. For example, in Programming for Choice, the interactive self-reflection methodology is a critical element of all programs. More leeway exists in negotiating the kinds of educational and promotional materials that should be used. Clarity regarding negotiation limits before beginning the process of scaling-up is vital for assuring reliable, large-scale replication.
3. *Accommodating new stakeholders.* Program implementers need to be flexible when accommodating new stakeholders throughout the process, especially as more individuals and communities become interested in a program. Maintaining a representational balance of participating stakeholders is not always simple. Ideally, there is a coordinating committee with representatives from various community and stakeholder groups. This committee encourages community-building through distributed leadership mechanisms and enhances responsiveness and reciprocal accountability, especially among local stakeholders (Maxcy & Nguyen, 2006).

The funding structure of the United Nations required that the program be overseen by a specific United Nations agency, and the United Nations Fund for

Population Activities (UNFPA) was identified as the agency. This organization's mandate in Mexico further obligated the program to run through Mexico's Consejo Nacional de Población (CONAPO). Both UNFPA and IMIFAP wanted to work specifically in some of the poorest regions of Mexico, and because IMIFAP had previously undertaken programs in Hidalgo, Chiapas was politically relevant, and both states had high levels of poverty, the decision was made to identify communities in these states for the scaling-up. To incorporate new players and accommodate new government stakeholders central to collaboration and eventual program ownership, a technical support group was formed of UNFPA, IMIFAP, and more than a dozen state and federal government agencies.

Needs assessment and problem definition with the Comprehensive Community Development program found that the concepts and methods were both successful and desired by the new target communities and collaborating institutions. Most of the necessary program changes identified at this stage were at the content level and reflected the program's extension to rural areas: images and examples needed to be adapted for relevance in the rural context, as well as the school-based program units shortened to fit the structure of rural schools.

ADVOCACY & DISSEMINATION

In the scaling-up stage, negotiations with political authorities as well as private and public sector financial institutions must occur. These simultaneous negotiations are required to successfully expand the program and to achieve its transference. They often occur while program developers are determining the level of equivalence that exists. Moreover, conversations with the mass media take place parallel to other mediations to ascertain that contextual support is provided. Dissemination geared toward improving contextual conditions for behavior change should be conducted at the level at which the expansion has been established. Programmers and past program participants may go on radio and television shows to publicize the results of the original program. To the same end, publications for scientific journals, presentations to grassroots groups, and material dissemination to authorities can occur.

Significant and extended negotiations were called for in the Comprehensive Community Development program given the sheer number of institutions that were collaborating. Of most contention in the negotiations was the development of program materials. Collaborating institutions pushed for the participation of all parties in this process and wanted to include a multitude of additional materials and trainings of affiliates; this was largely driven by political motivations. To maintain program integrity, however, we had to delineate specifically what was acceptable to include. The agreement reached was that IMIFAP would develop the school-based and women-focused materials, to be reviewed by collaborators. For the microfinance and male-focused programs, a collaborating institution would develop them, and IMIFAP would undertake revisions. A dilemma we faced was how communities and governments could develop ownership over the program while IMIFAP maintained rights to the program in order to replicate it in the future. This is a dilemma that continues with programs today.

During negotiations, IMIFAP stood strong on involving the community early on, basing the program in life skills and participatory methodology, and including frequent accompaniment of facilitators. Recognizing the importance to political collaborators of building their image through the program, IMIFAP had to give leeway on the level of accompaniment with partners working in the community-based programs. Little negotiation on evaluation strategy was necessary because all collaborators wanted to undertake both process and impact evaluations.

Following this negotiation, extensive talks were held with local radio stations so that the program information and messages could reach the entire state. A multitude of press conferences were also held so that stakeholders would recognize the reach of the program into talk shows and news broadcasts. Unfortunately, because of personnel changes with the media outlets with which we were working, the ultimate presence in the press was limited.

EVALUATION

Evaluation at this stage involves looking at: indicators (whether indicators to assess the impact are appropriate and well-built), design (to determine if the program design is consistent with the aim), and operations (mainly whether steps in the scaling-up of the program have been adequate, particularly regarding the expected effectiveness of the program). Questions to be asked at this stage include: "Will there be a similar impact on behavior change at this larger scale as there was before?" "Is the scaling-up planned so that the new target population's needs are addressed and respected?" "Are all parties involved?" "How can behavioral changes that resulted from the program be maintained when accompaniment and follow-up with a large population is costly and not represented in the primary interests of donors and authorities?" During the scaling-up process, evaluation seeks to determine if the program remains efficient and effective. Ultimately, an impact evaluation study will be necessary to demonstrate the effectiveness of the scaled-up implementation. Such a study preferably should also assess the long-term impact of a program.

In answering the questions pertinent to this stage, it was clear from the needs assessment that the new target population's needs would be addressed by the program, and ongoing communication with program participants enabled continual inquiry into this issue. A similar impact on behavior change as that which occurred in the small-scale implementation was feasible on the larger scale as well, with the extensive funding and collaboration with local government, a strong presence could be achieved in each community. Program maintenance and follow-up were ensured through the involvement of local governments and the training of government employees who could continue to replicate the program after official implementation had concluded. Process and impact evaluation was undertaken by an independent evaluation agency, and extensive meetings and sharing of evaluation instruments previously utilized by IMIFAP brought clarity of program purpose, contents, and materials to the evaluators. As has become clear, the Comprehensive Community Development program involved all pertinent stakeholders, though implementation and evaluation suffered as a result; we learned that programs involving such broad collaboration would benefit from a single agency holding final decisions. Impact evaluation found the program outcomes included enhanced skills and behavior patterns in children, initiative and empowerment on the part of women, and for many, a mindset of personal agency within a framework of responsibility.

Conclusions

A systematic approach to the development and implementation of Programming for Choice entails a conceptual foundation, as outlined in earlier parts of the book. The process requires clear and consistent ideas about how a program should be constructed and implemented. Moreover, it is important to establish a consensus among the stakeholders about the steps necessary to ensure that programs are administered so that a community can reach its potential. The strategy outlined in this chapter should serve as a guideline and should be adapted to fit the context where it is applied. The advantage of a step-by-step program implementation is that it provides room for improvement throughout the process. It also enables program developers to demonstrate the merits of each stage to both the target populations and other stakeholders.

We would like to draw attention to some additionally salient points about this strategy. The main principle in organizing the development of a program is the distinction of the four stages, listed in Figure 9–2: Summary of Program Development and Implementation Stages. Of course, other orderings are possible. For example, it could be argued that our first stage is not necessarily the beginning of a project (as we mentioned, there are generally prior activities). However, there are two reasons for excluding the additional stages in the formal strategy description. The first is that these prior activities are unstructured, exploratory, and largely come about in an *ad hoc* fashion. For example, in the "If I Am OK" program, the plans were triggered by the sponsor's invitation for proposals. The second reason is that the way in which projects are arrived at tends to not be indicative of a program's quality.

We encourage teams to develop their own strategies to suit their particular program. However, there are a few aspects of a strategy that (in our view) cannot be compromised:

> **Develop a clear methodological "roadmap":** Twenty years ago, extensive program evaluation was rare, and even nowadays reports that consist of program staff "impressions" as the main empirical evidence are not uncommon. Yet there is rich evaluation literature that constitutes the methodological backbone to the strategy presented here. An approach to evaluation is needed in which targeted program outcomes can be assessed in objective terms. Randomized controlled trials constitute one strategy for providing such objective proof but this design is not always feasible or desirable for practical reasons. We advocate a more comprehensive, mixed-methods approach to assessment, with qualitative and quantitative elements of process evaluation. Through careful planning and close monitoring of all activities, the quality of programs is likely to improve, making comprehensive evaluation a sound investment.
>
> **Establish a central role for advocacy and dissemination:** Like evaluation, advocacy and dissemination activities appear throughout all four stages of the model. While compared to evaluation there is limited literature on these activities, they too need to be carefully planned and maintained to gain support, to inform results, and to involve all parties.

Address the context and the target groups: In the "If I Am OK" program, we mentioned a range of supporting measures, including radio messages, posters, program bags and buttons, and numerous well-publicized meetings to announce the program and issue diplomas. These stand to lower contextual barriers for participants, making it easier for them to undertake and replicate what they have learned and practiced in a program.

Ground the Programming for Choice strategy in the underlying conceptual foundation (FrEE): The framework and the strategy are joint components. The emphasis on interactive program methodology, for example, is geared to bring about a greater sense of control and personal agency.

Balance the foundational elements of Programming for Choice: The strategy presented in this chapter is based in scientific research (theory and methods), professional experience, and common sense. Professional expertise plays an essential role in the translation of needs into program. In this chapter, we have tried to describe how programs are developed and implemented, and Chapter 6 went into more depth on developing program contents. Program development is where art meets science, and experience comes into play. The most effective program developers are able to balance theory and practice; the ideal with the realistic.

Notes

1. Senior Regional Monitoring and Evaluation Advisor for UNICEF
2. In 1998 GlaxoSmithKline was called SmithKline Beecham.
3. The most recent census data, from the 2005 Conteo de Población y Vivienda, found that the population remains at 3.5 million.
4. The most recent census data, from the 2005 Conteo de Población y Vivienda, found that 53% of homes have a water distribution system, and only 35%of homes have dirt floors.
5. Materials should be plasticized or made of other durable resources to ensure their longevity, whenever possible.

References

Altieri, M., Fonseca, S. A., Caballero, J. J., & Hernández, J. J. (2006). *Manejo del agua y restauración productiva en la región indígena mixteca de Puebla y Oaxaca [The management of water and productive restoration in the Indigenous Mixteca region of Puebla and Oaxaca]*. Washington, DC: International Bank for Reconstruction and Development and World Bank.

Anaya, M., Leenen, I., Givaudan, M., & Pick, S. (2008). México-Centroamerica: Educación en sexualidad, salud y habilidades para la vida. Fase III: Reporte Final [Mexico-Central America: Education on sexuality, health and life skills. Phase III: Final Report], *Report presented to the World Bank*. Mexico City: IMIFAP.

Banks, G. (2009). *Evidence-based policy-making: What is it? How do we get it.* Paper presented at the ANZSOG/ANU Public Lecture Series. Canberra. Retrieved June 1, 2009, from www.pc.gov.au/__data/assets/pdf_file/0003/85836/cs20090204.pdf.

Binswanger, H. P. (2000, June 23). Scaling up HIV/AIDS programs to national cover-age. *Science*, 288(5474), 2173–2176.

Consejo Nacional de Población [CONAPO] [National Population Council] (2009). Estadísticas de salud sexual y reproductiva [Sexual and reproductive health statistics]. Retrieved May 24, 2009, from Consejo Nacional de Población: www.conapo.gob.mx/.

de Anda, F. (2007, August 9). Promueve Emilio abstinencia sexual [Emilio promotes sexual abstinence]. *Reforma*, p. 2.

Drummond, M. F., Sculpher, M. J., Torrance, G. W., O'Brien, B. J., & Stoddart, G. L. (2005). *Methods for the economic evaluation of health care programs* (3rd ed.). Oxford: Oxford University Press.

Fetterman, D. M. (1996). Empowerment evaluation: An introduction to theory and practice. In D. M. Fetterman, S. J. Kaftarian & A. Wandersman (Eds.), *Empowerment evaluation: Knowledge and tool for self-assessment and accountability* (pp. 3–48). Thousand Oaks, CA: Sage Publications.

Fisher, A., Foreit, J., Laing, J., Stoeckel, J., & Townsend, J. (2002). *Designing HIV/AIDS intervention studies. An operations research handbook.* New York: Population Council.

García, G., Pick, S., & Romero, A. (submitted). Instrumentación nacional y evaluación de impacto de un programa para la promoción de la salud, la agencia personal y el empoderamiento [National implementation and impact assessment of a program to promote health, personal agency and empowerment].

Givaudan, M., Barriga, M., Pick, S., Leenen, I., & Martinez, R. (2009). Desarrollo integral comunitario en México, en los estados de Hidalgo y Chiapas, con énfasis en salud sexual y reproductiva y derechos de mujeres, reporte final [Comprehensive community development in the Mexican states of Hidalgo and Chiapas, with emphasis on sexual and reproductive health and women's rights, final report], *Report presented to the United Nations Fund for Population Activities.* Mexico City: IMIFAP.

Givaudan, M., Pick, S., Leenen, I., & DuBois, L. (submitted). Health education and life skills: Building life skills and knowledge in rural children in Mexico.

Instituto Nacional de Estadística, Geografía e Informática [INEGI] [National Institute of Statistics, Geography and Computing (2005). Conteo de población y vivienda 2005 [Count of population and living standards 2005]. Retrieved May 24, 2009, from Instituto Nacional de Estadística, Geografía e Informática: www.inegi.org.mx.

Instituto Nacional de Estadística, Geografía e Informática [INEGI] [National Institute of Statistics, Geography and Computing] (2000a). Estadísticas a propósito del día internacional de las poblaciones indígenas: Datos nacionales [Statistics for the International Day of Indigenous Populations: National Statistics]. Retrieved August 12, 2008, from Instituto Nacional de Estadística, Geografía, e Informática: www.generoysaludreproductiva.gob.mx/IMG/pdf/indigena04.pdf.

Instituto Nacional de Estadística, Geografía e Informática [INEGI] [National Institute of Statistics, Geography and Computing] (2000b). *XII Censo general de población y vivienda [XII general census of population and living standards].* Mexico City: Instituto Nacional de Estadística, Geografía e Informática.

Instituto Nacional de Estadística, Geografía e Informática [INEGI] [National Institute of Statistics, Geography and Computing] (2008). Estadísticas a propósito del día de la madre: Datos de Oaxaca [Statistics for Mother's Day: Data from Oaxaca]. Retrieved July 17, 2008, from Instituto Nacional de Estadística, Geografía, e Informática: www.inegi.gob.mx/.

Kagitcibasi, C. (1995). Is psychology relevant to global human development issues? Experience from Turkey. *American Psychologist*,50 (4), 293–300.

Lazarsfeld, P., & Katz, E. (1955). *Personal influence: The part played by people in the flow of mass communications*. Glencoe, IL: Free Press.

Leenen, I., García, G., Elizalde, L., Gaál, F., Givaudan, M. (2009). Implementación, evaluación y presentación de resultados de la capacitación para la orientación y promoción social para los Prestadores de Servicio de PAL. Reporte de la fase B. [Implementation, evaluation, and presentation of training outcomes for the orientation and social promotion for the PAL Service Providers. Report of phase B]. *Report presented to the Universidad Autónoma de Aguascalientes*. Mexico City: IMIFAP.

Leenen, I., Pick, S., Tacher, A., Givaudan, M., & Prado, A. (submitted). Facilitating sexual and reproductive health among migrants in Central America.

Leenen, I., Venguer, T., Vera, J., Givaudan, M., Pick, S., & Poortinga, Y. H. (2008). Effectiveness of a comprehensive health education program in a poverty-stricken rural area of Guatemala. *Journal of Cross-Cultural Psychology*,39 (2), 198–214.

Martínez, A., Givaudan, M., & Pick, S. (1995). Training and supervision in family life and sexuality education programs and provision of teaching materials in Latin America, *Report presented to the David and Lucile Packard Foundation*. Mexico City: IMIFAP.

Maxcy, B. D., & Nguyen, T. S. (2006). The politics of distributing leadership: Reconsidering leadership distribution in two Texas elementary schools. *Educational Policy*, 20(1), 163–196.

Mittman, B. S. (2001). *Qualitative methods and rigorous management research: (How) are they compatible?* (White paper prepared for the Department of Veterans Affairs Management Research). Sepulveda, CA: Center for the Study of Healthcare Provider Behavior.

Monk, D. H., & King, J. (1993). Cost analysis as a tool for education reform. In S. L. Jacobson & R. Berne (Eds.), *Reforming education: The emerging systemic approach*. Newbury Park, CA: Corwin Press.

Moynihan, R., Oxman, A. D., Lavis, J. N., & Paulsen, E. (2008). Evidence-informed health policy: Using research to make health systems healthier. Retrieved May 28, 2009, from www.epidemiologia.anm.cdu.ar/pdf/Evidence-IInformedHealthPolicy.pdf

Osorio, P. (submitted). Exporting strategies: A cross-cultural adaptation of a pregnancy prevention curriculum for teenagers.

Osorio, P., & Givaudan, M. (2006). Mexico Central America: Education in sexuality, health and life skills, Phase II, *Report presented to the World Bank*. Mexico City: IMIFAP.

Pick de Weiss, S., Aguilar, J. A., Rodriguez, G., Reyes, J., Collado, M. E., Pier, D., Acevedo, M. P., & Vargas, E. (1994). *Planeando tu vida: Nuevo programa de educación sexual para adolescentes [Planning your life: A new sexuality education program for adolescents]* (Greek language ed.). Athens, Greece: Vitrakis Publishers.

Pick, S. (2007). Extension of theory of reasoned action: Principles for health promotion programs with marginalized populations in Latin America. In I. Ajzen, D. Albarracín & R. Hornik (Eds.), *Prediction and change of health behavior: Applying the reasoned action approach* (pp. 223-241). Mahwah, NJ: Lawrence Erlbaum Associates.

Pick, S., Barriga, M., & Givaudan, M. (submitted). Agency, empowerment, health and life skills development among rural women in Mexico.

Pick, S., Givaudan, M., Olicón, V., Beltrán, M., & Oka, S. (2006). *My voice, my life. A training program to prevent teen pregnancy*. Mexico City: Editorial IDEAME.

Pick, S., Leenen, I., Givaudan, M., & Prado, A. (in press). "Yo quiero, yo puedo... prevenir la violencia": Programa breve de sensibilización sobre violencia en el noviazgo. [I want to, I can ... prevent violence: Raising awareness of dating violence through a brief intervention.] *Salud Mental*.

Pick, S., & Poortinga, Y. H. (2005). Marco conceptual y estrategia para el diseño e instrumentacion de programas para el desarrollo: Una visión científica, política y psicosocial [Conceptual framework and strategy for the design and implementation of development programs: A scientific, political and psycho-social vision]. *Revista Latinoamericana de Psicologia, 37* (3), 445–459.

Pick, S., & Reyes, J. (1994). Training project for Latin American health and population institutions, *Report presented to the John D. and Catherine T. MacArthur Foundation*. Mexico City: IMIFAP.

Ramón, J., Bendezu, A., Pick, S., & Givaudan, M. (2000). Replicación y evaluación del programa de la vida familiar y educación sexual Yo quiero, Yo puedo, con maestros de 5° y 6° grado en áreas marginalizadas de Perú [Replication and evaluation of family life and sexual education program I want to, I can, with teachers from 5th and 6th grade in marginalized areas of Peru], *Report presented to the World Bank*. Mexico City: IMIFAP.

Ramón, J., Zarate, M., Pick, S., & Givaudan, M. (2002). Fortalecimiento y expansión de un programa integral de educación sexual y habilidades para la vida, en Bolivia y Panamá a través de la capacitación, supervisión y evaluación de multiplicadores [Strengthening and expansion of a comprehensive sexuality education and life skills program in Bolivia and Panama through training, supervision and evaluation of replicators]. Phase II, *Report presented to the World Bank*. Mexico City: IMIFAP.

Ratne, M., & Nguyen, T. M. L. (2005). *Reproductive health in Asia. Effective advocacy for adolescent sexual and reproductive health. Guidelines for building advocacy skills*. Hanoi: United Nations Fund for Population Activities, CARE International in Vietnam, and Central Youth Union.

Rossi, P. H., Lipsey, M. W., & Freeman, H. E. (2004). *Evaluation: A systematic approach* (7th ed.). Thousand Oaks, CA: Sage Publications.

Segone, M. (2006). Democratic approach to evaluation. In M. Segone (Ed.), *New trends in development evaluation* (pp. 39–47). Geneva: United Nations Children's Fund.

Segone, M. (2008a). Editorial. In M. Segone (Ed.), *Bridging the gap: The role of monitoring and evaluation in evidence-based policy making* (pp. 7–12). Geneva: United Nations Children's Fund.

Segone, M. (2008b). Evidence-based policy making and the role of monitoring and evaluation within the new aid environment. In M. Segone (Ed.), *Bridging the gap: The role of monitoring and evaluation in evidence-based policy making* (pp. 16–45). Geneva: United Nations Children's Fund.

Shadish, W. R., Cook, T. D., & Campbell, D. T. (2002). *Experimental and quasi-experimental designs for generalized causal inference*. Boston: Houghton Mifflin.

Shadish, W. R., Cook, T. D., & Leviton, L. C. (1991). *Foundations of program evaluation: Theories of practice*. Newbury Park, CA: Sage Publications.

Silow-Carroll, S., & Alteras, T. (2005). Community-based oral health programs: A need and plan for evaluation, *Report presented to the W. K. Kellogg Foundation*. Washington, DC: Economic and Social Research Institute.

Sohail, M., Maunder, D. A. C., & Cavill, S. (2006). Effective regulation for sustainable public transport in developing countries. *Transport Policy,13* (3), 177–190.

Tacher, A., Beltrán, M., Givaudan, M., & Pick, S. (2008). Colaboración de organizaciones México-Guatemala-Honduras para el fortalecimiento de capacidades humanas: Fase I [Collaboration of Mexican, Guatemalan and Honduran organizations for
the strengthening of human capabilities: Phase I], *Report presented to W. K. Kellogg
Foundation* (pp. 1–40). Mexico City: IMIFAP.

Tacher, A., Leenen, I., Pick, S., Givaudan, M., & Prado, A. (2009). Facilitating sexual
and reproductive health among migrants in Central America, *Report presented to
the World Bank.* Mexico City: IMIFAP.

Universidad Autónoma de Aguascalientes (2009). Implementación del Modelo de
transmisión de conocimientos para el desarrollo de capacidades entre el personal de
Diconsa, los Consejos Comunitarios y los Comités Rurales de Abasto. Informe
ejecutivo final, *Reporte presentado a Diconsa.* Ciudad de México: IMIFAP.

van de Vijver, F. J. R., & Hambleton, R. K. (1996). Translating tests: Some practical
guidelines. *European Psychologist,*1 (2), 89–99.

van de Vijver, F. J. R., & Leung, K. (1997). *Methods and data analysis for cross-
cultural research.* Newbury Park, CA: Sage Publications.

van de Vijver, F. J. R., & Poortinga, Y. H. (2005). Conceptual and methodological
issues in adapting tests. In R. K. Hambleton, P. F. Merenda & C. D. Spielberger
(Eds.), *Adapting educational and psychological tests for cross-cultural assessment*
(pp. 39–63). Mahwah, NJ: Lawrence Erlbaum Associates.

Venguer, T., Leenen, I., Morales, N., Givaudan, M., Pick, S., Poortinga, I., & Martínez, R.
(2002). Multiplicación de un programa integral de educación para la salud en
mujeres jóvenes del estado de Oaxaca. [Replication of a comprehensive health education program for young women in the Oaxaca region of Mexico], *Final report
presented to SmithKline-Beecham.* Mexico City: IMIFAP.

Venguer, T., Pick, S., & Fishbein, M. (2007). Health education and agency: A comprehensive program for young women in the Mixteca region of Mexico. *Psychology,
Health & Medicine,* 12(4), 389–406.

Vera, J., Venguer, T., Givaudan, M., & Pick, S. (2002). Encuentro: México-Guatemala:
Educación de la sexualidad y habilidades para la vida [Encounter: Mexico-
Guatemala: Sexuality and life skills education], *Report presented to the World Bank.*
Mexico City: IMIFAP.

Weiss, C. (1998). *Evaluation. Methods for studying programs and policies* (2nd ed.).
Upper Saddle River, NJ: Prentice Hall.

Whitty, G. (2006). Education(al) research and education policy making: is conflict
inevitable? *British Educational Research Journal,* 32(2), 159–176.

CHAPTER 10

Conclusion

It is in our own hands, to construct the people that can make a difference
for the region and for the poor. Democracy is not only the right to vote
on Election Day; it means the right to choose and that means freedom.
—Alejandro Toledo, former president of Peru (2007, p. 6)

We began this book with testimonies and evidence from evaluation studies
illustrating how certain individuals experience diminished freedoms in Mexico.
Constrictive norms and environments in Latin America often harbor patterns
that impede optimal development, both in the fabric of communities and in
administrative and institutional structures. We described how in many communities, we have seen not only economic factors but also psychological and
social barriers come into play. These impede the enhancement of capabilities
and the full realization of individual potential, perpetuating the poverty cycle.

An optimally functioning democratic society entails a citizenry that partici-
pates in constructing its future. We have stressed the importance of laws, infrastructure, clinics, and schools in creating the structural context in which people
lead their daily lives. Policies and programs can enhance choice, personal
agency, and intrinsic empowerment so that people may form a strong social
core. Change in systems of paternalism and rule-boundedness—especially at
the local level—is realized through the actions of agentically empowered citizens and leaders. As Rubio emphasized, "A country must decide if it will go
on to support a political system oriented towards control from the top or if it
will build the structures for a democratic system, centered on the citizen"
(Rubio, 2006).[1] Building human capital takes more than schooling; it also
requires empowering young people with opportunities to participate as active
citizens from an early age. Informing and facilitating their decision making so
they can make choices that enhance their well-being "adds to their success as
workers and entrepreneurs, as parents, and as citizens. And for those who have
to recover from poor decisions or poor circumstances providing second
chances—to make up for missed opportunities—can keep young people from
being irrevocably left behind" (World Bank, 2007, p. 211).

Sen's people-centered approach transforms traditional notions about the
role of human factors in macro-economic development. His Capability Approach

240

is a conceptualization, a mode of thinking, rather than a formula for development (Robeyns, 2005). With this book, we extend his conceptualization, grounding our approach in behavior change theory to demonstrate how the Capability Approach can be made operational from a psychosocial perspective. This human basis for sustainable development, although comprising only one of the many perspectives of development programming and policy, has been under-represented in the development arena.

A Psychosocial Approach

In her Harvard graduation speech, J.K. Rowling stated: "Poverty entails fear, and stress, and sometimes depression; it means a thousand petty humiliations and hardships" (2008). She expresses the intensification of psychosocial stress that impoverished individuals commonly experience. Although the psychological principles underlying our approach apply to people in communities all over the world, the poor often stand to benefit most from their application. Therefore, most examples in the book have specifically referred to people living under conditions of poverty and extreme poverty.

Each individual possesses a unique combination of internal, social, and familial realities that shape who she is and how contextual constraints and opportunities affect her (Wilson & Aponte, 1985). For example, a person who has recently fallen into poverty will likely respond differently than a person who has lived in poverty for generations. Someone who is gaining strides in their personal development will react differently than a person of the same level of income who is sliding further into poverty (Gans, 1968). At the same time, high levels of uncertainty, unpredictability, and externally-imposed choice are generally associated with poverty. External power is imposed and maintained through tight social norms, rules, and expectations.

In many poor communities, this reality challenges an individual's ability to plan and undertake decisions, and makes it more difficult to carry out those decisions. Under restrictive social conditions, it makes little sense to take initiative because action rarely leads to results. When it does, it's often unclear who is responsible for the action or the consequences. Tight external control engenders high degrees of shame, guilt, and fear, which can be manipulated to restrict people's functionings and effectively limit their freedoms. We have argued that investing in the capacity of the individual and targeting psychosocial factors can drive changes in some of these barriers—i.e. unfreedoms. This relatively small investment can have an effective and sustainable impact on individual and community development.

The Framework for Enabling Empowerment: Concept and Strategy

The Framework for Enabling Empowerment (FiEE) summarizes the principles that we believe should guide programs aimed at the development of capabilities and appropriation of opportunities, aimed at breaking the poverty cycle. The concept underlying FrEE is that people are provided with knowledge and given the opportunity to practice the skills they tend to underuse, so that they become comfortable using them and they see the potential of applying them in a range of situations of varying degrees of difficulty. The appropriation of skills also entails a responsibility to address the consequences of their utilization; achieving this level of situational maturity often requires a reconceptualization of the self. When acquired through a participatory, long-term process, behaviors are more likely to endure. The opportunity of individuals and communities to repeatedly reduce psychological and contextual barriers and apply a series of skills to prevent and solve problems in different domains of their lives (e.g., in relation to health, education, and income-related issues) makes these behaviors more inherent. They become a routine part of the way things are done and the way the world is perceived. Thus, the framework is presented in a circular fashion, rather than linear, and elements of FrEE reinforce one another.

Psychosocial research and empirical work have informed the development of FrEE, and it is our hope that future testing of the framework will cast greater light on the processes involved and potential outcomes. The essence of the framework lies in addressing specific situations. Behavior change begins in a real-life situation where there exists a discrepancy between the action a person "should" take (as informed by customs and norms) and the choice that she *would like to* and *can* actually make. It is easy to take such psychological concepts for granted, especially in well-educated and privileged communities where people believe they have the right to choose, to plan, and to achieve the outcomes they desire. Yet our research demonstrates that this is often not the case (*see* Chapter 7). For this reason, we explained the initial stage of FrEE, in which people first understand and accept that they are entitled to choose (*see* Chapters 4 and 7). We emphasized outcomes and achievement (i.e., doing and being functionings) to provide a foundation from which people will be likely to seek the tools necessary to enhance their capabilities.

FrEE emphasizes that people gain access to opportunities by applying skills and knowledge in concrete situations that they experience as challenging or out of reach. Attitudes expressed in common phrases, such as "This is not for people like me" or "*me da pena*" [it makes me feel ashamed], can be overcome through experience. When an individual realizes that something is within the reach of her capabilities—for example, through practicing new skills as part of a training program or through positive experiences in the real world— psychological barriers are reduced. Acquiring knowledge about rights (and having the social support to do so) and being able to discuss one's needs with others also contribute to diminishing social and psychological barriers. Behaviors targeted in programs are modified in stages, from pre-contemplation of change to contemplation, preparation for action, action, and ultimately maintenance of the new course of action (Prochaska & DiClemente, 1982; Prochaska & Velicer, 1997). As individuals experience success in diverse concrete situations, they develop a sense of personal agency and are able to expand their range of capabilities.

A key concept in FrEE is personal agency, which describes both the process and the state through which an individual carries out decisions in a responsible, informed, and autonomous fashion. We indicated that our preference for the term *personal agency* is partly inspired by the currency of the term in developmental economics and psychology; in this sense, it serves as a bridge to connect the microlevel approaches of psychology with the macrolevel approaches of developmental economics. Personal agency integrates several elements of personal qualities from social psychology and the literature on personality research, including control, autonomy, self-efficacy, self-esteem, and self-determination. This emphasis on the self is fundamental to sustainable human development; empowerment programs based solely on external rather than personal motivators may reinforce dependency, rather than personal agency, because of the external locus of control.

A mindset of personal agency requires thinking beyond isolated behaviors, to perceive oneself as part of a community and as an agent, rather than an object, of change. Programs that address several domains of activity facilitate a more comprehensive conceptualization of oneself as an agent. They do so by supporting the application of the developed skills across a number of situations, thus building wider competencies and creating opportunities to execute new behaviors. This process requires not only common skills but also the reduction of psychological and social barriers.

When psychosocial barriers are sufficiently reduced, personal agency can evolve to the point where individuals begin to see themselves simultaneously as part of the context and influential within it. We named this process intrinsic empowerment (*see* Chapter 4). Drawing from the fields of socio-economic research and psychology, intrinsic empowerment combines the ideas of empowerment and personal agency as part of a fluid context. It is a specific form of empowerment that is intrinsically derived and therefore, we argue, is more likely to be sustainable. Together, individuals empowered with these psychological characteristics have the capacity to profoundly impact communities and institutions within their communities. The concepts involved here are built on the premises laid out across the book: The way a person behaves is a consequence of both his capabilities *and* his context. If capabilities exist so individuals can consider and put alternatives into action, then the characteristics of the individual and the community will have a greater potential to change and do so in a sustainable fashion.

FrEE makes Sen's Capability Approach operative as far as it clarifies the active role of the individual in converting commodities into functionings and rights into entitlements. It also explains how a functioning attained through external means is an isolated achievement—which is not necessarily accompanied by a capability—and therefore, the functioning will not lead to further achievements. FrEE provides a practical framework for influencing social factors so that unfreedoms are reduced and freedoms are enhanced. As a result, the context is made supportive and may even generate further capabilities. In FrEE, the person is directly involved in creating and accessing opportunities that respond to her needs.

Programming for Choice

We have demonstrated how the Capability Approach can be put into practice in underdeveloped and marginalized communities using FrEE. Programming for Choice, which contextualizes FrEE, was presented as the vehicle for making the framework operational. The development of Programming for Choice begins with taking an inventory of people's needs. In this way, expressed needs form the foundation of program content and developers respect the ethical issues associated with bringing external norms into a community. From the information gathered in this stage, an initial version of the program is designed and piloted together with educational and promotional materials. The program is crafted to teach skills and impart knowledge, using a participatory methodology through which behavior change is undertaken and reflected upon, and psychological barriers are decreased, as outlined by FrEE.

To most effectively introduce broad agency, which leads to not only personal but also contextual improvements in well-being, Programming for Choice should be comprehensive. As the Pan American Health Organization concludes, "Strategies that affect the larger political, media, family and community environment are also needed for long-term sustainable change" (Mangrulkar, Whitman, & Posner, 2001, p. 6). By addressing a range of actors simultaneously, Programming for Choice helps cultivate a community context supportive of the targeted changes more effectively than those targeting a single population. They also lead to deeper socio-cultural changes. A similar effect can be achieved with multistrategic aspects of programming. When messages are transmitted through multiple avenues, a Gestalt effect appears in which the sum is greater than the parts. The provision of sensitization to different public and private sectors allows for common programming strategies and collaboration, improving cost-effectiveness. It also increases the likelihood that program strategies will be integrated into a transversal human development policy. As Levy writes: "Designing effective social policies requires a horizontal view of programs and policies that cuts across ministries, agencies, and levels of government" (2008, p. 284).

Ideally, programs should be implemented through local program facilitators, which will increase acceptance and feelings of ownership and sustainability; it also decreases costs and supports the local economy. To ensure maintenance of the behavioral changes, development organizations should follow up with feedback and continued evaluation for at least a few years after the completion of a program. Of course, such support is most relevant during the initial stages, when people are most likely to revert back to their old ways.

The stages of program development are highly integrated. Ongoing advocacy and dissemination are conducted concurrently. After all, a program aimed at personal and community change depends on social support and cannot—and should not—function in isolation from a participant's context. Furthermore, these activities are instrumental to securing funding and eventually scaling-up the program. Programs are also continuously evaluated. Although program developers sometimes perceive evaluation as a threat, a culture of evaluation needs to be encouraged. Programs cannot be improved or justifiably replicated without a solid basis in feedback. Only when programming has been found to contribute significantly to behavior change is there enough evidence to support a broader implementation. It is this scaling-up of effective programs that forms the basis for effective policy. FrEE and the Programming for Choice strategy integrate a theoretical perspective with concrete steps for action.

Policy

Moving successful psychosocial programs into the realm of policy holds the potential to fill the evidence-based policy gap widely apparent in developing countries. To date, public policy programs and development projects have focused primarily on improving structural capacity but have underestimated the role of the individual in this process—namely, in terms of personal agency and intrinsic empowerment. There is a reciprocal relationship between the micro- and macrolevels of interaction that needs to be incorporated into successful policymaking: A supportive context is likely to enhance individual capabilities, just like individual growth can have a positive impact on the immediate environment. The policy decisions that acknowledge such issues are often made for political reasons, without an empirical or evidence-based foundation. Frequently they are based on the accumulation and interpretation of information, not necessarily on a systematic analysis of knowledge and needs, or the evaluation results of related programs.

Poor communication between researchers and policymakers regularly leads to implementation difficulties (Trostle, Bronfman, & Langer, 1999), especially when programs are scaled-up. Policies tend to outline the end goal, neglecting to provide guidance about how to successfully mobilize resources and expand a program's scale while preserving continuous visibility and the program's original objectives (Pick, Givaudan, & Reich, 2008). A beautifully designed policy can fail if the implementation is poorly conducted. Differences between target populations, as well as a discrepancy in the availability of resources, may necessitate adaptations of the concept, method, or content to facilitate a successful program transfer. The potential disconnect between policy and implementation results in an inadequate response to the needs of the community, rendering policies purely symbolic and lacking the desired impacts. In the process of accommodating new stakeholders, negotiation within established limits and the strategic inclusion of all players will permit greater success as programs are scaled-up. Both policy and programming need to be clearly designed and evaluated, with the connection between the two clearly established and addressed in the implementation.

Long-term changes in communities and institutions will not occur without modifications in the mindsets of both community members and the individuals making decisions. And yet, the role of policymakers, government officials, and local bureaucrats is often overlooked. This oversight severely limits advances in the formulation and implementation of policies because, however attractively conceptualized, a policy's implementation depends on the people working in the particular community where it will be deployed. Promoting personal agency within government leadership and among public sector bureaucrats revolutionizes traditional notions of public figures. Intrinsic empowerment promotes and is an outcome of leadership that is creative, autonomous, flexible, proactive, and responsible for its decisions and behaviors. However, these characteristics contradict traditional notions of the archetypical role of the bureaucrat (Weber, 1978). It is crucial for these individuals, and the institutions they represent, to recognize the importance of enabling personal agency, even among street-level bureaucrats. Only when they become comfortable with their own capabilities can their actions benefit the target populations. For this to be possible, changes need to be made at both the individual and, urgently, at the political level. As two key Mexican researchers in the field of development have stated: "Ultimately, the firm adoption of a socially inclusive development strategy depends on the social pact that is established" (Moreno Brid & Puchet Anyul, 2008, p.322).[2]

The conceptual framework and the strategy described in this book have established a systematic process for reducing the discrepancy between science and its application in the development field. This occurs when policies are formed around needs-based programs that ensure detailed evaluation not only of outcomes but also of their development and implementation. The field of implementation analysis[3] has much to contribute toward this end (Michie et al., 2007). Additionally, we hope that the program methodology laid out in this book helps to "close the gap" through programming that involves political figures and bureaucrats as well as the average citizen. The ultimate goal of employing independent programming to inform policy is to successfully scale-up and institutionalize programs that have been evaluated (and proven successful) at the local level.

Much of the institutional knowledge used to structure these programs and conduct their evaluations is embedded within the traditional domain of CSOs. Therefore, government–CSO collaboration makes sense and stands to benefit both parties. Particularly in low-income countries where administrative capacity is often weak, many factors—including poor resource environments and fluctuations in state activity and services—have limited, and continue to limit, the ability of governments to address socio-economic problems. Therefore, achieving national coverage of social development lies beyond the capabilities of most governments acting alone (DeJong, 2001). In Mexico and in other countries where education, healthcare, and other services provided by the government vary substantially in quality, one of the most important roles of a CSO is to help bridge the gap between the service provision and the service users (i.e., the target population). Ultimately, however, the CSO must seek to provide a sort of temporary scaffolding that supports the target population. The government plays an integral role once the program is established, providing necessary resources and political support to scale-up these programs. CSOs are uniquely positioned to work with the government to more closely link research, policy, and programming.

The Way Forward: The Future Outlook for Programming for Choice

Most empirical data presented in this book is based on the experiences of the Mexican Institute for Family and Population Research (IMIFAP). However, the testimonies and the results of outcome evaluation studies are relevant to the themes of development programs worldwide and to the evaluation literature. Creating and sustaining human development ultimately helps to build effective schools, develop a citizenry that upholds laws, decentralize policies through sound mechanisms, and improve the functionality of government. Human development also produces a citizenry that is increasingly participatory, competitive and responsible; able to design, offer, and access cost-effective services; make decisions and respond to their consequences; and exercise freedoms.

We have worked in 14 countries across Latin America and the Caribbean, as well as in the United States, Europe, and Asia. We have had informal conversations with individuals from other developing countries, primarily in Latin American and Africa, as well as in India, Greece, and U.S Latino communities. Our understanding from these experiences is that although critical factors may be slightly different across countries, such as accessibility of institutions and resistance to change, the general themes remain the same. We hope that the development strategy we have presented here will be tested both in Mexico and elsewhere and, where appropriate, adapted and applied cross-culturally.

In Chapter 4, where we described FrEE, we briefly referred to the empirical evidence that supports the major concepts and distinctions underlying the framework. There we mentioned three sources of such evidence. The first, scattered throughout the book, are the numerous, illustrative testimonies that describe changes in the lives of program participants as an effect of IMIFAP programs. The innumerable testimonies, of which only a small portion could be included, provide the backbone support for FrEE. We hope that they speak for themselves and portray the plausibility of the psychological change mechanisms that we have outlined in this book. The second source of evidence is controlled evaluation studies that have shown clear empirical evidence of behavior change and have been published in project reports, chapters in various books, and peer-reviewed journal articles. Here, we repeat a few of these references (Beltrán, Elizalde, & Givaudan, 2009; García, Pick, & Romero, submitted; Givaudan, Barriga, & Pick, 2008; Givaudan, García, & Pick, 2007; Givaudan, Leenen, & Pick, submitted; Givaudan & Osorio, 2009; Givaudan, Vitela, & Osorio, 2008; IMIFAP, 2008; Leenen et al., 2008; Osorio-Belmon, submitted; Osorio-Belmon & Givaudan, submitted; Osorio-Belmon & Leenen, submitted; Osorio & Givaudan, 2008; Pick, Barriga, & Givaudan, submitted; Pick et al., submitted; Pick, Givaudan, & Poortinga, 2003; Pick, Leenen, & García, submitted; Pick et al., in press-a; Pick, Leenen, & Teegarden, submitted; Pick & Osorio, submitted; Pick, Poortinga, & Givaudan, 2003; Pick et al., 2008; Pick et al., in press-b; Universidad Autónoma de Aguascalientes, 2008a, 2008b, 2008c, 2009; Venguer, Pick, & Fishbein, 2007).

The final source of evidence, the quantitative measurement of personal agency and intrinsic empowerment, has proven difficult because they are latent variables. Up to now, they have manifested in a very broad range of ways that include making autonomous decisions, taking one's children to be vaccinated, and even participating in village celebrations. In addition, there are pros and cons to using a specific versus a more general measure of personal agency and intrinsic empowerment. If one measures at the specific level, then she may not be grasping the full extent of the change; if one goes with the more general measures, then precision as to the significance of the changes may be lost. Advancement in methods will bring even greater insight into these processes and outcomes, heretofore demonstrated largely through observation and testimony. In Chapter 4 we referred to an article by Pick et al. (2007) in which the distinction between two separate factors for personal agency and agentic empowerment (renamed intrinsic empowerment) was validated. At the time of writing of this chapter, data collection for six evaluation studies that use such scales was in progress or recently completed. Initial results look positive (García, Pick, & Romero, submitted; Givaudan, Leenen, & Pick, submitted; Pick, Barriga, & Givaudan, submitted; Pick, Leenen, & García, submitted; Universidad Autónoma de Aguascalientes, 2009). The most recent study presents a psychometrically valid scale developed with a nationally representative sample of 320 participants and shows that while levels of personal agency vary across regions and sociocultural levels, on average 60% of Mexicans have a low level of personal agency (Romero et al., 2010). The next step will require developing measurement tools for the concepts.

We hope that the framework and strategy provided here will be further tested, developed, adapted, and applied cross-culturally, so that as researchers we can give back—through constructive policies, market, education, and health reforms as well as collaborative program implementation—to the marginalized communities that stand to benefit most from our research. We do not present a fully operationalized model. This book is about practice, about what we have found in the field while working from theories of psychology, and about the approach of Amartya Sen that has been conceptualized in FrEE. In addition, the systematic and repeated nontargeted changes in the populations within which we work provided the impetus for this book. What we present is a proposal, a conceptual model for breaking the poverty cycle and vehicle for its use—a way of understanding and conceptualizing changes we have found as a result of our programs. Through the replication of successful approaches, we as researchers can return the investments of our many funders and supporters to the marginalized communities that should benefit most from our findings.

Social scientists have long understood that psychological factors are key to shaping social functioning. With the advance of behavioral economics in recent decades, this awareness has increased. Key global political players such as the World Bank and the United Nations have adopted approaches compatible with Programming for Choice (UNDP, 2004; World Bank & CDD). So far, these adjustments have occurred primarily at the conceptual level and less in hands-on practice, but it is only a matter of time before major development organizations begin to incorporate more concrete elements of the human focused approach. The next step will be for governments and civil society institutions to join in the effort to expand choice, personal agency, and intrinsic empowerment. It is only through a more integrated and comprehensive approach that capabilities will be developed and sustainable identities as agents of change promoted in the developing world. Only in this way will we enhance the human basis of development, and break the poverty cycle in a sustainable fashion.

Notes

1. The original Spanish reads, "El país tiene que decidir si va a seguir apuntalando un sistema político orientado al control desde arriba o si va a construir el andamiaje para un sistema democrático, centrado en el ciudadano."
2. "En la última instancia, adoptar con firmeza una estrategia de desarrollo socialmente incluyente depende del pacto social que se establezca."
3. Major works in the field of implementation analysis include (Hasenfeld & Brock, 1991; Lipsky, 1978; Matland, 1995; Mazmanian & Sabatier, 1989; Michie et al., 2007; Pressman & Wildavsky, 1973; Ryan, 1999).

References

Beltrán, M., Elizalde, L., & Givaudan, M. (2009). Formación en habilidades para la vida y metodología participativa para personal de salud [Life skills training and participatory methodology for health workers], *Report presented to Public Health Services of Mexico City*. Mexico City: IMIFAP.

DeJong, J. (2001). A question of scale? The challenge of increasing the scale of nongovernmental organisations' HIV/AIDS efforts in developing countries. Washington, DC: Horizons/Alliance Project on Scaling Up HIV/AIDS Programs, Population Council.

Gans, H. J. (1968). Culture and class in the study of poverty: An approach to antipoverty research. In D. P. Moynihan (Ed.), *On understanding poverty: Perspectives from the social sciences* (pp. 201–228). New York: Basic Books.

García, G., Pick, S., & Romero, A. (submitted). Instrumentación nacional y evaluación de impacto de un programa para la promoción de la salud basado en la agencia y el empoderamiento [National implementation and evaluation of the impact of a program for health promotion based in agency and empowerment].

Givaudan, M., Barriga, M. A., & Pick, S. (2008). The children left behind: Researching the impact of migration on the development of children and developing, piloting and evaluating a program that answers their special needs, *Report presented to the Bernard van Leer Foundation*. Mexico City: IMIFAP.

Givaudan, M., García, A., & Pick, S. (2007). Programa de prevención de cáncer cérvico uterino en áreas de extrema pobreza rural de Michoacán [Cervical cancer prevention program in areas of extreme rural poverty in Michoacan state], *Report presented to the Inter-American Development Bank*. Mexico City: IMIFAP.

Givaudan, M., Leenen, I., & Pick, S. (submitted). Health education and life skills: Building life skills and knowledge in rural children in Mexico.

Givaudan, M., & Osorio, P. (2009). Yo quiero, yo puedo... prevenir y controlar obesidad, diabetes y enfermedades cardiovasculares. Reporte final [I want to, I can ... prevent and control obesity, diabetes and cardiovascular diseases. Final report], *Report presented to the Pfizer Foundation*. Mexico City: IMIFAP.

Givaudan, M., Vitela, A., & Osorio, P. (2008). Estrategia fronteriza de promoción y prevención para una mejor salud [Border strategy of promotion and prevention for improving health], *Report presented to the Pfizer Foundation*. Mexico City: IMIFAP.

Hasenfeld, Y., & Brock, T. (1991). Implementation of social policy revisited. *Administration and Society*, 22(4), 451–479.

Instituto Mexicano de Investigación de Familia y Población [IMIFAP] (2008). México-Centroamerica: Educación en sexualidad, salud y habilidades para la vida. Fase III: Reporte Final [Mexico-Central America: Education on sexuality, health and life skills. Phase III: Final Report], *Report presented to the World Bank*. Mexico City: IMIFAP.

Leenen, I., Venguer, T., Vera, J., Givaudan, M., Pick, S., & Poortinga, Y. H. (2008). Effectiveness of a comprehensive health education program in a poverty-stricken rural area of Guatemala. *Journal of Cross-Cultural Psychology*, 39(2), 198–214.

Levy, S. (2008). *Good intentions, bad outcomes: Social policy, informality, and economic growth in Mexico*. Washington, DC: Brookings Institution Press.

Lipsky, M. (1978). Standing the study of public policy implementation on its head. In W. D. Burnham & M. W. Weinburg (Eds.), *American Politics and Public Policy* (pp. 391–402). Cambridge, MA: MIT Press.

Mangrulkar, L., Whitman, C., & Posner, M. (2001). *Life skills approach to child and adolescent human development*. Washington, DC: Pan American Health Organization.

Matland, R. (1995). Synthesizing the implementation literature: The ambiguity-conflict model of policy implementation. *Journal of Public Administration Research and Theory*, 5(2), 145–174.

Mazmanian, D., & Sabatier, P. (1989). *Implementation and public policy: With a new postscript*. Lanham, MD: University Press of America.

Michie, S., Pilling, S., Garety, P., Whitty, P., Eccles, M. P., Johnston, M., & Simmons, J. (2007). Difficulties implementing a mental health guideline: An exploratory investigation using psychological theory. *Implementation Science*, 2(8), 1–8.

Moreno Brid, J. C., & Puchet Anyul, M. (2008). Objetivos, alcances y limitaciones de la intervención del Estado en la Economía en América Latina y el Caribe para impulsar un desarrollo socialmente incluyente [Objectives, achievements and limitations of the intervention of the State in the Economy of Latin America and the Caribbean to promote a socially inclusive development] *Democracía, estado, ciudadanía: Hacía un estado de y para la democracía en América Latina* (pp. 309–324). Lima, Peru: United Nations Development Program.

Osorio-Belmon, P. (submitted). Exporting strategies: A cross-cultural adaptation of a pregnancy prevention curriculum for teenagers.

Osorio-Belmon, P., & Givaudan, M. (submitted). "I want to, I can ... prevent and control obesity, diabetes and cardiovascular disease": Effects of a life skills intervention in the northern border region of Mexico.

Osorio-Belmon, P., & Leenen, I. (submitted). The role of financial education among rural women: Saving for microenterprise.

Osorio, P., & Givaudan, M. (2008). Formación en microcréditos para mujeres indígenas y rurales en Oaxaca [Training in microfinance for rural indigenous women in

Oaxaca State, Mexico], *Report presented to the Finnish Embassy in Mexico, Fund for Local Cooperation*. Mexico City: IMIFAP.

Pick, S., Barriga, M., & Givaudan, M. (submitted). Agency, empowerment, health and life skills development among rural women in Mexico.

Pick, S., Givaudan, M., Leenen, I., & Koojmans, A. (submitted). I want to, I can ... prevent cancer: Building knowledge and changing norms, attitudes and behaviors among rural Mexican women.

Pick, S., Givaudan, M., & Poortinga, Y. H. (2003). Sexuality and life skills education: A multistrategy intervention in Mexico. *American Psychologist*, 58(3), 230–234.

Pick, S., Givaudan, M., & Reich, M. (2008). NGO-government partnerships for scaling up: Sexuality education in Mexico. *Development in Practice*, 18(2), 164–175.

Pick, S., Leenen, I., & García, G. (submitted). Programa piloto para la promoción de la salud en comunidades marginadas, a través del desarrollo de agencia y empoderamiento [Pilot program for health promotion in marginalized communities, through the development of agency and empowerment].

Pick, S., Leenen, I., Givaudan, M., & Prado, A. (in press-a). I want to, I can ... prevent violence: Raising awareness of dating violence through a brief intervention. *Salud Mental*.

Pick, S., Leenen, I., & Teegarden, L. (submitted). Prevención de cáncer cervical y de mama en áreas de pobreza extrema en Michoacán, México [Cervical and breast cancer prevention in areas of extreme poverty in Michoacan, Mexico].

Pick, S., & Osorio, P. (submitted). The impact of an educational intervention in rural female users of microfinance services: Building entrepreneurial skills.

Pick, S., Poortinga, Y. H., & Givaudan, M. (2003). Integrating intervention theory and strategy in culture-sensitive health promotion programs. *Professional Psychology: Research & Practice*, 34(4), 422–429.

Pick, S., Romero, A., Arana, D., & Givaudan, M. (2008). Programa formativo para prevenir la violencia a nivel primaria y secundaria [Training program for the prevention of violence at the primary and secondary school levels], *Report presented to the Chamber of Deputies of the Congress of the Union, 60th Legislature*. Mexico City: IMIFAP.

Pick, S., Romero, A., de la Parra, A., & Givaudan, M. (in press-b). Evaluación del impacto de un programa de prevención de violencia en adolescentes [Evaluation of the impact of a violence prevention program on adolescents]. *Revista Interamericana de Psicología*.

Pick, S., Sirkin, J., Ortega, I., Osorio, P., Martínez, R., Xocolotzin, U., & Givaudan, M. (2007). Escala para medir las capacidades de agencia personal y empoderamiento (ESAGE) [Scale for the measurement of personal agency and empowerment]. *Revista Interamericana de Psicología*, 41(3), 295–304.

Pressman, J. L., & Wildavsky, A. B. (1973). *Implementation: How great expectations in Washington are dashed in Oakland: Or, Why it's amazing that Federal programs work at all, this being a saga of the Economic Development Administration as told by two sympathetic observers who seek to build morals on a foundation of ruined hopes*. Berkeley: University of California Press.

Prochaska, J. O., & DiClemente, C. C. (1982). Transtheoretical therapy: Toward a more integrative model of change. *Psychotherapy: Theory, Research & Practice*, 19(3), 276–288.

Prochaska, J. O., & Velicer, W. F. (1997). Misinterpretations and misapplications of the transtheoretical model. *American Journal of Health Promotion*, 12(1), 11–12.

Robeyns, I. (2005). The Capability Approach: A theoretical survey. *Journal of Human Development*, 6(1), 93–114.

Romero, A., Leenen, I., & Givaudan, M. (2010). Identificación de factores sociales que influyen en el bienestar de los beneficiarios de los programas sociales [Identification of social factors that influence the wellbeing of social program beneficiaries]. *Report presented to SEDESOL*. Mexico City: IMIFAP.

Rowling, J. K. (2008). The fringe benefits of failure, and the importance of imagination, *Commencement Address at Harvard College*. Cambridge, MA.

Rubio, L. (2006, June 18). Control. *Reforma*, p. 19, Retrieved June 7, 2008 from www.reforma.com.mx

Ryan, N. (1999). Rationality and implementation analysis. *Journal of Management History*, 5(1), 36–52.

Toledo, A. (2007). *The future of Latin America: A political perspective*. Paper presented at the Harvard Business School IX Latin American Conference. Cambridge, MA.

Trostle, J., Bronfman, M., & Langer, A. (1999). How do researchers influence decision-makers? Case studies of Mexican policies. *Health Policy and Planning*, 14(2), 103–114.

United Nations Development Program [UNDP] (2004). *Nepal human development report 2004: Empowerment and poverty reduction*. Kathmandu, Nepal.

Universidad Autónoma de Aguascalientes (2008a). Implementación del Modelo de transmisión de conocimientos para el desarrollo de capacidades entre el personal de Diconsa, los Consejos Comunitarios y los Comités Rurales de Abasto. Primer reporte parcial: Sensibilización [Implementation of a knowledge transmission model for capacity development of Diconsa, Community Council and Rural Supply Committee personnel. First partial report: Developing awareness], *Report presented to Diconsa*. Mexico City: IMIFAP.

Universidad Autónoma de Aguascalientes (2008b). Implementación del Modelo de transmisión de conocimientos para el desarrollo de capacidades entre el personal de Diconsa, los Consejos Comunitarios y los Comités Rurales de Abasto. Segundo reporte parcial: Formación [Implementation of a knowledge transmission model for capacity development of Diconsa, Community Council and Rural Supply Committee personnel. Second partial report: Training], *Report presented to Diconsa*. Mexico City: IMIFAP.

Universidad Autónoma de Aguascalientes (2008c). Implementación del Modelo de transmisión de conocimientos para el desarrollo de capacidades entre el personal de Diconsa, los Consejos Comunitarios y los Comités Rurales de Abasto. Tercer reporte parcial: Réplica y Acompañamiento [Implementation of a knowledge transmission model for capacity development of Diconsa, Community Council and Rural Supply Committee personnel. Third partial report: Replication and follow-up], *Report presented to Diconsa*. Mexico City: IMIFAP.

Universidad Autónoma de Aguascalientes (2009). Implementación del Modelo de transmisión de conocimientos para el desarrollo de capacidades entre el personal de Diconsa, los Consejos Comunitarios y los Comités Rurales de Abasto. Informe ejecutivo final. [Implementation of a knowledge transmission model for capacity development of Diconsa, Community Council and Rural Supply Committee personnel. Final executive report], *Report presented to Diconsa*. Mexico City: IMIFAP.

Venguer, T., Pick, S., & Fishbein, M. (2007). Health education and agency: A comprehensive program for young women in the Mixteca region of Mexico. *Psychology, Health & Medicine*, 12(4), 389–406.

Weber, M. (1978). Bureaucracy *Economy and Society* (Vol. 2, pp. 956–1005). Berkeley, CA: University of California Press.

Wilson, W. J., & Aponte, R. (1985). Urban poverty. *Annual Review of Sociology*, 11, 231–258.

World Bank (2007). *World development report: Development and the next generation.* Washington, DC: World Bank.

World Bank, & Community Driven Development [CDD]. Community mobilization and capacity building: Key facets Retrieved December 26, 2008, from http://go. worldbank.org/FZA4DP2XW0.

APPENDIX A

Examples of Programming for Choice that Have Enhanced Personal Agency and Intrinsic Empowerment

This appendix will serve as an introduction to some of the Mexican Institute of Family and Population Research (IMIFAP) programs whose outcomes exceeded the directly targeted changes in knowledge, skills, and behaviors. It is these nontargeted changes that lead to the conceptualization of this book. We present the programs discussed in the testimonies of Chapter 3, in chronological order of their development and implementation. First we discuss "I Want to, I Can ... Prevent Pregnancies,"[1] and "I Want to, I Can ... Prevent Violence,"[2] followed by the "I Want to, I Can ... Integral Human Development"[3] program for school children and the accompanying "I Want to, I Can ... Learn to Be Dad and Mom"[4] program for parents, then "I Want to, I Can ... Care for My Health and Exercise My Rights"[5] and "I Want to, I Can ... Start My Own Business."[6] Finally, we introduce "Comprehensive Community Development." We describe the programs as they were structured initially, to give the clearest idea as to what participants' testimonies in the book are referring. We have since made adaptations in length and contents as well as standardized program names so that all are called "I Want to, I Can."

Program: "I Want to, I Can ... Prevent Pregnancies"
(Originally: "Planning Your Life," 1988)

Training manual: Pick de Weiss, S., Aguilar, J., Rodríguez, G., Reyes, J., Collado, M.E., Pier, D., Acevedo, M.P., Vargas, E. & Vargas, E. (1988). *Planeando tu vida: Nuevo programa de educación sexual para adolescentes* [*Planning your life: A new sexuality education program for adolescents*]. Mexico City: Editorial Planeta (7th edition, 1995, 22nd printing, 2008).

Question-and-answer book: Pick de Weiss, S., & Vargas Trujillo, E. (1990). *Yo adolescente: Respuestas claras a mis grandes dudas* [*I, adolescent: Clear answers to my greatest doubts*]. Mexico City: Editorial Planeta.

Context

In Mexico, as in most parts of Latin America, teen pregnancy has represented a public health problem for a long time. In the mid-to-late 1980s, 17% of all children born were born to women between the ages of 15 and 19 years (SEGOB, 1990). Available data from adolescents in Mexico City indicated that women started having sexual relations at around 16 years old and men somewhat earlier, at around 14 or 15 years old. However, both groups had little information in terms of the use of birth control methods and function of the reproductive system. In addition, significant taboos surrounded issues of sexuality.

"Planning Your Life" (renamed "I Want to, I Can ... Prevent Pregnancies") (Pick et al., 1990) stemmed from a diagnostic study conducted in Mexico City in the 1980s by IMIFAP (Pick, Andrade Palos, & Gribble, 1989; Pick, Díaz-Loving, & Atkin, 1988). Groups of adolescents of low and middle-to-low socio-economic levels were interviewed, with the goal of identifying determinants of sexual behaviors. The results suggested that the sexual health and behaviors for pregnancy prevention of adolescents in Mexico were strongly influenced by variables such as knowledge and attitudes about sexuality and contraception, family's and friends' perceptions about sexuality (social norms), and skills in decision making, communication, and assertiveness (Pick, Díaz-Loving, & Atkin, 1988; Pick et al., 1991).

Objectives

"Planning Your Life" aims to address the national context of unwanted adolescent pregnancies. The program's objectives include understanding one's own sexuality; talking about sexuality with one's partner, children, and parents; and being able to make autonomous decisions regarding contraceptive use.

Content and Methods

The course integrates biological aspects of sexuality as well as psycho-social elements, using accessible language, self-reflection, and incorporation of the community, family, and authorities. The content of the course covers anatomy and physiology of the reproductive organs, menstruation, birth control methods (including abstinence), places where individuals can find information about birth control methods, physical and psycho-social aspects of sexuality, as well as sexually transmitted infections and their prevention. Aspects related to self-control are also covered, as well as training in assertiveness, personal values, planning activities, and decision making. The program additionally reinforces working toward future goals.

A central component of this and all later IMIFAP programming is a focus on community participation, input, and action rather than on "interventions." The community's role is so extensive that by the end, programs are not recognized as external interventions but rather as a cooperative effort between the community and the program developers.

Results

Beyond the increased likelihood of contraceptive use in adolescents who took the course before having had sexual intercourse for the first time, participants showed significant nontargeted changes. Notably, some of these changes were only peripherally related to the thematic material covered in the program. These adolescents worked to further the programs introduced by IMIFAP: They organized presentations in the community on violence prevention, employment, and drug prevention, and soon thereafter a number of the community members who had originally been opposed to the program began to participate. The young women showed increased participation in the community and local government, increased employment, and demand for better access to water sources, reduction of teacher absenteeism, and improvement in quality of health services.

After implementation of "Planning Your Life," the Ministry of Public Education, in its 1994 reform for educational modernization, took the IMIFAP program as a basis for official ninth-grade curricula. This development pointed to a new understanding of both the significance of youth education in sexual health and rights, and the importance of policies promoting comprehensive education to enhance knowledge acquisition as well as skills in observation, analysis, and critical thinking. These themes were and still are a central component in IMIFAP's approach, including in the current version of this program (Pick & Givaudan, 2004).

Program: "I Want to, I Can ... Prevent Violence"
(Originally "Breaking the Chain of Violence," 1999)

Training manual: Fawcett, G. & Isita, L. (1999). *Rompamos la cadena de la violencia. Un taller para mujeres sobre violencia en la relación de pareja* [*Let's break the chain of violence: A workshop for women about violence in couple relationships*]. Mexico City: Editorial IDEAME.

Question-and-answer book: Pick, S., & Givaudan, M. (2006). *Violencia: Cómo identificar y evitar la violencia en cualquiera de sus formas.* [*Violence: How to identify and avoid violence in any of its forms*]. Mexico City: Editorial IDEAME.

Context

When the previous program was being administered, participants brought up the issue of domestic violence so often it became clear that a program dedicated to this topic was necessary. Statistics supported the concerns vocalized by participants. In one neighborhood in Mexico City, 33% of women reported having lived in a violent relationship. Of these women, 66% had been physically abused, 76% had been psychologically abused, and 21% had been sexually abused (Shrader & Valdez, 1992). In the Mexican state of Jalisco, 57% of women had experienced some sort of interpersonal violence (Ramírez & Uribe, 1993). Community norms, attitudes, and beliefs often kept women trapped in abusive relationships. Additionally, national infrastructure to address domestic violence was insufficient; women who were victims of violence largely lacked a place to find help or a source of income. A clear gap existed between needs and service provision.

Objectives

To address the needs expressed by the women, "Breaking the Chain of Violence" was developed (Fawcett et al., 1999; Fawcett & Isita, 1999; Fawcett, Isita, & Pick, 1999). The program aims to help women recognize abuse and encourage communities to respond to abused women in a supportive rather than judgmental way. Much of this goal is based in getting women to talk among themselves about violence. Specific objectives include creating a team of community women who can provide support and information to abused women; helping those abused women who participate in the program to recognize abuse and identify different sources of support; shifting community perceptions of domestic violence from a private problem to a community issue; and reducing the blame often placed on female victims of abuse.

Content and Methods

The "Breaking the Chain of Violence" program adopted a multifaceted strategy, based on an ecological approach (Heise, 1998) and community action (Bracht, 1990). Focus groups facilitated the development of a methodology that would be successful within the community, highlighting the need for exercises that would encourage the open expression of norms, attitudes, and beliefs. In-depth interviews with women who had lived, or were currently living, with a violent partner served to identify the strategies adopted by abused women to survive and/or end abuse. The final version of the program involves workshops for women that focus on information and skill development in a participatory way that requires self-reflection. Community-focused programming includes peer outreach, small-scale media, popular theater, and special events (Fawcett et al., 1999).

Results

As in the "I Want to, I Can ... Prevent Pregnancies" program, significant nontargeted changes in the areas of communication and personal agency occurred in addition to the intended outcomes of the program (Fawcett, Isita, & Pick, 1999). Specifically, program participants spearheaded the provision of sexuality education courses to local authorities and to truckers of the gas company in charge of local gas delivery. They organized to improve government milk service provision and to start their own businesses, as well as starting sewing and computer classes at the local community center. Further, women began talking more about domestic violence and supporting each other on the issue. The program participants sought to influence the social norms in their community. They organized groups for men and adolescents, gave talks in the schools, held raffles to raise money for further training, and organized a fair focused around the issue of abuse. While programming allowed for the achievement of targeted outcomes, the combination of knowledge, skills and self-reflection within the workshops empowered participants to take the realized skills even further (Health promoters, personal communication, February 13, 2007).

Program: "I Want to, I Can ... Integral Human Development" (Originally "Yo, mi familia y mi medio ambiente," 1994)

Workbooks: Pick, S. & Givaudan, M. (1994). *Yo, mi familia y mi medio ambiente: Un libro de educación para la vida.* [*Me, my family and my environment: A life skills book*]. Series of 7 books for primary school grades kindergarten, 1, 2, 3, 4, 5, 6. Mexico City: Editorial Planeta.

Context

The initial motivation to create "I Want to, I Can ... Comprehensive Human Development" was that the education system in Mexico focused on rote memorization and involved little analytical learning or student participation. Children often complained of being bored in school, and even teachers reported lacking motivation to attend their own classes.[7] New research had found, however, that providing participatory and reflection-based programming to adolescents increased the likelihood of behavior change as compared to traditional programs with an emphasis on knowledge (Pick de Weiss & Andrade Palos, 1989).

The thematic education in schools, at the time, notably lacked sexuality education or drug, alcohol, and tobacco prevention programs of any kind. A low consciousness of gender equality prevailed. Meanwhile, research showed that providing comprehensive sexuality education programs before adolescents became sexually active increased the likelihood that they would adopt safe sex practices (Pick de Weiss et al., 1994). This highlighted a strong need for programming, including sexuality programming at even younger ages than IMIFAP was currently undertaking.

Objectives

The school-based "I Want to, I Can ... Comprehensive Human Development" program aims to encourage students' comprehensive development (Givaudan &

Pick, 2007a, 2007b, 2007c; Pick & Givaudan, 2007a, 2007b, 2007c, 2007d, 2007e, 2007f, 2007g, 2007h; Pick, Givaudan, & Beltrán, 2007). The program promotes skill and competency-building hand-in-hand with information and myth clarification. The strengthening of personal skills and psychosocial competencies serves specifically to develop comprehensive personal and community health promotion from childhood on. The initial contents were designed to create understanding of prevention and self-care in the areas of physical and mental health, social participation, and care for the environment (Pick & Givaudan, 1994a, 1994b, 1994c, 1994d, 1994e, 1994f, 1994g). By building skills and competencies and imparting information in a repeated fashion for different issues regarding health and individual development, the program promotes not only thematic knowledge but improvements in behavior and increased participation in the class and community activities. Later versions of the program also work to improve skills associated with participatory citizenship (Pick et al., 2000; Pick et al., 1999a, 1999b). Versions for the preschool, primary, and secondary school levels in urban (Givaudan & Pick, 2007a; Pick & Givaudan, 1996a, 1996b, 1996c, 1996d, 1996e, 1996f, 1996g, 1996h, 1996i, 1996j, 1996k, 2007a, 2007b, 2007c, 2007d, 2007e, 2007f, 2007g, 2007h, 2007i; Pick, Givaudan, & Beltrán, 2007) and rural areas (Pick & Givaudan, 2003a, 2003b, 2003c, 2003d) were developed.

Content and Methods

"I Want to, I Can … Comprehensive Human Development" dedicates specific lessons to each of the life skills recognized as protective factors for physical and mental health. The program focuses on strengthening self-knowledge, decision making, communication skills, analysis, problem solving, and critical thinking; other areas covered include management of affect, frustration, and stress as well as expression of feelings applied to daily problems at the personal, family, and societal levels. In addition to its focus on skill sets, the program offers specific information in the areas of hygiene, nutrition, sexuality, and caring for the environment (Givaudan & Pick, 2007a, 2007b, 2007c; Givaudan, Pick, & Beltrán, 2009a, 2009b; Pick & Givaudan, 1994a, 1994b, 1994c, 1994d, 1994e, 1994f, 1994g, 1996a, 1996b, 1996c, 1996d, 1996e, 1996f, 1996g, 1996h, 1996i, 1996j, 1996k, 2007a, 2007b, 2007c, 2007d, 2007e, 2007f, 2007g, 2007h, 2007i; Pick, Givaudan, & Beltrán, 2007). Additional versions have added drug use and alcohol abuse prevention (Givaudan, Beltrán, & Pick, 2006; Givaudan & Pick, 2006a, 2006b; Pick, Givaudan, & Beltrán, 2006), prevention of HIV/AIDS (Chaylian et al., 2002; Reyes et al., 1996), violence (Beltrán et al., 2007; Beltrán et al., 1999; Fawcett & Isita, 1999; Fawcett et al., 1999; Ruiz & Fawcett, 1999), obesity and diabetes (Peña et al., 2007), cancer (Fuertes, Acuña, & Venguer, 2001a, 2001b; Fuertes & Venguer, 2001a, 2001b), and school achievement (Givaudan et al., 2009).

Participatory techniques such as games and role-plays provide a basis for the programming: "Active homework" is assigned to the students so that lessons learned throughout the sessions can be applied at home and in the community. When it became clear that neither the teachers nor the students were accustomed to participatory methodologies, specific workshops for teacher training were additionally developed. "I Want to, I Can ... Comprehensive Human Development" was designed to be integrated into the official education program from preschool through secondary school levels, and its contents could be applied as a complement to other school subjects. At the lower and upper secondary school levels, the program became part of the official national curriculum "Civic and Ethics Formation" (Pick et al., 2000; Pick et al., 1999a, 1999b).

Results

Evaluation of the program, conducted with 245 boys and girls, found that there was significant increase in knowledge about menstruation and sexual organs, as well as enhancement of the children's ability to assume responsibility for their school grades and to communicate with their teachers about things they did not understand (Givaudan et al., 1997a). Further qualitative evaluation with 115 students, supported by the World Bank, noted the high degree of participation and motivation from teachers and parents involved in the program. Improvements in interfamily communication were attributed to the program (Givaudan et al., 1997b). An external evaluation of the program confirmed changes in attitudes about gender and improvements in communication and decision-making skills as well as in health practices (Bos, 1998) and in prevention of alcohol abuse (Givaudan & Pick, 2004).

Equally significant are the nontargeted outcomes reported by teachers and by the children and parents themselves when we talked with them. Children were reported to show higher school attendance, more frequent submission of homework on time, and increased class participation. Students indicated that they began to speak with their teachers about sexual abuse and violence and initiated a clean-up of the school grounds and community. The program's model of skills combined with knowledge, repetition, active homework, and contextual support enabled significant personal development. Spontaneous comments received referred, for example, to people feeling shy before the workshop and being afraid of getting punished for asking questions, whereas after the workshop, they began to talk with friends and family about what they learned and began building confidence and skills. Others made reference to the fact that they now felt it was acceptable to have knowledge about sexuality and to talk about it and considered it okay to make decisions and to oppose ideas of others when one did not agree with them. They also realized they now had the ability to do so (Givaudan et al., 2007).

Program: "I Want to, I Can ... Learn to Be Dad and
Mom" (Originally "Learning to Be Dad and Mom," 1995)

Training manual: Pick, S., Givaudan, M. & Martinez, A. (1995). *Aprendiendo a ser papá y mamá: De niñas y niños desde el nacimiento hasta los 12 anos [Learning to be dad and mom of girls and boys from birth until age 12*]. Mexico City: Editorial Planeta (3rd edition, in press).

Question-and-answer book: Givaudan, M. & Pick, S. (1995*). Yo papá, Yo mamá: La forma responsable de educar y disfrutar con tus hijos e hijas* [*I dad, I mom: The responsible way to educate and have fun with your sons and daughters*]. Mexico City: Editorial Planeta (3rd edition, in press).

Context

With the "I Want to, I Can ... Comprehensive Human Development" program including sexuality education in schools, parents began complaining. Asked by the school system to respond to these complaints, IMIFAP held a meeting with parents. At this meeting, the parents made clear their concern that their children now knew more about sexuality than they did; they wanted to create a more favorable environment to speak with their children about the contents of the program. This signaled the need to work simultaneously with fathers and mothers.

Objectives, Content, and Methods

To this end, "Learning to Be Dad and Mom" addresses the taboos that parents have regarding sexuality, as well as values, interests and sexual roles, and discipline and limits. The participatory-style classes include the importance of talking to one's children about these and other difficult issues and how to do so. The program also included a "dictionary" presenting alternative responses to difficult subject matters for different age groups (Solano, Pick, & Pick, 1995). The importance of placing limits, expressing affection, assertive communication, decision making and taking care of one's own personal development as a basis for taking care of others are also included. A similar program was later developed for parents with adolescent children, including a manual (Pick, Givaudan, & Martinez, 1998) and a question-and-answer book for parents (Fernández, Givaudan, & Pick, 2002).

Results

Evaluation of the program found that those parents who participated declared greater ease in relating to their sons and daughters (Givaudan, 1999). The results showed that the skills component of the program enabled parents to take what they had learned into other domains (Givaudan, López, & Pick, 1998; Givaudan et al., 1994; Ramón, Camacho, & Pick, 1997; Ramón, Givaudan, & Pick, 1997a, 1997b). The parental requests for sexuality education and the subsequent role of the program in supporting children's learning and development highlighted the importance of a multipopulation approach to programming (Givaudan et al., 1994; Pick de Weiss, 1993).

An additional outcome was that we looked into ways of extending this program and the "I Want to, I Can ... Comprehensive Human Development" program to the children of migrants and their caretakers. The extended program, entitled "I Want to, I Can … Learn and Have Fun in Preschool," focused on preschool children of migrants. Nontargeted outcomes of the program were reported by teachers and by the children and parents themselves. Children exhibited more self-confidence and better ability to interact with peers, as well as more respect for their classmates. Decision-making and problem-solving skills improved significantly. Children became more adept at dealing with peer pressure, and showed a desire to make their own decisions, rather than relying on those of their parents and teachers (Givaudan, Barriga, & Pick, 2008).

The program's effects were felt not only by students but by their parents and teachers as well. Improved skills in dealing with children, spending more time with them, getting to know them better, and giving them more freedom in choosing what to do with their time were among the results found. Parents mentioned allowing their child to choose what games to play at home, and teachers allowed their students more freedom in picking their activities and exercises for the day. Additionally, caregivers and teachers used more positive language, avoided negative comments toward children, and expressed their emotions more positively. Children were subsequently encouraged to reflect on their emotions and behaviors to come to terms with them in their own way. In general, parents and teachers reported it was much easier to maintain rules than before; children had come to respect them (Givaudan, Barriga, & Gaál, 2009; Givaudan, Barriga, & Pick, 2008).

Program: "I Want to, I Can … Care for My Health and Exercise My Rights" (Originally "If I Am OK, So Is My Family," 1999)

Venguer, T., Quezada, M., Pick, S., Cabral, J., Flores, A., Mireles, M., Montero, G. & Morales, N. (2000). *Si yo estoy bien mi familia también: Modulo de salud y empoderamiento. Manual teórico, manual de ejercicios, material didáctico, rotafolio, tríptico y cartel* [*If I am OK, so is my family: Health and Empowerment Module. Training Manual, Workbook, Didactic Material, Flipchart, Pamphlet and Poster*]. Mexico City: IMIFAP & IMSS-Oportunidades.

Venguer, T., Quezada, M., Pick, S., Cabral, J., Flores, A., Mireles, M., Montero, G. & Morales, N. (2000). *Si yo estoy bien mi familia también: Modulo de alimentación y empoderamiento. Manual teórico, manual de ejercicios, material didáctico, rotafolio, tríptico y cartel* [*If I am OK, so is my family: Nutrition and Empowerment Module. Training Manual, Workbook, Didactic Material, Flipchart, Pamphlet and Poster*]. Mexico City: IMIFAP & IMSS-Oportunidades.

Venguer, T., Quezada, M., Pick, S., Cabral, J., Flores, A., Montero, G. & Morales, N. (2000). *Si yo estoy bien mi familia también: Modulo de higiene, saneamiento y empoderamiento. Manual teórico, manual de ejercicios, material didáctico, rotafolio, tríptico y cartel* [*If I am OK, so is my family: Hygiene, Sanitation and Empowerment Module. Training Manual, Workbook, Didactic Material, Flipchart, Pamphlet and Poster*]. Mexico City: IMIFAP & IMSS-Oportunidades.

Venguer, T., Quezada, M., Pick, S., Cabral, J., Flores, A., Montero, G. & Morales, N. (2000). *Si yo estoy bien mi familia también: Modulo de sexualidad, salud reproductiva y empoderamiento. Manual teórico, manual de ejercicios, material didáctico, rotafolio, tríptico y cartel* [*If I am OK, so is my family: Sexuality, Reproductive Health and Empowerment Module. Training Manual, Workbook, Didactic Material, Flipchart, Pamphlet and Poster*]. Mexico City: IMIFAP & IMSS-Oportunidades.

Venguer, T., Quezada, M., Pick, S., Cabral, J., Flores, A., Montero, G. & Morales, N. (2000). *Si yo estoy bien mi familia también: Modulo de desarrollo y empoderamiento para niñas y niños. Manual teórico, manual de ejercicios, material didáctico, rotafolio, tríptico y cartel* [*If I am OK, so is my family: Development and Empowerment for Children Module. Training Manual, Workbook, Didactic Material, Flipchart, Pamphlet and Poster*]. Mexico City: IMIFAP & IMSS-Oportunidades.

Venguer, T., Quezada, M., Pick, S., Cabral, J., Flores, A., Montero, G. & Morales, N. (2000). *Si yo estoy bien mi familia también: Modulo de salud, nutrición y empoderamiento para niñas y niños. Manual teórico, manual de ejercicios, material didáctico, rotafolio, tríptico y cartel* [*If I am OK, so is my family: Sexuality, Reproductive Health and Empowerment Module. Training Manual, Workbook, Didactic Material, Flipchart, Pamphlet and Poster*]. Mexico City: IMIFAP & IMSS-Oportunidades.

Context

The "If I Am OK, So Is My Family" program was developed from the identified needs and problem definitions of rural and indigenous communities (Venguer et al., 1999a, 1999b, 2000, 2001, 2002), a population not previously targeted by IMIFAP programs. In the highlands of the Oaxacan Mixteca region of Mexico, information collected from public resources, focus groups with women, and semi-structured interviews with local and federal health and education authorities highlighted several impediments to changes in specific behaviors. A fundamental impediment was the limited conception of each individual taking preventative health steps (Venguer et al., 2000). Relationships between domains, such as nutrition or reproductive health and well-being, were poorly understood. Significant inequality of opportunity as well as minimal economic, education, health, and participatory opportunities further limited the population. Mixteca had the highest rate of malnutrition in the country and 37% of incomes fell below the minimum wage (INEGI, 2000). Social norms attached shame and fear to the simple expression of one's ideas and to the undertaking of initiatives such as a trip to the health clinic. Health as a basic right was simply not in the scheme of things (Venguer et al., 2000; Venguer, Pick, & Fishbein, 2007).

Objectives

The program has a parallel goal to previous IMIFAP programs in its aim to enable women, here rural and indigenous, to gain control over their health.

The curriculum promotes gender equality and focuses on the skills central to all IMIFAP programs: communication, decision making, self-knowledge, and emotional intelligence. In addition, four specific domains were addressed: general health issues (Venguer et al., 2000b); nutrition and diet (Venguer et al., 2000a); hygiene and sanitation (Venguer et al., 2000b); and sexuality and reproductive health and rights (Venguer et al., 2000d). Additional domains pertinent to children's health issues were also included (Venguer et al., 2000a, 2000c).

Content and Methods

To reach the largest number of women possible and maintain cost-effectiveness, the program was implemented as a closely supervised and accompanied cascade with three levels of "replicators." IMIFAP program staff trained the first level of replicators, government-paid health technicians who worked as community action promoters; these promoters, in turn, trained a second level of 500 government-paid rural health assistants working in the Oaxaca health system. These assistants then each trained between six and eight volunteers who presented the program in their own village to small groups of women. IMIFAP staff members monitored activities at all stages of the program, often administering questionnaires and making community visits to ensure the maintenance of program quality. Presentation styles in the workshops centered on interaction rather than instruction. Program activities directed at the social context facilitated changes in behavior and enabled the maintenance of these changes. During the period that workshops were in progress, two radio stations broadcasted messages with key elements of the program (in three phases: sensitization, information, and recommendations for concrete actions) on an hourly basis, accompanied by a program-specific jingle created in collaboration with women from different communities (Venguer et al., 2000, 2002).

Results

Several findings testify to the effectiveness of the program. Both *ad hoc* results and a questionnaire and observations study (undertaken through home visits looking at demographic information, knowledge, and behaviors in various domains) illustrated that relevant changes in behavior occurred. The more salient results included high rates of attendance at the workshops—over 90% of the participating 39,000 girls and women—and statistically significant increases in Pap smears, contraceptive use, latrine use, nutrition, and communication with one's partner and children regarding sexuality. Moreover, a follow-up assessment after 18 months showed that, in general, these changes were maintained (Venguer, Pick, & Fishbein, 2007).

Community organizing was a predominant nontargeted effect of the program. Participants, all female, took the initiative to organize women in the community to get Pap smears, establish a community kitchen to provide breakfast to children and the elderly, and organize community celebrations.

Personal transformations in the women were further seen. Authorities, as well as the community promoters and women themselves, reported that the participants began to interact with authority figures in an entirely new manner, making formal requests to the local and municipal governments for support in their various initiatives. At an institutional level, a large part of the curriculum was adopted in a number of states by the Mexican governmental initiative *IMSS-Oportunidades* (Venguer, Pick, & Fishbein, 2007).

Program: "I Want to, I Can ... Start My Own Business" (Originally "Entrepreneurship for Growth," 2003)

Training manuals: Bernal, M., García, Y. & Venguer, T. (2003). *Programa para la promoción del desarrollo exitoso de la microempresa en el medio rural. Manual para instructores(as). Módulo I. Habilidades psicolaborales. Módulo II. Competencias técnicas* ["Microenterprise development program in rural contexts". Manual for instructors. Module I. Psycho-laboral skills. Module II, Technical competencies]. Mexico City: IMIFAP.

Flipchart: Bernal, M., García, Y. & Venguer, T. (2003). *Programa para la promoción del desarrollo exitoso de la microempresa en el medio rural* [Program for the promotion of the successful development of microenterprises in rural areas]. Mexico City: IMIFAP.

Context

Despite the presence of small-business loans targeted at women in Mexico, many of the recipients were not utilizing the money to start or enhance an ongoing business. In the 1990s, Nacional Financiera (a Mexican government financial institution providing such loans) consulted informally with IMIFAP regarding this situation, and in response IMIFAP conducted an informal evaluation. Findings showed that women were afraid to take risks and be competitive, did not feel entitled to make decisions, and were fearful of both succeeding and failing with their investments. It was evident that a source of income was necessary for these women, however, because once female participants had enacted such changes in their lives as using contraceptives, having Pap smears, vaccinating their children, and eating better, they came to IMIFAP looking to participate in income-generating projects.

Objectives

The goal of "Entrepreneurship for Growth" was to implement a program that would make lending more successful: to create better borrowers of credit. The program combines life skills-building with the provision of small loans to teach and furthermore to empower individuals to start their own micro-enterprise, or small business. Aims of life skills training for the participants include increasing risk-taking and decision-making capabilities, promoting self-efficacy and self-esteem, increasing participants' sense of internal control, improving motivation to be successful, and developing technical, management, and leadership skills. As with all IMIFAP programs, the ultimate goal is an improvement in participants' quality of life and a new identity as agents of their own lives.

Content and Methods

Originally, 20 rural communities of the Mixteca region of Oaxaca participated in the program, with a total of 600 women (Bernal et al., 2006). The workshops, running between 2002 and 2005, integrated "If I Am OK, So Is My Family" curriculum with training in the life skills and technical skills that correlated with small-business establishment and maintenance (Bernal et al., 2007). Additional activities were crucial to development of the program and included training promoters, organizing, supervising and assisting community banks and small businesses, and providing loans to participants. The program nowadays has extended and is being carried out in 55 communities in two states of Mexico and in remote rural areas of Honduras and Guatemala (Osorio & Givaudan, 2008a; Osorio & Pick, 2009).

Results

Project evaluation, which occurred as an ongoing process throughout project implementation as well as at the conclusion, focused on attendance, skill attainment, and overall impact of the program. Focus groups allowed for the collection of qualitative information related to the impact of the program and revealed psycho-social impacts, specifically significant improvements in decision-making skills, creativity, and self-efficacy. Business success was determined through calculations of economic indicators such as average profit and savings. Sustainable businesses developed after a year and a half, and within these businesses, there was a 96% loan return rate, as well as an average monthly savings rate of 20% among the program participants. Furthermore, the businesses began to employ other community members (IMIFAP, 2005). Five hundred and fifty small businesses were established and 20 community banks were also created. This number has since grown to approximately 130 community banks and 1,600 businesses (Osorio & Givaudan, 2008b; Pick & Osorio-Belmon, submitted).

The workshops, in combination with business development, create a sense of personal agency within the women that leads them to push for further changes within the community. The women come forward to report having succeeded in closing down the local brothel; replicating workshops on violence, cervical cancer, and family planning; serving as community representatives; and successfully lobbying for improved local infrastructure. The women not only begin businesses, but their understanding of themselves as individuals and their relationships with their community entirely changes (Osorio & Givaudan, 2008b; Osorio & Pick, 2008a, 2008b).

Program: "Comprehensive Community Development" (2002–2008)

PROGRAM FOR WOMEN

Venguer, T., Quezada, M., Pick, S., Cabral, J., Flores, A., Mireles, M., Montero, G. & Morales, N. (2000). *Si yo estoy bien mi familia también: Modulo de salud y empoderamiento. Manual teórico, manual de ejercicios, material didáctico, rotafolio, tríptico y cartel* [*If I am OK, so is my family: Health and Empowerment Module. Training Manual, Workbook, Didactic Material, Flipchart, Pamphlet and Poster*]. Mexico City: IMIFAP & IMSS-Oportunidades.

Venguer, T., Quezada, M., Pick, S., Cabral, J., Flores, A., Mireles, M., Montero, G. & Morales, N. (2000). *Si yo estoy bien mi familia también: Modulo de alimentación y empoderamiento. Manual teórico, manual de ejercicios, material didáctico, rotafolio, tríptico y cartel* [*If I am OK, so is my family: Nutrition and Empowerment Module. Training Manual, Workbook, Didactic Material, Flipchart, Pamphlet and Poster*]. Mexico City: IMIFAP & IMSS-Oportunidades.

Venguer, T., Quezada, M., Pick, S., Cabral, J., Flores, A., Montero, G. & Morales, N. (2000). *Si yo estoy bien mi familia también: Modulo de higiene, saneamiento y empoderamiento. Manual teórico, manual de ejercicios, material didáctico, rotafolio, tríptico y cartel* [*If I am OK, so is my family: Hygiene, Sanitation and Empowerment Module. Training Manual, Workbook, Didactic Material, Flipchart, Pamphlet and Poster*]. Mexico City: IMIFAP & IMSS-Oportunidades.

Venguer, T., Quezada, M., Pick, S., Cabral, J., Flores, A., Montero, G. & Morales, N. (2000). *Si yo estoy bien mi familia también: Modulo de sexualidad, salud reproductiva y empoderamiento. Manual teórico, manual de ejercicios, material didáctico, rotafolio, tríptico y cartel* [*If I am OK, so is my family: Sexuality, Reproductive Health and Empowerment Module. Training Manual, Workbook, Didactic Material, Flipchart, Pamphlet and Poster*]. Mexico City: IMIFAP & IMSS-Oportunidades.

PROGRAM FOR MEN

Training Manual: Castellanos, J. (2007) *Salud, género y empoderamiento para hombres: Manual para promotores y promotoras.* [Health, Gender and Empowerment for Men: Manual for Promoters.] Mexico: Editorial IDEAME.

Workbook: Bernal, M., & Castellanos, J. (2007) *Salud, género y empoderamiento para hombres: Rotafolio para promotores y promotoras* .[Health, Gender and Empowerment for Men: Flip Chart for Promoters.] Mexico City: IDEAME.

MICROENTERPRISE PROGRAM

Training Manual: Bernal, M., García, Y., & Venguer, T. (2004). *Programa para la promoción del desarrollo exitoso de la MICROEMPRESA en el medio rural.* [Program for the Promotion of Successful Microenterprise Development in the Rural Setting.] Mexico City: Editorial IDEAME.

Workbook: Bernal, M., García, Y., & Venguer, T. (2003). *Programa para la promoción del desarrollo exitoso de la MICROEMPRESA en el medio rural.* [Program for the Promotion of Successful Microenterprise Development in the Rural Setting Mexico City: Editorial IDEAME.

PROGRAM FOR CHILDREN

Training Manual: Givaudan, M., Pick, S., & Vazquez, F. (2003) *Habilidades para la vida y salud: 3° a 6° de primaria.* Guía para el maestro. [Life Skills and Health. 3rd to 6th Grades of Primary School. Teachers' Guide.] Mexico City: Editorial IDEAME.

Workbook: Pick, S. & Givaudan, M. (2003) *Habilidades para la vida y salud: Programa escolar para niñas y niños.* 3° de primaria. [Life Skills and Health: School-Based Program for Children. 3rd Grade of Primary School.] Mexico City: Editorial IDEAME.

Workbook: Pick, S. & Givaudan, M. (2003) *Habilidades para la vida y salud: Programa escolar para niñas y niños.* 4° de primaria. [Life Skills and Health: School-Based Program for Children. 4th Grade of Primary School.] Mexico City: Editorial IDEAME.

Workbook: Pick, S. & Givaudan, M. (2003) *Habilidades para la vida y salud: Programa escolar para niñas y niños.* 5° de primaria. [Life Skills and Health: School-Based Program for Children. 5th Grade of Primary School.] Mexico City: Editorial IDEAME.

Workbook: Pick, S. & Givaudan, M. (2003) *Habilidades para la vida y salud: Programa escolar para niñas y niños.* 6° de primaria. [Life Skills and Health: School-Based Program for Children. 6th Grade of Primary School.] Mexico City: Editorial IDEAME.

Context

Women have been the most affected by the exclusion and different kinds of poverties in many communities. Their gender has kept them at the margin of decision making, as much in public policy as in the family sphere. Among indigenous populations, in particular, the problems are aggravated. Government programs for vulnerable populations focus on providing social assistance rather than addressing the roots of the problems. The "Comprehensive Community Development" project understood that to address the gender inequalities and marginalization and exclusion experienced by women, it was necessary to promote male participation and responsibility as well as equality between women and men. By way of significant changes in gender roles, both men and women would gain a clearer understanding of their rights and responsibilities in all spheres of public and private life.

Objectives

The "Comprehensive Community Development" program is IMIFAP's largest comprehensive program to date. Its aim was the creation of a community development model of intrinsic empowerment, health, and economic productivity that integrated the individual, the family, and the community to bring about a higher quality of life for marginalized families. For women and men, it aimed to improve quality of life through changes in behaviors and, through this, build their intrinsic empowerment in the areas of health and rights; in the case of women, it would also promote microfinance ventures; for children, it aimed to foster knowledge and the development of psycho-social skills so that the children would be healthy, productive, and responsible in their actions.

Content and Methods

The program, incorporating the health and education systems and mass media, entailed components that started out as four separate programs. This strategy supported synergy and behavioral changes in the community. Various components of the program were developed, implemented, and evaluated, equally at the level of needs-based content as at the level of supporting materials. The program was then carried out through a closely accompanied cascade process. Initially, it was planned that the project would be carried out in the state of Hidalgo. In the first year, the project's coverage grew, and it was simultaneously implemented in the state of Chiapas.

Results

The "Comprehensive Community Development" program had positive effects in target families and communities. It is estimated that each trained individual had an impact on a minimum of 3 additional people, totaling 413,200 individuals benefiting from the program. Among children, program effects were seen through their knowledge, attitudes, and behaviors regarding health protection and quality-of-life improvement (Givaudan, Pick, Leenen, & DuBois, submitted). Among men, the results indicate that the program has a positive effect in the way in which men think about their relationship with their family, their responsibility within the family, and the way in which they communicate with their spouse and their children (Givaudan et al., 2009). Women showed a positive impact in knowledge, attitudes and behaviors associated with nutrition, hygiene, and sexual health (Pick, Barriga, & Givaudan, submitted). By this point in IMIFAP program development, outcomes of personal agency and intrinsic empowerment were integrated into program evaluation instruments (Givaudan, Pick, Leenen, & DuBois, submitted). Increases in personal agency and intrinsic empowerment were seen across all target populations and exemplified in testimonies (Givaudan et al., submitted).

The programs for men and women achieved the training of close to 3,000 government personnel—including directors, assistants, auxiliary personnel, and community promoters—strengthening the possibilities of sustainability in the medium and long term (IMIFAP, 2009). The program has since been expanded with a focus on hygiene and nutrition to 11,000 rural communities (Universidad Autónoma de Aguascalientes, 2008a, 2008b, 2008c) and with a focus on nutrition for children under age 5 years in the 300,000 poorest households (Universidad Autónoma de Aguascalientes, 2009). The results show statistically significant increases in knowledge across various domains, including hygiene and nutrition, in behaviors such as personal hygiene and eating nutritiously, in assertiveness, and in personal agency and intrinsic empowerment (Leenen et al., 2009; García, Pick, & Romero, submitted).

Notes

1. The original name of this program was "Planning Your Life."
2. Originally, "Breaking the Chain of Violence."
3. Originally, "I Want to, I Can."
4. Originally, "Learning to Be Dad and Mom."
5. Originally, "If I Am OK, So Is My Family."
6. Originally, "Entrepreneurship for Growth."
7. To a great degree, this is still the case. Mexico's education system is heavily based in rote memorization and both children and teachers report being bored and lacking motivation in the classroom (Corral Jurado, 2009; Taylor, 2009).

References

Beltrán, M., Bernal, M., Olivares, J., & Torres, C. (2007). *Yo quiero, yo puedo ... prevenir violencia. Programa para la promoción de la equidad de género para adolescentes de México y Centroamérica [I want to, I can ... prevent violence. Program for the promotion of gender equality for adolescents in Mexico and Central America].* Mexico City: Editorial IDEAME.

Beltrán, M., Bolaños, E., Fawcett, G., & Isita, L. (1999). *Yo quiero, yo puedo ... prevenir violencia. Versión para mujeres rurales e indígenas [I want to, I can ... prevent violence. Version for women in indigenous and rural areas].* Mexico City: Editorial IDEAME.

Bernal, M., Castellanos, J., García, Y., Givaudan, M., Pick, S., Olivares, J., Torres, C., & Venguer, T. (2007). *Yo quiero, yo puedo ... empezar mi negocio. Programa de formación de microempresas y salud. Manual para promotores. [I want to, I can ... start my own business. Microenterprise and health training program. Manual for facilitators.].* Mexico City: Editorial IDEAME.

Bernal, M., Martínez, R., Ortega, I., Ruesga, C., Givaudan, M., & Pick, S. (2006). Programa de microempresas con mujeres rurales de Oaxaca [Microenterprise program with rural women in Oaxaca], *Report presented to the W. K. Kellogg Foundation.* Mexico City: IMIFAP.

Bos, V. (1998). *Promoting resilience in Mexican children: Theoretical foundation and evaluation of a school program.* Unpublished masters thesis, Leiden University, Leiden, Netherlands.

Bracht, N. (Ed.). (1990). *Health promotion at the community level.* Newbury Park, CA: Sage Publications.

Chaylian, S., Givaudan, M., Venguer, T., & Leenen, I. (2002). *Prevención del VIH/SIDA. Manual teórico/práctico [HIV/AIDS prevention. A theoretical/practical manual].* Mexico City: Editorial IDEAME.

Corral Jurado, J. (2009, April 14). Reforma educativa: ¿podrá Lujambio? [Educational reform: Can Lujambio do it?]. *El Universal,* p. A17.

Fawcett, G., Heise, L. L., Isita-Espejel, L., & Pick, S. (1999). Changing community responses to wife abuse. A research and demonstration project in Iztacalco, Mexico. *American Psychologist, 54*(1), 41–49.

Fawcett, G., & Isita, L. (1999). Rompamos la cadena de la violencia. Un taller para mujeres sobre violencia en la relación de pareja [Let's break the chain of violence. A workshop for women about violence in couple relationships]. Mexico City: Editorial IDEAME.

Fawcett, G., Isita, L., & Pick, S. (1999). Changing community norms toward wife abuse: A research and demonstration project in Iztacalco, Mexico, *Report presented to the International Center for Research on Women*. Mexico City: IMIFAP.

Fawcett, G., Venguer, T., Miranda, L., & Fernández, F. (1999). *Los servicios de salud ante la violencia doméstica. Manual para instructores (as) [Health services in the face of domestic violence. Manual for instructors]*. Mexico City: Editorial IDEAME.

Fernández, F., Givaudan, M., & Pick, S. (2002). *Deja volar a tu adolescente. Libro para papás y mamás. [Let your teenager fly. A book for dads and moms]*. Mexico City: Editorial IDEAME.

Fuertes, C., Acuña, J. C., & Venguer, T. (2001a). *Es cosa de dos: sesiones dirigidas a hombres para la prevención y detección temprana del cáncer cérvicouterino [We're in this together: Sessions for men on the prevention and early detection of cervical cancer]*. Mexico City: Editorial IDEAME.

Fuertes, C., Acuña, J. C., & Venguer, T. (2001b). *Es trabajo de equipo: sesión dirigida al personal de salud para la prevención y detección temprana del cáncer cérvicouterino [Working as a team: Workshop for health personnel for the prevention and early detection of cervical cancer]*. Mexico City: Editorial IDEAME.

Fuertes, C., & Venguer, T. (2001a). *Porque me quiero, me cuido: un taller integral para la prevención y detección temprana del cáncer cérvico uterino [Because I care about myself, I take care of myself: A comprehensive workshop for the prevention and early detection of cervical cancer]*. Mexico City: Editorial IDEAME.

Fuertes, C., & Venguer, T. (2001b). *Porque me quiero, me cuido: un taller integral para la prevención y detección temprana del cáncer cérvico uterino: manual dirigido a promotoras para el trabajo con mujeres [Because I care about myself, I take care of myself: A comprehensive workshop for the prevention and early detection of cervical cancer: Manual directed towards promoters for work with women]*. Mexico City: Editorial IDEAME.

García, G., Pick, S., & Romero, A. (submitted). Instrumentación nacional y evaluación de impacto de un programa para la promoción de la salud, la agencia personal y el empoderamiento [National implementation and impact assessment of a program to promote health, personal agency and empowerment].

Givaudan, M. (1999). Evaluación del programa de sexualidad y vida familiar para padres "Aprendiendo a ser papá y mamá" [Evaluation of the sexuality and family life program for parents "Learning to be dad and mom"], *Report presented to the Summit Foundation*. Mexico City: IMIFAP.

Givaudan, M., Barriga, M., & Gaál, F. (2009). Yo quiero, yo puedo ... aprender y divertirme en preescolar. Una estrategia para fortalecer la resiliencia en comunidades con alto índice de migración en México [I want to, I can ... learn and have fun in preschool. A strategy to strengthen resilience in communities with high indices of migration in Mexico], *Report presented to the Bernard van Leer Foundation*. Mexico City: IMIFAP.

Givaudan, M., Barriga, M., Pick, S., Leenen, I., & Martinez, R. (2009). Desarrollo integral comunitario en México, en los estados de Hidalgo y Chiapas, con énfasis en salud sexual y reproductiva y derechos de mujeres, reporte final [Comprehensive community development in the Mexican states of Hidalgo and Chiapas, with emphasis on sexual and reproductive health and women's rights, final report], *Report presented to the United Nations Fund for Population Activities*. Mexico City: IMIFAP.

Givaudan, M., Barriga, M. A., & Pick, S. (2008). The children left behind: Researching the impact of migration on the development of children and developing, piloting and evaluating a program that answers their special needs, *Report presented to the Bernard van Leer Foundation*. Mexico City: IMIFAP.

Givaudan, M., Beltrán, M., & Pick, S. (2006). *Yo quiero, yo puedo. Material de apoyo para docentes. Estrategias para la prevención de adicciones [I want to, I can. Support material for teachers. Strategies to prevent addictions]*. Mexico City: Editorial IDEAME.

Givaudan, M., Karakowsky, Y., Villanueva, T., & Prado, A. (2009). *Yo quiero, yo puedo ... tener éxito en la escuela. Nivel primaria. Carpeta de actividades [I want to, I can ... have success in school. Primary school level. Activities manual]*. Mexico City: Editorial IDEAME.

Givaudan, M., Leenen, I., Tacher, A., Pick, S., & Martínez, R. (2007). Life skills curriculum as an HIV/STI prevention strategy, *Report presented to the National Institute of Health*. Mexico City: IMIFAP.

Givaudan, M., López, K., & Pick, S. (1998). Evaluation of the sex and family life program for parents: Aprendiendo a ser papá y mamá [Learning to be dad and mom], *Report presented to the Summit Foundation*. Mexico City: IMIFAP.

Givaudan, M., & Pick, S. (2004). A preventative program for substance abuse in Mexico: Best practices. *Prevention Perspectives*, Retrieved August 12, 2008, from www.mentorfoundation.org.

Givaudan, M., & Pick, S. (2006a). *Yo quiero, yo puedo. 1° de Secundaria. Con enfásis en prevención de adicciones. [I want to, I can. Seventh grade. With emphasis on preventing addictions]*. Mexico City: Editorial IDEAME.

Givaudan, M., & Pick, S. (2006b). *Yo quiero, yo puedo. 2° de Secundaria. Con enfásis en prevención de adicciones. [I want to, I can. Eighth grade. With emphasis on preventing addictions]*. Mexico City: Editorial IDEAME.

Givaudan, M., & Pick, S. (2007a). *Yo quiero, yo puedo. Programa de educación para la vida. Preescolar 1 [I want to, I can. Life skills education. Preschool grade 1]*. Mexico City: Editorial IDEAME.

Givaudan, M., & Pick, S. (2007b). *Yo quiero, yo puedo. Programa de educación para la vida. Preescolar 2 [I want to, I can. Life skills education. Preschool grade 2]*. Mexico City: Editorial IDEAME.

Givaudan, M., & Pick, S. (2007c). *Yo quiero, yo puedo. Programa de educación para la vida. Preescolar 3 [I want to, I can. Life skills education. Preschool grade 3]*. Mexico City: Editorial IDEAME.

Givaudan, M., Pick, S., & Beltrán, M. (2009a). *Yo quiero, yo puedo. Nivel primaria. Manual para maestros (as) [I want to, I can. Primary school level. Teacher's manual]* (Vol. II: 4th–6th). Mexico City: Editorial IDEAME.

Givaudan, M., Pick, S., & Beltrán, M. (2009b). *Yo quiero, yo puedo. Nivel primaria. Manual para maestros (as) [I want to, I can. Primary school level. Teacher's manual]* (Vol. I: 1st–3rd). Mexico City: Editorial IDEAME.

Givaudan, M., Pick, S., Leenen, I., & DuBois, L. (submitted). Health education: Building life skills and knowledge in rural children in Mexico.

Givaudan, M., Ramón, J., Camacho, D., & Pick, S. (1997a). Qualitative evaluation of the Yo quiero, yo puedo program for 5th and 6th grades, *Report presented to the World Bank*. Mexico City: IMIFAP.

Givaudan, M., Ramón, J., Camacho, D., & Pick, S. (1997b). Replication of the family life and sex education program Yo quiero, yo puedo in marginalized areas of Mexico City, *Report presented to the Compton Foundation*. Mexico City: IMIFAP.

Givaudan, M., Weiss, E., Pick de Weiss, S., Alvarez, M., Collado, M. E., & Gupta, G. R. (1994). Strengthening intergenerational communication within the family: An AIDS prevention strategy for adolescents, *Report presented to the International Center for Research on Women*. Mexico City: IMIFAP.

Heise, L. (1998). Violence against women: An integrated, ecological framework. *Journal of Violence Against Women*, 4(3), 262–290.

Instituto Mexicano de Investigación de Familia y Población [IMIFAP] (2005). Development and piloting of a small scale business training program in rural Oaxaca, *Report presented to the W. K. Kellogg Foundation*. Mexico City: IMIFAP.

Instituto Mexicano de Investigación de Familia y Población [IMIFAP] (2009). Desarrollo Integral Comunitario en México, en los estados de Hidalgo y Chiapas, con énfasis en salud sexual y reproductiva y derechos de mujeres, Reporte Final [Comprehensive Community Development in Mexico, in the states of Hidalgo and Chiapas, with emphasis on sexual and reproductive health and women's rights, Final Report], *Report presented to the United Nations Fund for Population Activities*. Mexico City: IMIFAP.

Instituto Nacional de Estadística, Geografía e Informática [INEGI] [National Institute of Statistics, Geography and Computing] (2000). Estadísticas a propósito del día internacional de las poblaciones indígenas: Datos nacionales [Statistics for the International Day of Indigenous Populations: National Statistics]. Retrieved August 12, 2008, from Instituto Nacional de Estadística, Geografía, e Informática: www.generoysaludreproductiva.gob.mx/IMG/pdf/indigena04.pdf.

Leenen, I., García, G., Elizalde, L., Gaál, F., Givaudan, M. (2009). Implementación, evaluación y presentación de resultados de la capacitación para la orientación y promoción social para los Prestadores de Servicio de PAL. Reporte de la fase B. [Implementation, evaluation, and presentation of training outcomes for the orientation and social promotion for the PAL Service Providers. Report of phase B]. *Report presented to the Universidad Autónoma de Aguascalientes*. Mexico City: IMIFAP.

Osorio, P., & Givaudan, M. (2008a). Formación en microcréditos para mujeres indígenas y rurales en Oaxaca [Training in microfinance for rural indigenous women in Oaxaca State, Mexico], *Report presented to the Finnish Embassy in Mexico, Fund for Local Cooperation*. Mexico City: IMIFAP.

Osorio, P., & Givaudan, M. (2008b). Yo quiero, yo puedo … empezar mi negocio: Estado de Oaxaca [I want to, I can … start my own business: In the state of Oaxaca], *Report presented to Geneva Global*. Mexico City: IMIIFAP.

Osorio, P., & Pick, S. (2008a). Fortalecimiento del capital social de 16 comunidades de alta y muy alta marginación de la región Mixteca (Oaxaca) a través del desarrollo de habilidades psicosociales y conocimientos que faciliten procesos asociativos [Strengthening of the social capital of 16 communities with high and very high levels of marginalization in the Mixteca (Oaxaca) region through the development of psychosocial skills and knowledge that facilitate the formation of civil associations] *Report presented to SEDESOL*. Mexico City: IMIFAP.

Osorio, P., & Pick, S. (2008b). Programa integral de salud y empoderamiento para mejorar la calidad de vida de 65 mujeres indígenas que habitan en San Martín Itunyoso, Oaxaca [Comprehensive health and empowerment program to improve the quality of life of 65 indigenous women in San Martin Itunyoso, Oaxaca], *Report presented to INDESOL*. Mexico City: IMIFAP.

Osorio, P., & Pick, S. (2009). I want to, I can … start my own business: Development of microbusinesses in the Mexican State of Hidalgo, *Report presented to Procter & Gamble Alumni*. Mexico City: IMIFAP.

Peña, A., Zamora, M., Tafoya, F., Beltrán, M., Olivares, J., Sosa, E., & Torres, C. (2007). *Yo quiero, yo puedo … prevenir y controlar obesidad, diabetes y enfermedades cardiovasculares. Manual [I want to, I can … prevent and control obesity, diabetes and cardiovascular diseases. Manual]*. Mexico City: Editorial IDEAME.

Pick de Weiss, S. (1993). Development of support for national sexuality education in Mexico, *Report presented to the Moriah Fund, the Prospect Hill Foundation and the John Merck Fund*. Mexico City: IMIFAP.

Pick de Weiss, S., & Andrade Palos, P. (1989). Development and longitudinal evaluation of comparative sexuality education courses, *Report presented to the United States Agency for International Development*. Mexico City: IMIFAP.

Pick de Weiss, S., Andrade Palos, P., Townsend, J., & Givaudan, M. (1994). Evaluación de un programa de educación sexual sobre conocimientos, conducta sexual y anticoncepción en adolescentes [Evaluation of a sexuality education program on knowledge, behavior and contraception in adolescents]. *Salud Mental, 17*(17), 25–31.

Pick, S., Aguilar, J. A., Rodríguez, G., & Montero, M. (1990). *Planeando tu vida: Programa de educación sexual para adolescentes [Planning your life: Sexual education program for adolescents]*. Mexico, City: Editorial Pax México.

Pick, S., Andrade Palos, P., & Gribble, J. (1989). *Bases para el desarrollo y evaluación de programas de educación sexual [Bases for the development and evaluation of sexuality education programs]*. Paper presented at the International Conference of Adolescent Fertility in Latin America and the Caribbean. Oaxaca, Mexico.

Pick, S., Barriga, M., & Givaudan, M. (submitted). Agency, empowerment, health and life skills development among rural women in Mexico.

Pick, S., Díaz-Loving, R., & Atkin, L. (1988). Adolescentes en la Ciudad de México: Estudio psicosocial de prácticas anticonceptivas y embarazo no deseado [Adolescents in Mexico City: Psychosocial study of contraceptive practices and unwanted pregnancy], *Report presented to the Pan American Health Organization and the United Nations Fund for Population Activities*. Mexico City: IMIFAP.

Pick, S., & Givaudan, M. (1994a). *Yo, mi familia y mi medio ambiente: un libro de educación para la vida. Cuarto de primaria [Me, my family and my environment: A life skills book. Fourth grade]*. Mexico City: Editorial Planeta.

Pick, S., & Givaudan, M. (1994b). *Yo, mi familia y mi medio ambiente: un libro de educación para la vida. Quinto de primaria [Me, my family and my environment: A life skills book. Fifth grade]*. Mexico City: Editorial Planeta.

Pick, S., & Givaudan, M. (1994c). *Yo, mi familia y mi medio ambiente: un libro de educación para la vida. Segundo de primaria [Me, my family and my environment: A life skills book. Second grade]*. Mexico City: Editorial Planeta.

Pick, S., & Givaudan, M. (1994d). *Yo, mi familia y mi medio ambiente: un libro de educación para la vida. Sexto de primaria [Me, my family and my environment: A life skills book. Sixth grade]*. Mexico City: Editorial Planeta.

Pick, S., & Givaudan, M. (1994e). *Yo, mi familia y mi medio ambiente: un libro de educación para la vida. Tercero de primaria [Me, my family and my environment: A life skills book. Third grade]*. Mexico City: Editorial Planeta.

Pick, S., & Givaudan, M. (1994f). *Yo, mi familia y mi medio ambiente: un libro de educación para la vida. Preescolar [Me, my family and my environment: A life skills book. Kindergarten]*. Mexico City: Editorial Planeta.

Pick, S., & Givaudan, M. (1994g). *Yo, mi familia y mi medio ambiente: un libro de educación para la vida. Primero de primaria [Me, my family and my environment: A life skills book. First grade]*. Mexico City: Editorial Planeta.

Pick, S., & Givaudan, M. (1996a). *Yo quiero, yo puedo. Programa de educación para la vida. Cuarto de primaria [I want to, I can. Life skills education. Fourth grade]*. Mexico City: Editorial IDEAME.

Pick, S., & Givaudan, M. (1996b). *Yo quiero, yo puedo. Programa de educación para la vida. Preescolar [I want to, I can. Life skills education. Preschool].* Mexico City: Editorial IDEAME.

Pick, S., & Givaudan, M. (1996c). *Yo quiero, yo puedo. Programa de educación para la vida. Preescolar: guía para el maestro [I want to, I can. Life skills education. Preschool: Teacher's manual].* Mexico City: Editorial IDEAME.

Pick, S., & Givaudan, M. (1996d). *Yo quiero, yo puedo. Programa de educación para la vida. Primero de primaria [I want to, I can. Life skills education. First grade].* Mexico City: Editorial IDEAME.

Pick, S., & Givaudan, M. (1996e). *Yo quiero, yo puedo. Programa de educación para la vida. Primero de secundaria [I want to, I can. Life skills education. Seventh grade].* Mexico City: Editorial IDEAME.

Pick, S., & Givaudan, M. (1996f). *Yo quiero, yo puedo. Programa de educación para la vida. Quinto de primaria [I want to, I can. Life skills education. Fifth grade].* Mexico City: Editorial IDEAME.

Pick, S., & Givaudan, M. (1996g). *Yo quiero, yo puedo. Programa de educación para la vida. Segundo de primaria [I want to, I can. Life skills education. Second grade].* Mexico City: Editorial IDEAME.

Pick, S., & Givaudan, M. (1996h). *Yo quiero, yo puedo. Programa de educación para la vida. Segundo de secundaria [I want to, I can. Life skills education. Eighth grade].* Mexico City: Editorial IDEAME.

Pick, S., & Givaudan, M. (1996i). *Yo quiero, yo puedo. Programa de educación para la vida. Sexto de primaria [I want to, I can. Life skills education. Sixth grade].* Mexico City: Editorial IDEAME.

Pick, S., & Givaudan, M. (1996j). *Yo quiero, yo puedo. Programa de educación para la vida. Tercero de primaria [I want to, I can. Life skills education. Third grade].* Mexico City: Editorial IDEAME.

Pick, S., & Givaudan, M. (1996k). *Yo quiero, yo puedo. Programa de educación para la vida. Tercero de secundaria [I want to, I can. Life skills education. Ninth grade].* Mexico City: Editorial IDEAME.

Pick, S., & Givaudan, M. (2003a). Habilidades para la vida y salud. Desarrollo integral comunitario. (Programa escolar para niñas y niños). 3° de primaria [Life and health skills. Comprehensive community development. (School program for boys and girls). Third grade]. Mexico City: Editorial IDEAME.

Pick, S., & Givaudan, M. (2003b). Habilidades para la vida y salud. Desarrollo integral comunitario. (Programa escolar para niñas y niños). 4° de primaria [Life and health skills. Comprehensive community development. (School program for boys and girls). Fourth grade]. Mexico City: Editorial IDEAME.

Pick, S., & Givaudan, M. (2003c). Habilidades para la vida y salud. Desarrollo integral comunitario. (Programa escolar para niñas y niños). 5° de primaria [Life and health skills. Comprehensive community development. (School program for boys and girls). Fifth grade]. Mexico City: Editorial IDEAME.

Pick, S., & Givaudan, M. (2003d). Habilidades para la vida y salud. Desarrollo integral comunitario. (Programa escolar para niñas y niños). 6° de primaria [Life and health skills. Comprehensive community development. (School program for boys and girls). Sixth grade]. Mexico City: Editorial IDEAME.

Pick, S., & Givaudan, M. (2004). *Soy adolescente: mis retos, mis riesgos y mis expectativas [I am an adolescent: My challenges, my risks and my expectations].* Mexico City: Editorial IDEAME.

Pick, S., & Givaudan, M. (2007a). *Yo quiero, yo puedo. Programa de educación para la vida. Cuarto de primaria [I want to, I can. Life skills education. Fourth grade].* Mexico City: Editorial IDEAME.

Pick, S., & Givaudan, M. (2007b). *Yo quiero, yo puedo. Programa de educación para la vida. Primero de primaria [I want to, I can. Life skills education. First grade].* Mexico City: Editorial IDEAME.

Pick, S., & Givaudan, M. (2007c). *Yo quiero, yo puedo. Programa de educación para la vida. Primero de secundaria [I want to, I can. Life skills education. Seventh grade].* Mexico City: Editorial IDEAME.

Pick, S., & Givaudan, M. (2007d). *Yo quiero, yo puedo. Programa de educación para la vida. Quinto de primaria [I want to, I can. Life skills education. Fifth grade].* Mexico City: Editorial IDEAME.

Pick, S., & Givaudan, M. (2007e). *Yo quiero, yo puedo. Programa de educación para la vida. Segundo de primaria [I want to, I can. Life skills education. Second grade].* Mexico City: Editorial IDEAME.

Pick, S., & Givaudan, M. (2007f). *Yo quiero, yo puedo. Programa de educación para la vida. Segundo de secundaria [I want to, I can. Life skills education. Eighth grade].* Mexico City: Editorial IDEAME.

Pick, S., & Givaudan, M. (2007g). *Yo quiero, yo puedo. Programa de educación para la vida. Sexto de primaria [I want to, I can. Life skills education. Sixth grade].* Mexico City: Editorial IDEAME.

Pick, S., & Givaudan, M. (2007h). *Yo quiero, yo puedo. Programa de educación para la vida. Tercero de primaria [I want to, I can. Life skills education. Third grade].* Mexico City: Editorial IDEAME.

Pick, S., & Givaudan, M. (2007i). Yo quiero, yo puedo: estrategia para el desarrollo de habilidades y competencias en el sistema escolar [I want to, I can: Strategy for the development of skills and competencies within the school system]. *Psicologia da Educação: Revista do Programa de Estudos Pós-Graduados em Psicologia da Educação/ Pontifícia Universidade Católica de São Paulo, 23,* 203–221.

Pick, S., Givaudan, M., & Beltrán, M. (2006). *Yo quiero, yo puedo. 3° de secundaria. Con enfásis en prevención de adicciones. [I want to, I can. Ninth grade. With emphasis on preventing addictions].* Mexico City: Editorial IDEAME.

Pick, S., Givaudan, M., & Beltrán, M. (2007). *Yo quiero, yo puedo. Programa de educación para la vida. Tercero de secundaria [I want to, I can. Life skills education. Ninth grade].* Mexico City: Editorial IDEAME.

Pick, S., Givaudan, M., & Martinez, A. (1998). *Deja volar a tu adolescente y será un gran adulto [Let your adolescent fly and he/she will be a great adult].* Mexico City: Editorial IDEAME.

Pick, S., Givaudan, M., Tenorio, A., & Fernández, F. (2000). *Formación cívica y ética: Yo quiero, yo puedo. 3° de secundaria [Civics and ethics training: I want to, I can. Ninth grade]* (2003, 4th ed.). Mexico City: Editorial Limusa.

Pick, S., Givaudan, M., Troncoso, A., & Tenorio, A. (1999a). *Formación cívica y ética: Yo quiero, yo puedo. 1° de secundaria [Civics and ethics training: I want to, I can. Seventh grade]* (2003, 5th ed.). Mexico City: Editorial Limusa.

Pick, S., Givaudan, M., Troncoso, A., & Tenorio, A. (1999b). *Formación cívica y ética: Yo quiero, yo puedo. 2° de secundaria [Civics and ethics training: I want to, I can. Eighth grade]* (2003, 5th ed.). Mexico City: Editorial Limusa.

Pick, S., Gribble, J., Atkin, L., & Andrade Palos, P. (1991). Sex, contraception, and pregnancy among adolescents in Mexico City. *Studies in Family Planning, 22*(2), 74–82.

Pick, S., & Osorio-Belmon, P. (submitted). The impact of an educational intervention in rural female users of microfinance services: Building entrepreneurial skills.

Ramírez, J. C., & Uribe, G. (1993). Mujer y violencia: Un hecho cotidiano [Women and violence: A daily occurrence]. *Salud Pública de México,* 35(2), 148–160.

Ramón, J., Camacho, D., & Pick, S. (1997). Parental support of sexuality education in Mexico: Implementation and multiplication of educational programs, *Report presented to the Moriah Foundation.* Mexico City: IMIFAP.

Ramón, J., Givaudan, M., & Pick, S. (1997a). Continuing replication of IMIFAP education programs for Mexican parents of children and adolescents, *Report presented to the Public Welfare Foundation.* Mexico City: IMIFAP.

Ramón, J., Givaudan, M., & Pick, S. (1997b). Replication of sexual health and family life education programs for parents in Mexico and Latin America, *Report presented to Public Welfare Foundation.* Mexico City: IMIFAP.

Reyes, J., Givaudan, M., Pick, S., Martínez, A., & Ramón, J. (1996). *Un equipo contra el sida [A team against AIDS].* Mexico City: Editorial IDEAME.

Ruiz, M. G., & Fawcett, G. (1999). *Rostros y máscaras de la violencia. Un taller sobre amistad y noviazgo para adolescentes [Faces and masks of violence. A workshop on friendship and dating for adolescents].* Mexico City: Editorial IDEAME.

Secretaría de Gobernación [SEGOB] [Ministry of Administration] (1990). *Programa Nacional de Población 1989-1994 [National Population Program 1989–1994].* Retrieved August 13, 2008, from www.segob.gob.mx/compilacion_juridica/webpub/Dec15.pdf.

Shrader, E., & Valdez, R. (1992). *Violencia hacia la mujer mexicana como problema de salud pública: La incidencia de la violencia doméstica en una microregión de la Ciudad Nezahualcóyotl [Violence against Mexican women as a public health problem: The prevalence of domestic violence in a microregion of Nezahualcóyotl City].* Mexico City: Centro de Investigación y Lucha Contra la Violencia Doméstica.

Solano, G., Pick, S., & Pick, S. (1995). *Déjame responderte: diccionario para que papá y mamá pueden hablarle a sus hijos e hijas de más de 200 temas que los ponen en aprietos [Let me answer you: A dictionary, so that dad and mom can talk to their children about more than 200 themes that put them on the spot].* Mexico City: Editorial IDEAME (2nd edition, 2007).

Taylor, L. (2009, May 22). Teaching Across Borders student writes from Mexico, Retrieved June 20, 2009, from http://educ.ucalgary.ca/transitions-across-borders-student-writes-mexico.

Universidad Autónoma de Aguascalientes (2008a). Implementación del Modelo de transmisión de conocimientos para el desarrollo de capacidades entre el personal de Diconsa, los Consejos Comunitarios y los Comités Rurales de Abasto. Primer reporte parcial: Sensibilización [Implementation of a knowledge transmission model for capacity development of Diconsa, Community Council and Rural Supply Committee personnel. First partial report: Developing awareness], *Report presented to Diconsa.* Mexico City: IMIFAP.

Universidad Autónoma de Aguascalientes (2008b). Implementación del Modelo de transmisión de conocimientos para el desarrollo de capacidades entre el personal de Diconsa, los Consejos Comunitarios y los Comités Rurales de Abasto. Segundo reporte parcial: Formación [Implementation of a knowledge transmission model for capacity development of Diconsa, Community Council and Rural Supply Committee personnel. Second partial report: Training], *Report presented to Diconsa.* Mexico City: IMIFAP.

Universidad Autónoma de Aguascalientes (2008c). Implementación del Modelo de transmisión de conocimientos para el desarrollo de capacidades entre el personal de Diconsa, los Consejos Comunitarios y los Comités Rurales de Abasto. Tercer reporte parcial: Réplica y Acompañamiento [Implementation of a knowledge transmission model for capacity development of Diconsa, Community Council and Rural Supply Committee personnel. Third partial report: Replication and follow-up], *Report presented to Diconsa*. Mexico City: IMIFAP.

Universidad Autónoma de Aguascalientes (2009). Implementación del Modelo de capacitación para la orientación y promoción social. Descripción técnica y plan de trabajo [Implementation of a knowledge transmission model for capacity development of Diconsa, Community Council and Rural Supply Committee personnel. Final executive report], *Report presented to Diconsa*. Mexico City: IMIFAP.

Venguer, T., Leenen, I., Morales, N., Givaudan, M., Pick, S., Poortinga, I., & Martínez, R. (1999a). Multiplicación de un programa integral de educación para la salud en mujeres jóvenes del estado de Oaxaca [Replication of a comprehensive health education program for young women in the state of Oaxaca, Mexico], *Report I presented to SmithKline-Beecham*. Mexico City: IMIFAP.

Venguer, T., Leenen, I., Morales, N., Givaudan, M., Pick, S., Poortinga, I., & Martínez, R. (1999b). Multiplicación de un programa integral de educación para la salud en mujeres jóvenes del estado de Oaxaca [Replication of a comprehensive health education program for young women in the state of Oaxaca, Mexico], *Report II presented to SmithKline-Beecham*. Mexico City: IMIFAP.

Venguer, T., Leenen, I., Morales, N., Givaudan, M., Pick, S., Poortinga, I., & Martínez, R. (2000). Multiplicación de un programa integral de educación para la salud en mujeres jóvenes del estado de Oaxaca [Replication of a comprehensive health education program for young women in the state of Oaxaca, Mexico], *Report III presented to SmithKline-Beecham*. Mexico City: IMIFAP.

Venguer, T., Leenen, I., Morales, N., Givaudan, M., Pick, S., Poortinga, I., & Martínez, R. (2001). Multiplicación de un programa integral de educación para la salud en mujeres jóvenes del estado de Oaxaca [Replication of a comprehensive health education program for young women in the state of Oaxaca, Mexico], *Report IV presented to SmithKline-Beecham*. Mexico City: IMIFAP.

Venguer, T., Leenen, I., Morales, N., Givaudan, M., Pick, S., Poortinga, I., & Martínez, R. (2002). Multiplicación de un programa integral de educación para la salud en mujeres jóvenes del estado de Oaxaca. [Replication of a comprehensive health education program for young women in the Oaxaca region of Mexico], *Final report presented to SmithKline-Beecham*. Mexico City: IMIFAP.

Venguer, T., Pick, S., & Fishbein, M. (2007). Health education and agency: A comprehensive program for young women in the Mixteca region of Mexico. *Psychology, Health & Medicine,* 12(4), 389–406.

Venguer, T., Quezada, M., Pick, S., Cabral, J., Flores, A., Mireles, M., Montero, G., & Morales, N. (2000a). *Si yo estoy bien mi familia también: módulo de alimentación y empoderamiento. Manual teórico, manual de ejercicios, material didáctico, rotafolio, tríptico y cartel [If I am OK, so is my family: Nutrition and empowerment module. Training manual, workbook, didactic material, flipchart, pamphlet and poster].* Mexico City: IMIFAP and IMSS-Oportunidades.

Venguer, T., Quezada, M., Pick, S., Cabral, J., Flores, A., Mireles, M., Montero, G., & Morales, N. (2000b). *Si yo estoy bien mi familia también: módulo de salud y empoderamiento. Manual teórico, manual de ejercicios, material didáctico, rotafolio, tríptico y cartel [If I am OK, so is my family: Health and empowerment module. Training manual, workbook, didactic material, flipchart, pamphlet and poster].* Mexico City: IMIFAP and IMSS-Oportunidades.

Venguer, T., Quezada, M., Pick, S., Cabral, J., Flores, A., Montero, G., & Morales, N. (2000a). *Si yo estoy bien mi familia también: módulo de desarrollo y empoderamiento para niñas y niños. Manual teórico, manual de ejercicios, material didáctico, rotafolio, tríptico y cartel [If I am OK, so is my family: Development and empowerment for children module. Training manual, workbook, didactic material, flipchart, pamphlet and poster].* Mexico City: IMIFAP and IMSS-Oportunidades.

Venguer, T., Quezada, M., Pick, S., Cabral, J., Flores, A., Montero, G., & Morales, N. (2000b). *Si yo estoy bien mi familia también: módulo de higiene, saneamiento y empoderamiento. Manual teórico, manual de ejercicios, material didáctico, rotafolio, tríptico y cartel [If I am OK, so is my family: Hygiene, sanitation and empowerment module. Training manual, workbook, didactic material, flipchart, pamphlet and poster].* Mexico City: IMIFAP and IMSS-Oportunidades.

Venguer, T., Quezada, M., Pick, S., Cabral, J., Flores, A., Montero, G., & Morales, N. (2000c). *Si yo estoy bien mi familia también: módulo de salud, nutrición y empoderamiento para niñas y niños. Manual teórico, manual de ejercicios, material didáctico, rotafolio, tríptico y cartel [If I am OK, so is my family: Sexuality, reproductive health and empowerment module. Training manual, workbook, didactic material, flipchart, pamphlet and poster].* Mexico City: IMIFAP and IMSS-Oportunidades.

Venguer, T., Quezada, M., Pick, S., Cabral, J., Flores, A., Montero, G., & Morales, N. (2000d). *Si yo estoy bien mi familia también: módulo de sexualidad, salud reproductiva y empoderamiento. Manual teórico, manual de ejercicios, material didáctico, rotafolio, tríptico y cartel [If I am OK, so is my family: Sexuality, reproductive health and empowerment module. Training manual, workbook, didactic material, flipchart, pamphlet and poster].* Mexico City: IMIFAP and IMSS-Oportunidades.

APPENDIX B

Acknowledgments

Papi, muchas gracias. You have exemplified that dreams are goals and goals can be reached. *Ma,* thank you for your optimism, sense of humor, and common sense. Thank you both for showing me that people can create their own opportunities and can set an example for others to do the same. Silvie, thank you for your companionship, and *Oma,* for your *joie de vivre.*

I would like to especially recognize and thank my colleagues at IMIFAP. Martha Givaudan, Héctor Pérez, and I have been working as a close team for almost 20 years—jointly overcoming political and ideological barriers to allow IMIFAP to reach over 19 million people. I especially wish to mention the support of María del Carmen Alvarez, who has been my dedicated assistant for over 20 years. My appreciation extends to the IMIFAP staff at large, including both current staff members and my past colleagues.[1] This book is the product of all of our work.

Henry David gave us the idea of starting an NGO over 25 years ago (I had not even heard the word before), and continued to give us tender loving care and advice over the years. Martin Fishbein at the University of Pennsylvania, a friend, a colleague, an adviser, and a co-idealist was there at every step of IMIFAP's growth, devoting a substantial amount of time to advise and support us. Lucy Reidl and Patricia Andrade at the National University of Mexico (UNAM) have provided creative insights for many years.

Without the enormous support of over 300 foundations, government institutions and corporations, IMIFAP would not be where it is today. I wish to mention our earliest funders, who provided us with instrumental support when IMIFAP was still conceptualizing most of its work. In the 1980s, our initial grant support came from the late José Antonio Solis at the Pan American Health Organization, and Willem Visser, then representative for Mexico and the Caribbean at the United Nations Fund for Population Activities (UNFPA).

A few months later came the technical and financial support from Bob Klein, John Townsend, Ricardo Vernon, and Thomas Frejka at the Population Council in Mexico. Thank you for believing in academic-based, applied research when the prevailing belief at the time was that academics and community-based practice should operate in silos.

Over the years, IMIFAP received vital funding and support from Adelle Simmons, Stewart Burden, and Karen Grown at the MacArthur Foundation; Allen Greenberg at the Buffett Foundation; Shira Saperstein at the Moriah Fund; and Nancy Alvey and Sam Taylor at USAID. Adelle, I will never forget your surprise when you attended some of the first "I Want to, I Can" courses and said something like, "If only we had such programs in my country!" Stewart and Karen patiently supported the whirlwind of developing, implementing, and evaluating life skills programs and institutionalizing sexuality education in Mexico. Allen, thank you for being the most challenging funder and for making us think and analyze at a deeper level. Shira, thank you for always listening. Sam and Nancy, your tough questioning and warmth were instrumental. The United Nations Foundation awarded us our largest grant, which allowed IMIFAP to go from testing individual programs to comprehensive community development. Arie Hoekman, Javier Dominguez, Alfonso Sandoval, and Sandra Samaniego from the United Nations Fund for Population Activities (UNFPA) supported us throughout the project. The Mentor Foundation and Fundación Gonzalo Rio Arronte have been instrumental in funding our efforts in alcohol and drug use prevention. Our work with young children would not have been possible without the support of SEDESOL and the Bernard van Leer Foundation.

Without the support of corporations, the work in rural and indigenous areas would never have been possible. Our most generous support has come from Smith Kline and Beecham (now GlaxoSmithKline). Thank you Marco Botey, Adrian Cruz, Javier Ponce, and Manouchehr Yazhari. I still remember Adrian's face when he saw the hotel we had reserved for him in the highlands of Oaxaca. He said, "I usually stay at the Four Seasons!" Well, Adrian, that was the Four Seasons of Huajuapan de León, Oaxaca; thank you all for being such good sports.

At the government level, the ideas from, and opportunities created by, influential individuals helped us institutionalize many of our programs. Former Mexican President Ernesto Zedillo provided us with both intelligent and practical guidance, and former Secretary of Education Manuel Bartlett challenged the traditional rules and expectations. Various government officials patiently tried to understand the role of psycho-social factors for the improvement of education, health, and social development in Mexico and opened many doors for us: Governors Rogelio Montemayor and Manuel Angel Nuñez, Ministers José Sarukhan and Julio Frenk, and Undersecretaries Benjamin Gonzalez Roaro, Jesus Liceaga, and Gustavo Merino; State Ministers Alberto Jonguitud, Oscar Pimentel, and Lourdes Quintanilla, former Director of *IMSS-Oportunidades* Javier Cabral, Manuel Cardenas, Marco Lopez, and Juan Carlos Rodriguez Pueblita at the Mexican Ministry for Social Development; Armando Barriguete and Arturo Cervantes at the Mexican Ministry of Health; and last, but certainly not least, Lydia Berrón and Mercedes Sanchez in the Ministry of Education of the State of Campeche; Salomón Chertorivski, Francisco Caballero, and Miguel Limón, all formerly at Diconsa and now at Seguro Popular in the Mexican Ministry of Health; and Edith Serrano at Diconsa. There is not space here to thank all of our supporters from over the years; they are listed on the IMIFAP website (www.imifap.org.mx); we want to extend here our deepest gratitude to each of them.

Critical contributions to IMIFAP's work have been provided for many years by professional associations, members of our board, and friends and colleagues in different parts of the world. We wish to especially recognize that of the American Psychological Association, the International Association of Applied Psychology (IAAP) and the Interamerican Society of Psychology (SIP). A heartfelt thanks to board members Diego Antoni, Mauricio Atri, Diana Beckman, Julieta Besquin, Abraham Bissu, Jorge Camil Starr, Alfredo Ciklik, Alfonso Corona, Pilar Denegri, Fernando Fernández de Cordoba, Edith Garcia, Patricia García López, Ronaldo Gimbel, Francisco Gomez, Lorena Guillé, Carmen Gutierrez, Alberto Islas, Ana Lopezmestre, Rudy Kahn, Alberto Kritzler, Ruben Kupferman, Elisabeth Malkin, Elias Mekler, Alfredo Navarrete, Amalia Noriega, Silvia Piso, Alejandro Ramírez, Ian Reider, Alberto Saracho, Alfredo Troncoso, Edmundo Vallejo, Ives von Gunten, Sara Woldenberg, and the late Alinka Zabludovsky.

One of the pleasures of writing a book has been the enlightening opportunity to collaborate with so many friends and colleagues. First and foremost, I wish to recognize the contribution of Ype H. Poortinga at Tilburg University in the Netherlands and Lovaine University in Belgium. We have spent days, weeks, and months analyzing, arguing, synthesizing, reanalyzing, rearguing, and re-synthesizing. His patience, care, and commitment have been instrumental throughout the entire process.

Numerous individuals have meticulously, and patiently, assisted with research, writing, editing, and referencing. Foremost, Jenna and I want to warmly recognize Shoshana Grossman-Crist, a recent graduate from Tufts University and a rising star, who has played an invaluable role in the production of a completed manuscript. She patiently and diligently edited each chapter, provided insightful comments, and managed many of the interns on the project. I would like to express my deepest gratitude to Harvard University, specifically the Harvard Center for Population and Development Studies and the Harvard School of Public Health, where I was a visiting scholar for 2 years and was able to write most of the book. Professors Amartya Sen, Michael Reich, and Laura Reichenbach provided valuable observations. I want to especially thank Mark Bornstein at the National Institute of Child Health and Human Development, who decided to support this work after just a workshop I gave on personal agency and intrinsic empowerment at an International Society for the Study of Behavioral Development conference in Gramado, Brazil. He assisted with my publisher search and put me in contact with Lori Handelman at Oxford University Press, who has been warm, timely, and efficient in her support every step of the way.

This book has benefited from extensive and meaningful input from many of the above mentioned colleagues and friends as well as from Pieter Drenth at the Free University in the Netherlands; Marco Ijzer at University of Minnesota in the United States; Gerjo Kok at Maastricht University in the Netherlands; Dina Krauskopf at FLACSO in Santiago, Chile; Judy Kuriansky from Columbia University in the United States; Juan Carlos Moreno Brid at CEPAL in Mexico City; Gustavo Souss at McKenzie Consulting in Buenos Aires, Argentina; Harry Triandis at the University of Illinois in the United States; Fons van de Vivjer at Tilburg University in the Netherlands; Harvey Waxman in private practice in Boston, Massachusetts, United States; and Sonia Weiss Pick at Bain & Co. in Mexico and Technoserve in Peru. Discussions on context with both Carolina Ruesga of Gesoc, A.C. and Jesus Viejo at Grupo Alfa (both in Mexico) were instrumental in providing the link between the different levels at which personal agency and intrinsic empowerment can be targeted. We also wish to recognize the significant comments received from Des Gasper at Institute of Social Studies in the Netherlands. The work of the following dedicated research assistants was instrumental: Karla Alonso, Erica Anhalt, Veyom Bahl, Sophia Bessias, Alice Beste, Iris Boutros, Nedialka Douptcheva, Lindsay DuBois, James Finegan, Anne Johnson, Adriana Garcia, Stephen Groves, Susan Heilig, Kathryn Lankester, Alice Manos, Stephanie Margulies, Nicole Mejia, Tomoko Ono, Jessica Parker, Gauri Saxena, Sarah Schaffer, Kristen Smith, Lauren Teegarden, Alyse Wheelock and Joanna Zuckerman Bernstein.

And last, but certainly not least, I thank my three kids Daniel, Arturo, and Sonia and the most recent addition to the family, Deborah. Your smiles, jokes, elegantly sarcastic comments, and, above all, your love and intelligence are the fuel that keeps me going. *Muchas gracias a mis chavos. Son lo máximo.*

Acknowledgments from Jenna Sirkin

I would like to thank Rotary International, especially New Hampshire and Vermont District 7870 and Joseph Matthews, Michael Swinford, and Jerry Hanauer. Your generous support of my Rotary Ambassadorial Scholarship in Mexico City enabled me to contribute to this research in a meaningful and intimate way. The Mexico City Rotary Clubs—notably, Lourdes Galindo and Ernesto Ibarra—were excellent hosts during my time abroad. My colleagues at IMIFAP and the extended Weiss and Pick families and friends have made Mexico my second home.

Sherman Teichman and Heather Barry at the Institute for Global Leadership at Tufts University inspired my curiosity about international development work, and provided critical support for my initial project in Mexico City in 2003. My thesis and academic advisors at Tufts University—Peter Winn, Claudia Kaiser-Lenoir, and Edith Balbach—fostered my interest and curiosity about Latin American development and health policy; Betty and Roger Borghesani generously granted me the opportunity to spend a summer at a CSO in Mexico while I was still a Tufts undergraduate. Thank you to my professors and colleagues from The Heller School at Brandeis University for their encouragement throughout the process of completing this book. I would especially like to thank my dissertation chair and program advisor for their mentorship, Deborah Gurewich and Stanley Wallack.

And most importantly, I am indebted to my loving family: Mom, Dad, Kayla, Grammy, Papa, Aunts, Uncles, and my inspirational friends. I would never have made it here without all of your support—you keep me grounded, challenge me to reach my goals, and make sure I enjoy life along the way.

Note

1. In making this acknowledgement to IMIFAP, unintentionally, some names may be omitted. I ask those friends and colleagues to forgive me. The field coordinators have been the heart and soul behind our program implementation: Pilar Acevedo, Mario Anaya, Daniela Arana, Marco Barriga, Mariola Beltrán, Soledad Chaylan, Alejandro Estrada, Gillian Fawcett, Francisco Fernández, Carmen Fuertes, Angélica García, Mireille Garcia, Javier Gómez, Gabriela Guzmán, Juan Carlos Hernández, Flor de María Jiménez, Angela Martínez, Patricia Merlo, Elsa Perez, Verónica Olicón, Pavel Osorio, Jessica Ramón, Maricarmen Ramírez, Tatiana Ramos, Jeanette Reyes, Alejandro Rodríguez, Cuauhtemoc Sánchez, Alexa Tacher, Carlota Tello, Ana Laura Vitela, and Mario Zárate; the logistics, coordinated by Tere Venguer and Carmen Contreras; Manuel Patiño's guidance in distributing educational and promotional materials; the computer assistance of Emilio Zavala; the data organization and capture team of Felipe Castellanos, Socorro Gatica, Carla Reyes, and Adriana Sandoval; the evaluation, research, and statistical expertise of Evelyn Aldaz, Marcela Alvarez, Ana Bendezú, Ma. Elena Collado, Laura Delgado, Georgina Garcia, Elsa Karina López, Cristina Martínez, Rocio Martínez, Claudia Navarro, Isaac Ortega, and Angélica Romero, coordinated by Iwin Leenen, showing us where our program strengths and weaknesses lay; and the systemization work of Ilan Adler, Gabriela Castellanos, Luis Elizalde, Fernando Gaal, Alejandro Levin, Guinduri Rossell, Antia Mendoza, Doris Weitz, and Ulises Xolocotzin, which has brought order to what has been an organic growth of IMIFAP. The dedication of Suzanne Cohen, Katie Flom Kline, Nadxielli Flores, Thalia Inhelder, Bob Klotz, Nicole Laborde, Andrea Noyes, Saya Oka, Andrea Prado, Laura Proctor, and Natalia Wills in development and grant writing has been fundamental to keeping the financial health of IMIFAP in place. I would finally like to thank our research, materials development, and field teams who ensure that IMIFAP's "I Want to, I Can" educational materials reflect peoples' needs and that our work reaches communities and schools throughout Mexico and Latin America: Abraham Acosta, Juan Carlos Acuña, Hermelinda Alcorta, Nancy Amador, Cecilia Anaya, Delil Athié, Cinthya Barba, Mariana Becerril, Israel Bianchi, Evelyn Blom, Elvira Bolaños, Jeremy Brown, Jaqueline Bustamante, Liliana Bustamante, Víctor Caamaño, Selene Calixto, Diana Camacho, Miriam Camacho, Antonio Candelas, Janneth Carballido, Diana Castellanos, Javier Castellanos, Rosa María Castellanos, Luis Jorge Castillo, Elizabeth Coll, Fernando Contreras, Sandra Cortes, Alfredo Cruz, Brenda Cruz, Pilar Cruz, Sally Davis, Gracia Dalton, Ana Yuria del Rio Samuel Díaz, Meghan Dilley, Alejandra Enciso, Giovanna Escobar, Zoe Fenig, Hilda Fernández, Yolanda Fernández, Fabiola Franco, Josefina Franzoni, Martha Fuentes, Adina Galante, Mónica Gamboa, Jennifer Gamlin, Susana García, Virginia García, Yolanda García, Elizabeth Gatica, Marcela

Givaudan, Lauren Gold, Yasmin Gómez, Eva Grinberg, Alejandro Guerrero, Ricardo Guevara, María Isabel Gutiérrez, Dana Haight, Alba Hernández, Paola Hernández, Rodrigo Hernández, Richard Hoff, Jessica Hughes, Leticia Isita, Yael Karakowsky, Sona Kumar, Susana Lara, Mariana León, Lourdes Leonelli, Alhelí López, Cristina Martínez, Marcela Martínez, Marcela Martinelli, Roberto Max, Antia Mendoza, Ricardo Mejía, Lidia Miranda, María Mireles, Paola Monroy, Norma Morales, Diana Moreno, Lea Mosena, Sergio Muñoz, Laura Nájera, Isabel Nicolás, Alejandro Ortiz, Alina Ostrosky, Angélica Palacios, Ernesto Peduzzi, Lorena Pérez, Citlali Pérez de la Barrera, Miriam Quintanillo, Hilda Ramírez, Ivette Ramos, Sandra Elena Ramos, Josefina Raya, Bárbara Reyes, Ana Rodríguez, María Isabel Rubio, Mónica Ruiz, Alicia Saldivar, Josephine Saltmarsh, Erika Sánchez, Mauricio Sánchez, Yolanda Sánchez, Elodia Santana, Berenice Sarralde, Fernanda Solórzano, Edgar Sosa, Lindsay Stradley, Doris Tarchópulos, Rebeca Toledo, Adriana Ugalde, Mónica Vanegas, Susana Vivanco Felicia Vázquez, María Vázquez, Judith Vera, Mayra Vera, and Jazmín Zárate. And none of this would have been possible without the administrative support of Luis Jorge Castillo, José Flores, Ricardo Gallegos, Adriana García, Rosalía García, Miguel Ángel León, Antolina Ortiz, Dolores Pérez, Greta Pérez, Estela Ramírez, Edna Reay, Enrique Romero, Javier Vicencio, Eva Villegas and Alexander Wais.

GLOSSARY

Autonomy: The capacity of being a self-governing agent; it is a component of personal agency.

Behaviors: Actions; the operationalization of choice. Result from the application of skills and knowledge and the reduction of psychological barriers.

Capabilities (Sen): The opportunities a person has to live various lifestyles. These depend on the individual's psychological and social circumstances. Also referred to as freedoms.

Capability Approach (Sen): The central principle is to enhance the alternatives or choices people have. The approach values human capabilities as a worthwhile goal rather than for the mere instrumental benefits of human capital formation. Includes three key concepts: entitlements, functionings, and capability. Also referred to as the "agent-oriented approach."

Constraints: Obstacles to informed, autonomous action.

Contextual constraints or barriers: External limitations on an individual's potential to make decisions and choices and/or to act on them; includes structural barriers such as poverty, lack of education or access to quality healthcare, social norms, oppression and the lack of law enforcement.

Psychological constraints or barriers: Internal limitations on an individual's potential to make decisions and choices and/or to act on them; includes feelings of insecurity or inferiority, in conjunction with obstacles derived from tight social norms that induce fear, shame, and guilt. Generally externally controlled and favored, adopted by the individual as a result of external pressure and lack of perceived alternatives.

Context: The circumstances in which people are living. Components (discussed in this book) include the domains of economics, education, health, and government systems.

Control: The degree to which behavioral outcomes depend on one's own behaviors and personal characteristics versus chance or unpredictable factors; motivation and ability to take responsibility depends on the predictability and level of control a person has over events and situations within his or her life. A component of personal agency.

Entitlements (Sen): The commodities over which a person has the right and potential to establish ownership and command; can be political, economic, or otherwise.

Externally determined empowerment: Empowerment in which behavior is motivated by external factors. Includes extrinsic and systemic empowerment.

Extrinsic empowerment: Where external factors motivate behavior, usually of a material kind. For example, attendance at a politician's rally may result from expectation of monetary rewards.

Systemic empowerment: Where social norms motivate behavior; people do things because they feel they are expected to act in a certain way. For example, students behave well because a teacher is present in the classroom, or a young woman carries out certain tasks simply because societal norms dictate that she do so.

FrEE (Framework for Enabling Empowerment): A practical means for bringing Sen's Capability Approach into practice. Based on the experience that programs directed at facilitating choice to address specific situations enable movement towards sustainable human (and therefore social, political, and economic) development. Components are knowledge, skills, reduction of psychological barriers, behavior change, personal agency, and intrinsic empowerment.

Freedoms (Sen): Also known as capabilities; provide people with a range of alternatives for action. The foundation for Sen's Capability Approach.

Functionings (Sen): Outcomes. The various things a person may value doing or being; an umbrella term for the activities and states or situations people spontaneously recognize to be important—such as nutrition, security, a meaningful job, and an identity.

Achieved functionings (Sen): What a person has actually done. Those functionings that have been pursued and realized, also called *realized functionings*.

Alternative functionings (Sen): The various functionings that a person possesses and from which she can choose. Making up an individual's capability set.

Being functionings (adapted from Sen): Personal, more stable characteristics, such as self-respect or personal agency.

Doing functionings: (adapted from Sen) Specific behaviors, such as eating vegetables, getting a vaccination or communicating in an assertive fashion.

Refined functionings (Sen): The behaviors that emerge from an internal process of building skills and knowledge. Indicating not only possession of achieved functionings but also potential alternative functionings. Differ from functionings that merely arise as the result of increased access to one commodity.

Intrinsic empowerment: Represents both the inner state and the process of extending personal agency beyond the individual level to impact one's context. Based on the reciprocal relationship between the individual's sense of agency and the existing contextual opportunities and constraints. Results from repeated success in exercising newly developed personal agency in particular spheres and enables a fuller realization of individual capabilities and human rights. Contrasts with forms of external empowerment, including systemic empowerment and extrinsic empowerment.

Opportunities: Facilities to informed, autonomous action.

Contextual opportunities: External facilities that enhance an individual's potential to make decisions and choices and/or to act on them; examples include education, jobs, quality health services, supportive social norms, and the enforcement of laws.

Psychological opportunities: Internal facilities that enhance an individual's potential to make decisions and choices and/or to act on them; i.e.,—feelings of security, in conjunction with social norms supportive of personal development.

Person: An individual distinct from, yet interdependent with, the context.

Personal agency: Both the process and the state through which a person carries out informed and intrinsically motivated decisions in an autonomous fashion; achieved through an individual's realization of choice. Expands on the concept of agency (the process by which a person carries out informed, motivated and autonomous decisions) to emphasize internal development and the changes that occur at the stable level of a person's characteristics.

Domain-specific personal agency: Personal agency exercised in specific domains, including education, economics, government, and health. This can be targeted in thematic programming.

General personal agency: Personal agency exercised across a range of domains. Involves multiple behaviors and can be applied to different needs. Generalizes from domain-specific personal agency when the individual experiences repeated success in making choices in concrete situations in specific domains.

Programming for Choice: The actual strategy for making FrEE operational; focuses on the individual as a means of challenging constraining norms and aims to bring about changes in targeted behaviors and, ultimately, personal agency and intrinsic empowerment.

Self-efficacy: One's belief in his or her ability to succeed; an aspect of psychological functioning enabling individuals to exercise a measure of control over their thoughts, feelings, and actions. A component of personal agency.

Skills: Abilities enabling people to carry out various behaviors and actions. The foundation for competencies, and thus the point of departure for programs that aim to expand choice; they are formed in response to situational demands and are put into action through behaviors.

Unfreedoms (Sen): Constraints or barriers to change as described in the language of Sen's Capability Approach. These arise when people lack either the opportunities or the capabilities to achieve what they value. Unfreedoms present in the context can restrict the extent to which the capability set can be developed.

Index